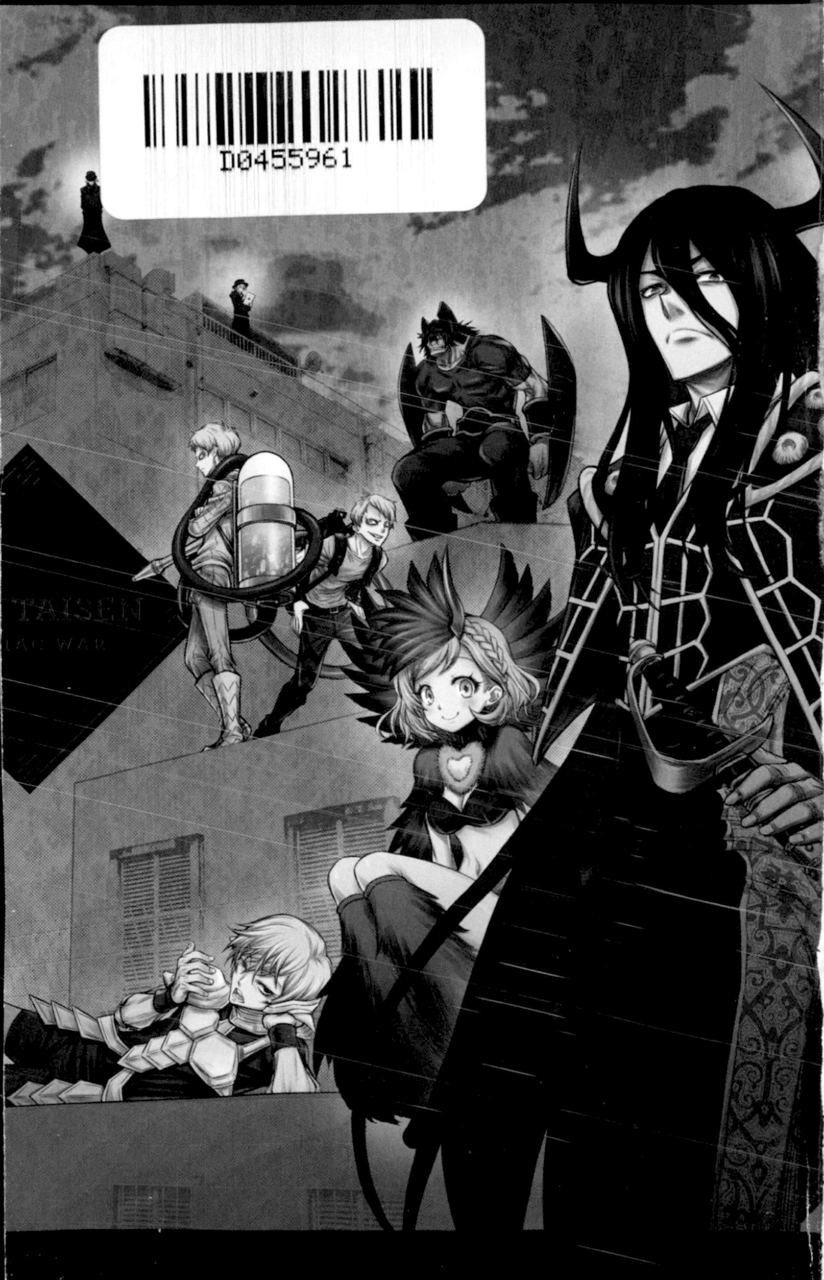
TAISEN
IAC WAR

MANGA BY
**AKIRA
AKATSUKI**

JUNI TAISEN

ZODIAC WAR

BASED ON THE NOVEL BY
NISIOISIN

CHARACTER DESIGNS BY
**HIKARU
NAKAMURA**

1

JUNI TAISEN

ZODIAC WAR

THE TWELVE FIGHTERS

1

The Zodiac War is held every twelve years.

2

Twelve fierce warriors take on the names of the Zodiac.

3

The sole victor will be granted any single wish.

4

The twelve warriors each possess unique superpowers.

The Fighter of the Rat

NEZUMI

Kills Inexorably

The Fighter of the Ox

USHII

Just Kills

The Fighter of the Tiger

TORA

Kills with Drunken Power

The Fighter of the Rabbit

USAGI

Kills with Distinction

The Fighter of the Dragon

TATSUMI BROTHER, the Elder

Kills for Money

The Fighter of the Horse

UUMA

Kills in Silence

The Fighter of the Monkey

SHARYŪ

Kills in Peace

The Fighter of the Dog

DOTSUKU

Kills with Bites

The Fighter of the Snake

TATSUMI BROTHER, the Younger

Kills for Money

The Fighter of the Sheep

HITSUJII

Kills with Deception

The Fighter of the Chicken

NIWATORI

Kills by Pecks

The Fighter of the Boar

INŌNOSHISHI

Kills in Abundance

CONTENTS

CHAPTER ONE THE TWELVE

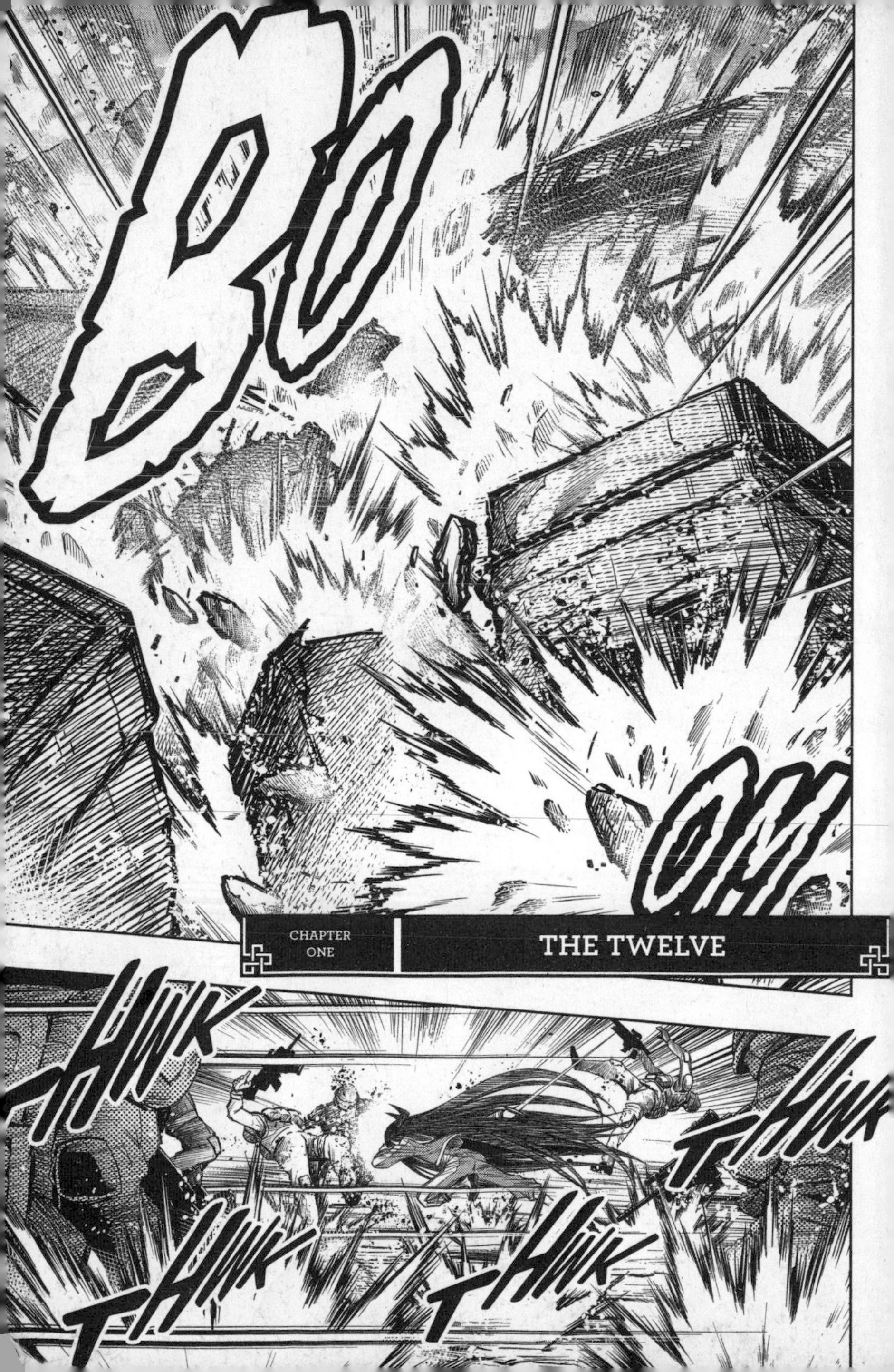
BOOM
CHAPTER ONE
THE TWELVE
THUNK
THUNK
THUNK
THUNK

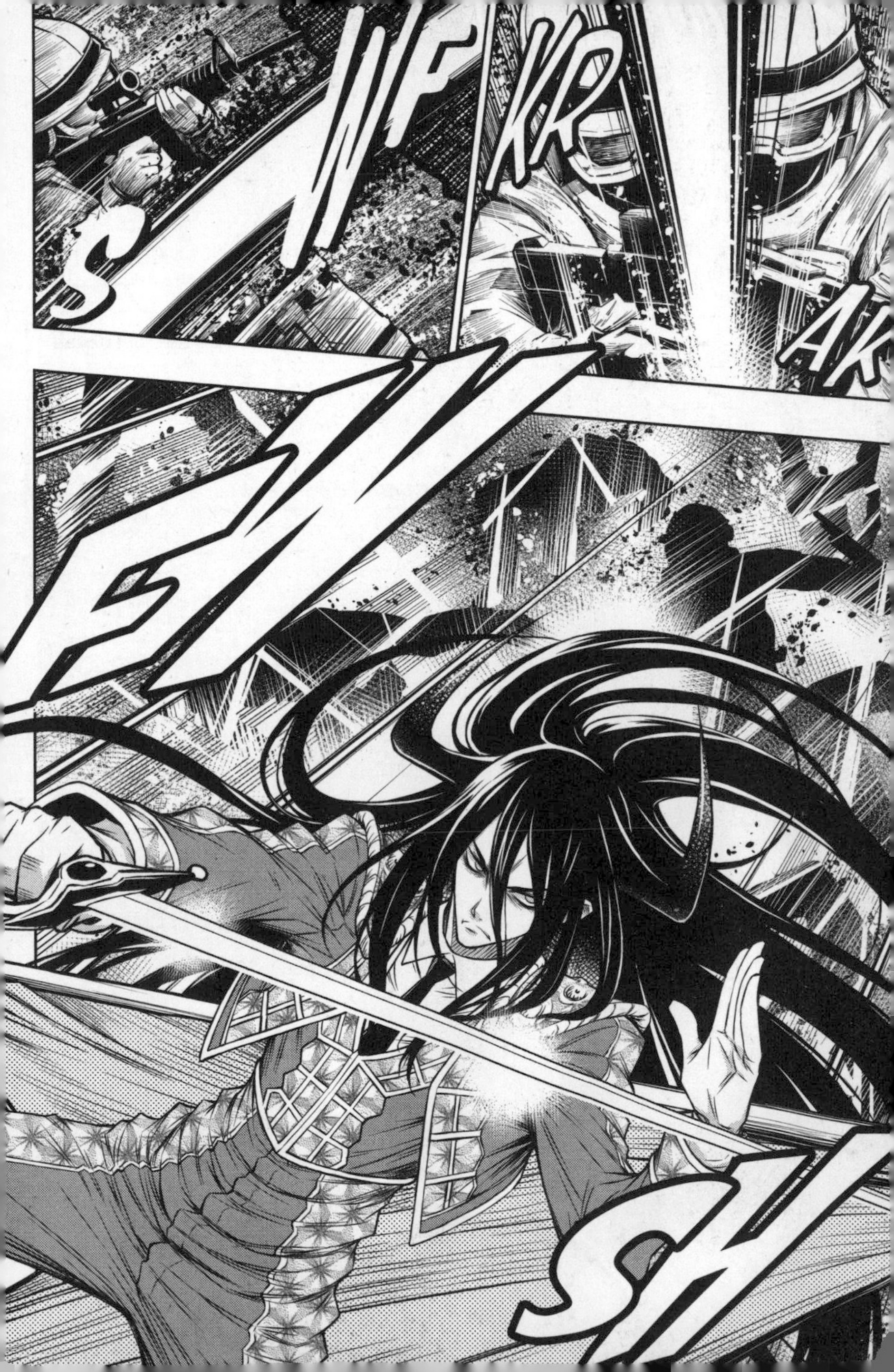
KR
AK

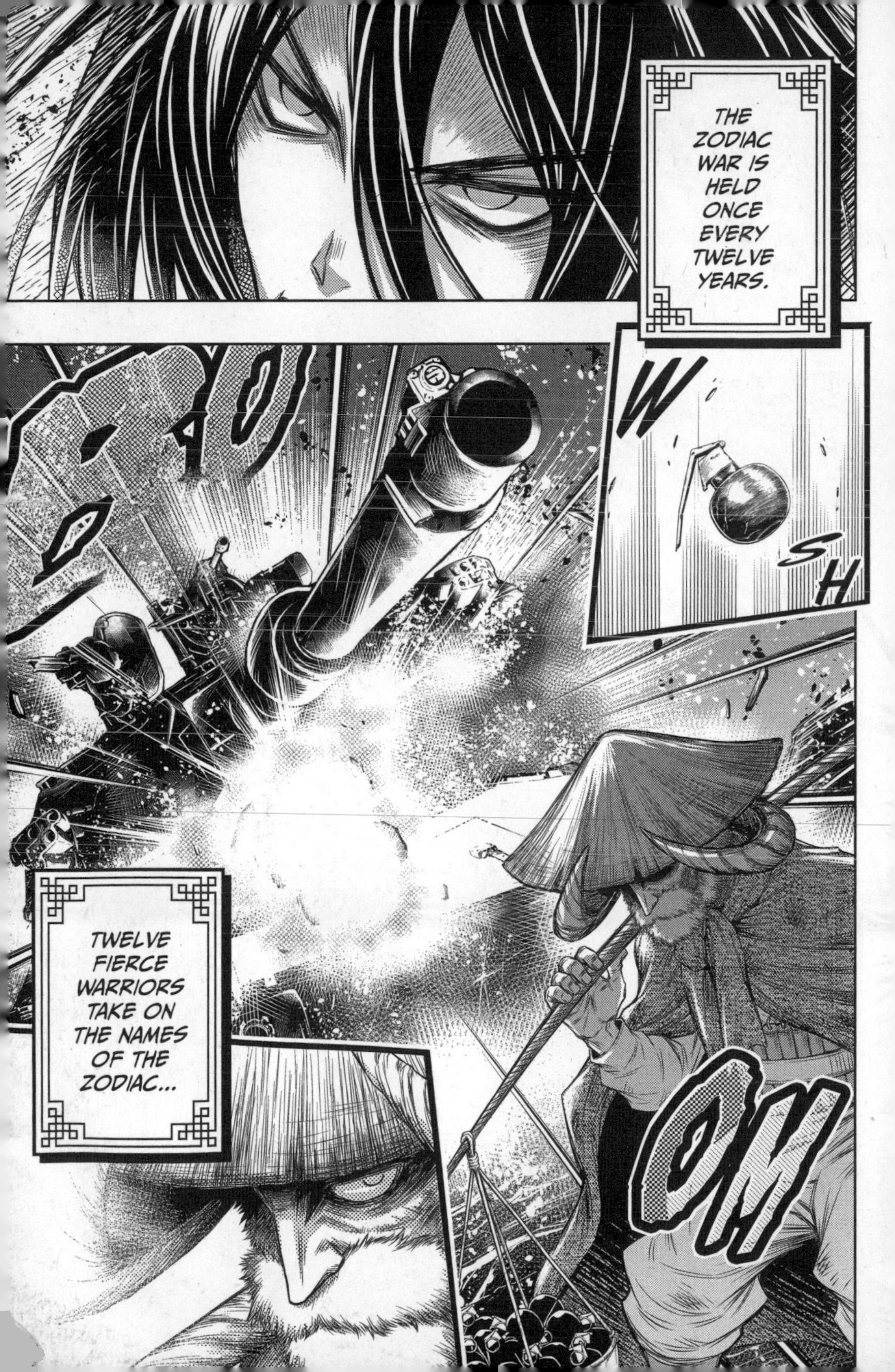
THE ZODIAC WAR IS HELD ONCE EVERY TWELVE YEARS.
W
SH
TWELVE FIERCE WARRIORS TAKE ON THE NAMES OF THE ZODIAC...
OM

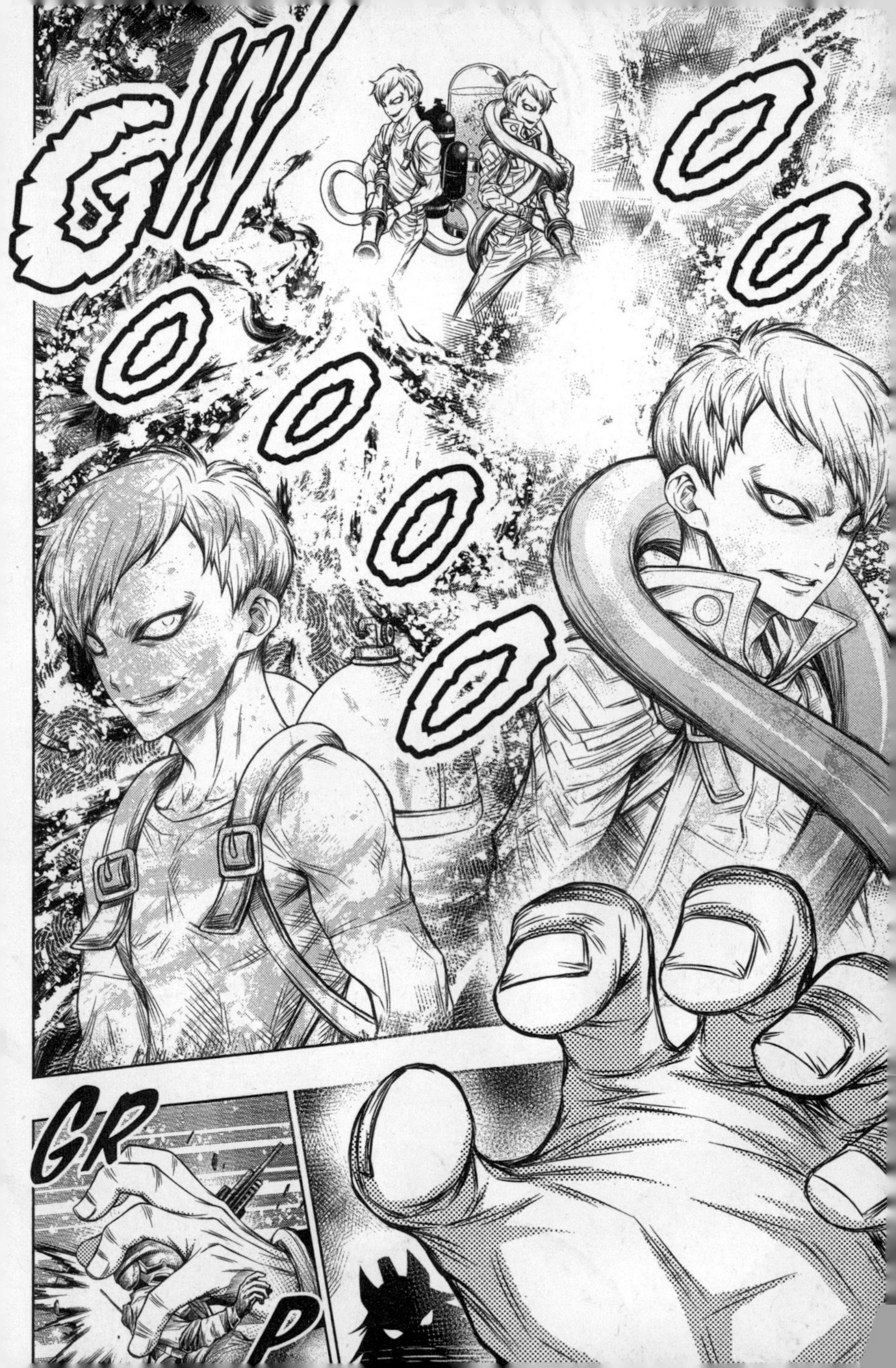
GWOOOOOO
GR
P

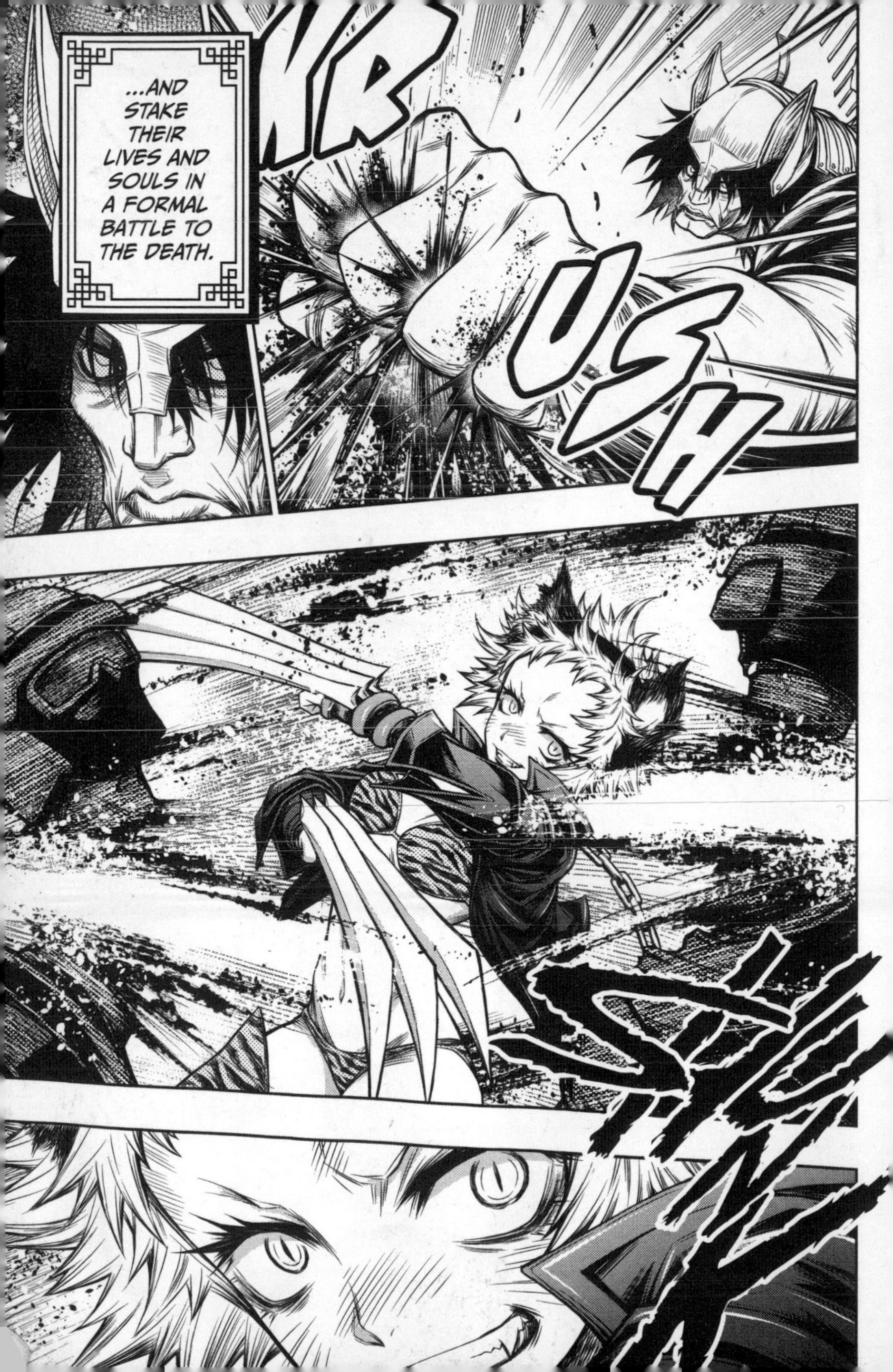
...AND STAKE THEIR LIVES AND SOULS IN A FORMAL BATTLE TO THE DEATH.

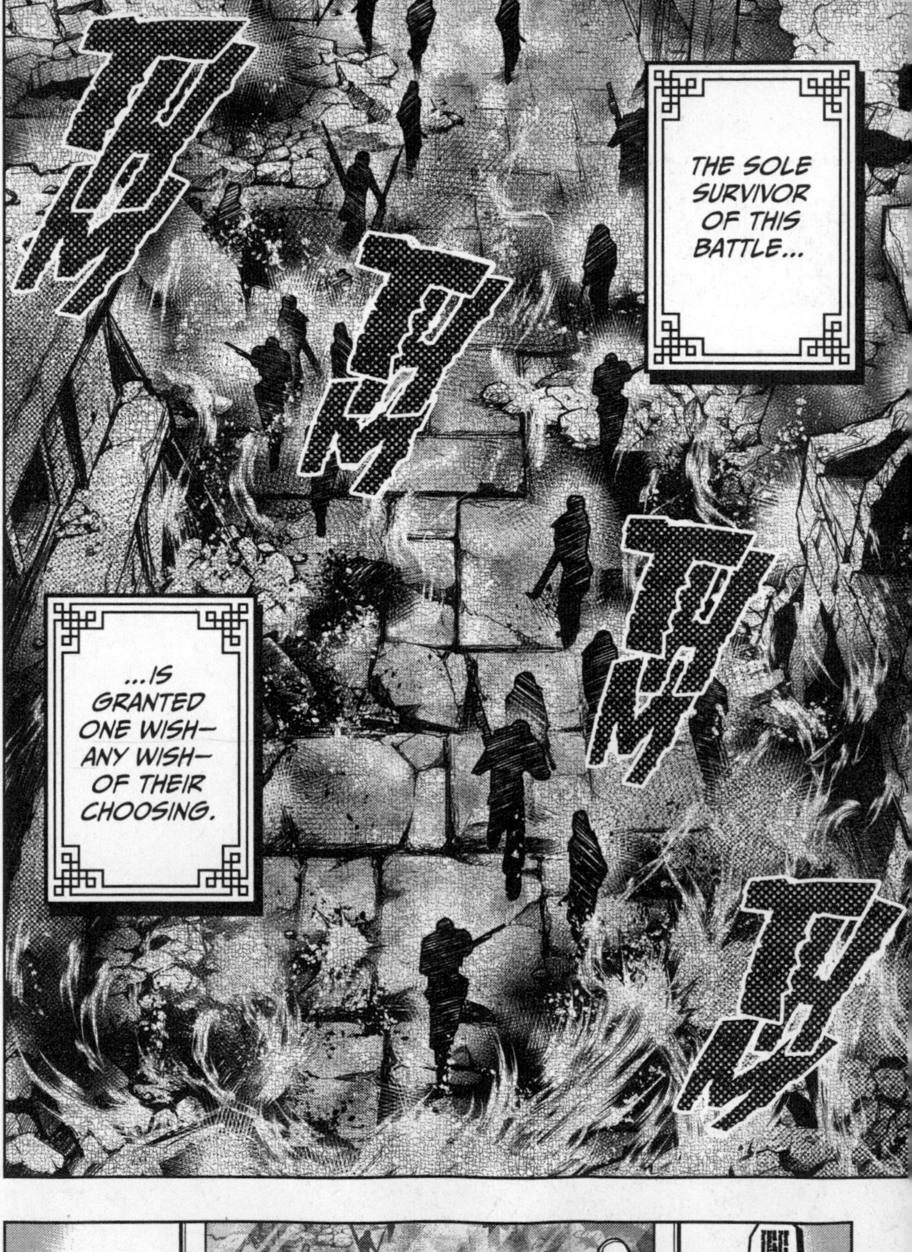
THE SOLE SURVIVOR OF THIS BATTLE...
...IS GRANTED ONE WISH—ANY WISH—OF THEIR CHOOSING.
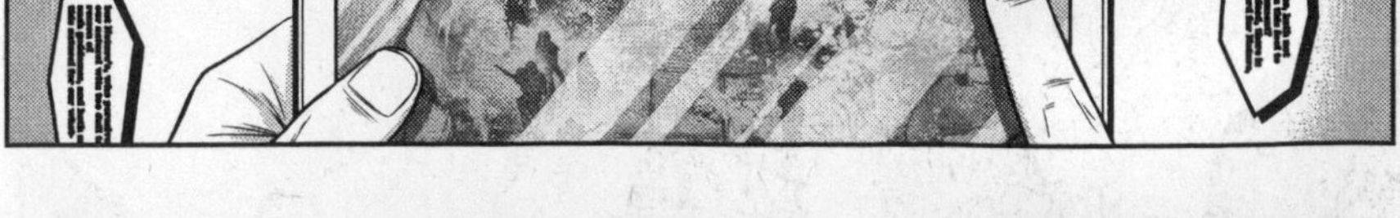

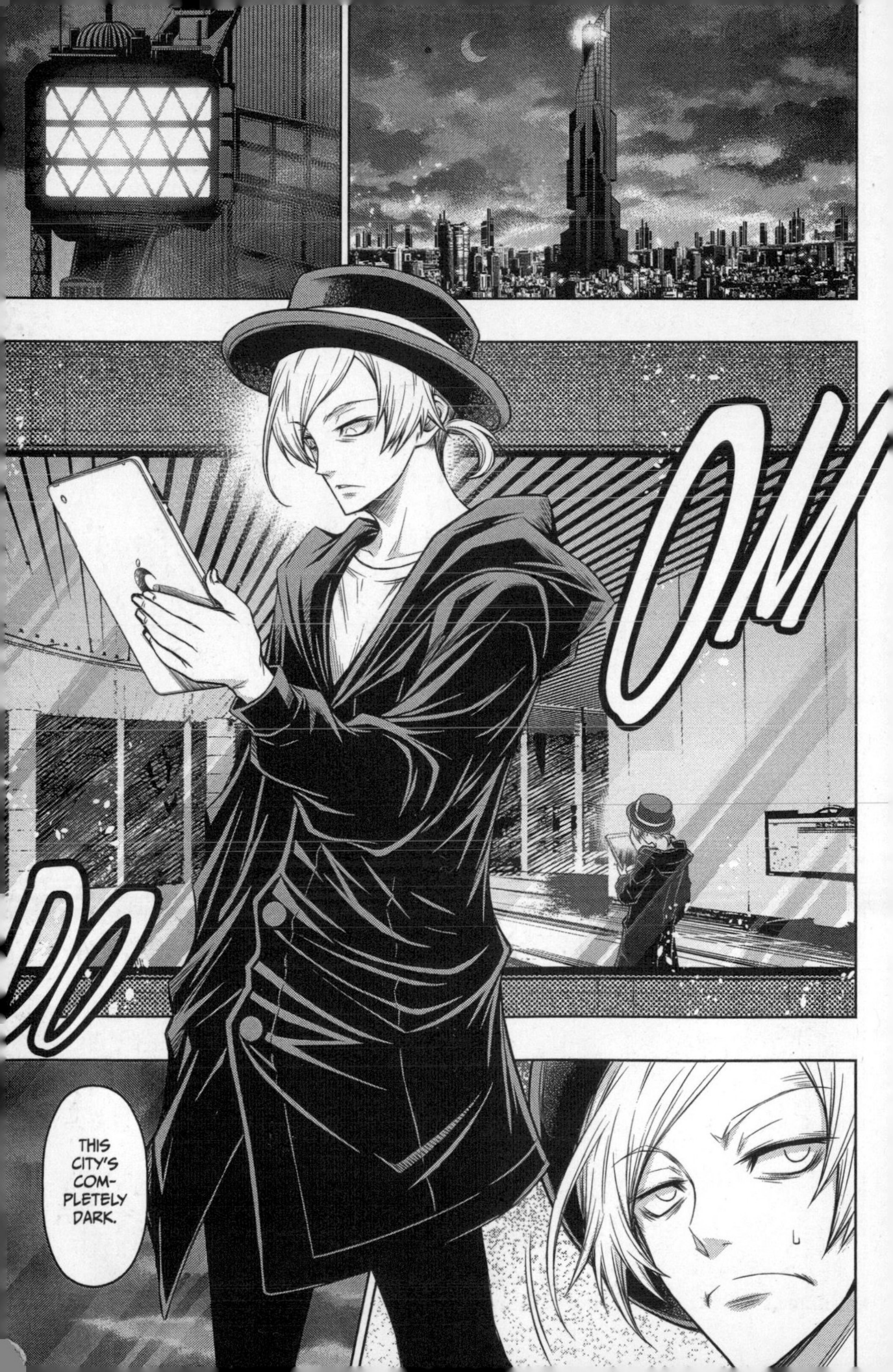
OM
M
THIS CITY'S COM-PLETELY DARK.

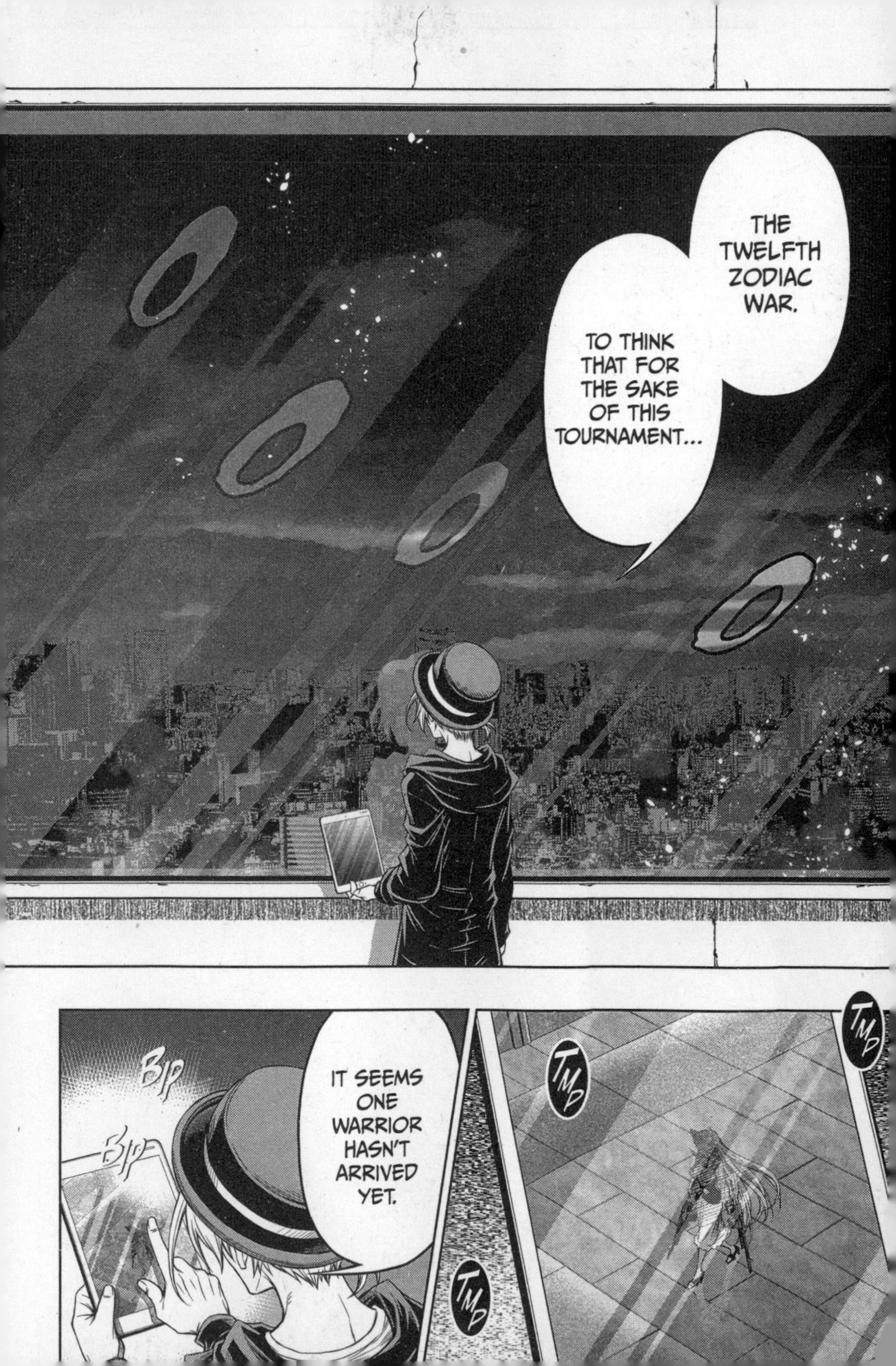
THE TWELFTH ZODIAC WAR.
TO THINK THAT FOR THE SAKE OF THIS TOURNAMENT...
TMP
TMP
TMP
BIP
BIP
IT SEEMS ONE WARRIOR HASN'T ARRIVED YET.

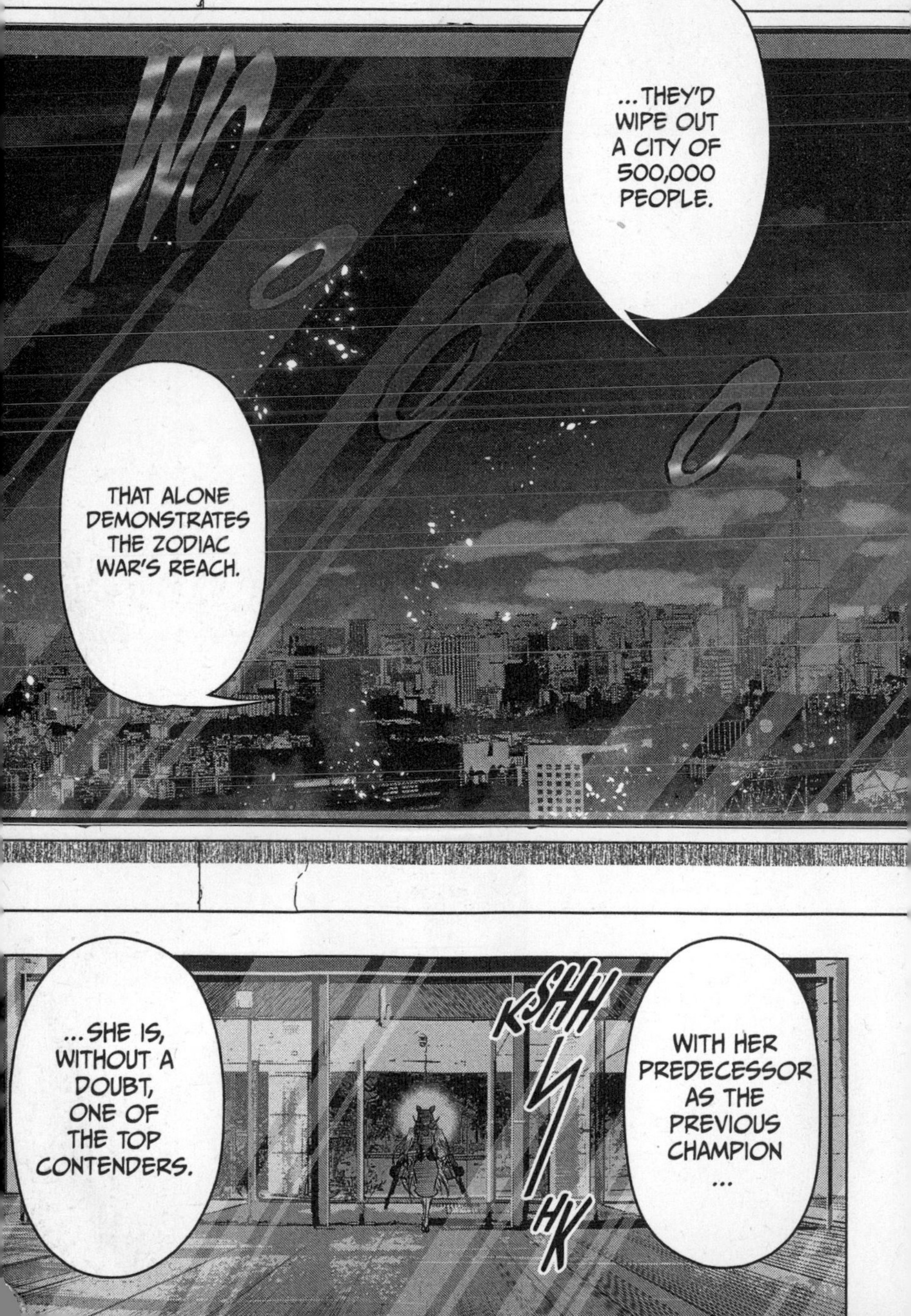
...THEY'D WIPE OUT A CITY OF 500,000 PEOPLE.
THAT ALONE DEMONSTRATES THE ZODIAC WAR'S REACH.
WITH HER PREDECESSOR AS THE PREVIOUS CHAMPION ...
KSHH
HK
...SHE IS, WITHOUT A DOUBT, ONE OF THE TOP CONTENDERS.

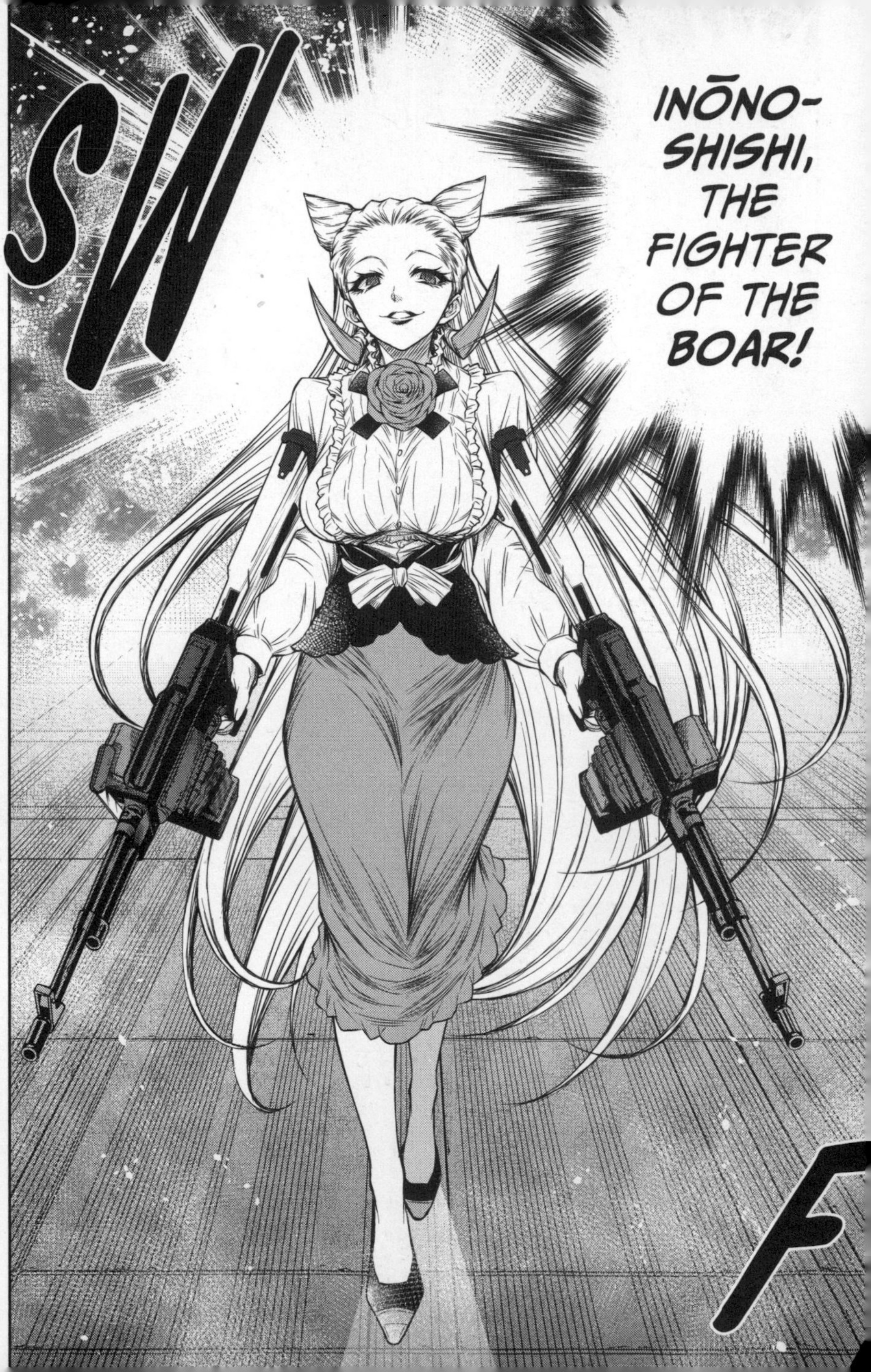
INŌNO-SHISHI, THE FIGHTER OF THE BOAR!

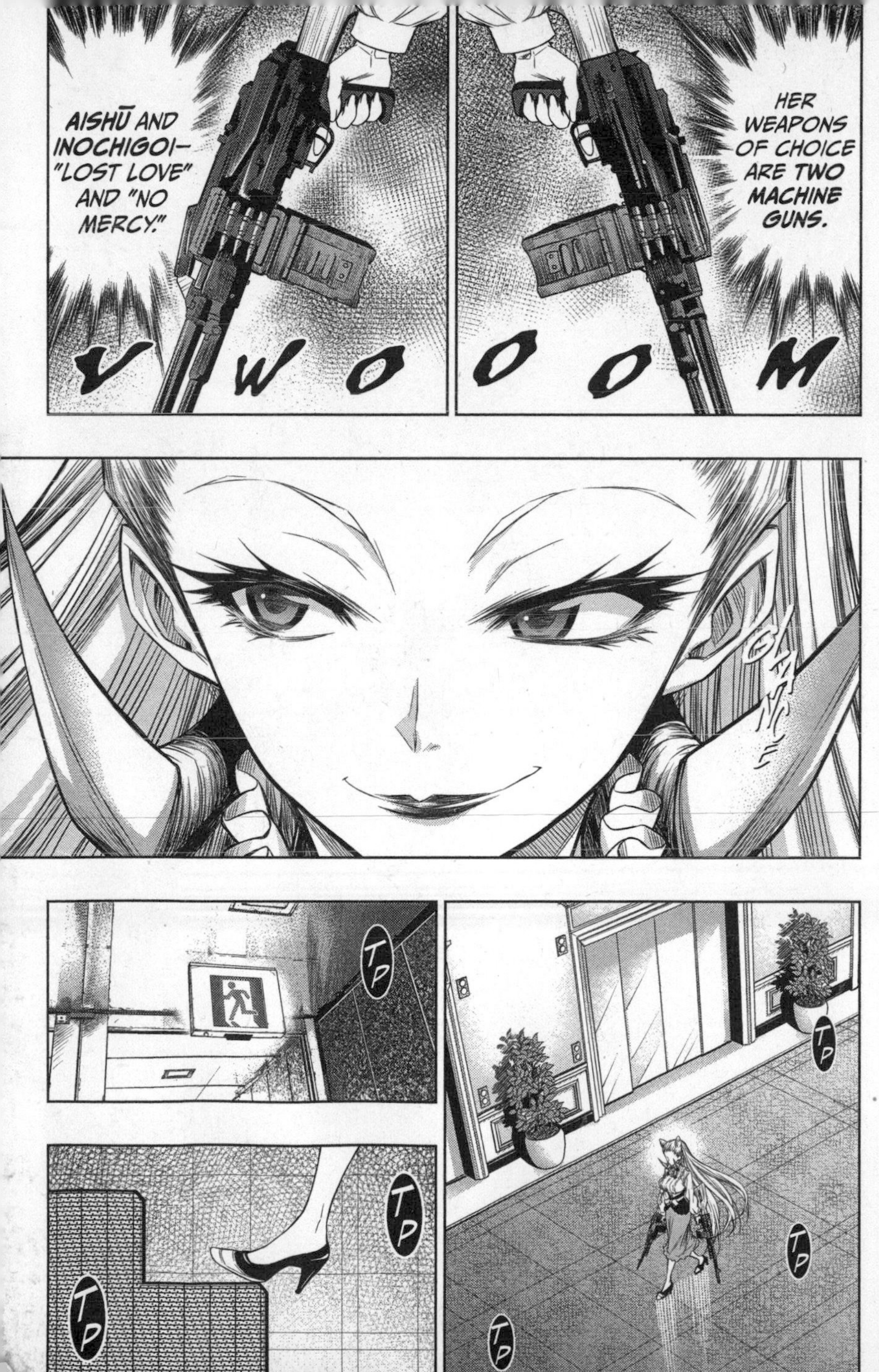
HER WEAPONS OF CHOICE ARE TWO MACHINE GUNS.
AISHŪ AND INOCHIGOI— "LOST LOVE" AND "NO MERCY."
VWOOOM
TP
TP
TP
TP
TP
TP

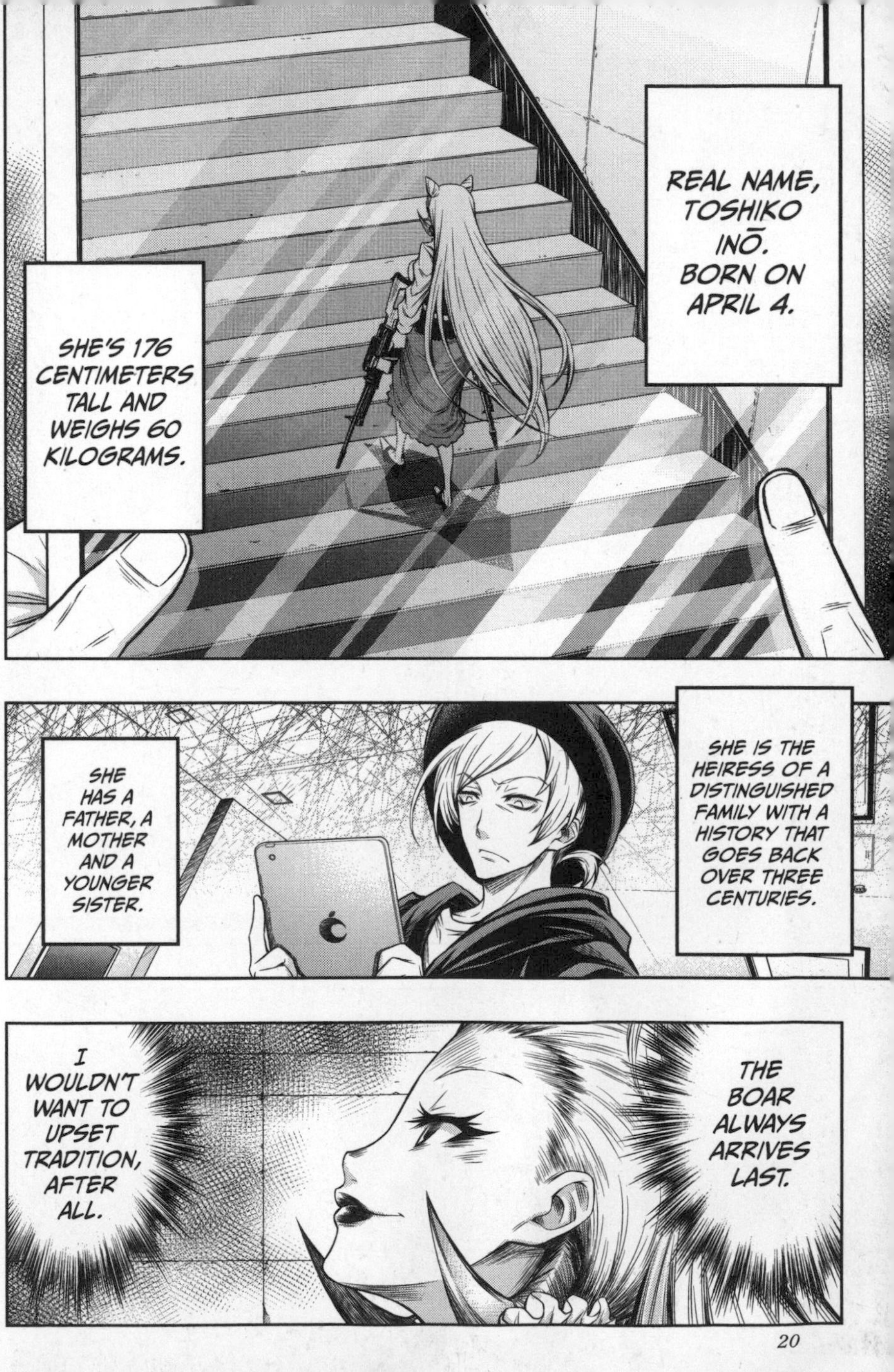
REAL NAME, TOSHIKO INŌ. BORN ON APRIL 4.
SHE'S 176 CENTIMETERS TALL AND WEIGHS 60 KILOGRAMS.
SHE IS THE HEIRESS OF A DISTINGUISHED FAMILY WITH A HISTORY THAT GOES BACK OVER THREE CENTURIES.
SHE HAS A FATHER, A MOTHER AND A YOUNGER SISTER.
THE BOAR ALWAYS ARRIVES LAST.
I WOULDN'T WANT TO UPSET TRADITION, AFTER ALL.

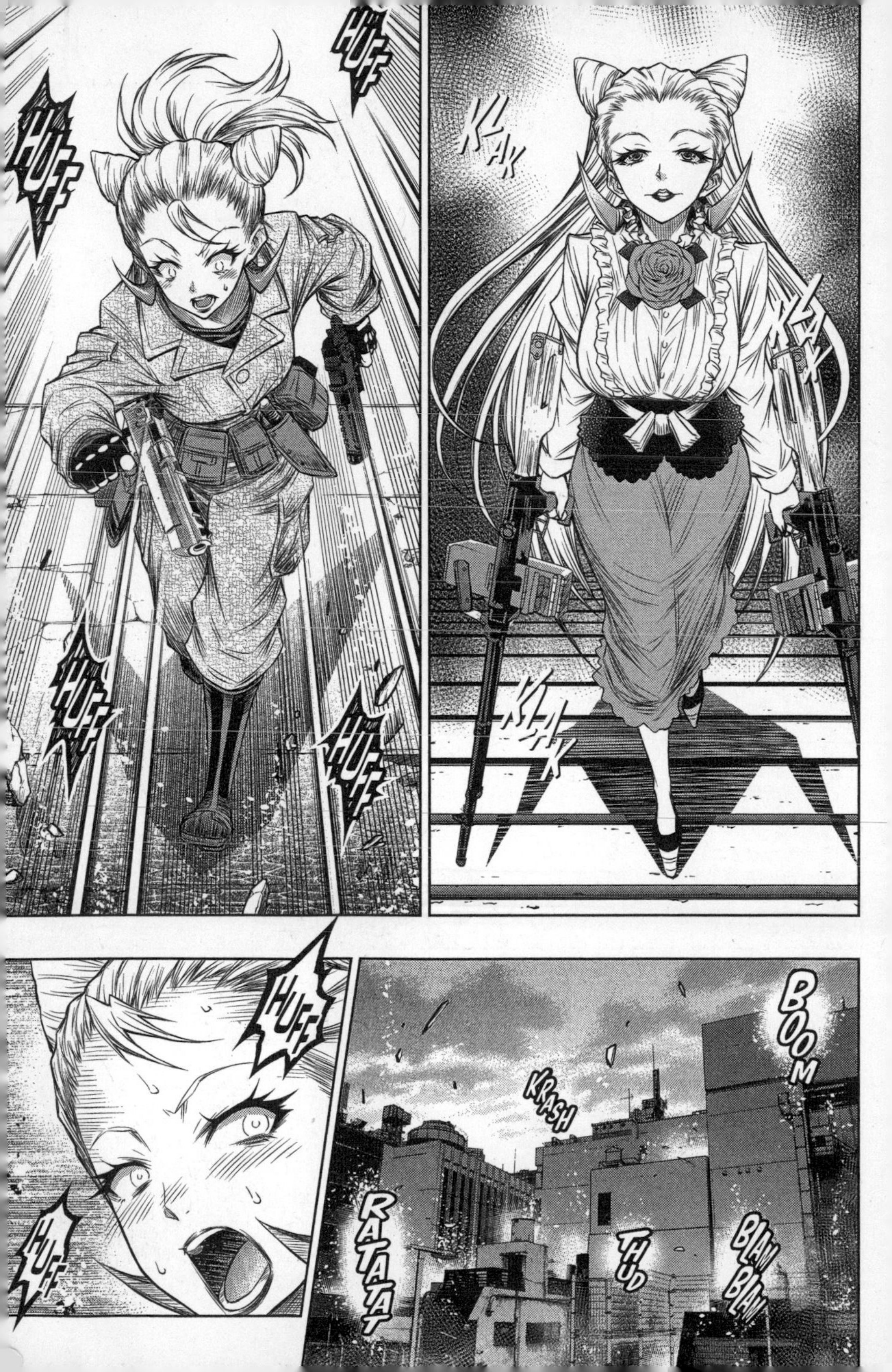
KLAK
KLAK
KLAK
HUFF
HUFF
HUFF
HUFF
BOOM
KRASH
BLAM BLAM
THUD
RATATAT
HUFF
HUFF

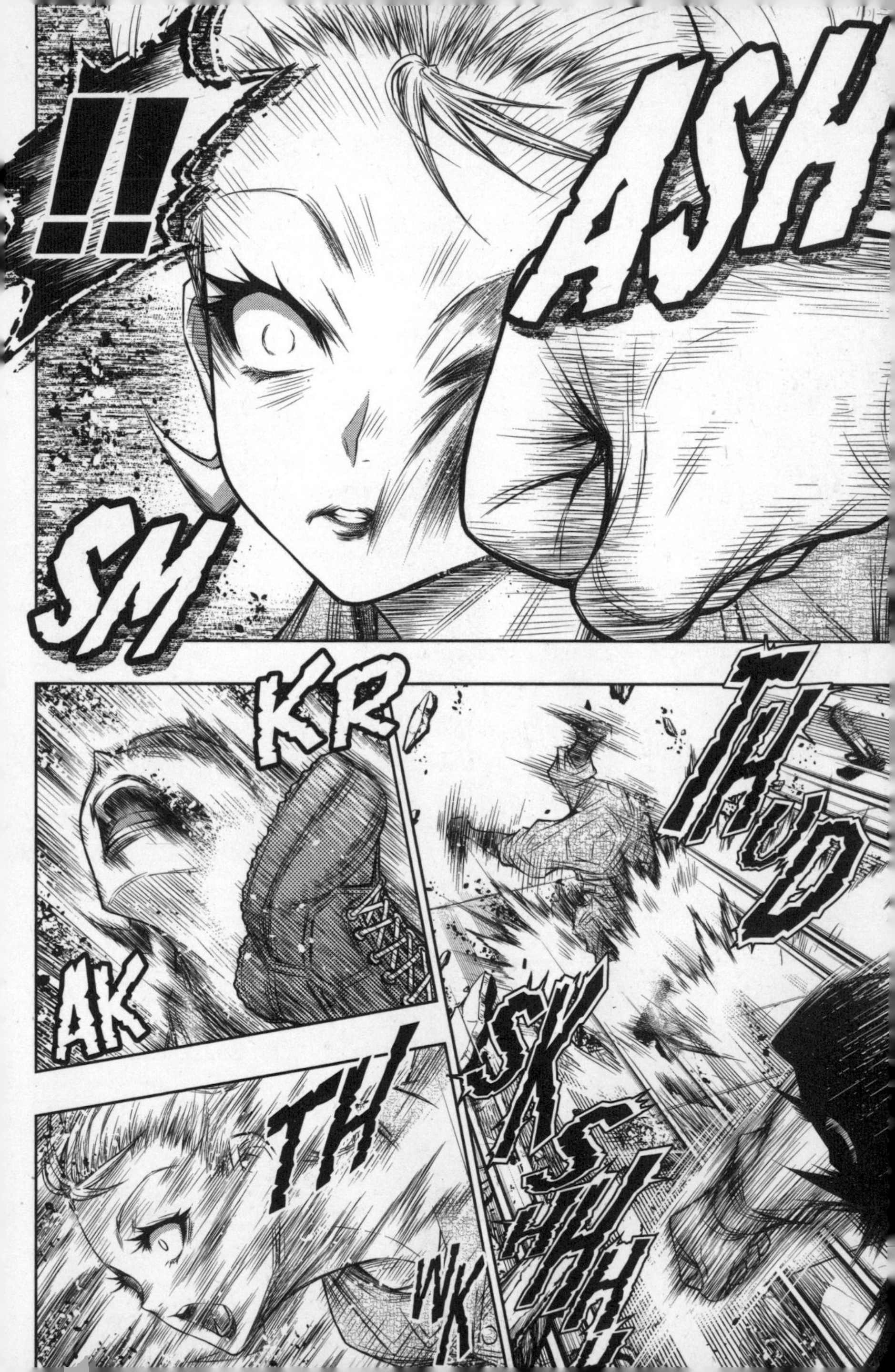

ASH
!!
SM
THUD
SK
SH
KR
AK
TH
WK

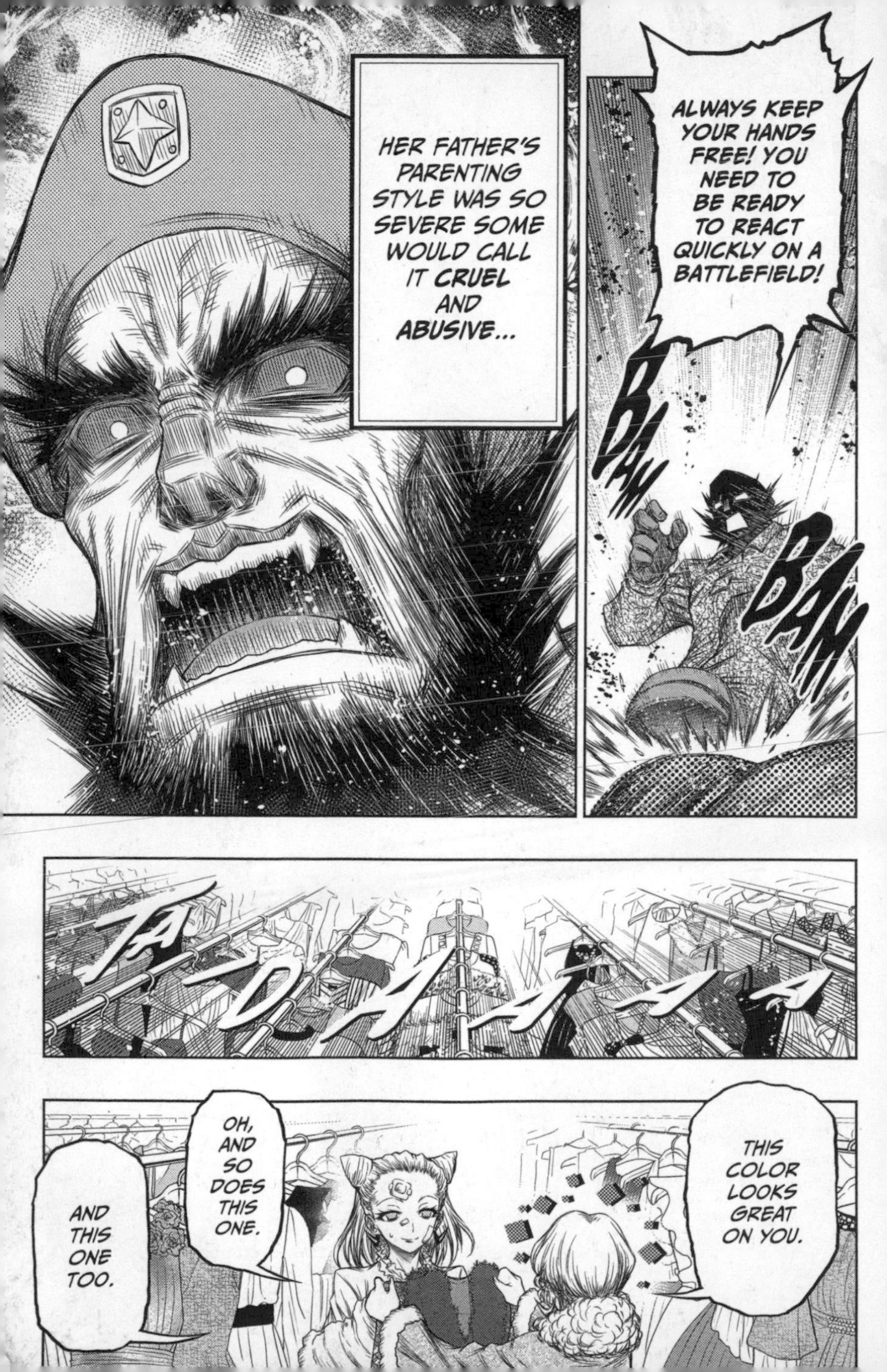
ALWAYS KEEP YOUR HANDS FREE! YOU NEED TO BE READY TO REACT QUICKLY ON A BATTLEFIELD!
BAM
BAM
HER FATHER'S PARENTING STYLE WAS SO SEVERE SOME WOULD CALL IT **CRUEL** AND **ABUSIVE**...
TA-D-A-A-A
THIS COLOR LOOKS GREAT ON YOU.
OH, AND SO DOES THIS ONE.
AND THIS ONE TOO.

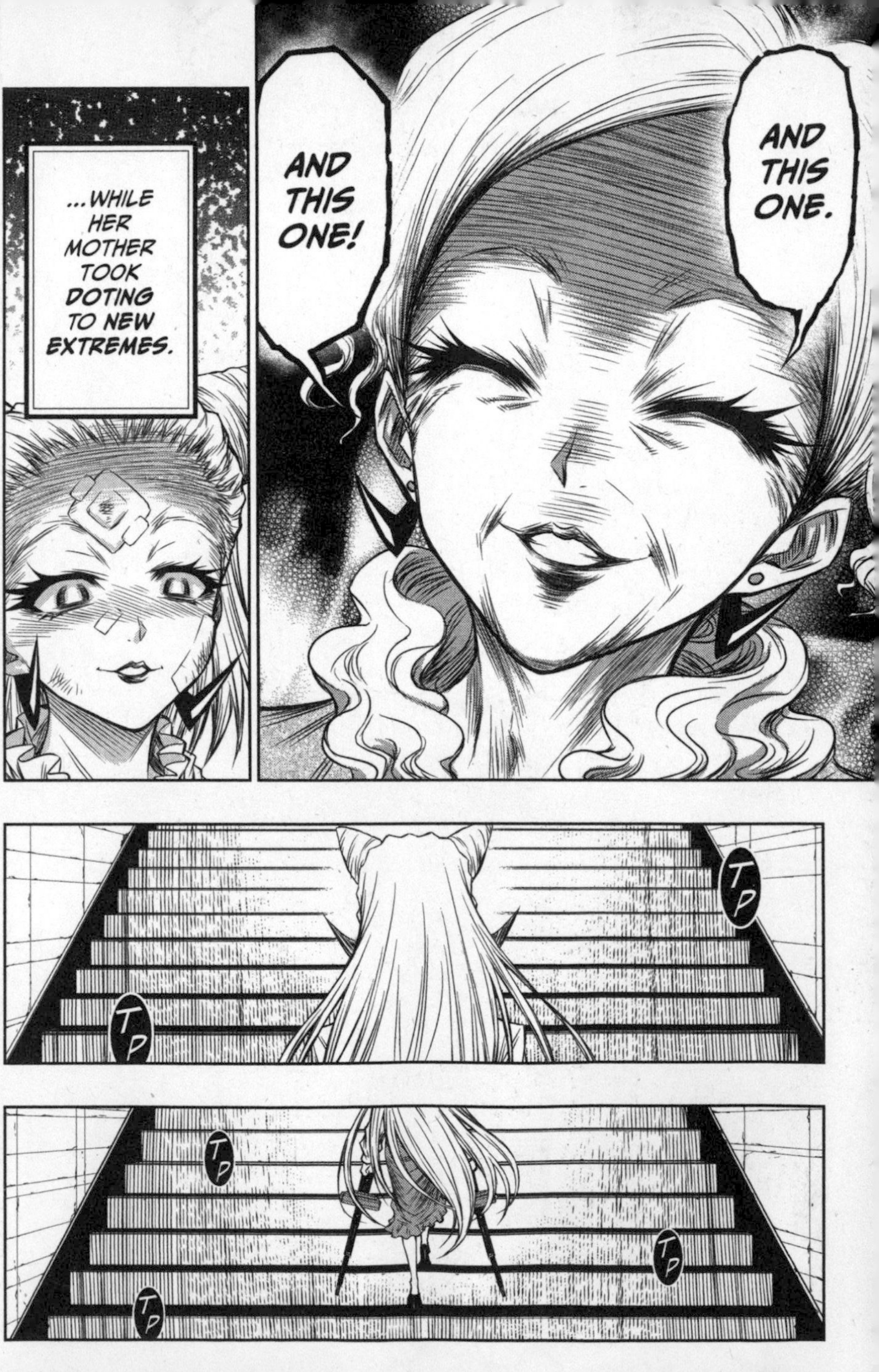
AND THIS ONE.
AND THIS ONE!
...WHILE HER MOTHER TOOK DOTING TO NEW EXTREMES.
TP
TP
TP
TP
TP

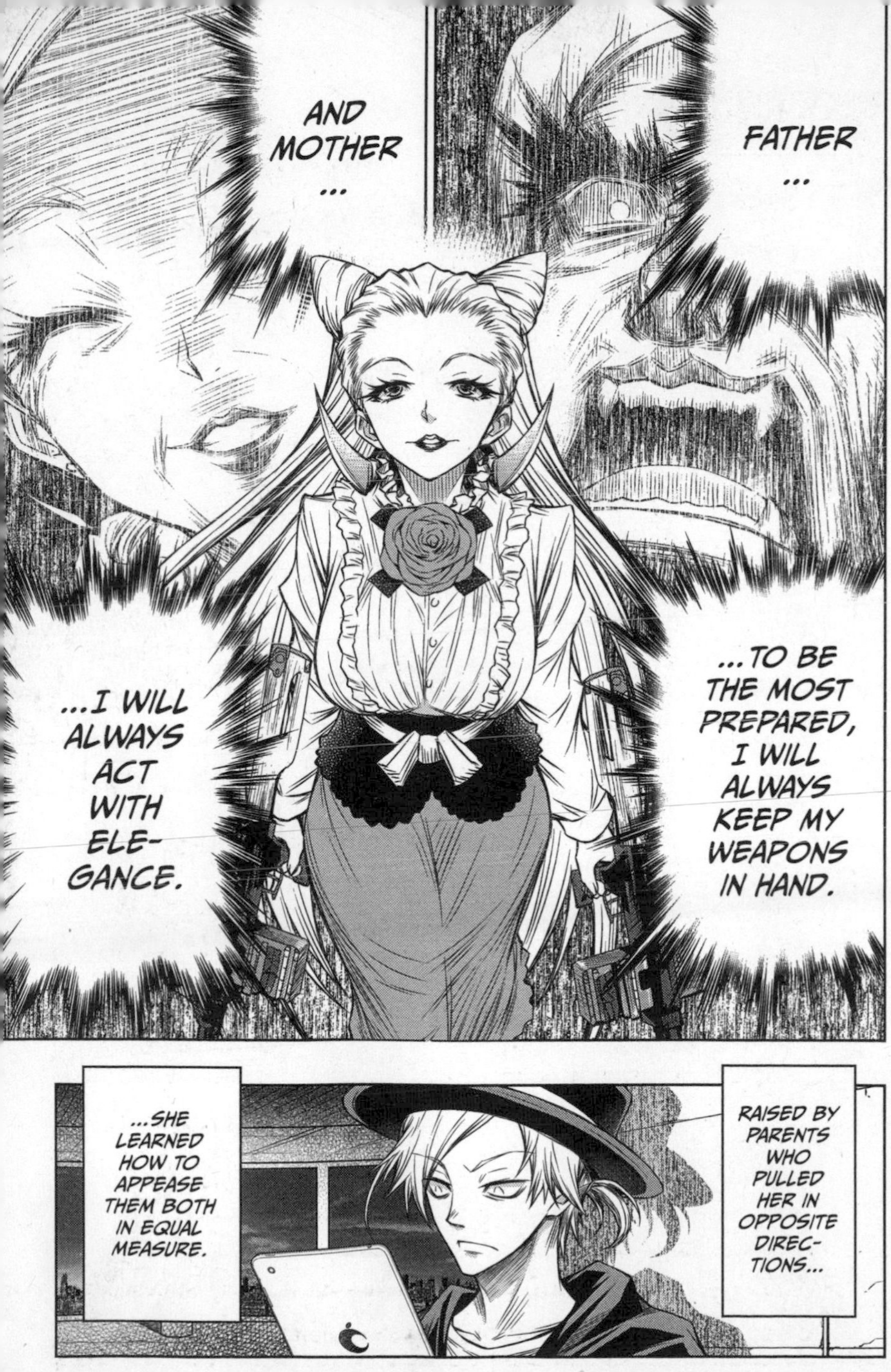
FATHER ...
AND MOTHER ...
...TO BE THE MOST PREPARED, I WILL ALWAYS KEEP MY WEAPONS IN HAND.
...I WILL ALWAYS ACT WITH ELE-GANCE.
RAISED BY PARENTS WHO PULLED HER IN OPPOSITE DIREC-TIONS...
...SHE LEARNED HOW TO APPEASE THEM BOTH IN EQUAL MEASURE.

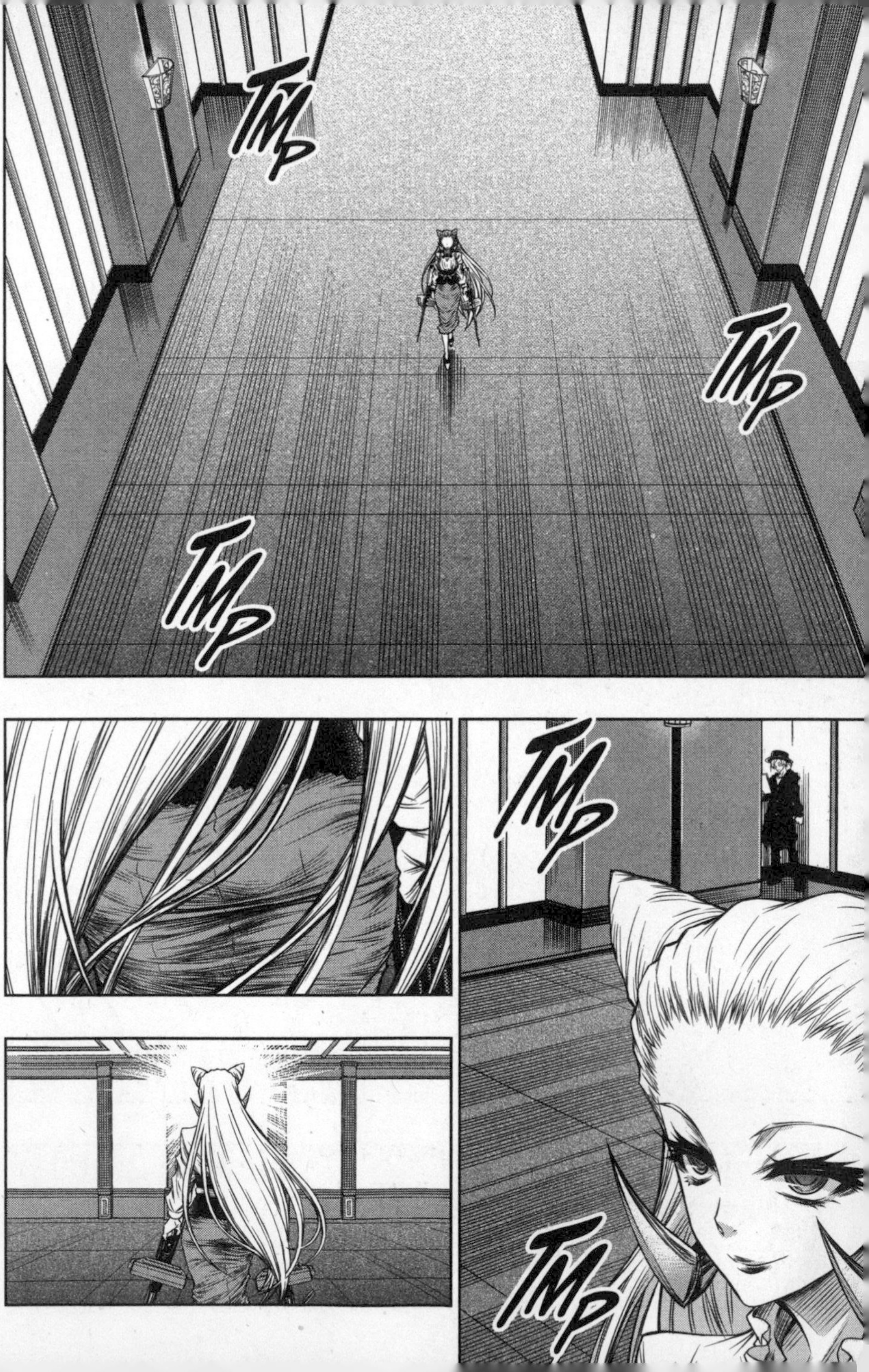
TMP
TMP
TMP
TMP
TMP

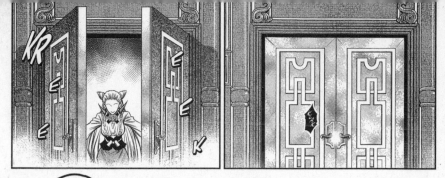

GOOD EVENING, EVERY- ONE.

I TRUST YOUR WAIT HAS BEEN PLEASANT.

I AM BOAR.

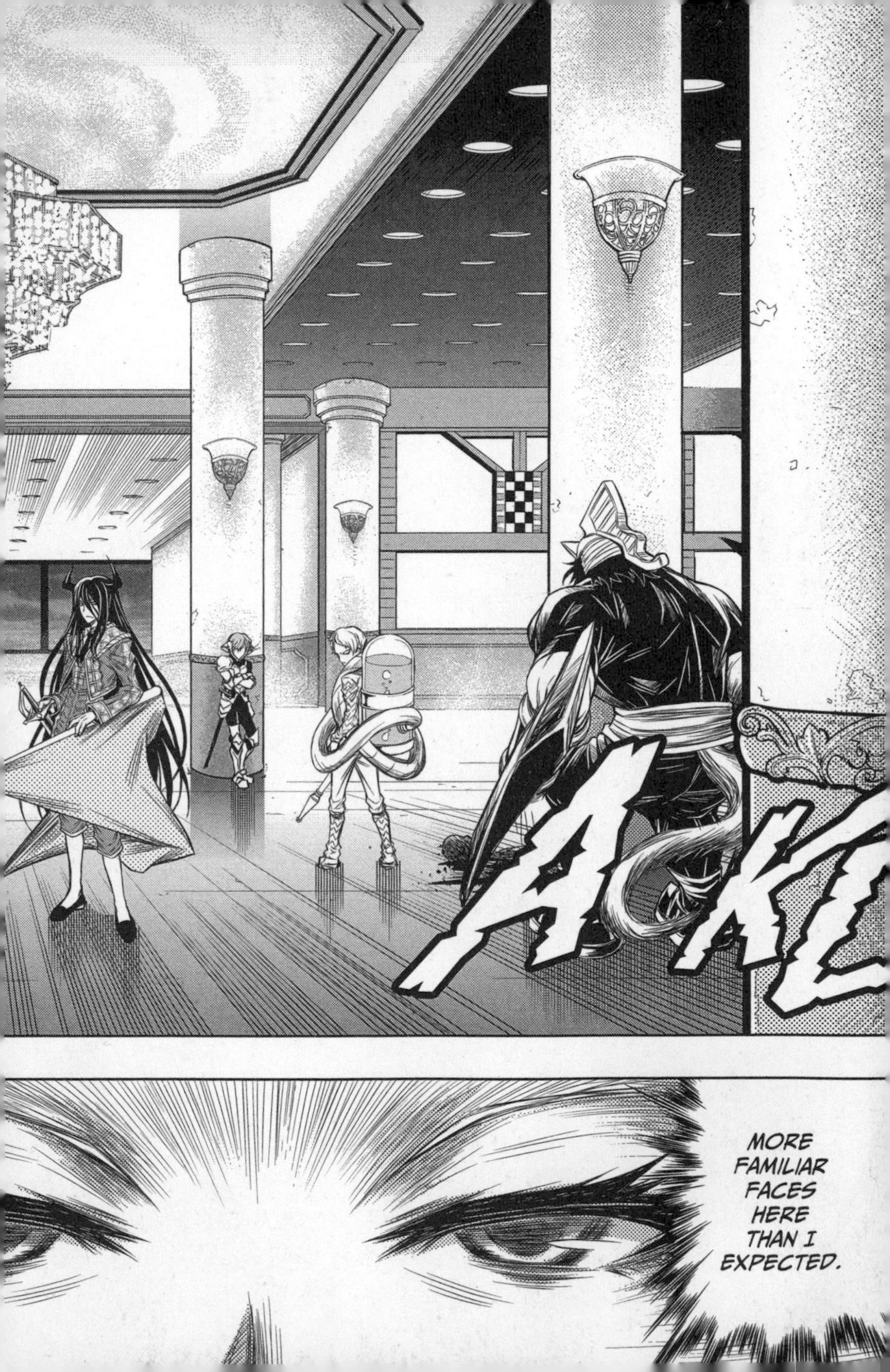
MORE FAMILIAR FACES HERE THAN I EXPECTED.

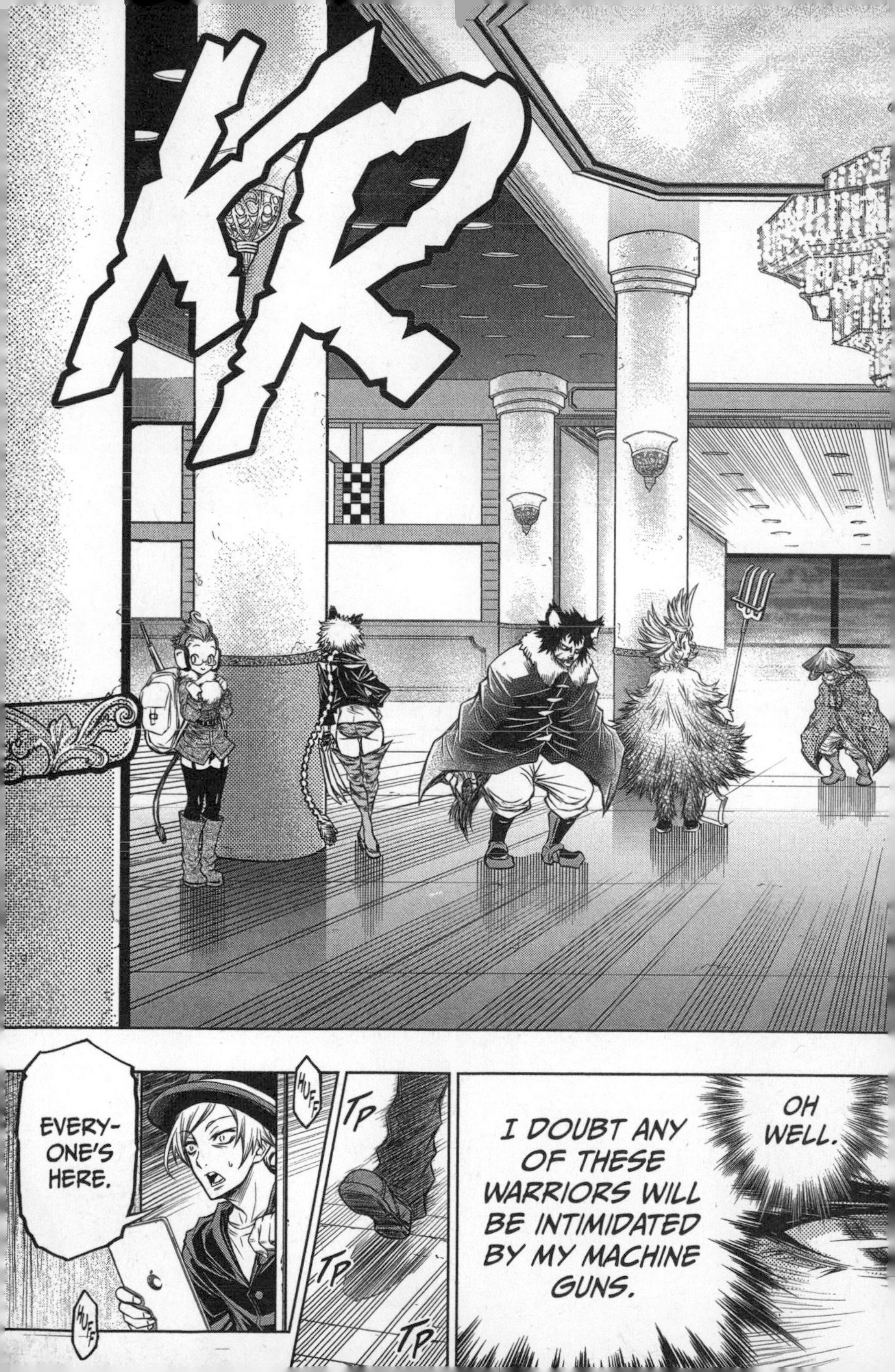
KR
OH WELL.
I DOUBT ANY OF THESE WARRIORS WILL BE INTIMIDATED BY MY MACHINE GUNS.
TP
TP
TP
HUFF
EVERY-ONE'S HERE.
HUFF

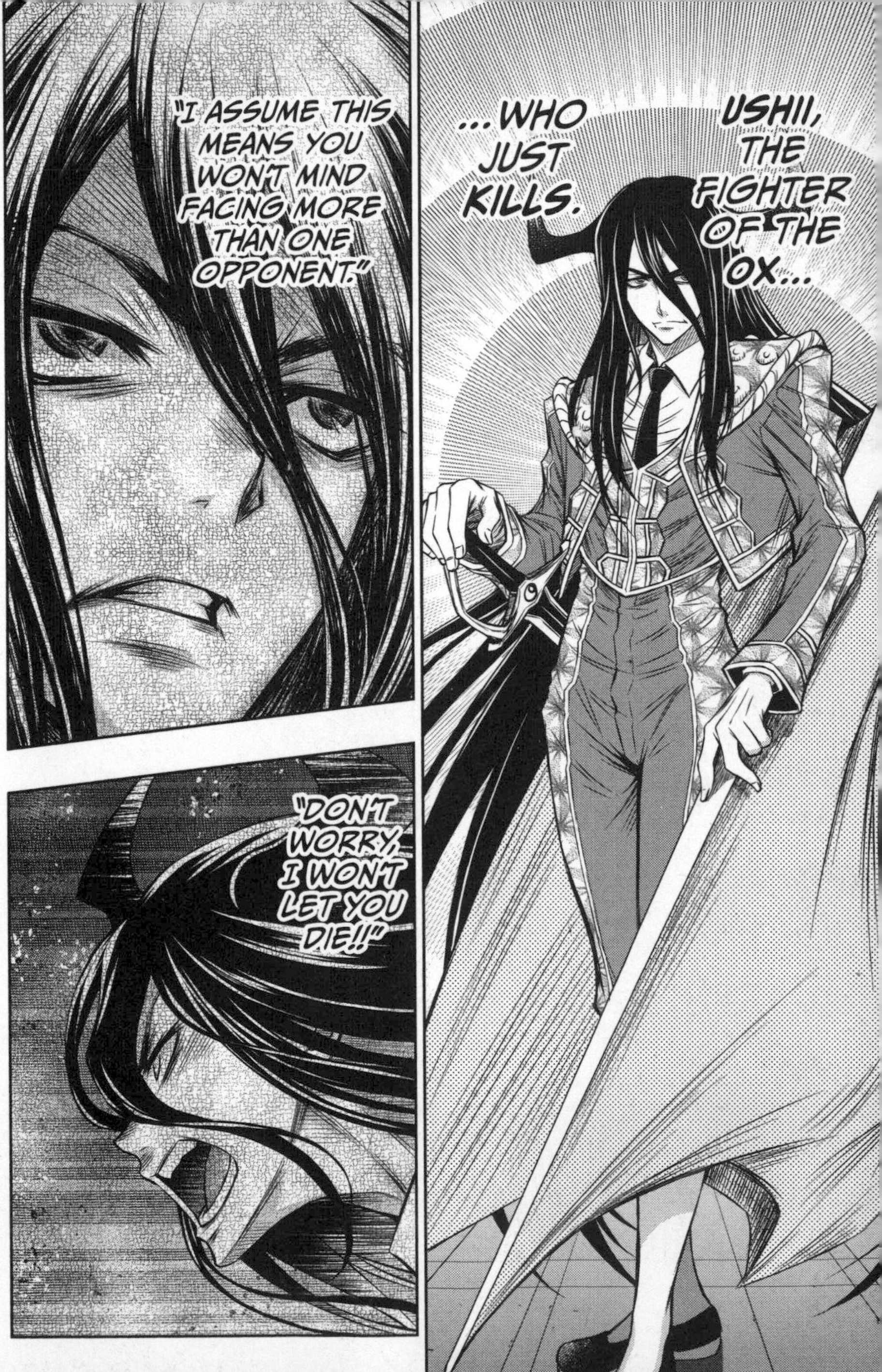
USHII, THE FIGHTER OF THE OX...
...WHO JUST KILLS.
"I ASSUME THIS MEANS YOU WON'T MIND FACING MORE THAN ONE OPPONENT."
"DON'T WORRY, I WON'T LET YOU DIE!!"

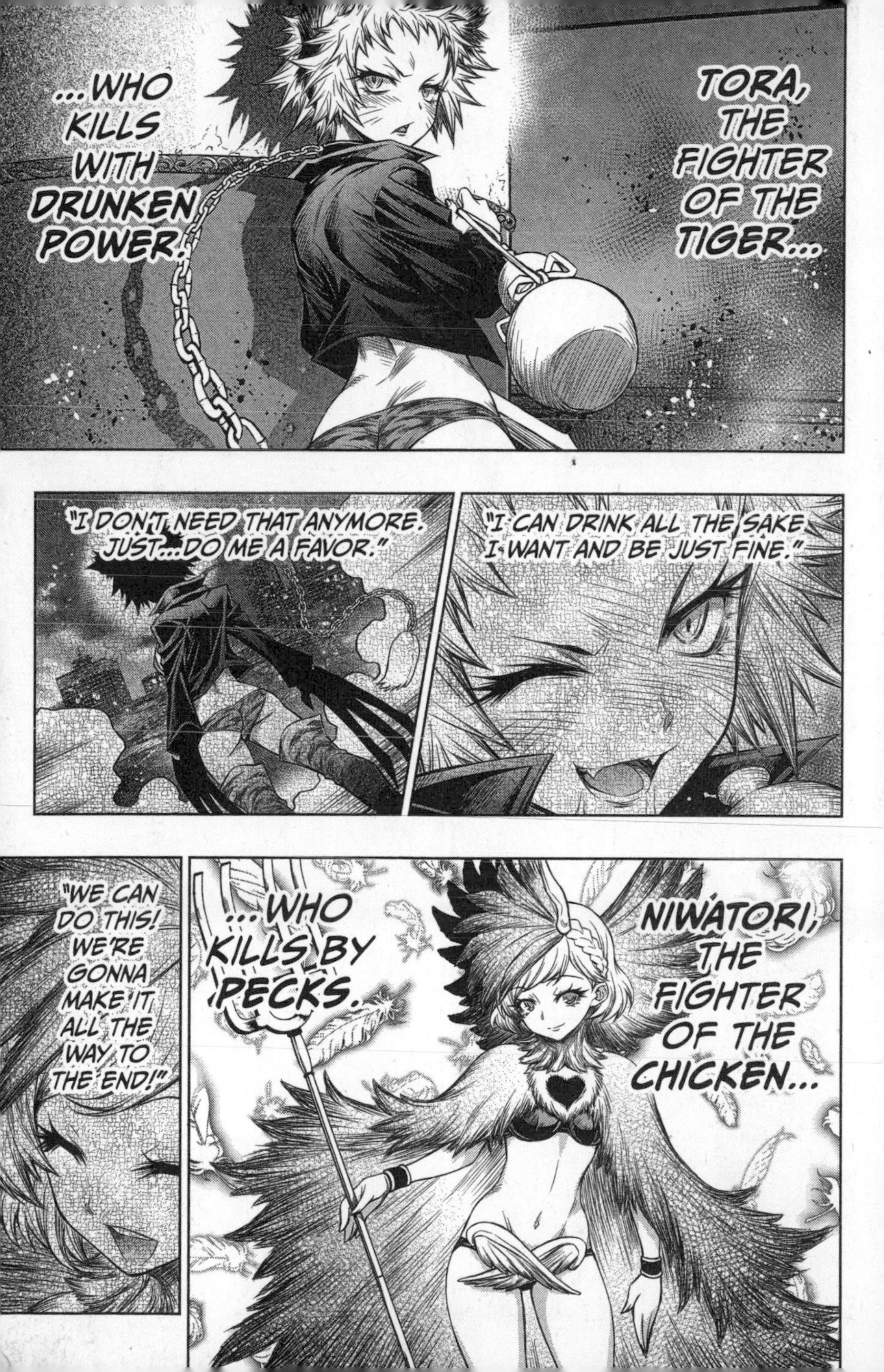
TORA, THE FIGHTER OF THE TIGER...
...WHO KILLS WITH DRUNKEN POWER.
"I CAN DRINK ALL THE SAKE I WANT AND BE JUST FINE."
"I DON'T NEED THAT ANYMORE. JUST...DO ME A FAVOR."
NIWATORI, THE FIGHTER OF THE CHICKEN...
...WHO KILLS BY PECKS.
"WE CAN DO THIS! WE'RE GONNA MAKE IT ALL THE WAY TO THE END!"

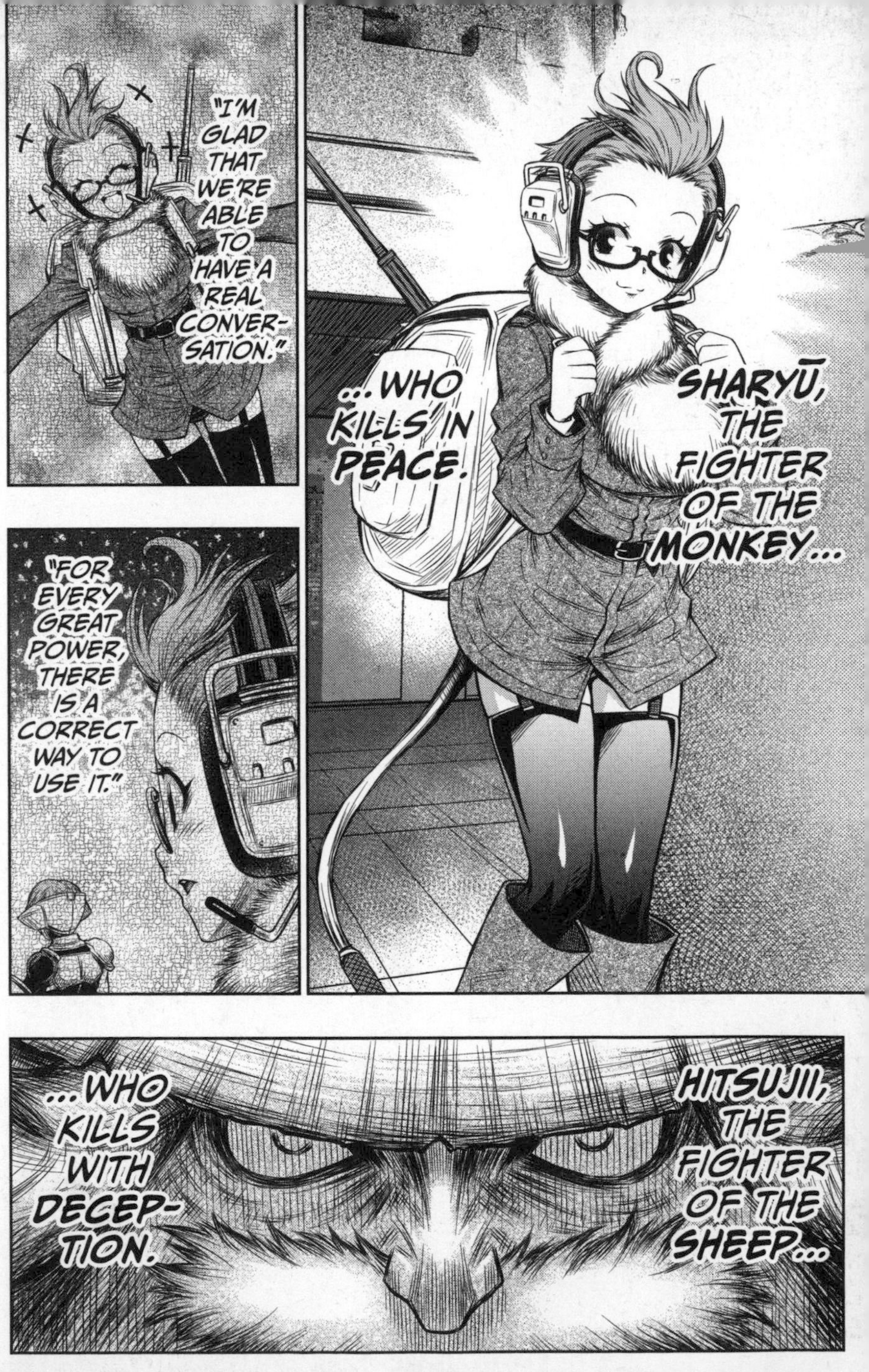
SHARYŪ, THE FIGHTER OF THE MONKEY...
...WHO KILLS IN PEACE.
"I'M GLAD THAT WE'RE ABLE TO HAVE A REAL CONVER-SATION."
"FOR EVERY GREAT POWER, THERE IS A CORRECT WAY TO USE IT."
HITSUJII, THE FIGHTER OF THE SHEEP...
...WHO KILLS WITH DECEP-TION.

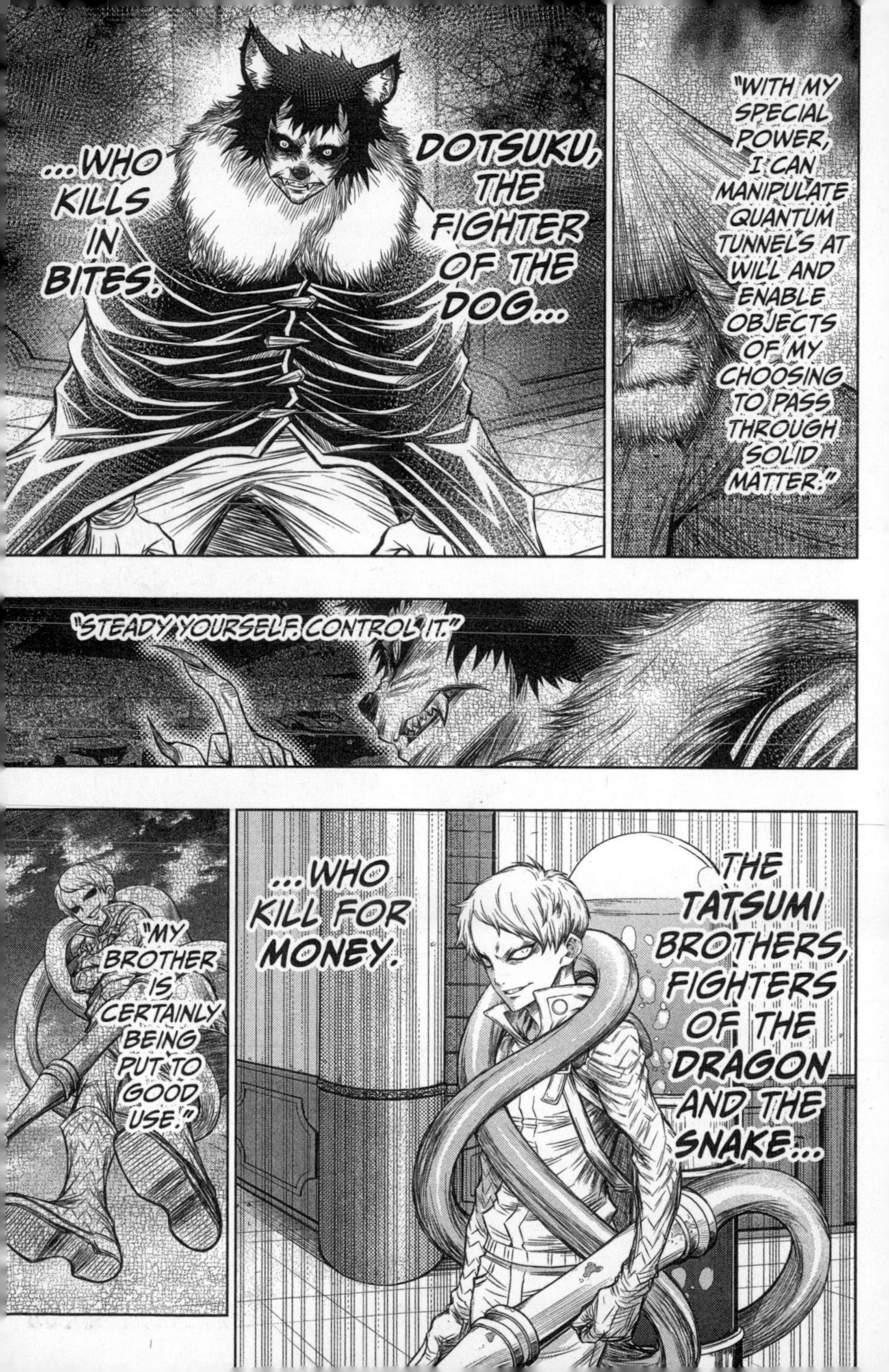
"WITH MY SPECIAL POWER, I CAN MANIPULATE QUANTUM TUNNELS AT WILL AND ENABLE OBJECTS OF MY CHOOSING TO PASS THROUGH SOLID MATTER."
DOTSUKU, THE FIGHTER OF THE DOG...
...WHO KILLS IN BITES.
"STEADY YOURSELF. CONTROL IT."
THE TATSUMI BROTHERS, FIGHTERS OF THE DRAGON AND THE SNAKE...
...WHO KILL FOR MONEY.
"MY BROTHER IS CERTAINLY BEING PUT TO GOOD USE."

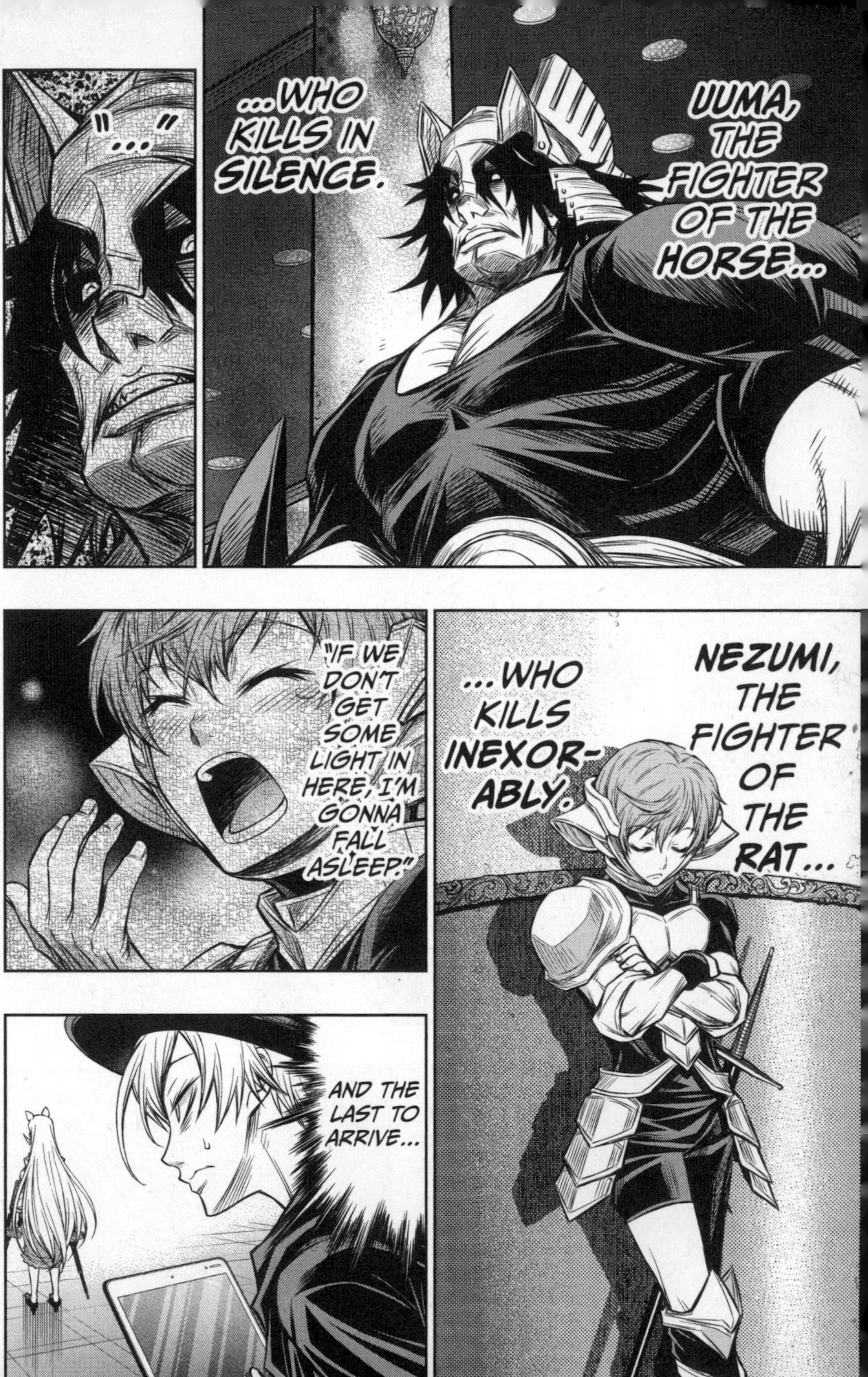
UUMA, THE FIGHTER OF THE HORSE...
...WHO KILLS IN SILENCE.
"..."
NEZUMI, THE FIGHTER OF THE RAT...
...WHO KILLS INEXORABLY.
"IF WE DON'T GET SOME LIGHT IN HERE, I'M GONNA FALL ASLEEP."
AND THE LAST TO ARRIVE...

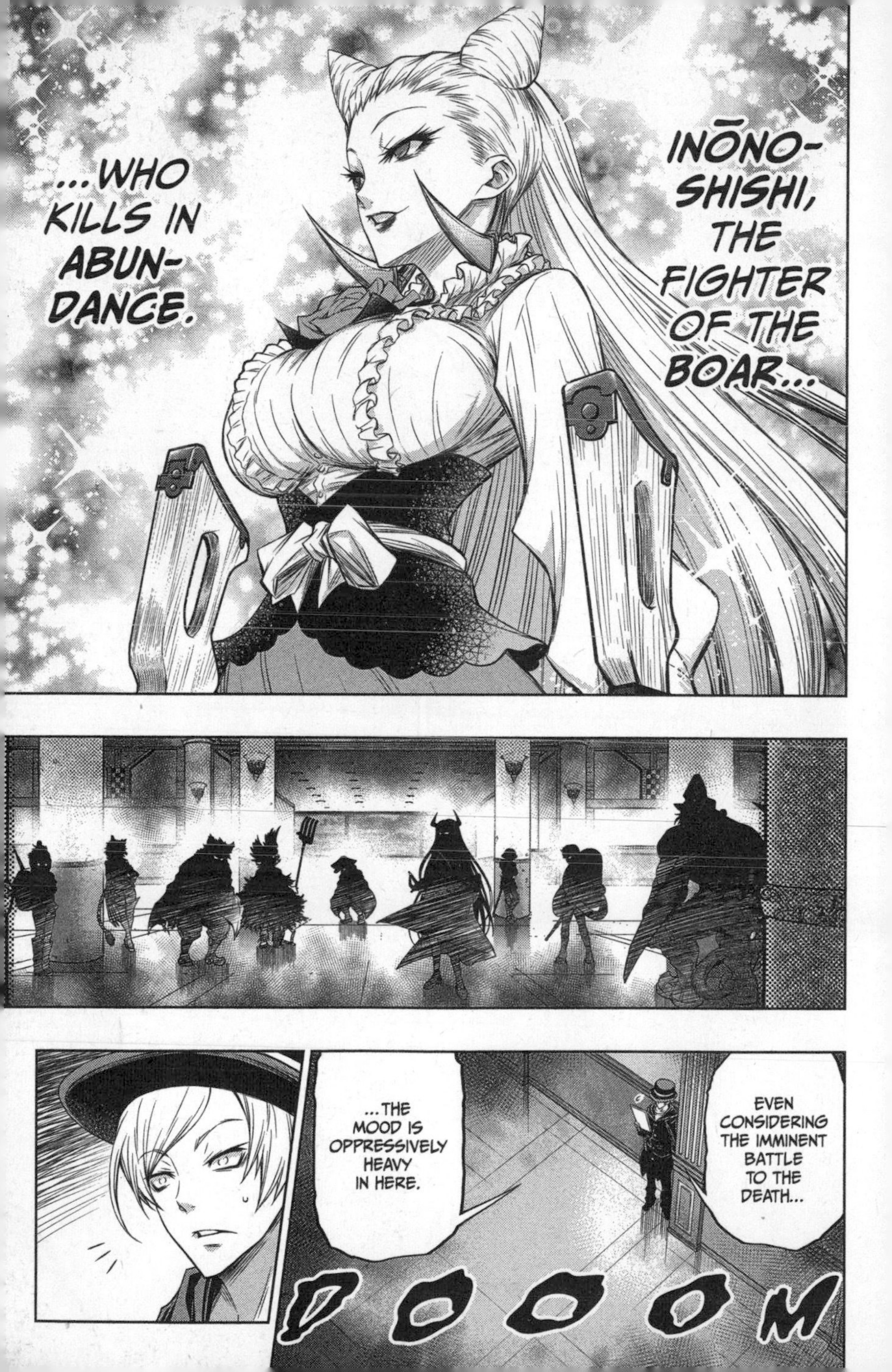
INŌNO-SHISHI, THE FIGHTER OF THE BOAR...
...WHO KILLS IN ABUN-DANCE.
EVEN CONSIDERING THE IMMINENT BATTLE TO THE DEATH...
...THE MOOD IS OPPRESSIVELY HEAVY IN HERE.
DOOOOM

UN

!!

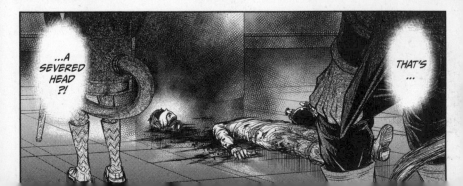

...A SEVERED HEAD ?!

THAT'S ...

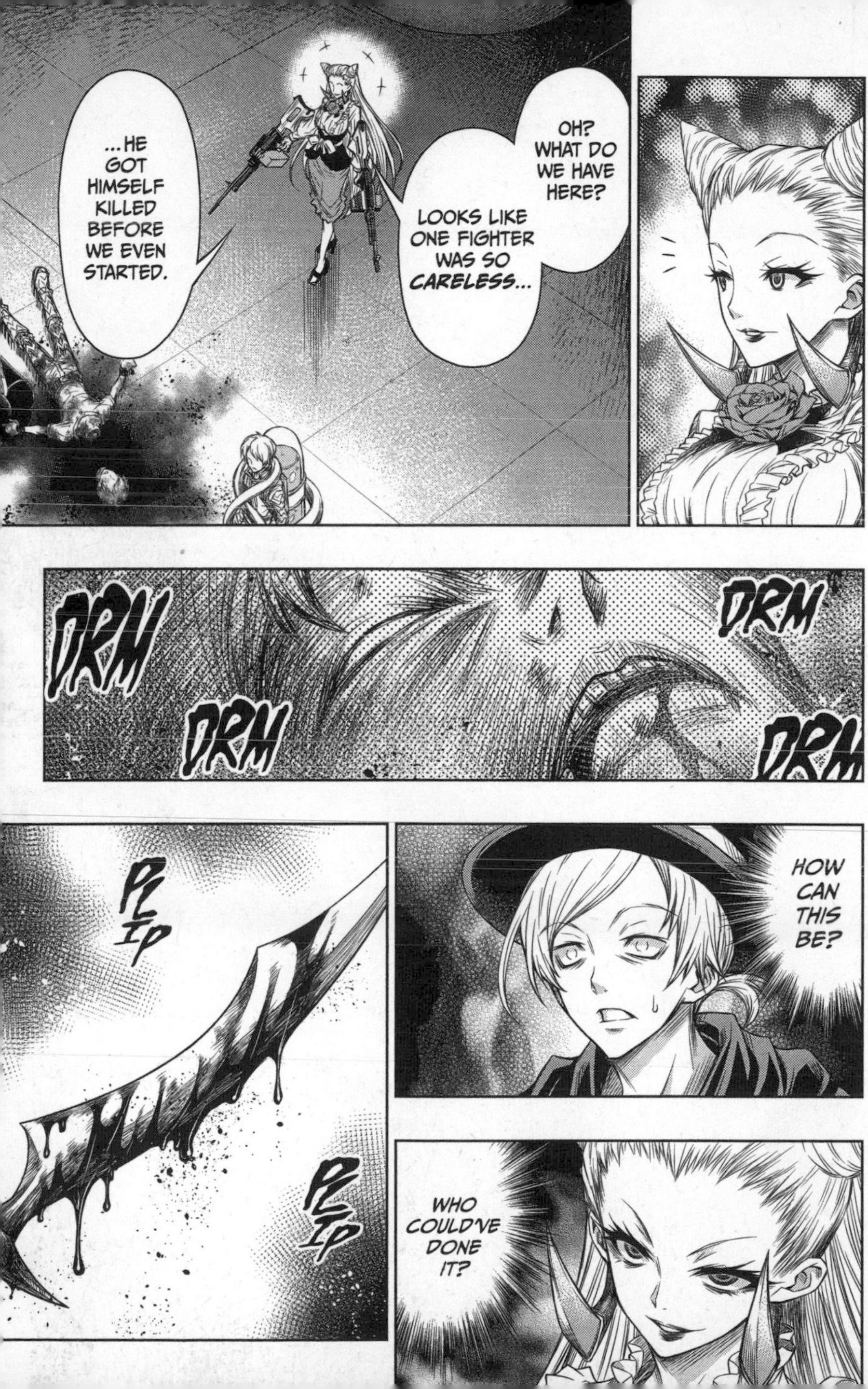
OH? WHAT DO WE HAVE HERE?
LOOKS LIKE ONE FIGHTER WAS SO *CARELESS*...
...HE GOT HIMSELF KILLED BEFORE WE EVEN STARTED.
DRM
DRM
DRM
DRM
HOW CAN THIS BE?
WHO COULD'VE DONE IT?
PLIP
PLIP

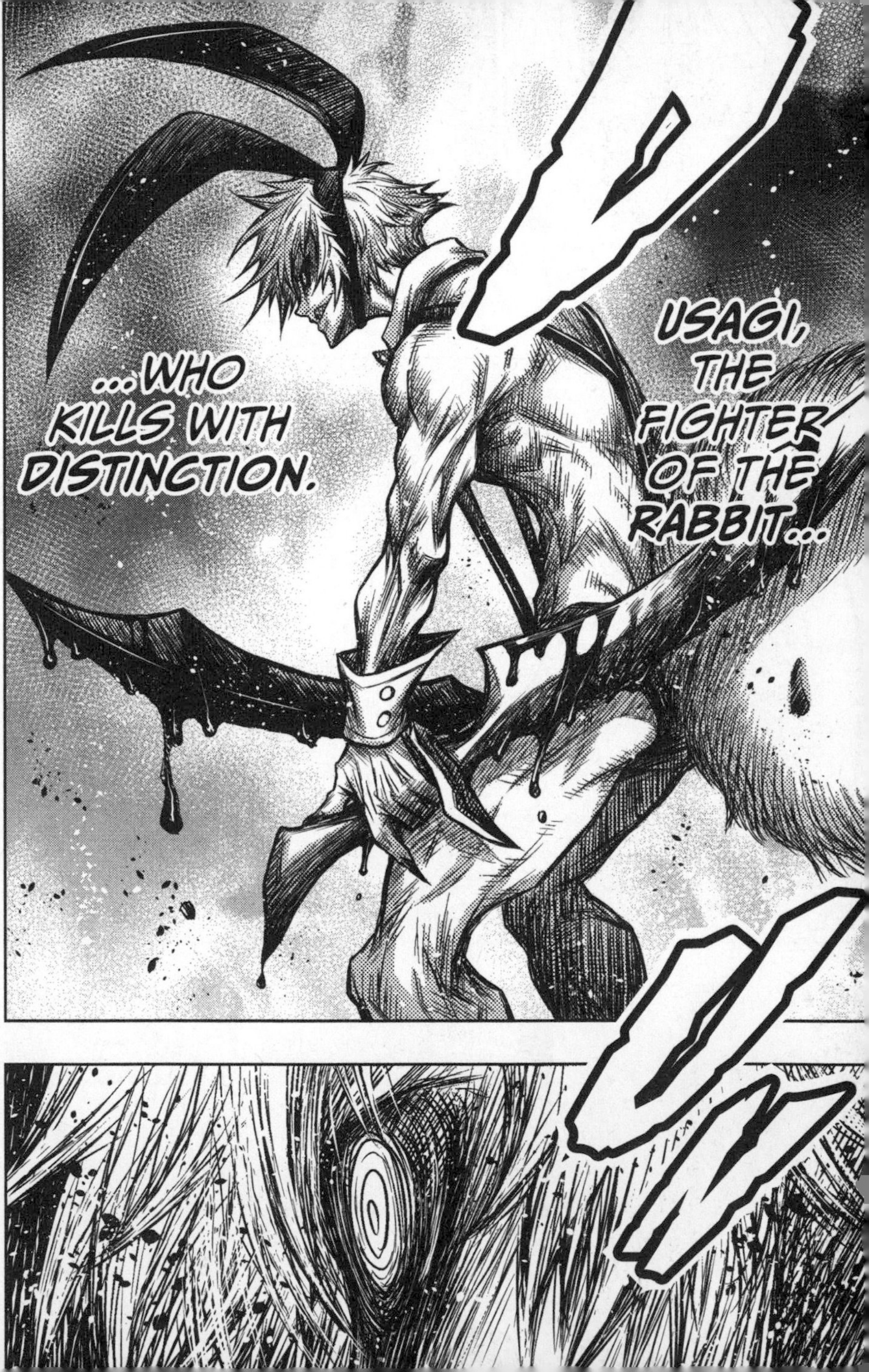
USAGI, THE FIGHTER OF THE RABBIT...
...WHO KILLS WITH DISTINCTION.

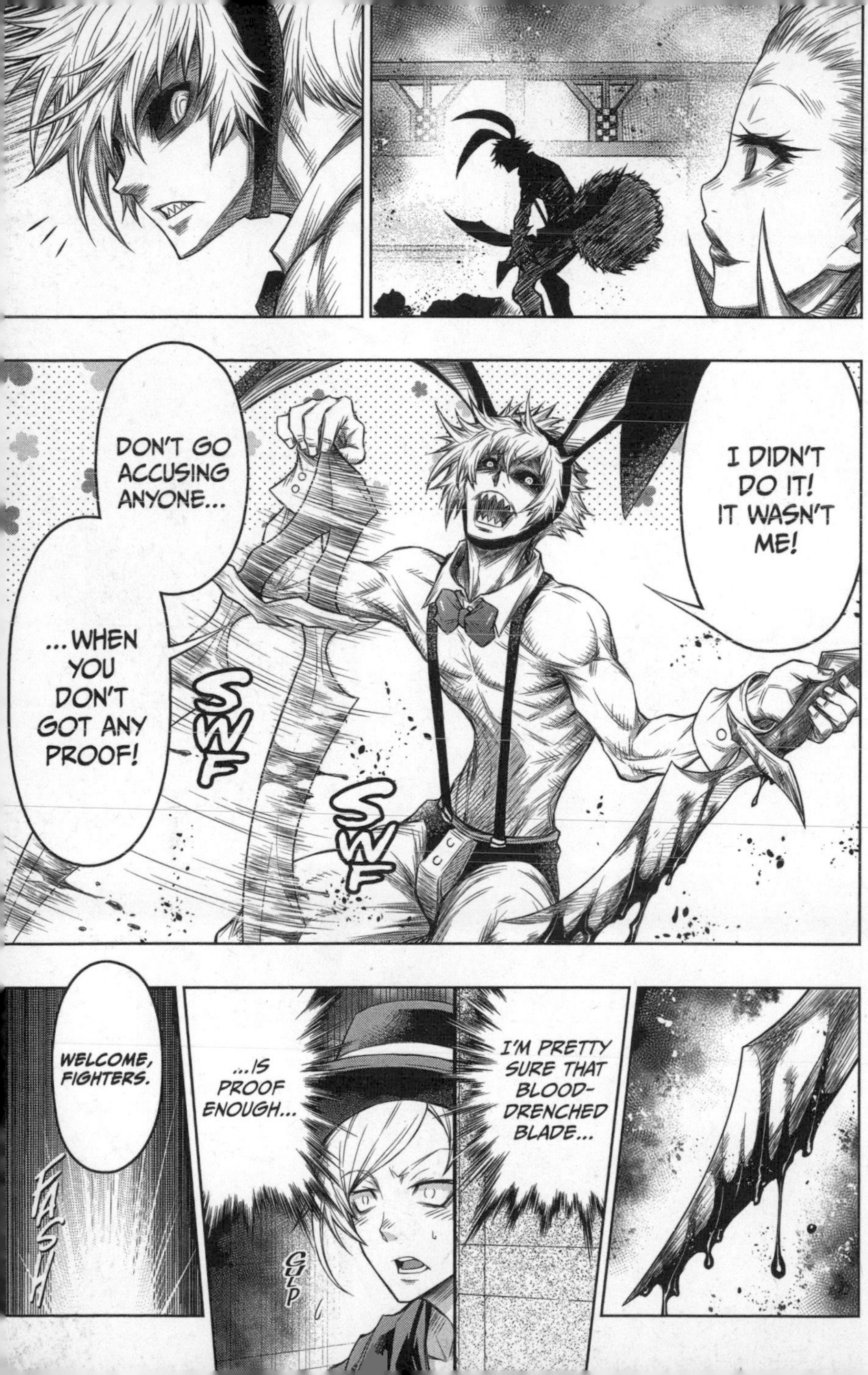
I DIDN'T DO IT! IT WASN'T ME!
DON'T GO ACCUSING ANYONE...
...WHEN YOU DON'T GOT ANY PROOF!
SWF
SWF
I'M PRETTY SURE THAT BLOOD-DRENCHED BLADE...
...IS PROOF ENOUGH...
GULP
WELCOME, FIGHTERS.
FASH

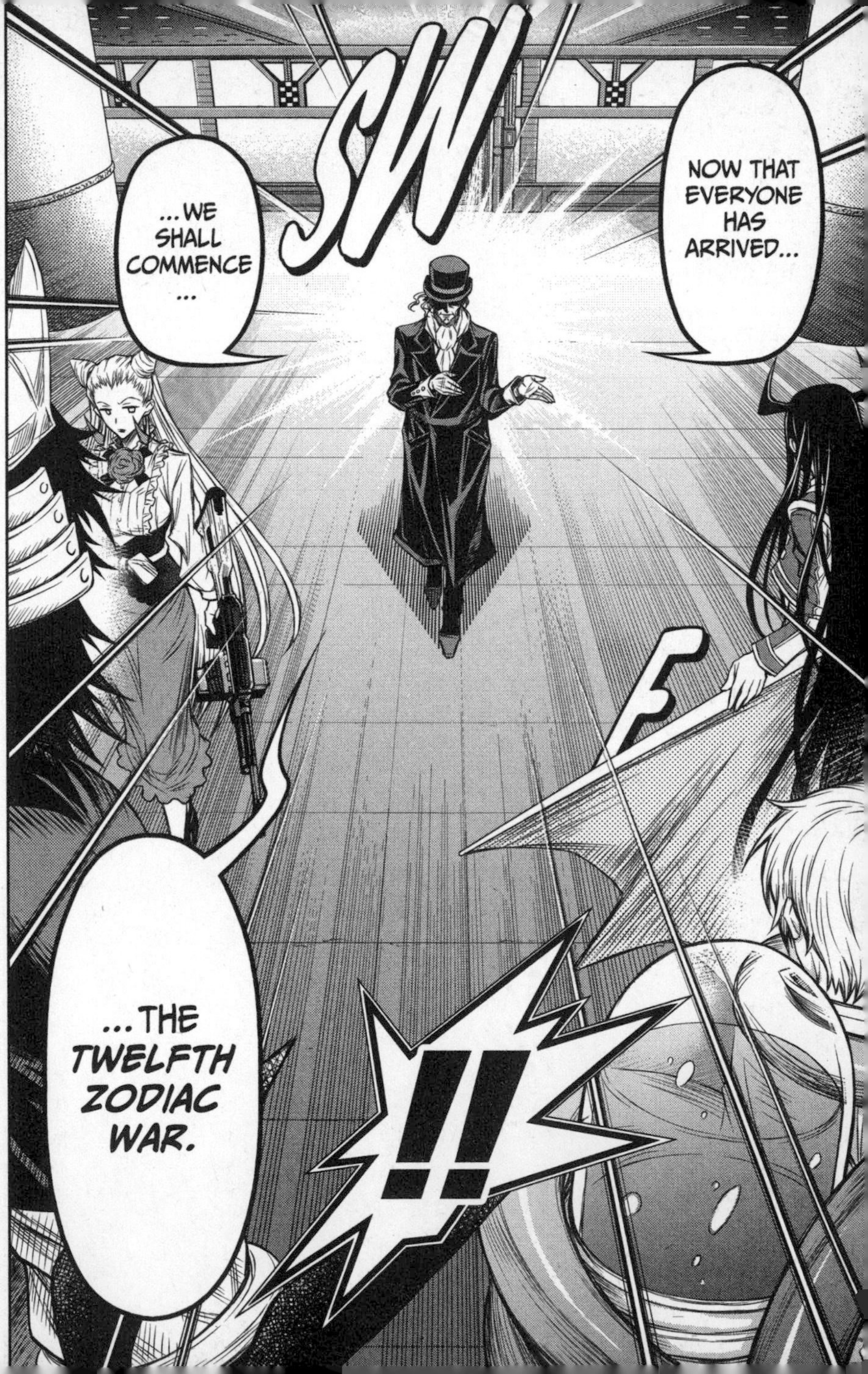
NOW THAT EVERYONE HAS ARRIVED...
...WE SHALL COMMENCE ...
...THE TWELFTH ZODIAC WAR.
!!

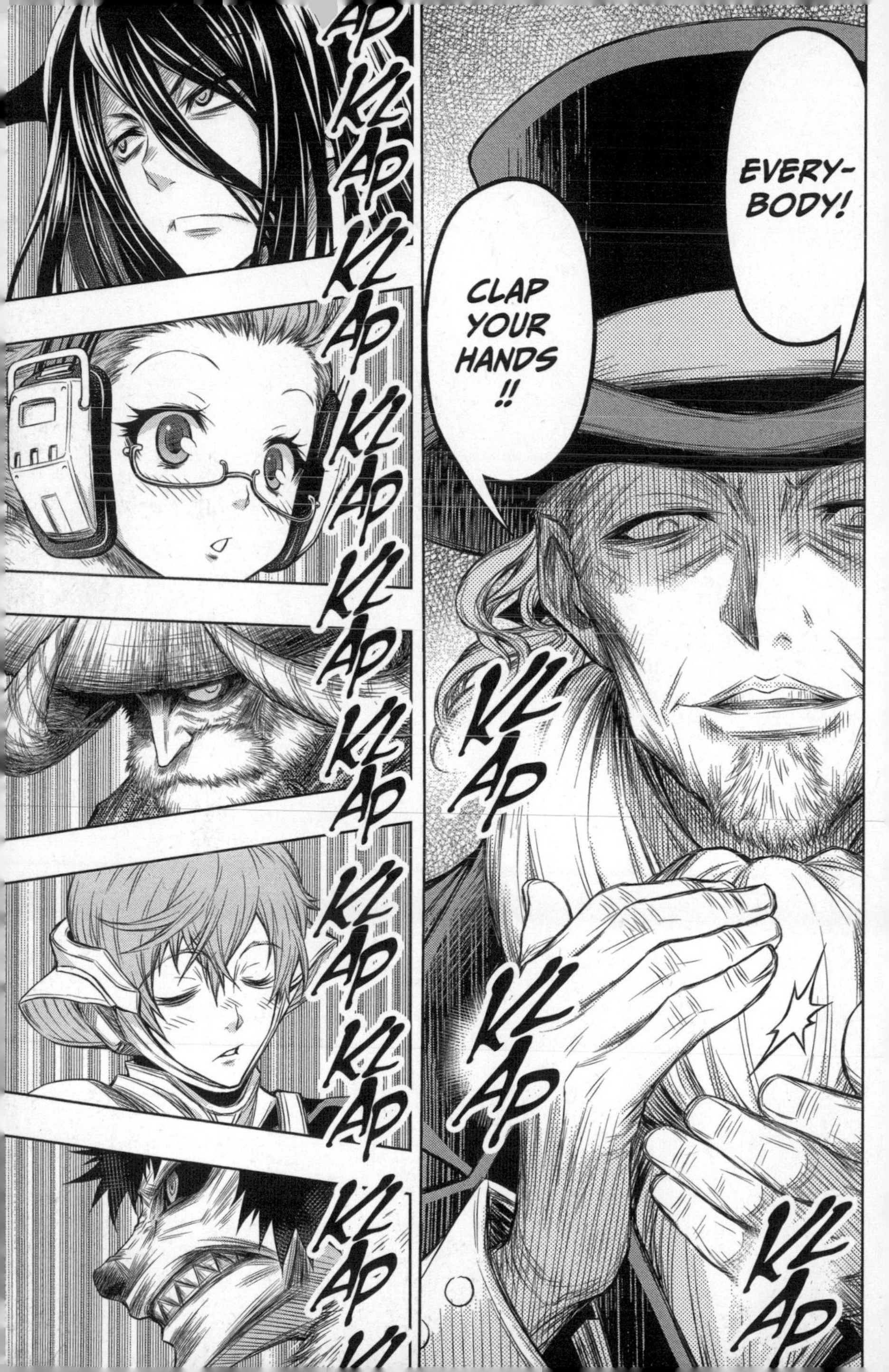
EVERY-BODY!
CLAP YOUR HANDS!!
KLAP
KLAP
KLAP

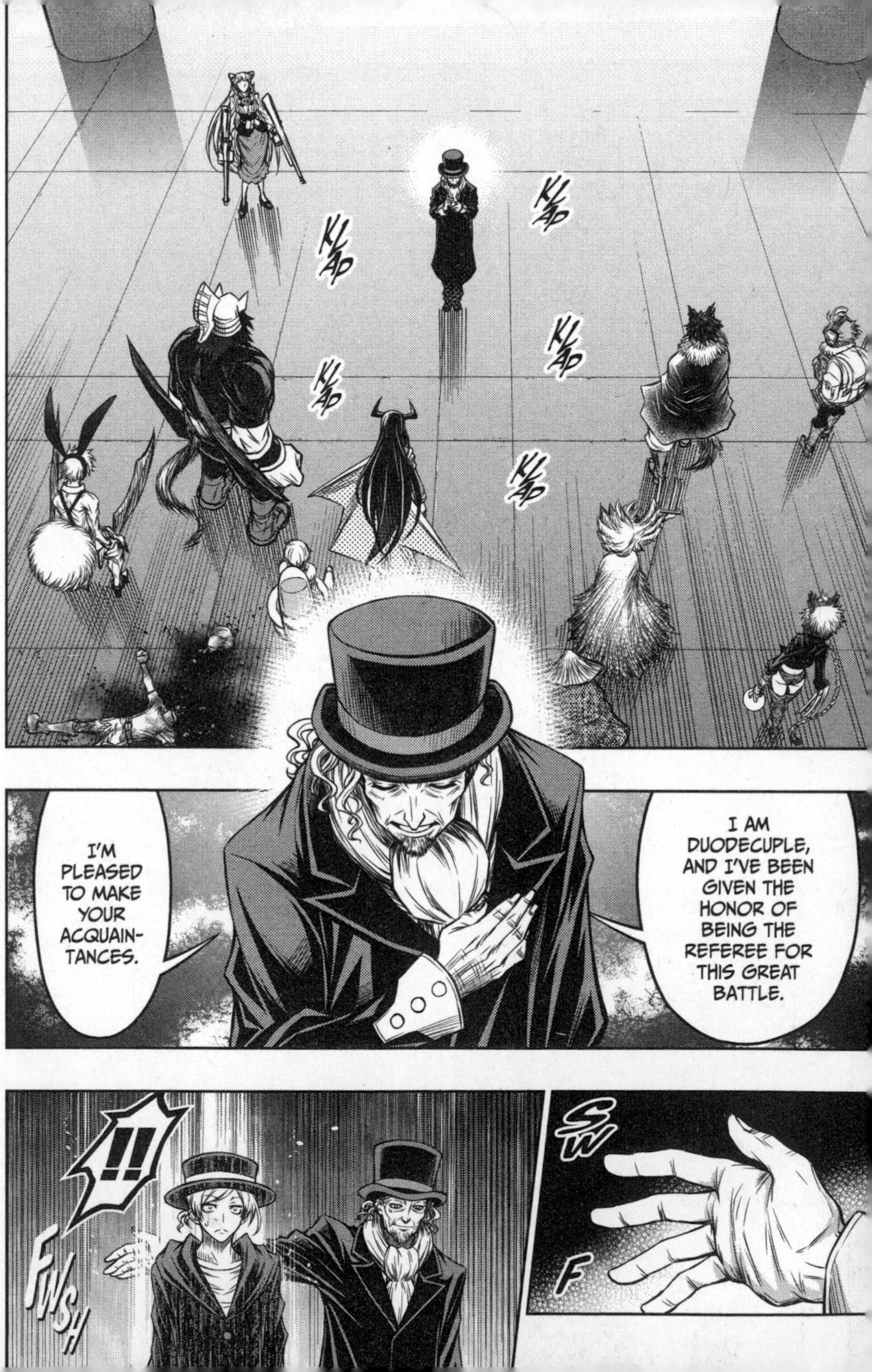
KLAP
KLAP
KLAP
KLAP
KLAP
I AM DUODECUPLE, AND I'VE BEEN GIVEN THE HONOR OF BEING THE REFEREE FOR THIS GREAT BATTLE.
I'M PLEASED TO MAKE YOUR ACQUAIN-TANCES.
SW
F
!!
FWSH

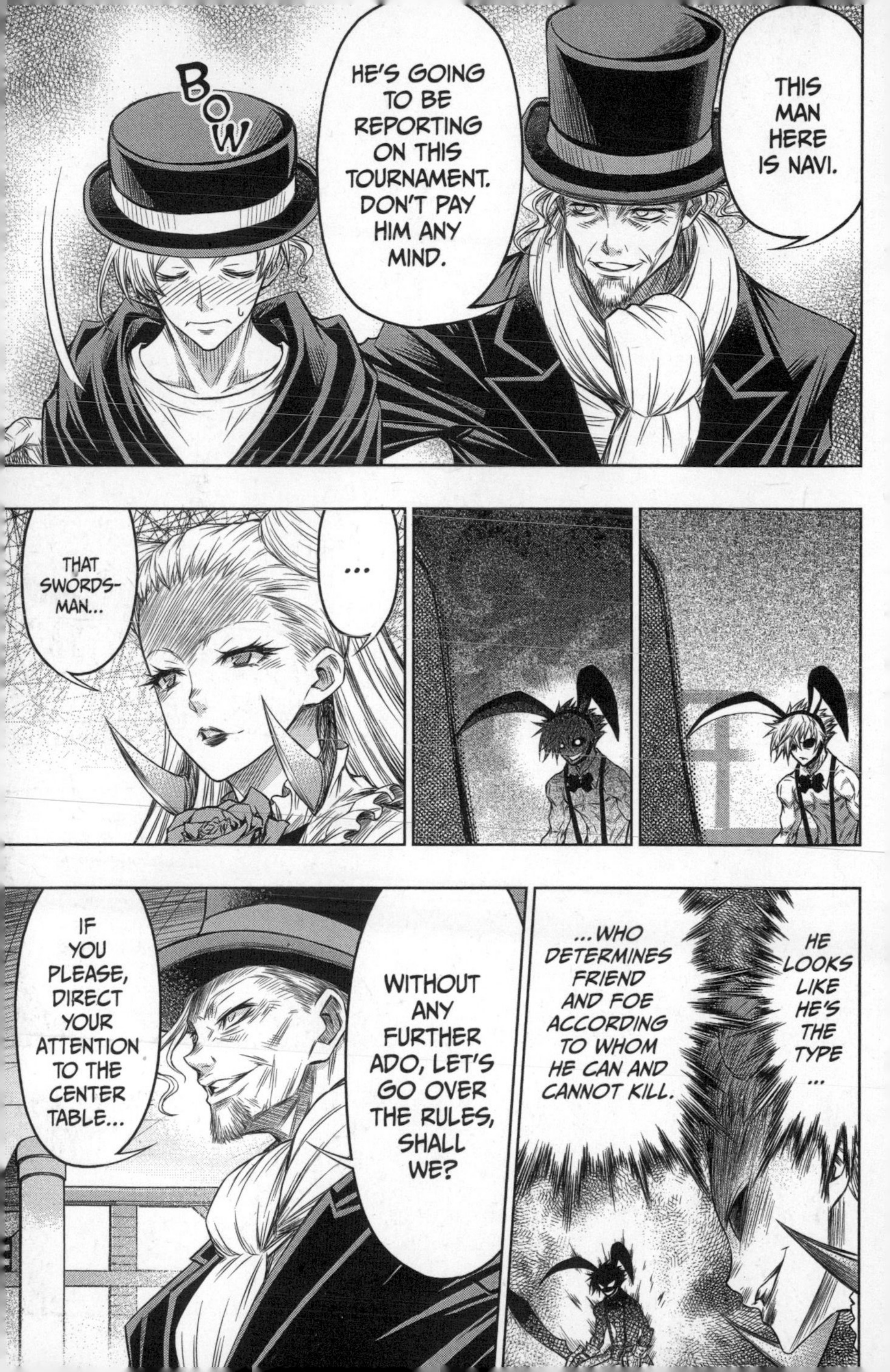
THIS MAN HERE IS NAVI.
HE'S GOING TO BE REPORTING ON THIS TOURNAMENT. DON'T PAY HIM ANY MIND.
BOW
...
THAT SWORDS-MAN...
HE LOOKS LIKE HE'S THE TYPE ...
...WHO DETERMINES FRIEND AND FOE ACCORDING TO WHOM HE CAN AND CANNOT KILL.
WITHOUT ANY FURTHER ADO, LET'S GO OVER THE RULES, SHALL WE?
IF YOU PLEASE, DIRECT YOUR ATTENTION TO THE CENTER TABLE...

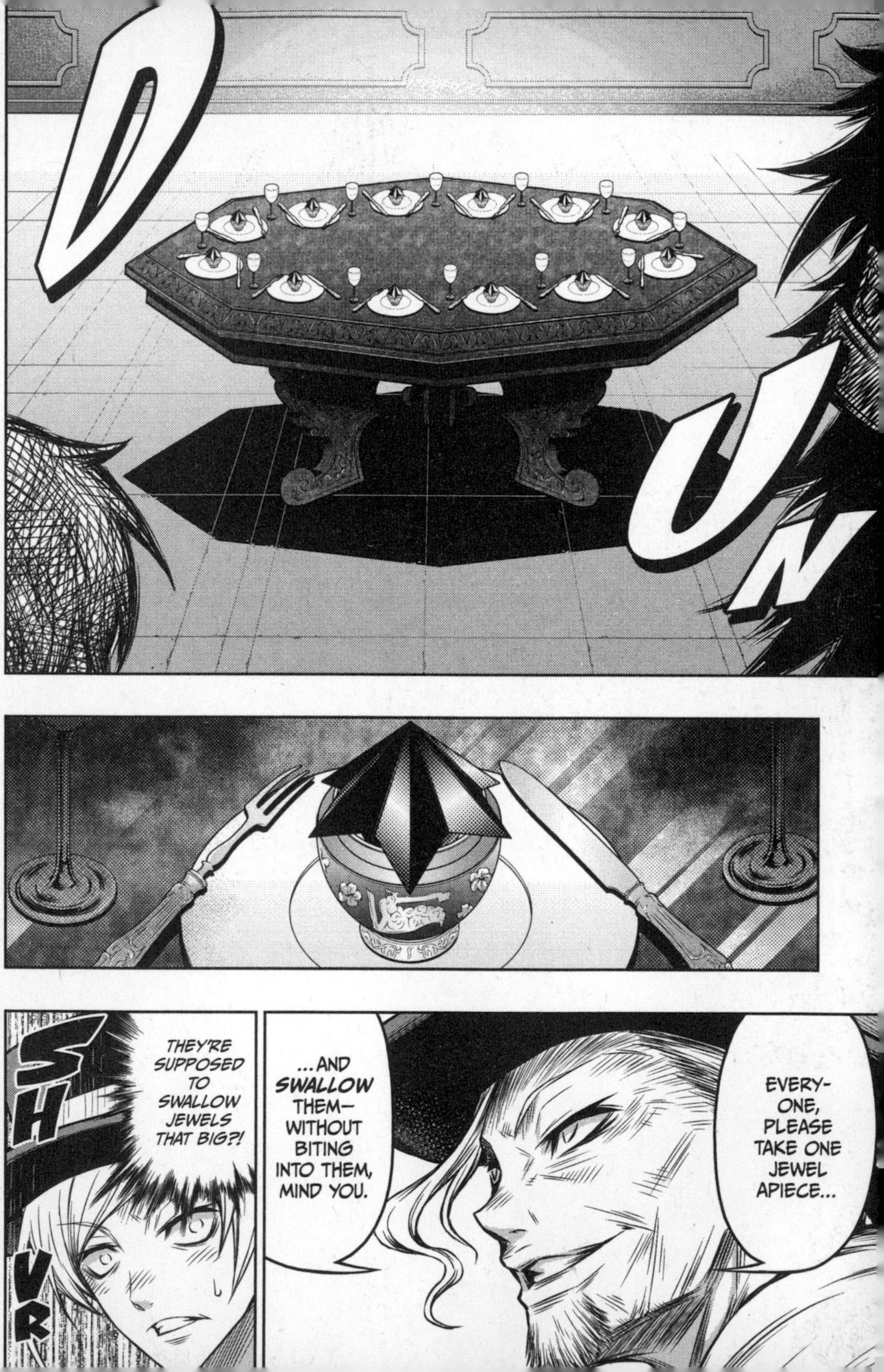
DUN
EVERY-ONE, PLEASE TAKE ONE JEWEL APIECE...
...AND **SWALLOW** THEM—WITHOUT BITING INTO THEM, MIND YOU.
THEY'RE SUPPOSED TO SWALLOW JEWELS THAT BIG?!
SHVR

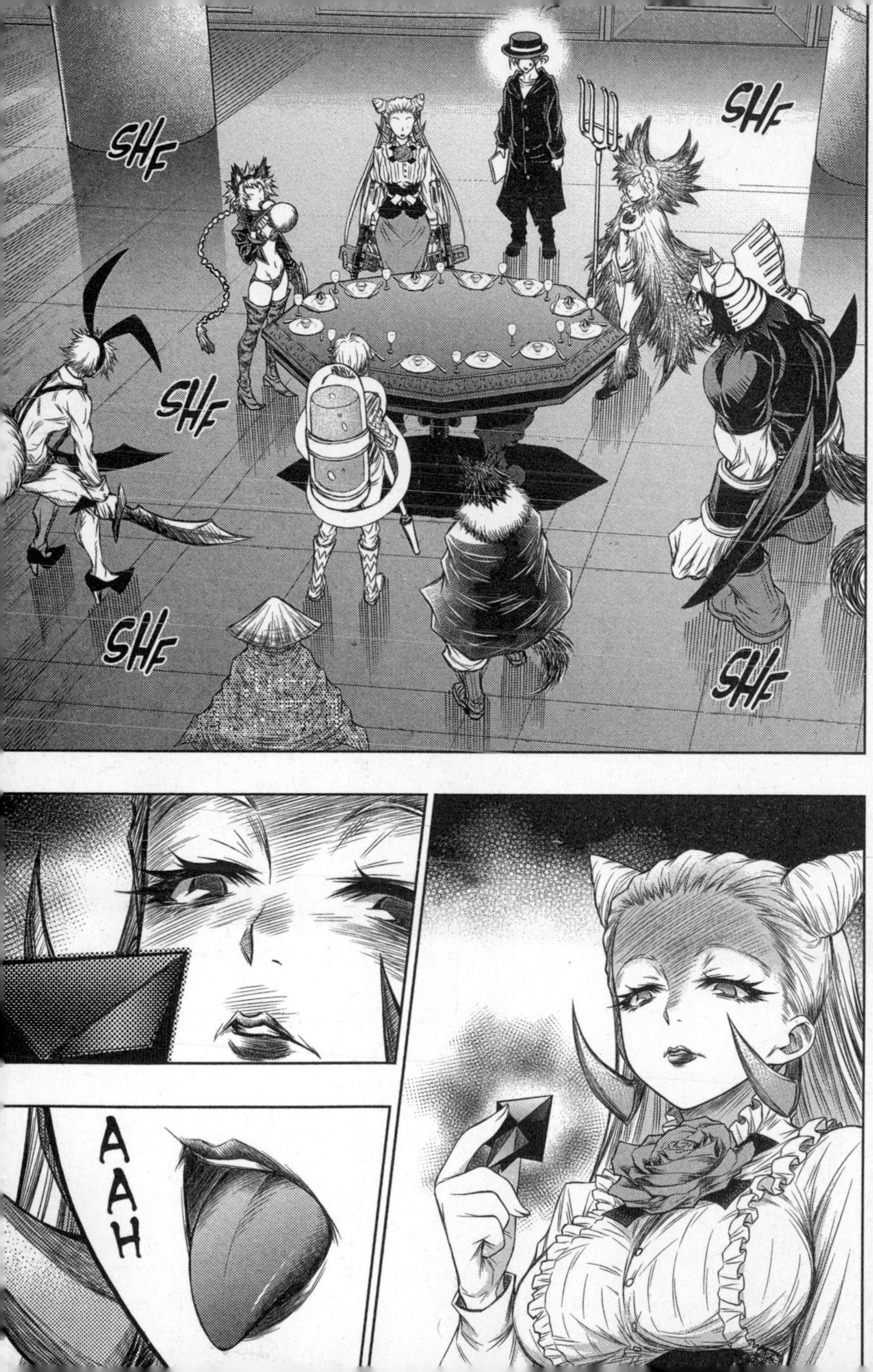
SHF
SHF
SHF
SHF
SHF
AAH

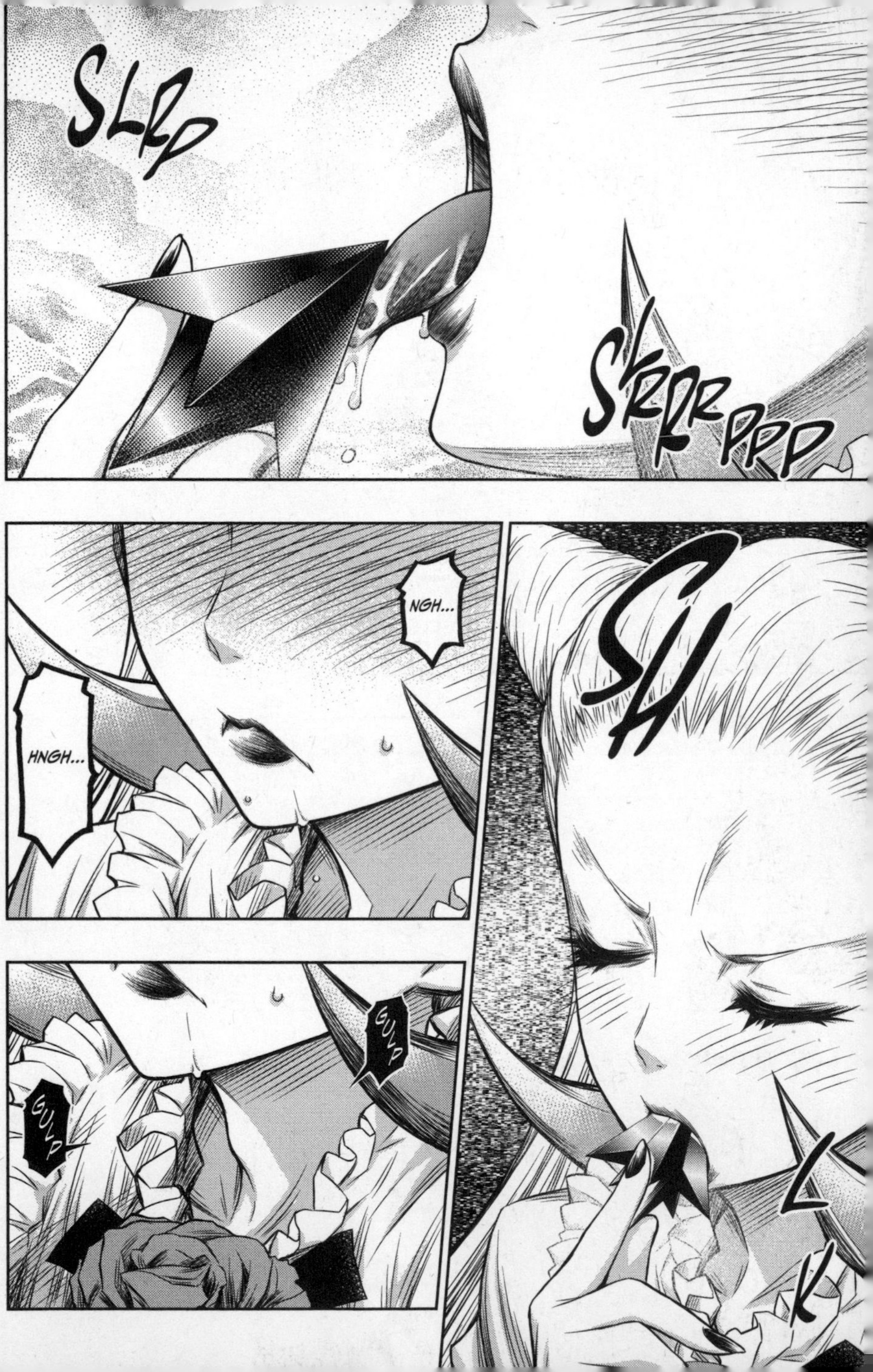
SKRRRPPP
SLRP
SH
LK
NGH...
HNGH...
GULP
GULP

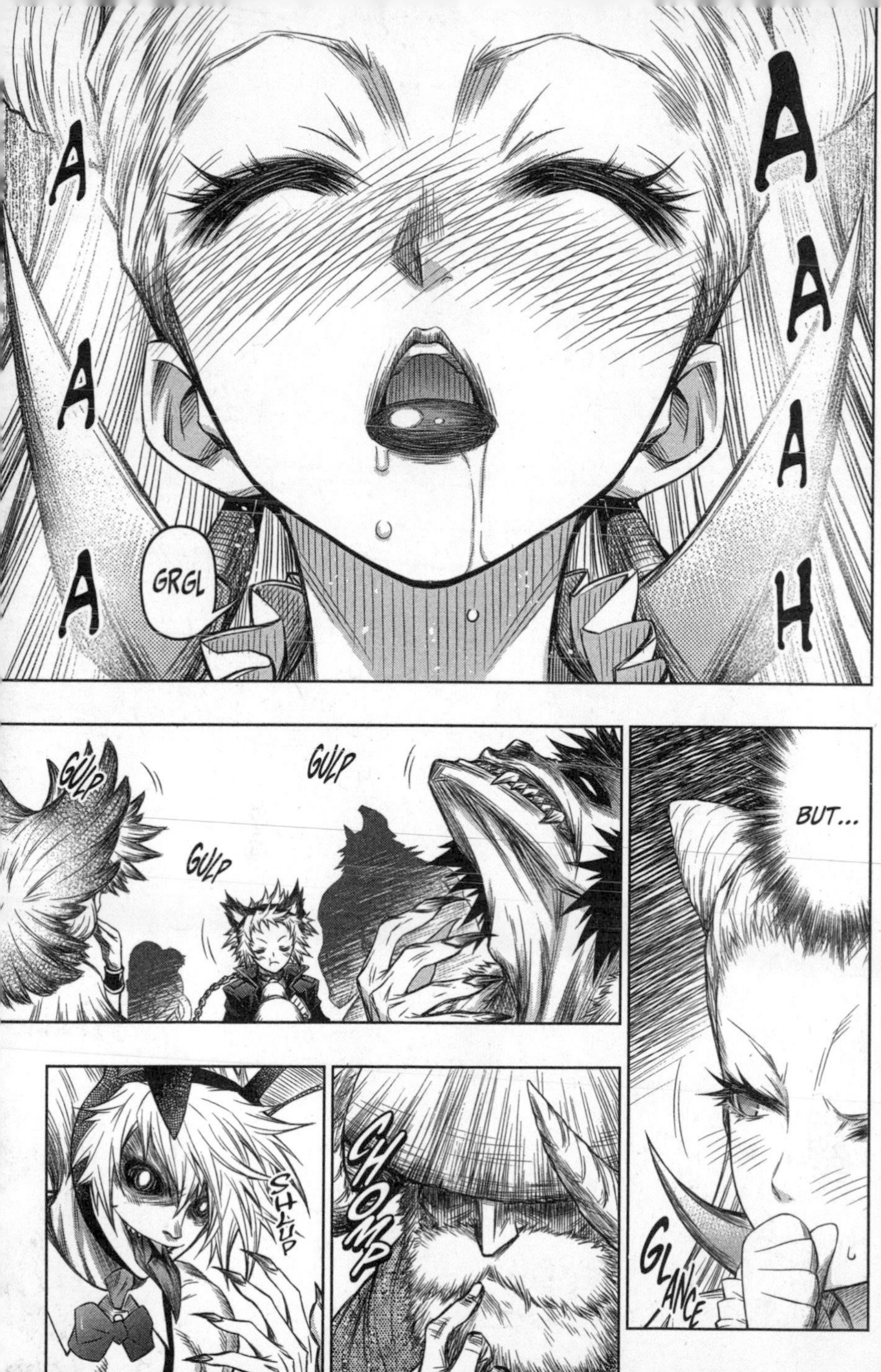
AAAAH
A A A
GRGL
BUT...
GLANCE
GULP
GULP
GULP
CHOMP
SHLUP

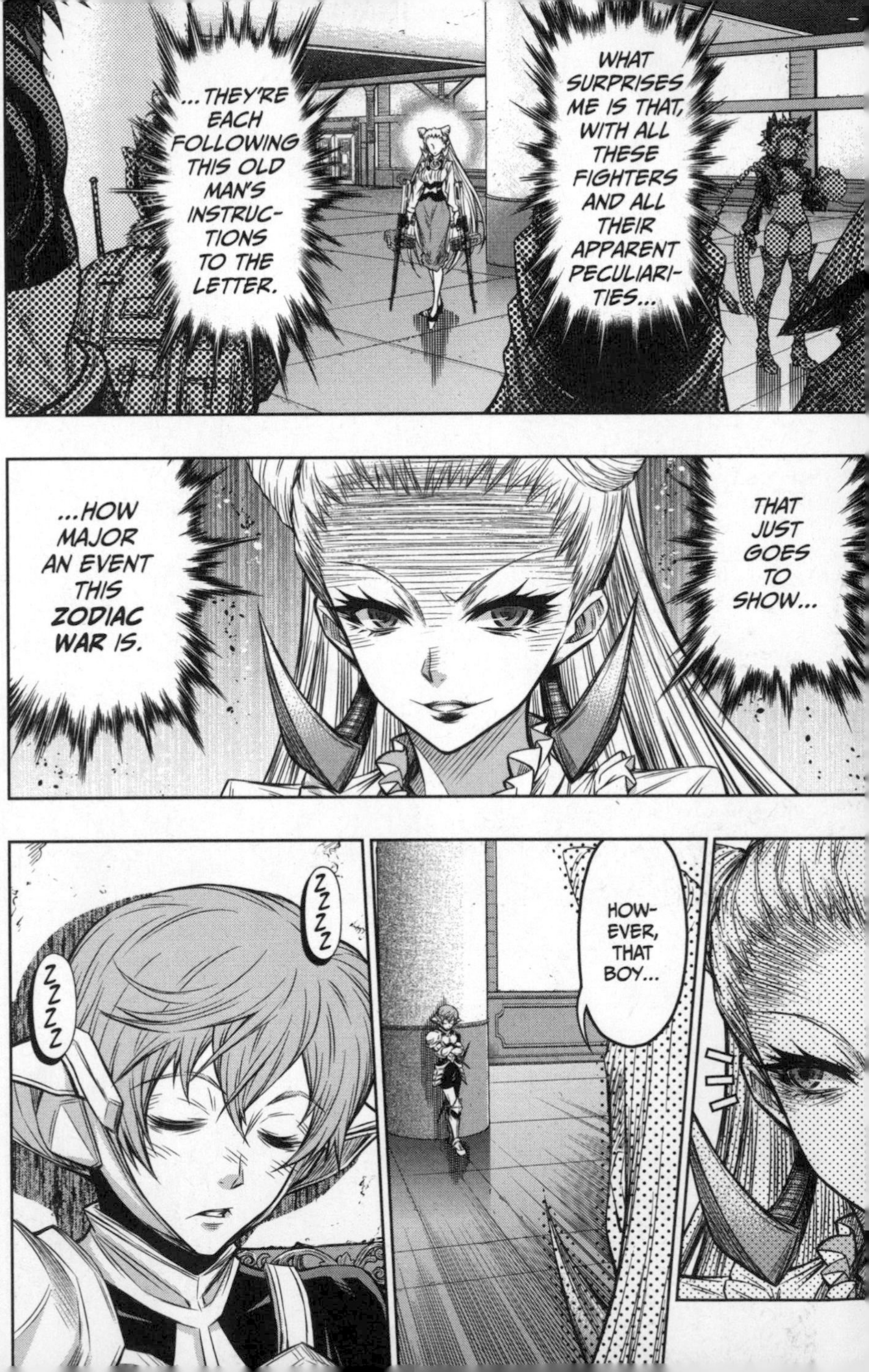
WHAT SURPRISES ME IS THAT, WITH ALL THESE FIGHTERS AND ALL THEIR APPARENT PECULIARI-TIES...
...THEY'RE EACH FOLLOWING THIS OLD MAN'S INSTRUC-TIONS TO THE LETTER.
THAT JUST GOES TO SHOW...
...HOW MAJOR AN EVENT THIS ZODIAC WAR IS.
HOW-EVER, THAT BOY...
ZZZZ
ZZZZ

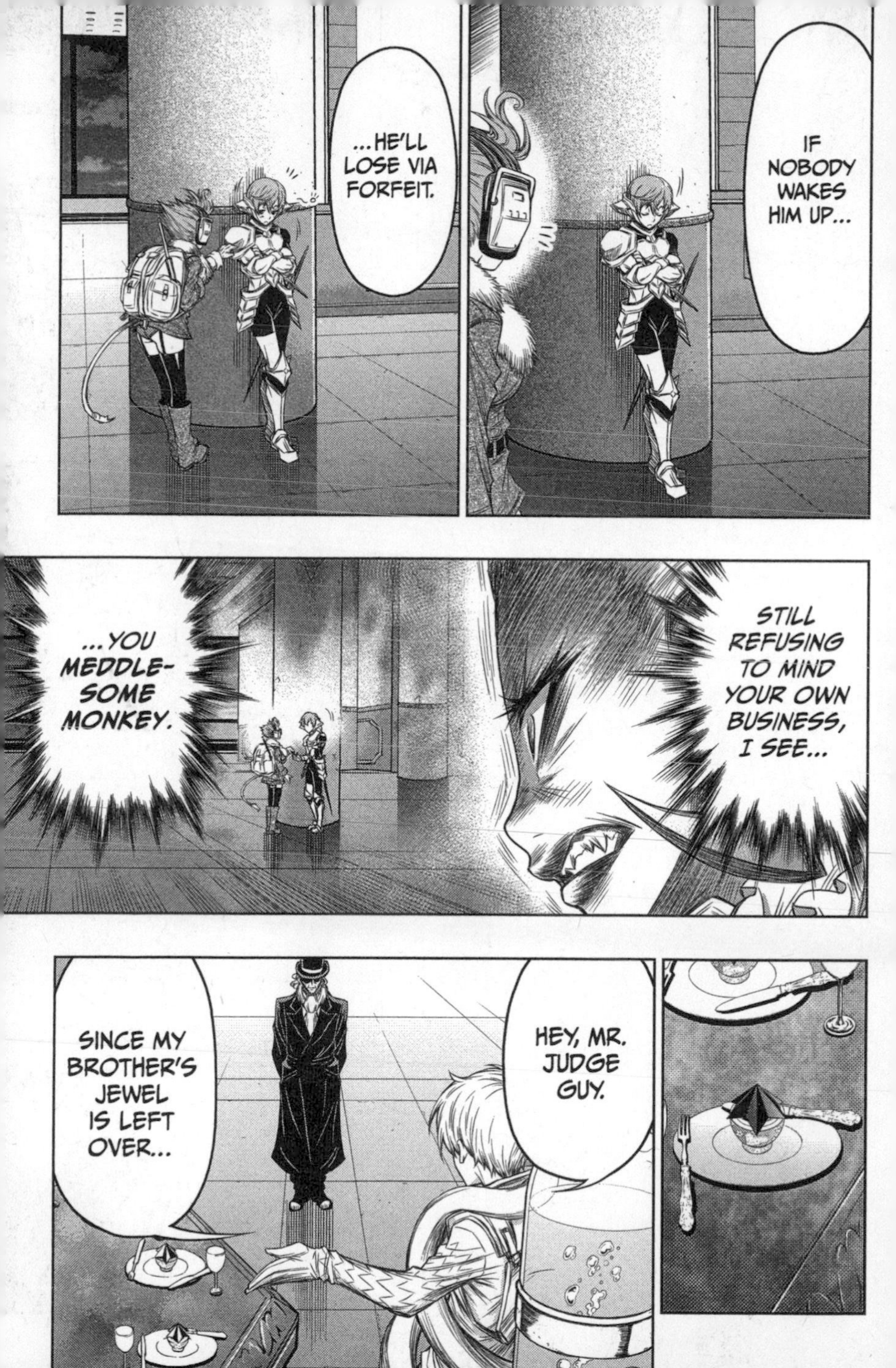
IF NOBODY WAKES HIM UP...
...HE'LL LOSE VIA FORFEIT.
STILL REFUSING TO MIND YOUR OWN BUSINESS, I SEE...
...YOU MEDDLESOME MONKEY.
HEY, MR. JUDGE GUY.
SINCE MY BROTHER'S JEWEL IS LEFT OVER...

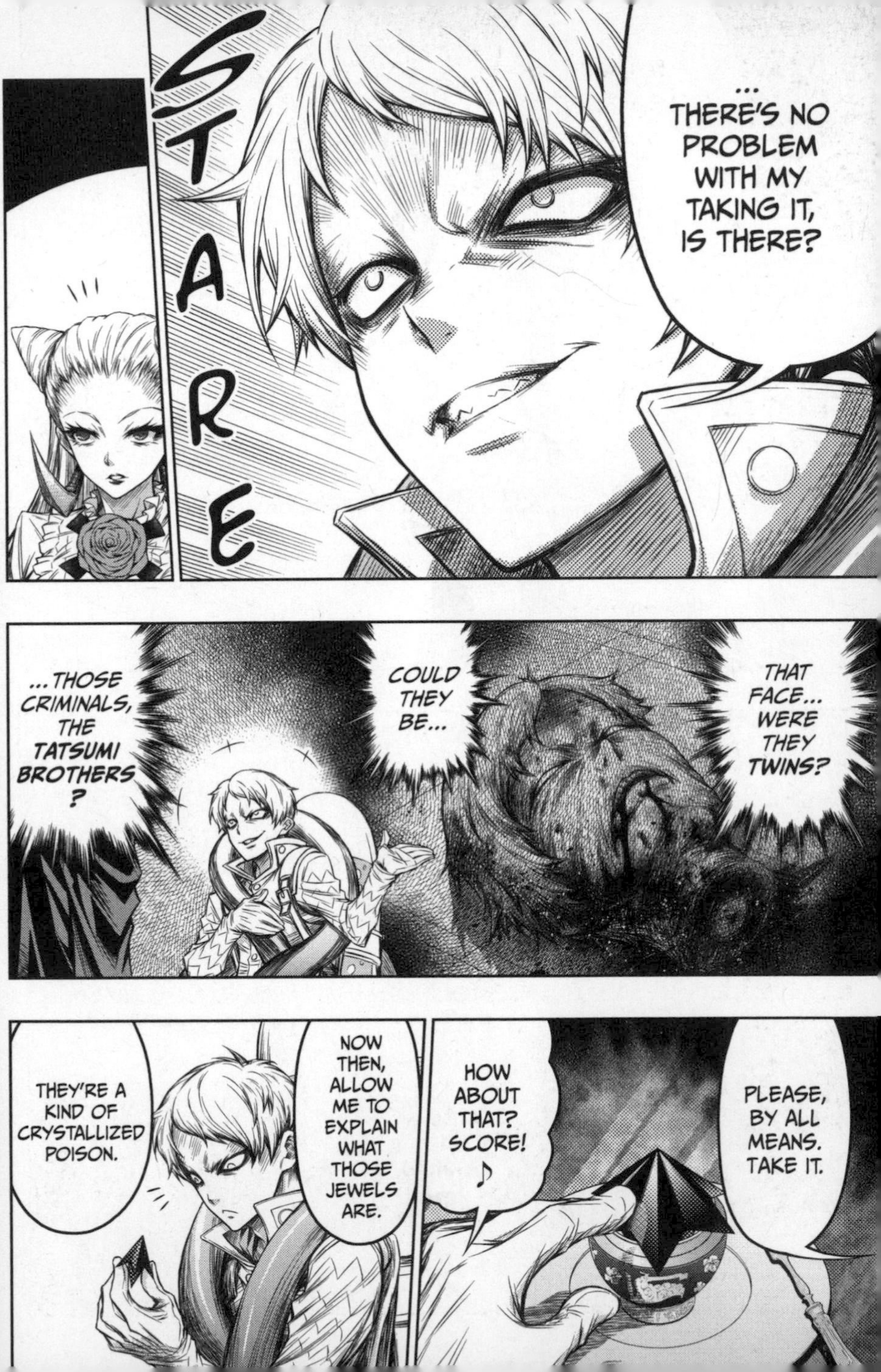
... THERE'S NO PROBLEM WITH MY TAKING IT, IS THERE?
STARE
THAT FACE... WERE THEY TWINS?
COULD THEY BE...
...THOSE CRIMINALS, THE TATSUMI BROTHERS?
PLEASE, BY ALL MEANS. TAKE IT.
HOW ABOUT THAT? SCORE! ♪
NOW THEN, ALLOW ME TO EXPLAIN WHAT THOSE JEWELS ARE.
THEY'RE A KIND OF CRYSTALLIZED POISON.

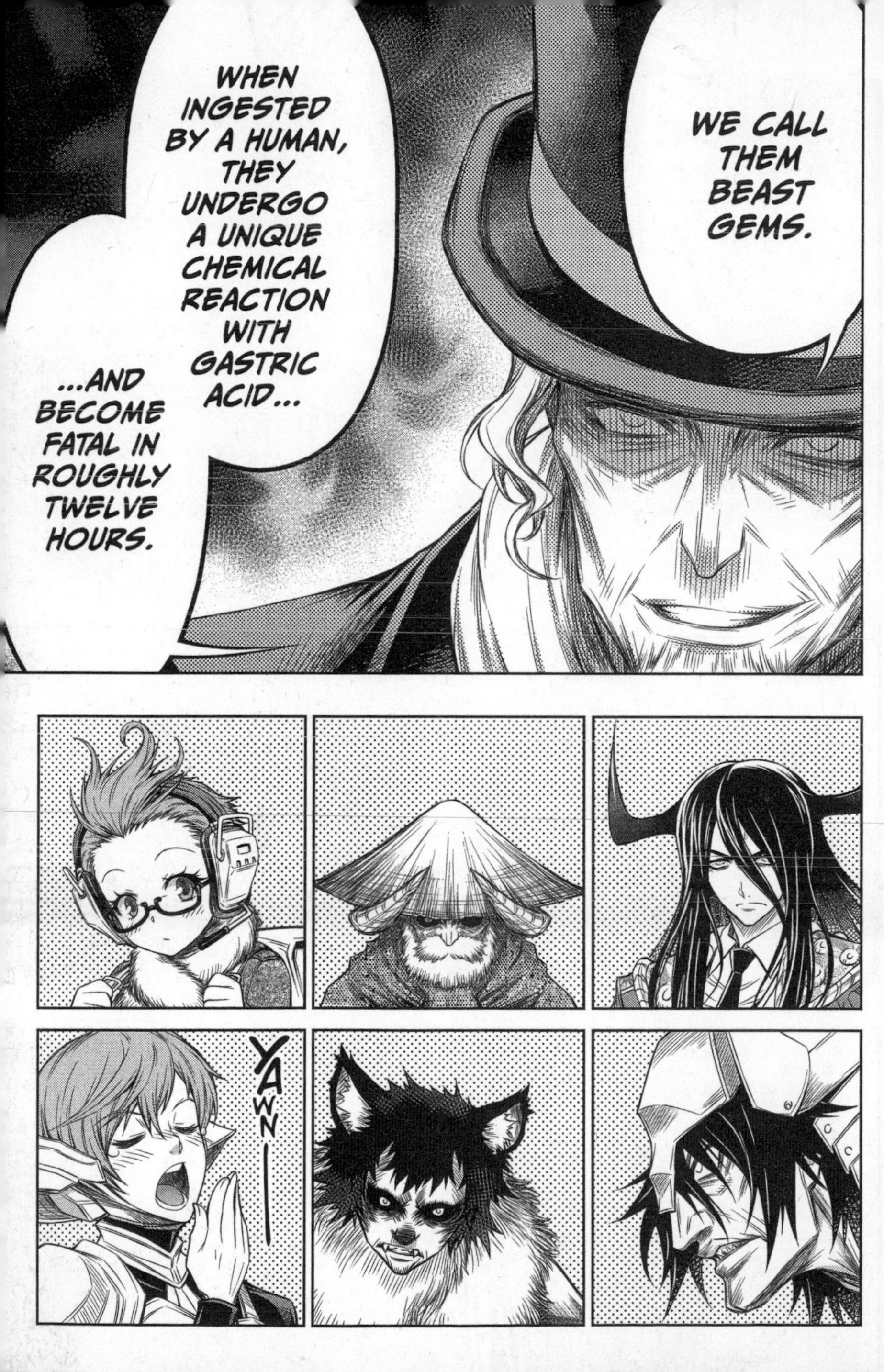
WE CALL THEM BEAST GEMS.
WHEN INGESTED BY A HUMAN, THEY UNDERGO A UNIQUE CHEMICAL REACTION WITH GASTRIC ACID...
...AND BECOME FATAL IN ROUGHLY TWELVE HOURS.
YAWN

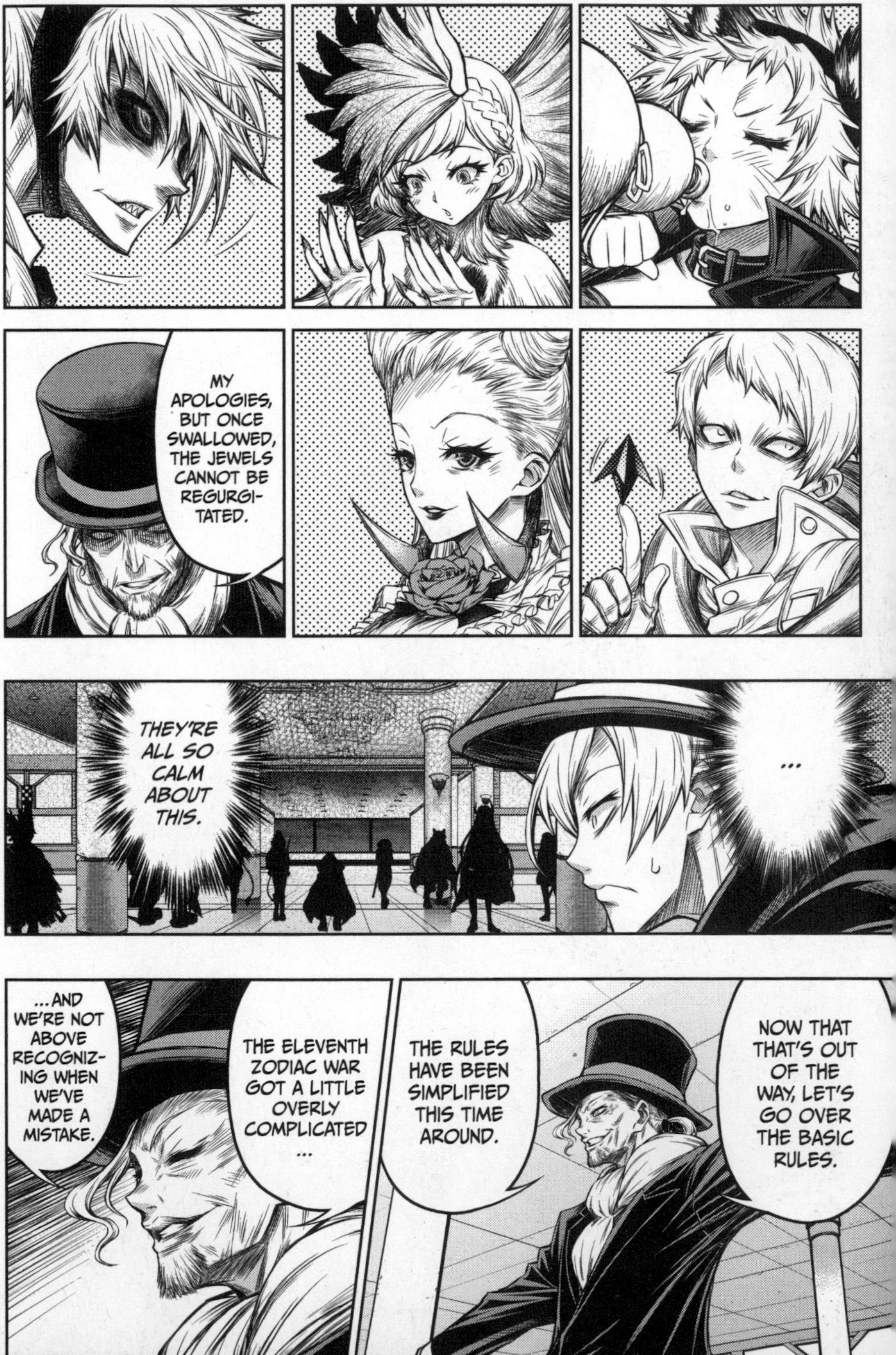
MY APOLOGIES, BUT ONCE SWALLOWED, THE JEWELS CANNOT BE REGURGITATED.
...
THEY'RE ALL SO CALM ABOUT THIS.
NOW THAT THAT'S OUT OF THE WAY, LET'S GO OVER THE BASIC RULES.
THE RULES HAVE BEEN SIMPLIFIED THIS TIME AROUND.
THE ELEVENTH ZODIAC WAR GOT A LITTLE OVERLY COMPLICATED...
...AND WE'RE NOT ABOVE RECOGNIZING WHEN WE'VE MADE A MISTAKE.

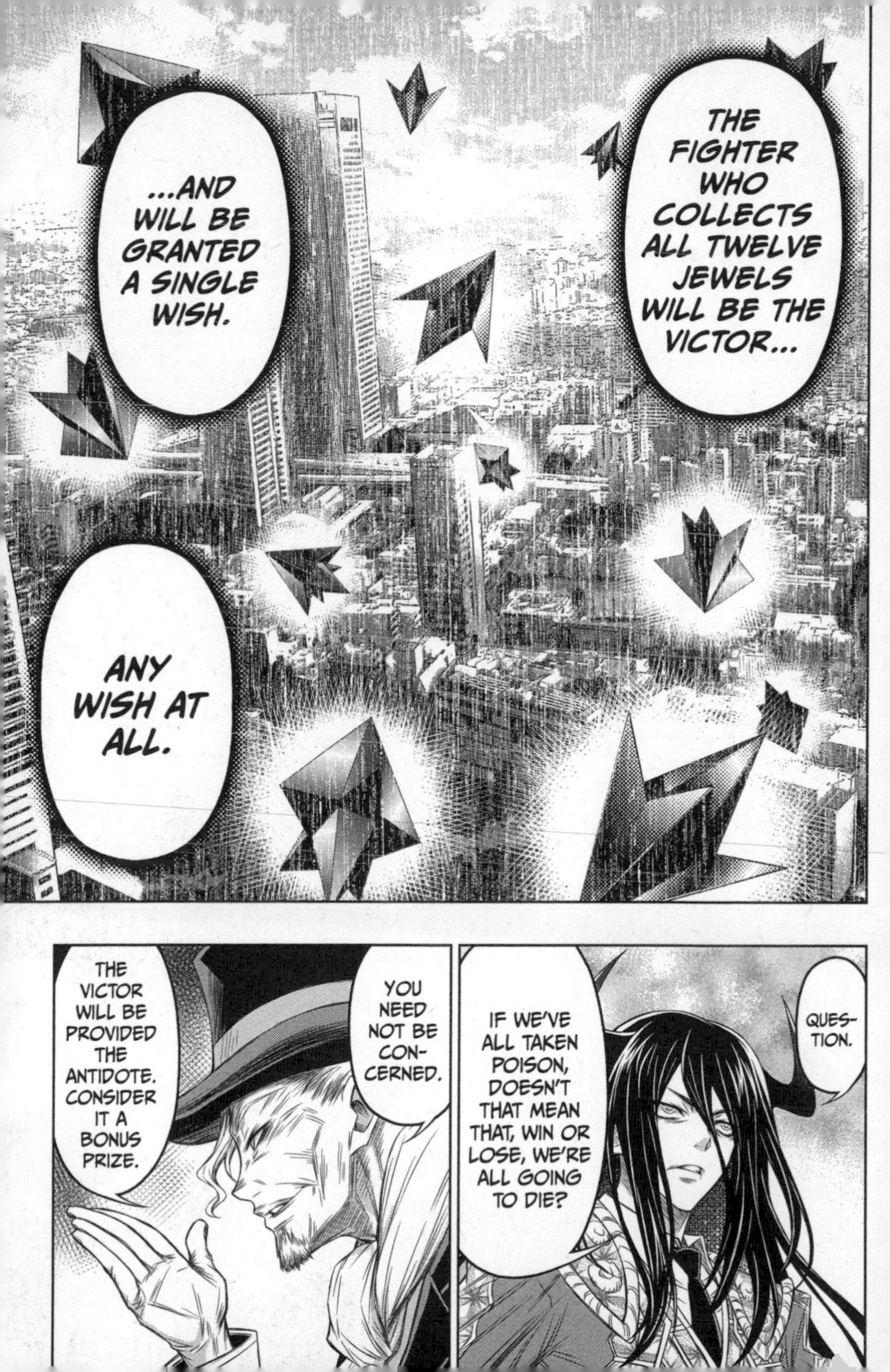
THE FIGHTER WHO COLLECTS ALL TWELVE JEWELS WILL BE THE VICTOR...
...AND WILL BE GRANTED A SINGLE WISH.
ANY WISH AT ALL.
QUES-TION.
IF WE'VE ALL TAKEN POISON, DOESN'T THAT MEAN THAT, WIN OR LOSE, WE'RE ALL GOING TO DIE?
YOU NEED NOT BE CON-CERNED.
THE VICTOR WILL BE PROVIDED THE ANTIDOTE. CONSIDER IT A BONUS PRIZE.

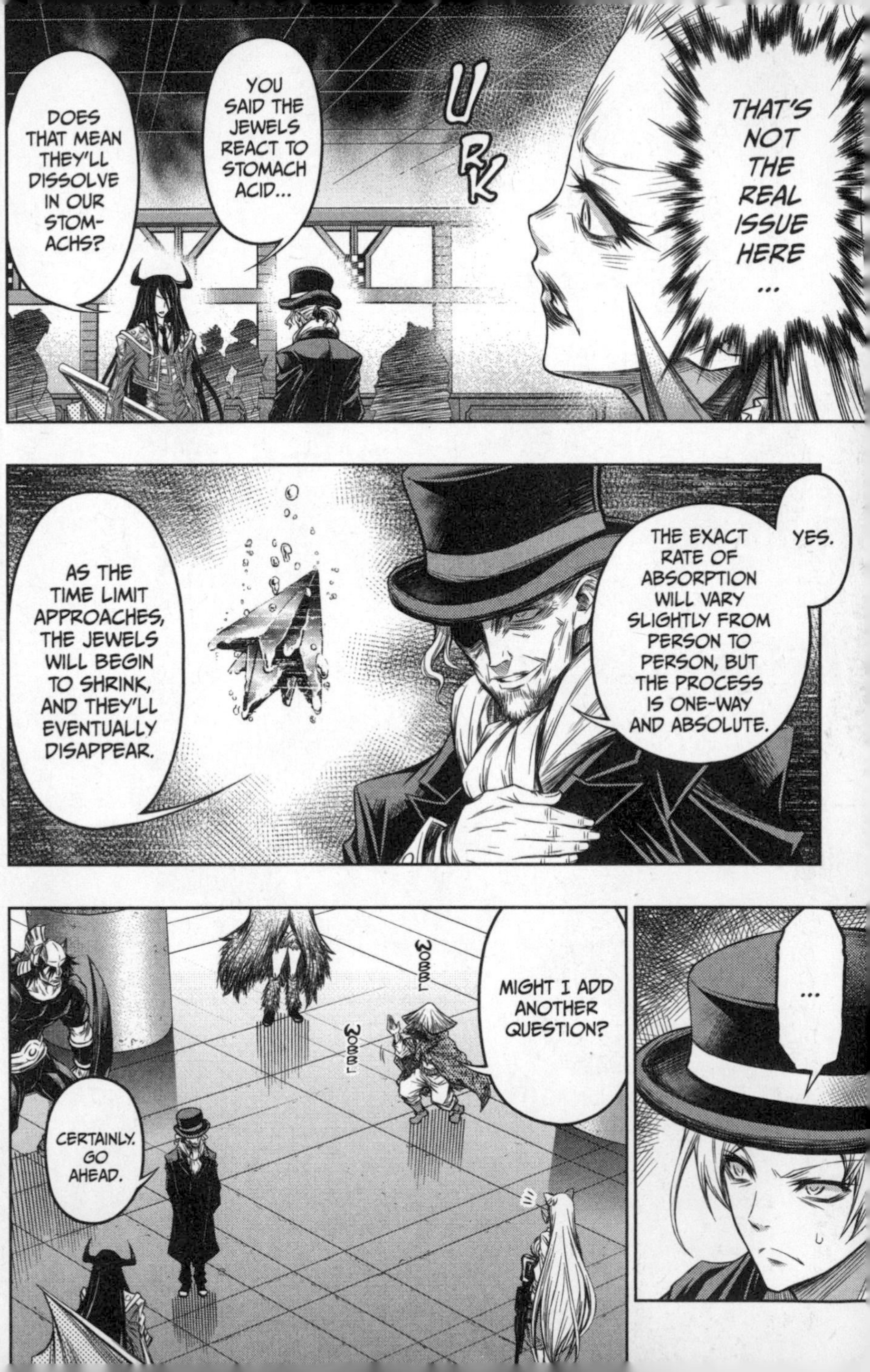
THAT'S NOT THE REAL ISSUE HERE ...
URK
YOU SAID THE JEWELS REACT TO STOMACH ACID...
DOES THAT MEAN THEY'LL DISSOLVE IN OUR STOMACHS?
YES.
THE EXACT RATE OF ABSORPTION WILL VARY SLIGHTLY FROM PERSON TO PERSON, BUT THE PROCESS IS ONE-WAY AND ABSOLUTE.
AS THE TIME LIMIT APPROACHES, THE JEWELS WILL BEGIN TO SHRINK, AND THEY'LL EVENTUALLY DISAPPEAR.
...
MIGHT I ADD ANOTHER QUESTION?
WOBBL
WOBBL
CERTAINLY. GO AHEAD.

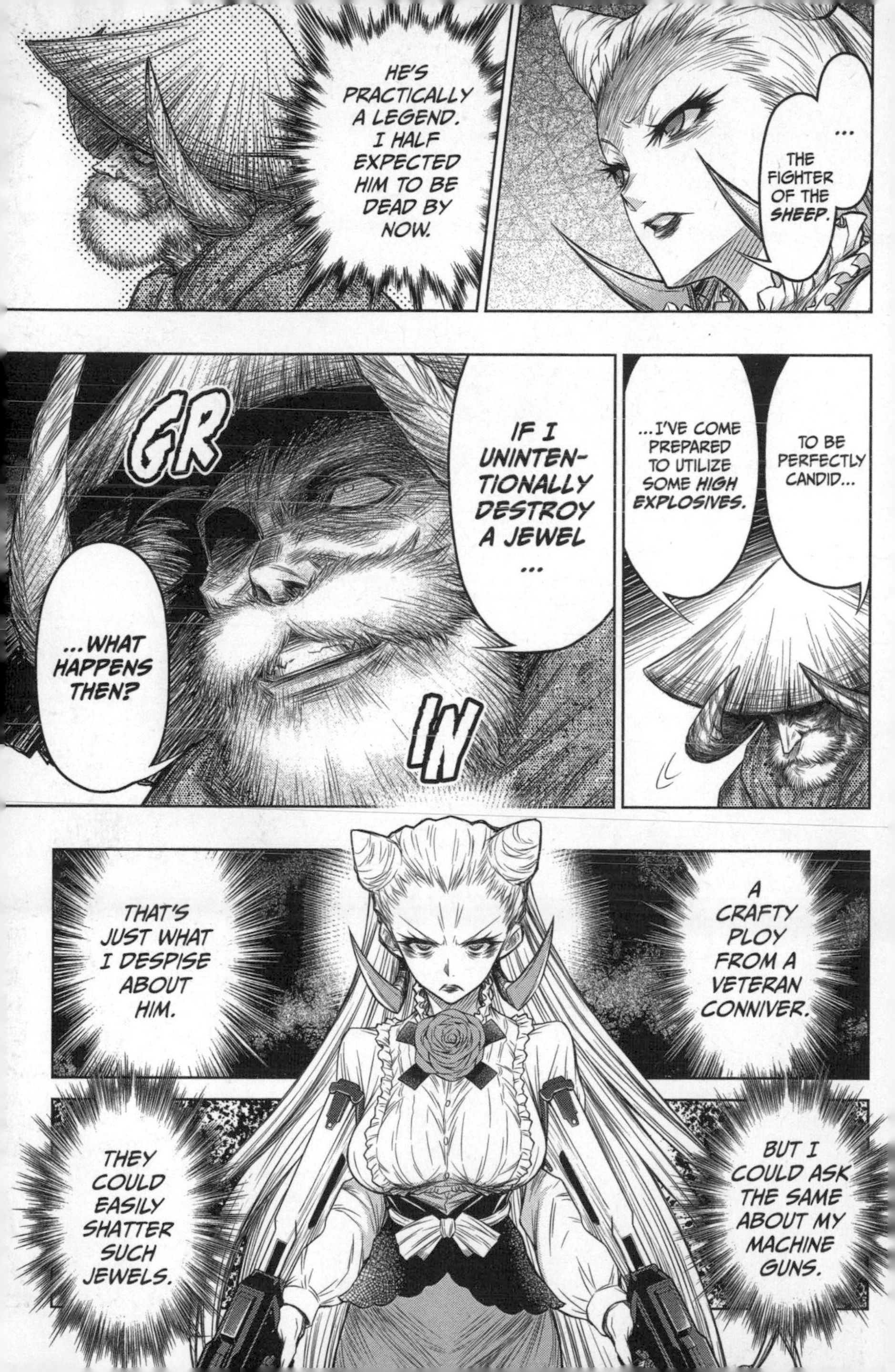
... THE FIGHTER OF THE SHEEP.
HE'S PRACTICALLY A LEGEND. I HALF EXPECTED HIM TO BE DEAD BY NOW.
TO BE PERFECTLY CANDID...
...I'VE COME PREPARED TO UTILIZE SOME HIGH EXPLOSIVES.
IF I UNINTEN-TIONALLY DESTROY A JEWEL ...
...WHAT HAPPENS THEN?
GR
IN
A CRAFTY PLOY FROM A VETERAN CONNIVER.
THAT'S JUST WHAT I DESPISE ABOUT HIM.
BUT I COULD ASK THE SAME ABOUT MY MACHINE GUNS.
THEY COULD EASILY SHATTER SUCH JEWELS.

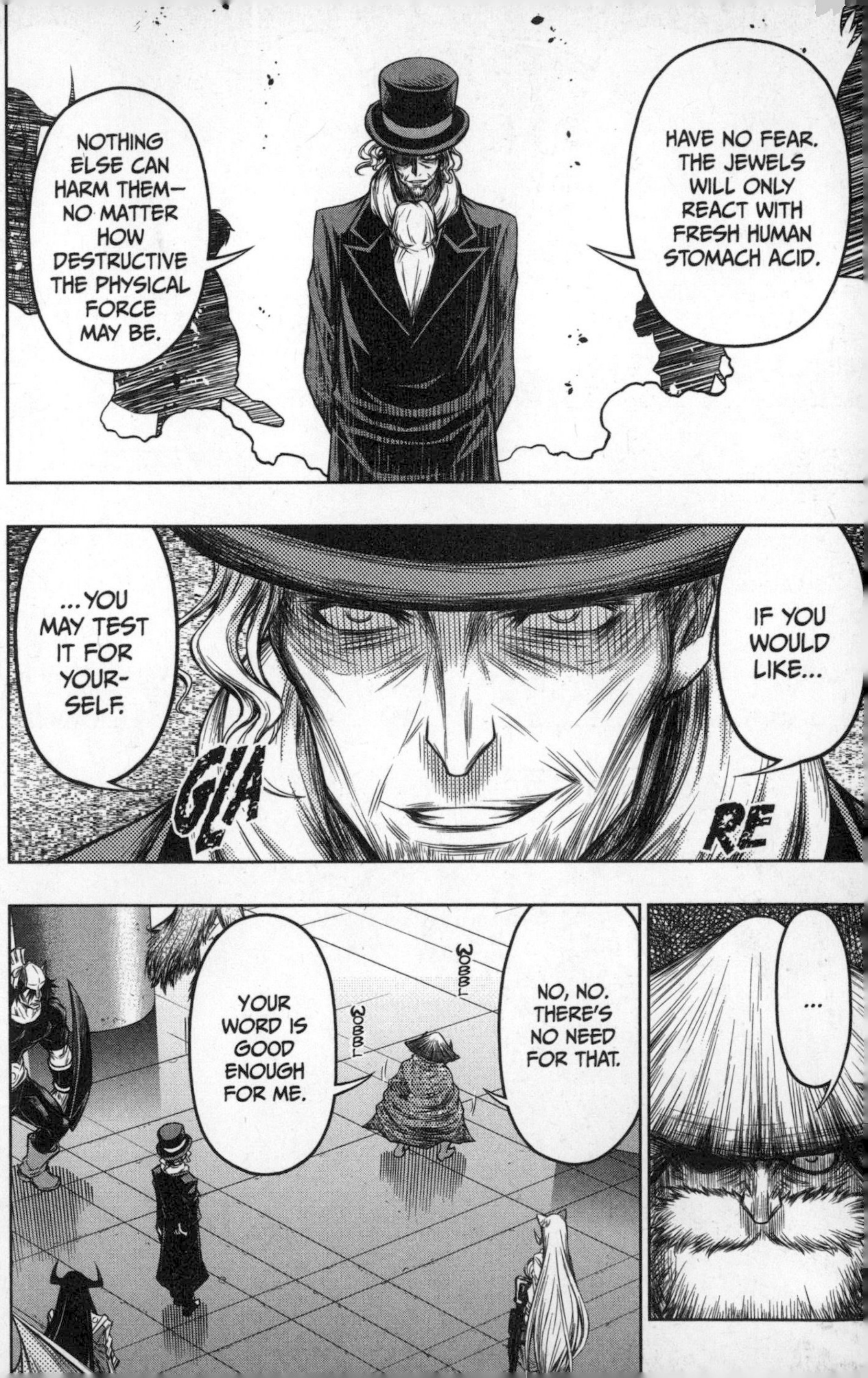
HAVE NO FEAR. THE JEWELS WILL ONLY REACT WITH FRESH HUMAN STOMACH ACID.
NOTHING ELSE CAN HARM THEM— NO MATTER HOW DESTRUCTIVE THE PHYSICAL FORCE MAY BE.
IF YOU WOULD LIKE...
...YOU MAY TEST IT FOR YOUR-SELF.
GIA
RE
...
NO, NO. THERE'S NO NEED FOR THAT.
WOBBL
WOBBL
YOUR WORD IS GOOD ENOUGH FOR ME.

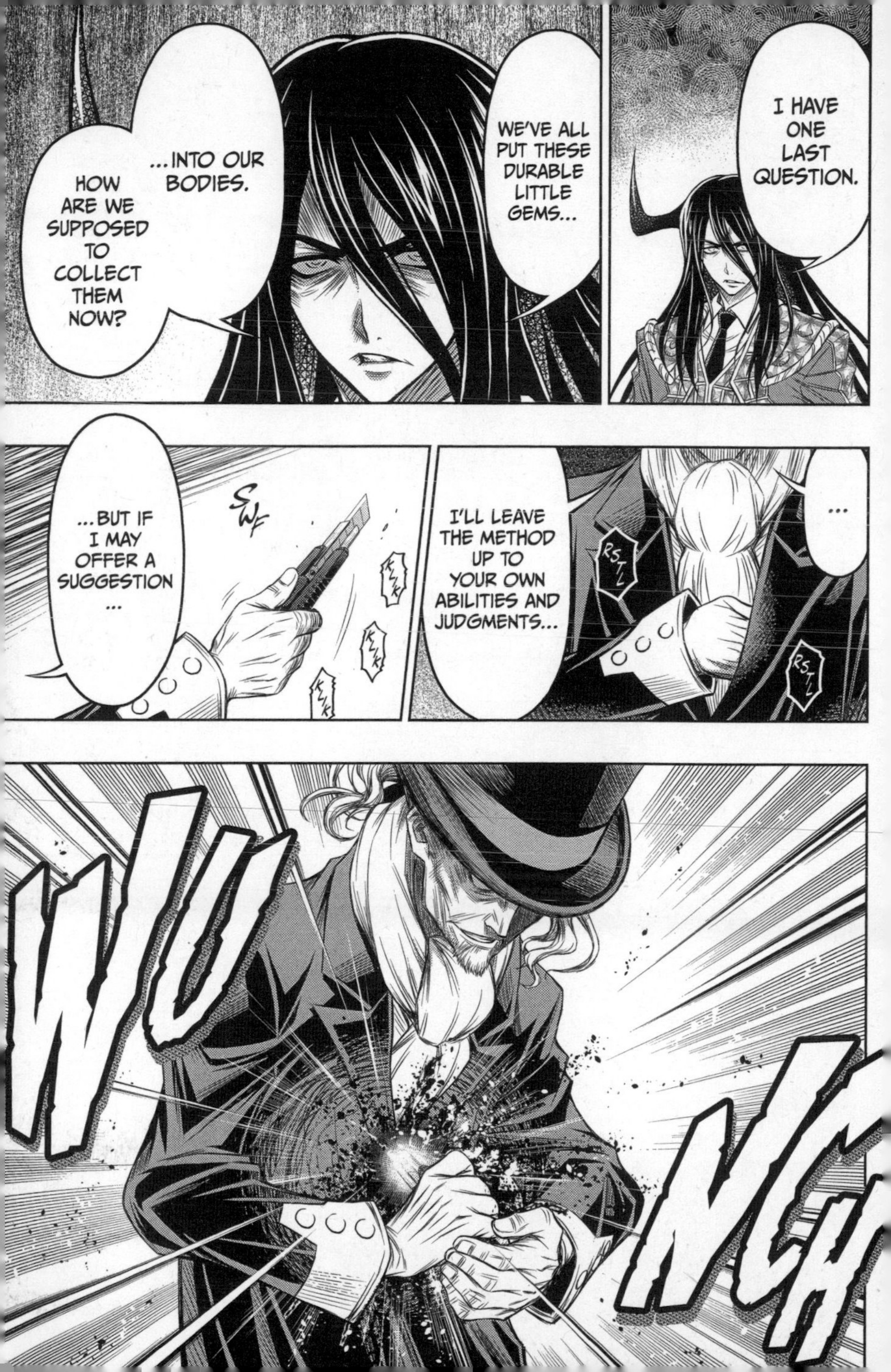
I HAVE ONE LAST QUESTION.
WE'VE ALL PUT THESE DURABLE LITTLE GEMS...
...INTO OUR BODIES.
HOW ARE WE SUPPOSED TO COLLECT THEM NOW?
...
RSTL
I'LL LEAVE THE METHOD UP TO YOUR OWN ABILITIES AND JUDGMENTS...
RSTL
SWF
KLIK
KLIK
KLIK
...BUT IF I MAY OFFER A SUGGESTION ...
WUNCH

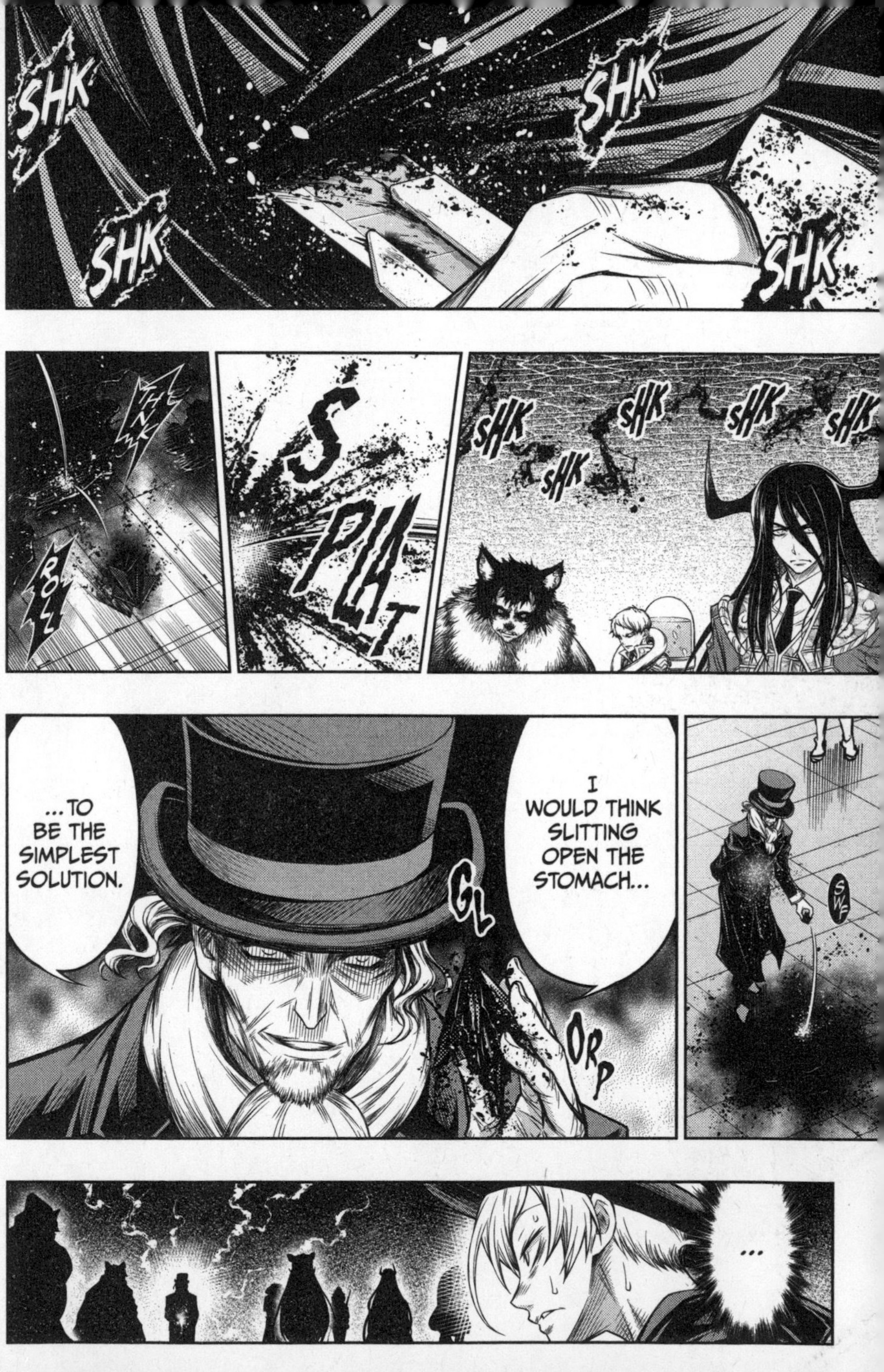
SHK
SHK
SHK
SHK
sHK
sHK
sHK
sHK
sHK
sHK
SPLAT
THNK
ROLL
SWF
I WOULD THINK SLITTING OPEN THE STOMACH...
GLORP
...TO BE THE SIMPLEST SOLUTION.
...

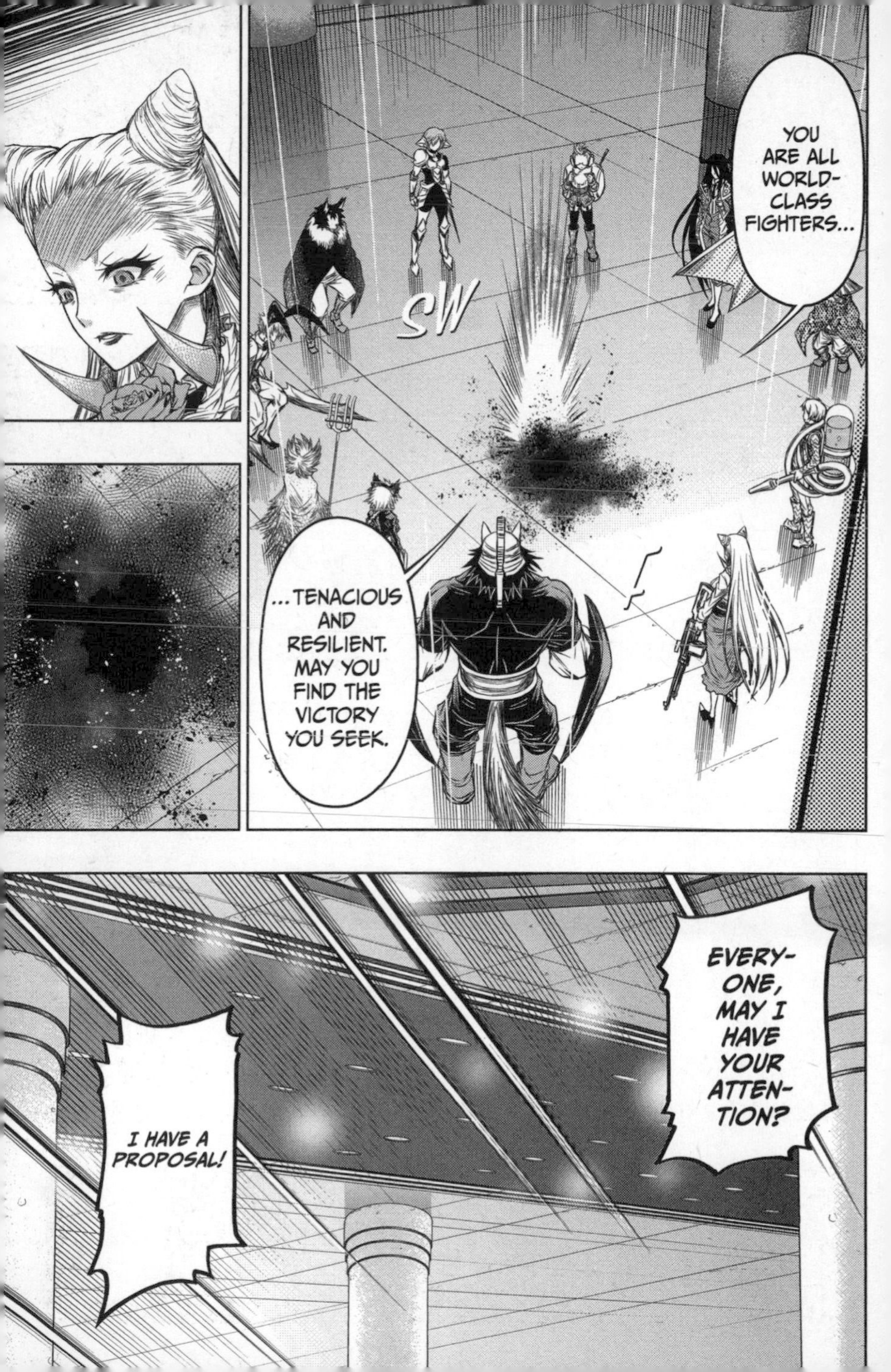
YOU ARE ALL WORLD-CLASS FIGHTERS...
SW
...TENACIOUS AND RESILIENT. MAY YOU FIND THE VICTORY YOU SEEK.
EVERY-ONE, MAY I HAVE YOUR ATTEN-TION?
I HAVE A PROPOSAL!

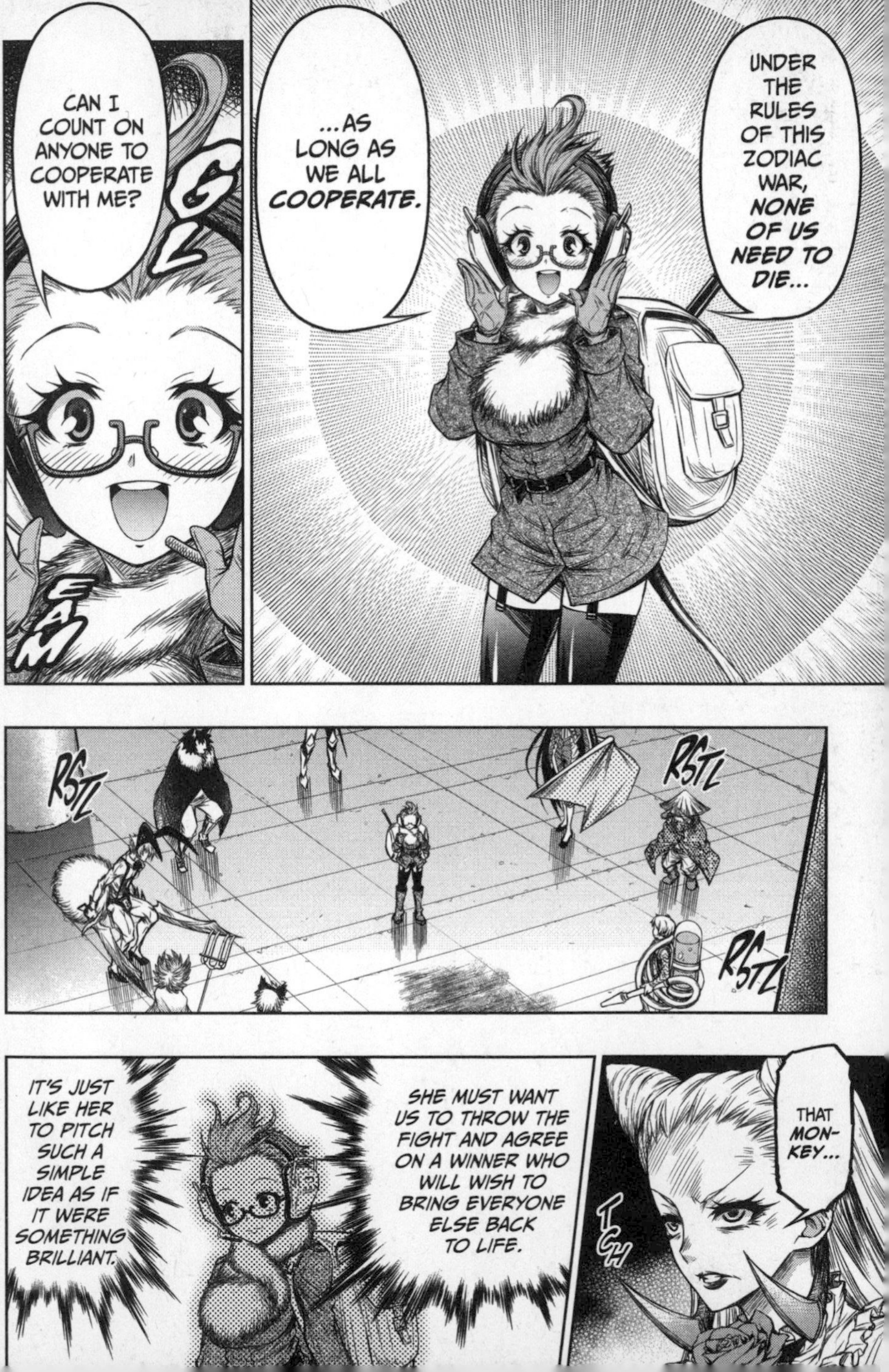
UNDER THE RULES OF THIS ZODIAC WAR, NONE OF US NEED TO DIE...
...AS LONG AS WE ALL COOPERATE.
CAN I COUNT ON ANYONE TO COOPERATE WITH ME?
GLEAM
RSTL
RSTL
RSTL
THAT MON-KEY...
TCH
SHE MUST WANT US TO THROW THE FIGHT AND AGREE ON A WINNER WHO WILL WISH TO BRING EVERYONE ELSE BACK TO LIFE.
IT'S JUST LIKE HER TO PITCH SUCH A SIMPLE IDEA AS IF IT WERE SOMETHING BRILLIANT.

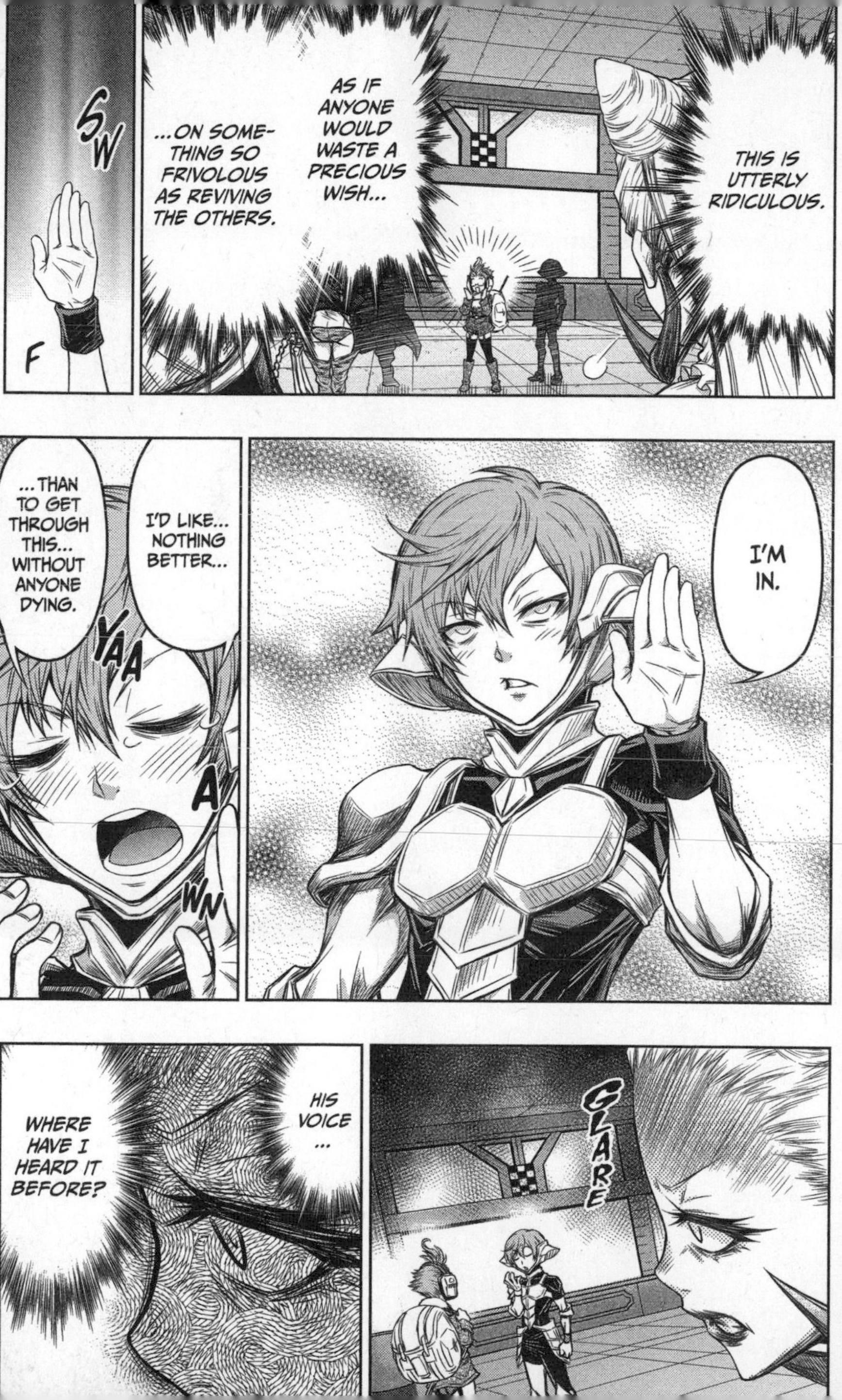
THIS IS UTTERLY RIDICULOUS.
AS IF ANYONE WOULD WASTE A PRECIOUS WISH...
...ON SOMETHING SO FRIVOLOUS AS REVIVING THE OTHERS.
SW
F
I'M IN.
I'D LIKE... NOTHING BETTER...
...THAN TO GET THROUGH THIS... WITHOUT ANYONE DYING.
YAA
A
WN
GLARE
HIS VOICE ...
WHERE HAVE I HEARD IT BEFORE?

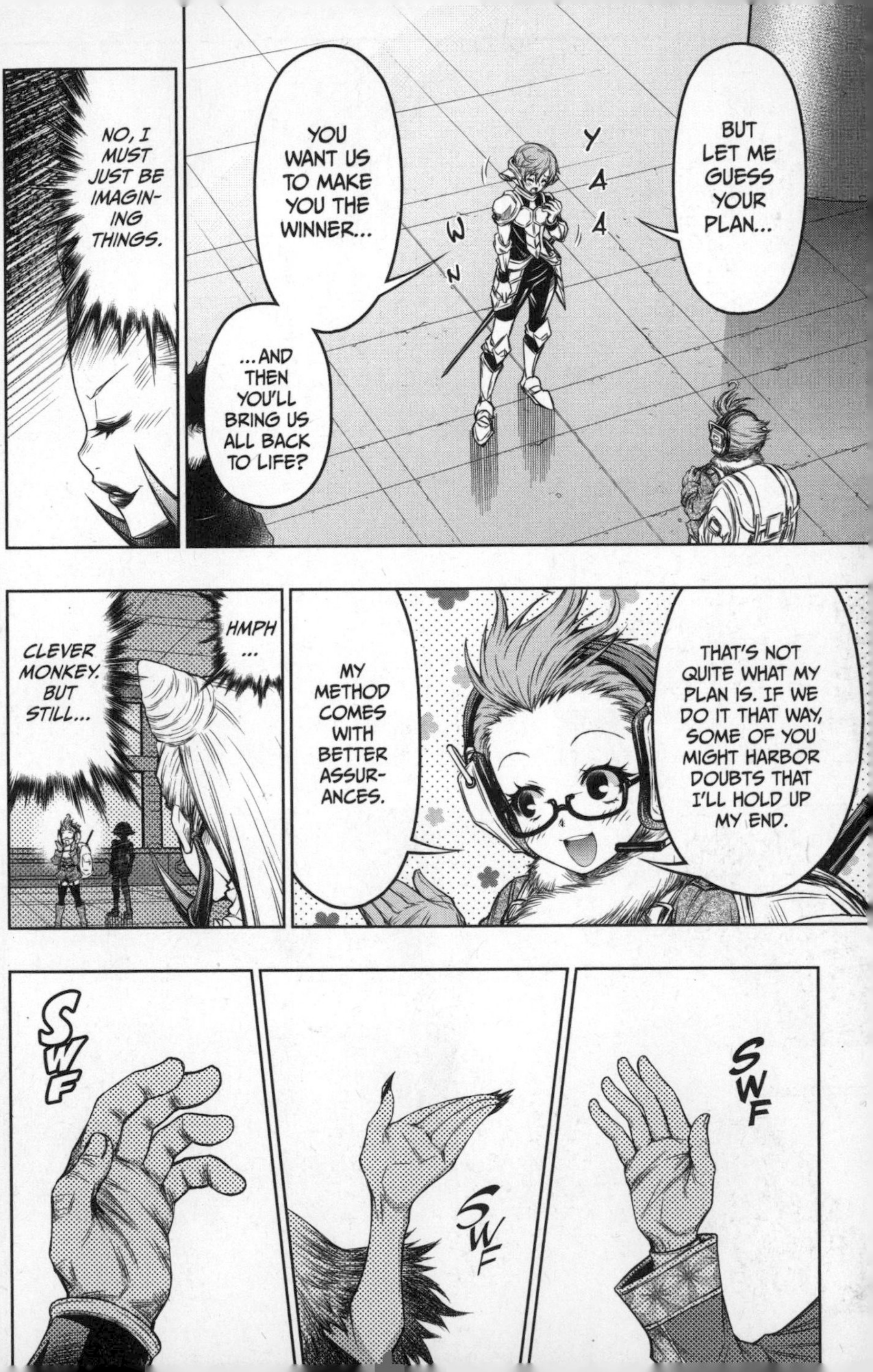
BUT LET ME GUESS YOUR PLAN...
YAAWN
YOU WANT US TO MAKE YOU THE WINNER...
...AND THEN YOU'LL BRING US ALL BACK TO LIFE?
NO, I MUST JUST BE IMAGINING THINGS.
THAT'S NOT QUITE WHAT MY PLAN IS. IF WE DO IT THAT WAY, SOME OF YOU MIGHT HARBOR DOUBTS THAT I'LL HOLD UP MY END.
MY METHOD COMES WITH BETTER ASSURANCES.
HMPH...
CLEVER MONKEY. BUT STILL...
SWF
SWF
SWF

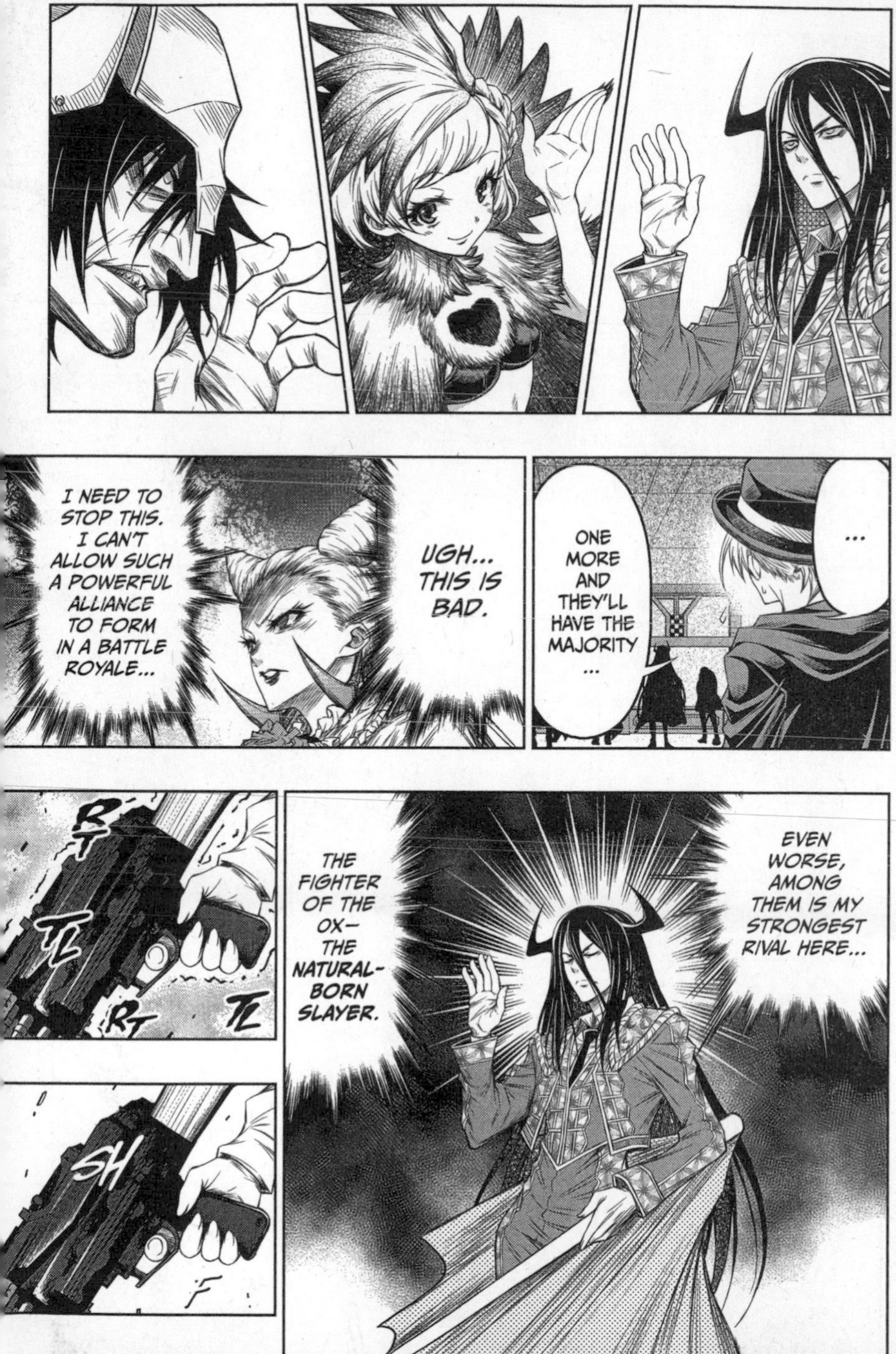
...
ONE MORE AND THEY'LL HAVE THE MAJORITY ...
UGH... THIS IS BAD.
I NEED TO STOP THIS. I CAN'T ALLOW SUCH A POWERFUL ALLIANCE TO FORM IN A BATTLE ROYALE...
EVEN WORSE, AMONG THEM IS MY STRONGEST RIVAL HERE...
THE FIGHTER OF THE OX— THE NATURAL-BORN SLAYER.
RT
TL
RT
TL
SH
F

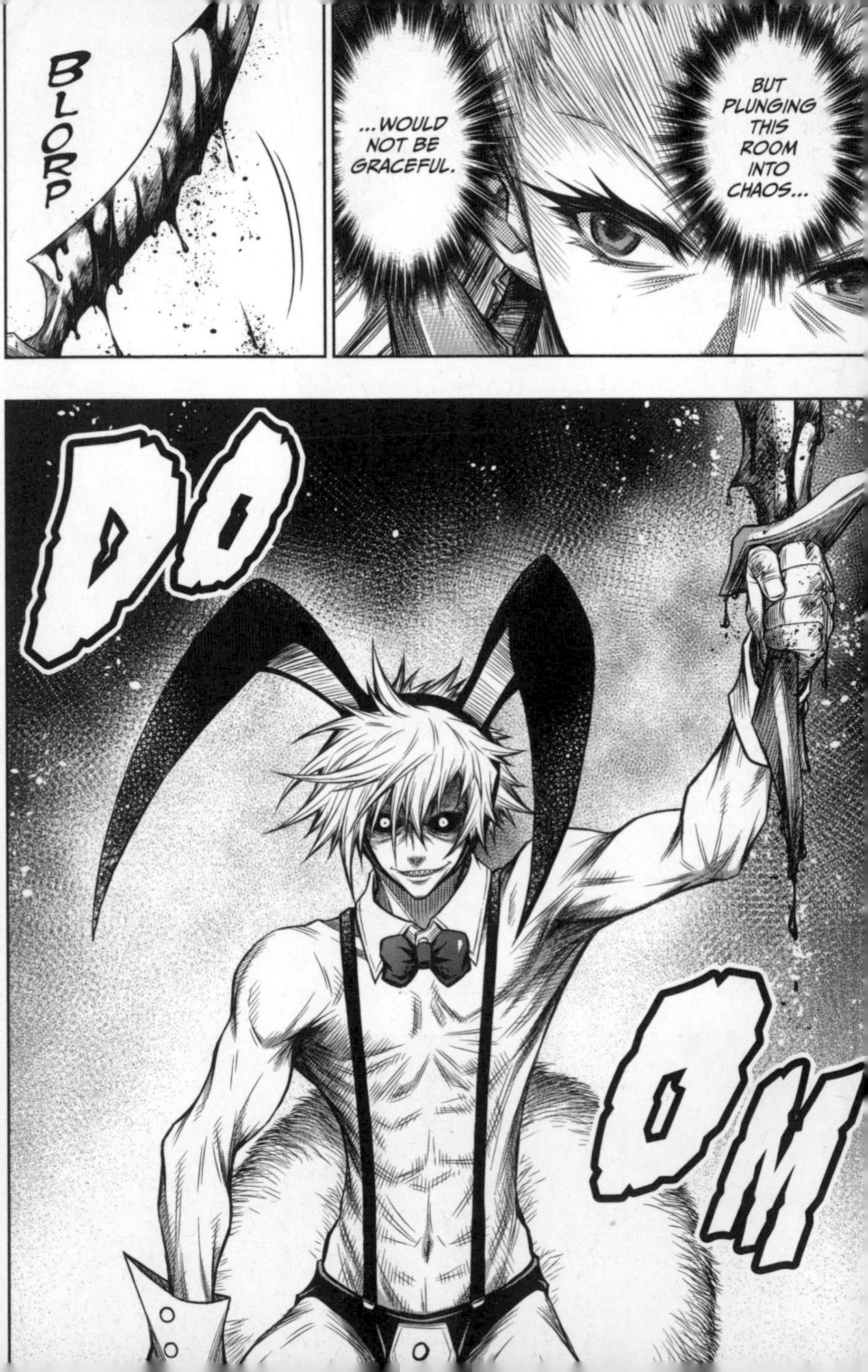
BUT PLUNGING THIS ROOM INTO CHAOS...
...WOULD NOT BE GRACEFUL.
BLORP
DO
OM

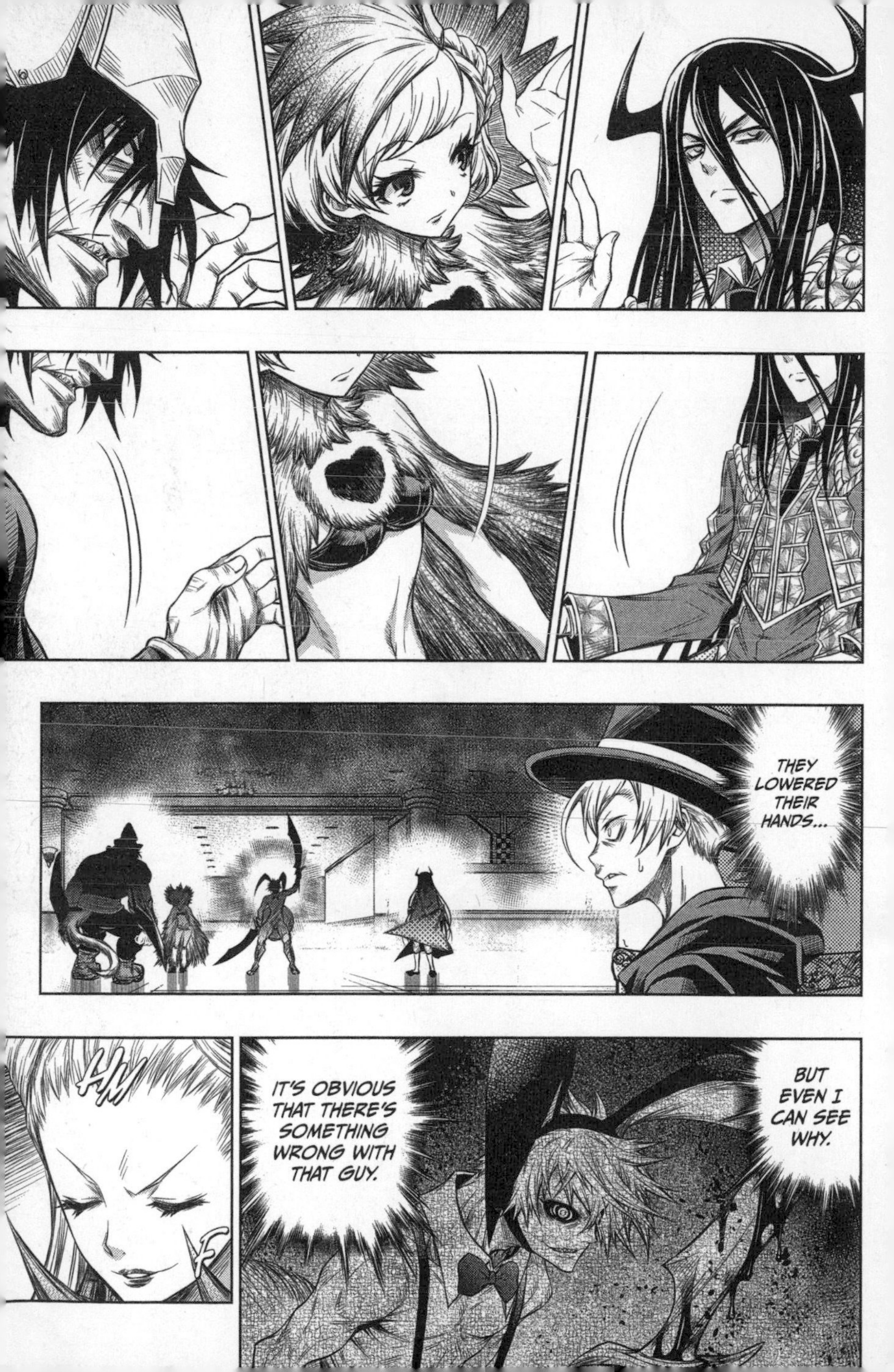
THEY LOWERED THEIR HANDS...
BUT EVEN I CAN SEE WHY.
IT'S OBVIOUS THAT THERE'S SOMETHING WRONG WITH THAT GUY.
HM
F

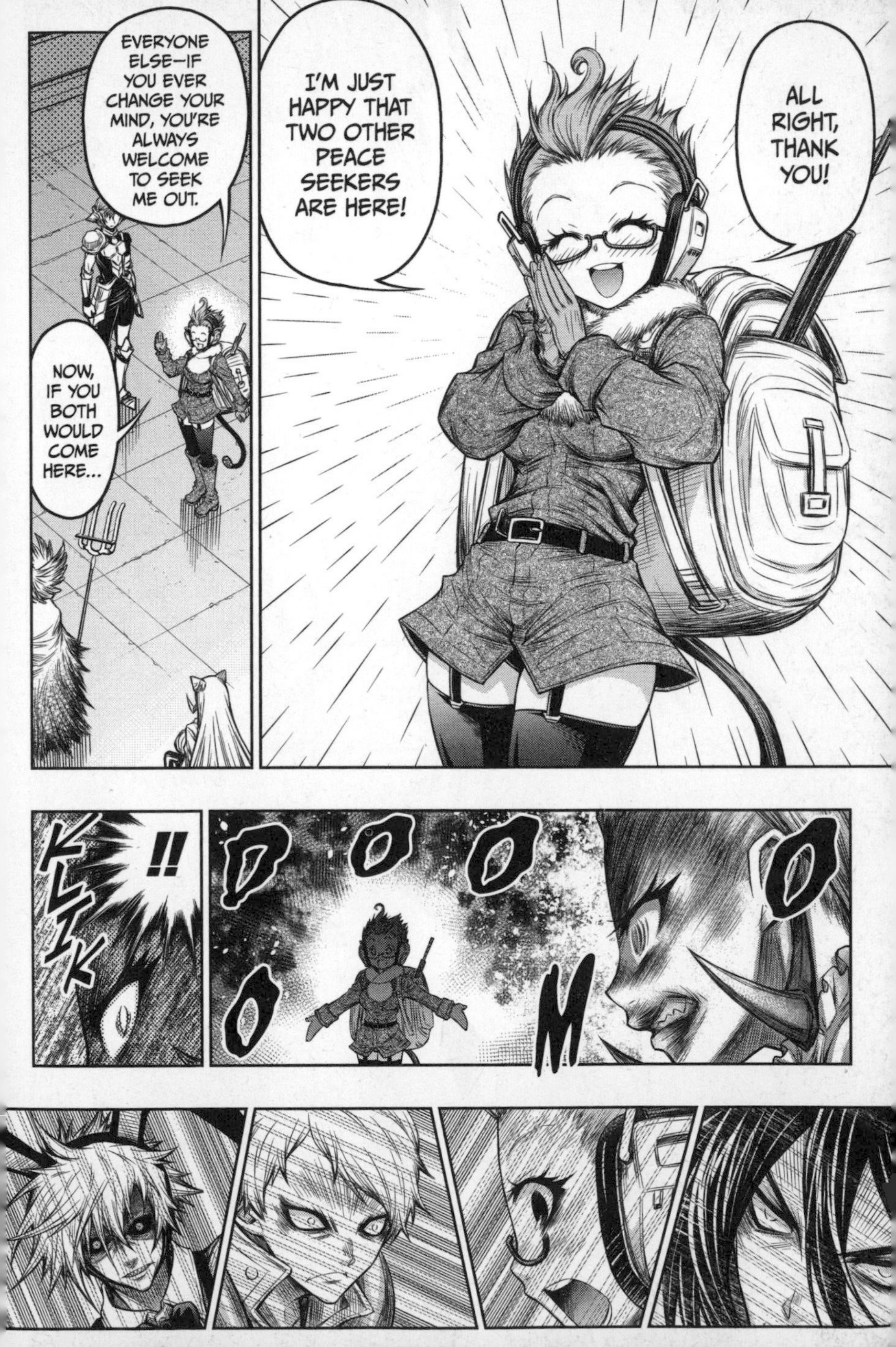
ALL RIGHT, THANK YOU!
I'M JUST HAPPY THAT TWO OTHER PEACE SEEKERS ARE HERE!
EVERYONE ELSE—IF YOU EVER CHANGE YOUR MIND, YOU'RE ALWAYS WELCOME TO SEEK ME OUT.
NOW, IF YOU BOTH WOULD COME HERE...
DOOOOM
KLIK
!!

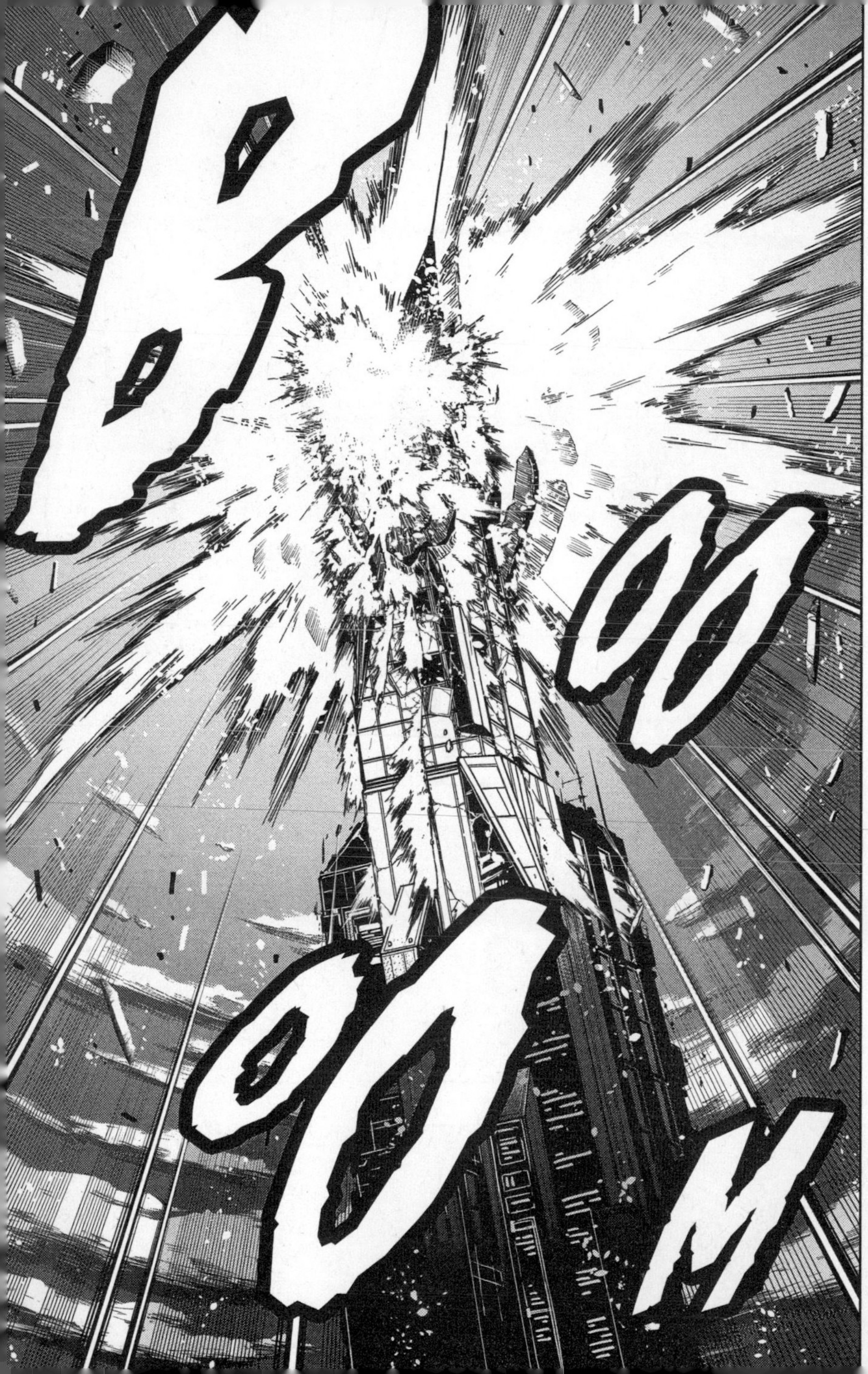
BOOM

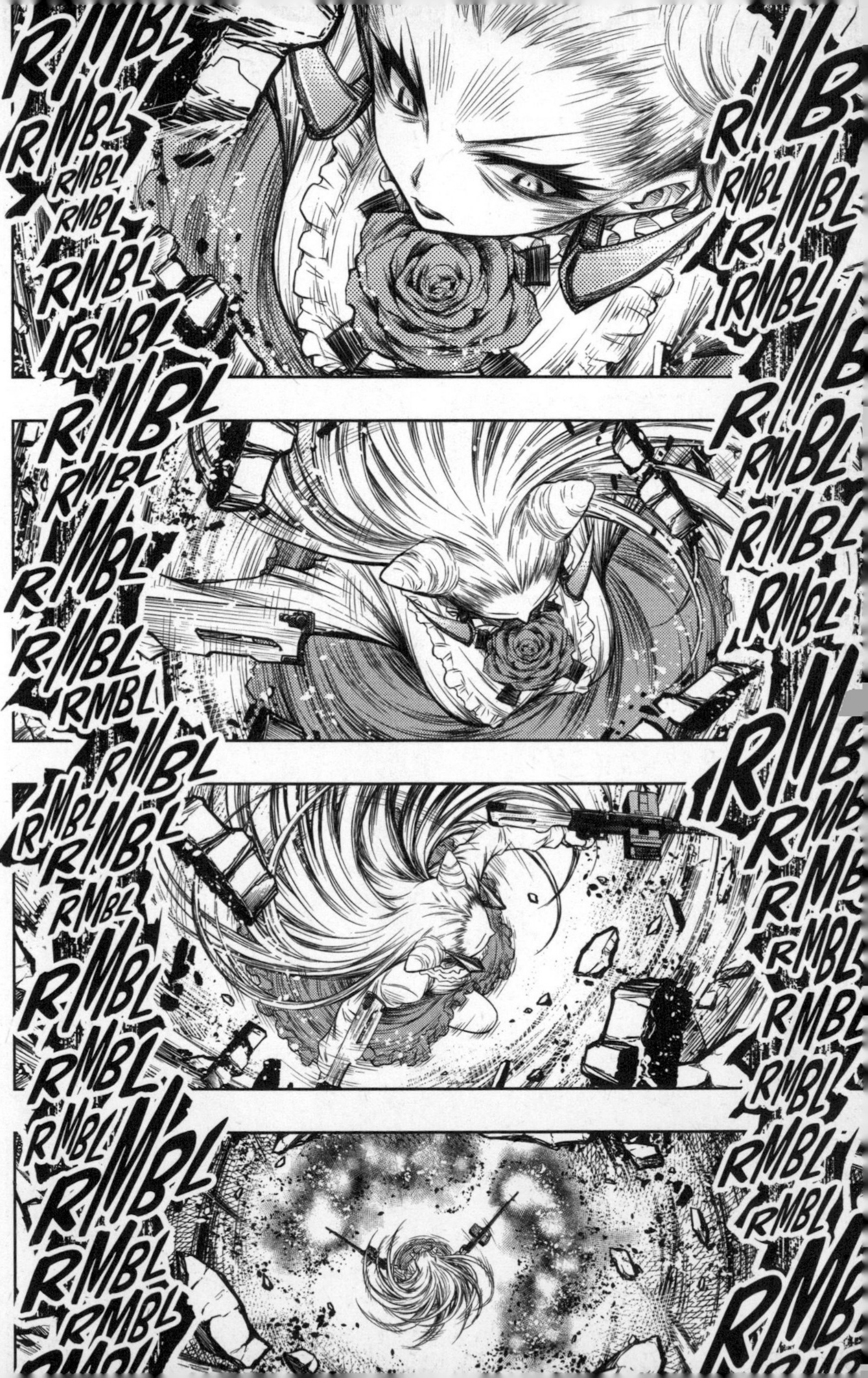
RMBL
RMBL
RMBL
RMBL
RMBL
RMBL
RMBL
RMBL

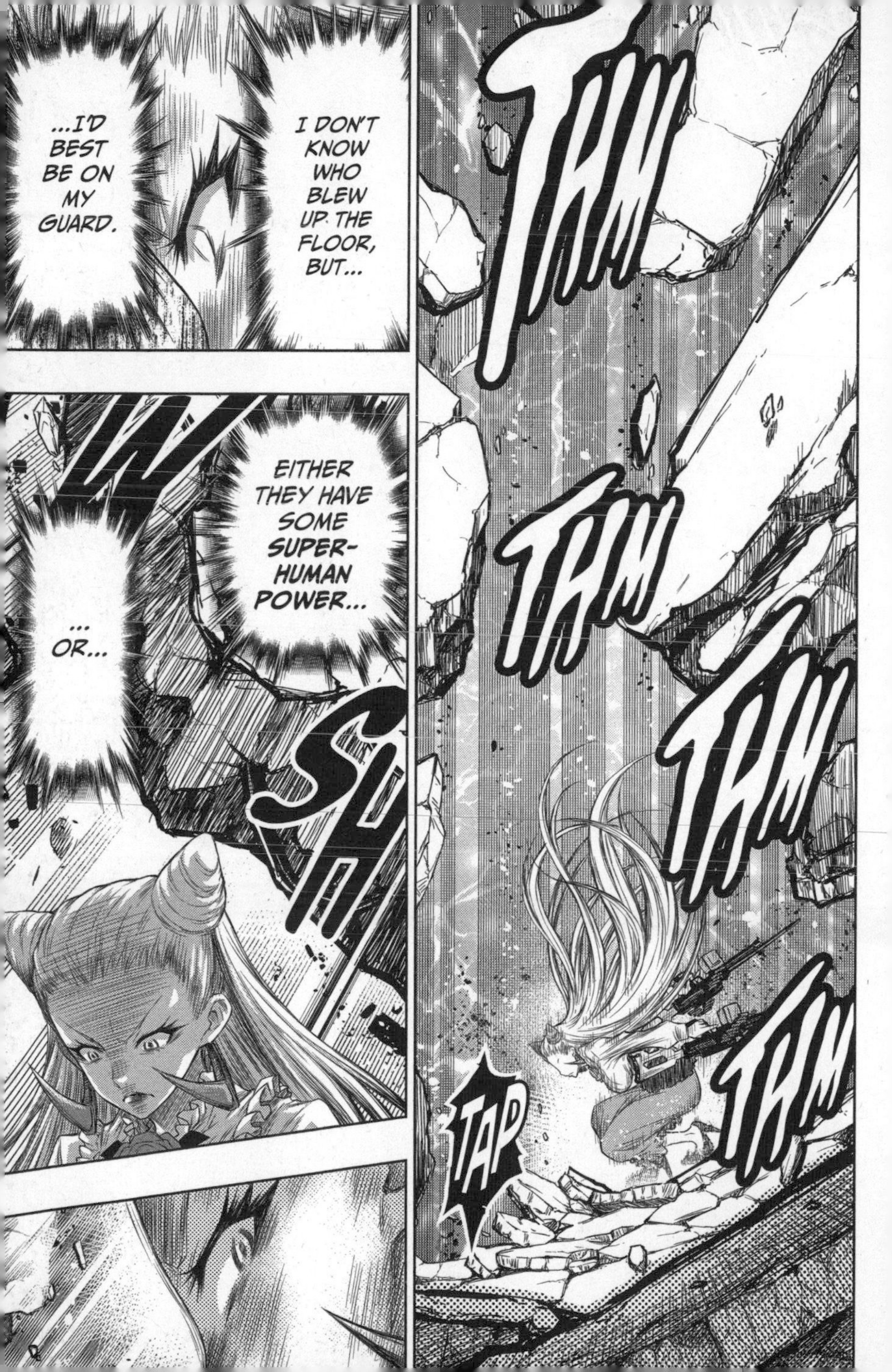
TAM
TAM
TAM
TAM
TAP
I DON'T KNOW WHO BLEW UP THE FLOOR, BUT...
...I'D BEST BE ON MY GUARD.
EITHER THEY HAVE SOME SUPER-HUMAN POWER...
... OR...
SH

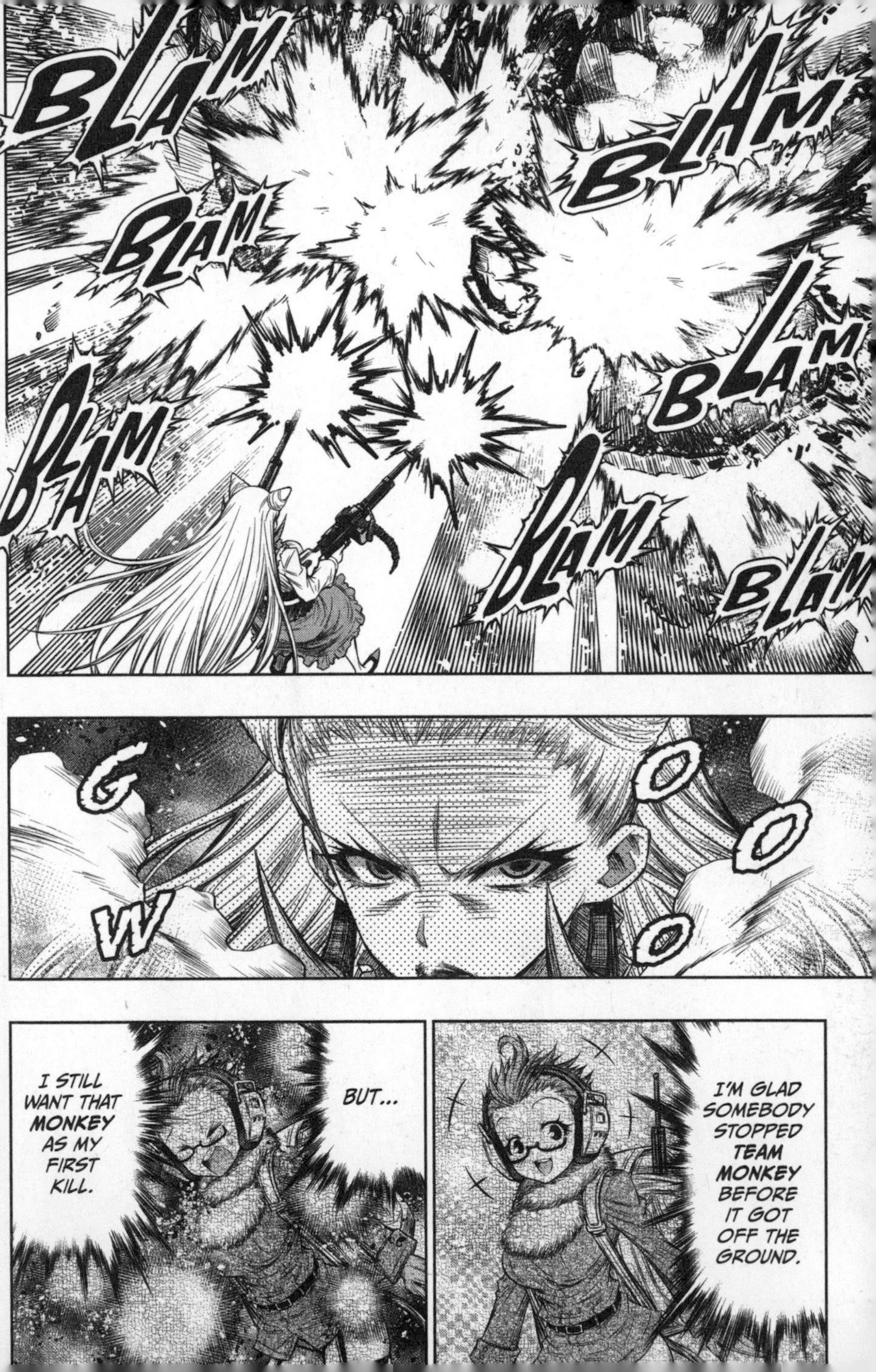
BLAM
BLAM
BLAM
BLAM
BLAM
BLAM
BLAM
OOO
GW
I'M GLAD SOMEBODY STOPPED TEAM MONKEY BEFORE IT GOT OFF THE GROUND.
BUT...
I STILL WANT THAT MONKEY AS MY FIRST KILL.

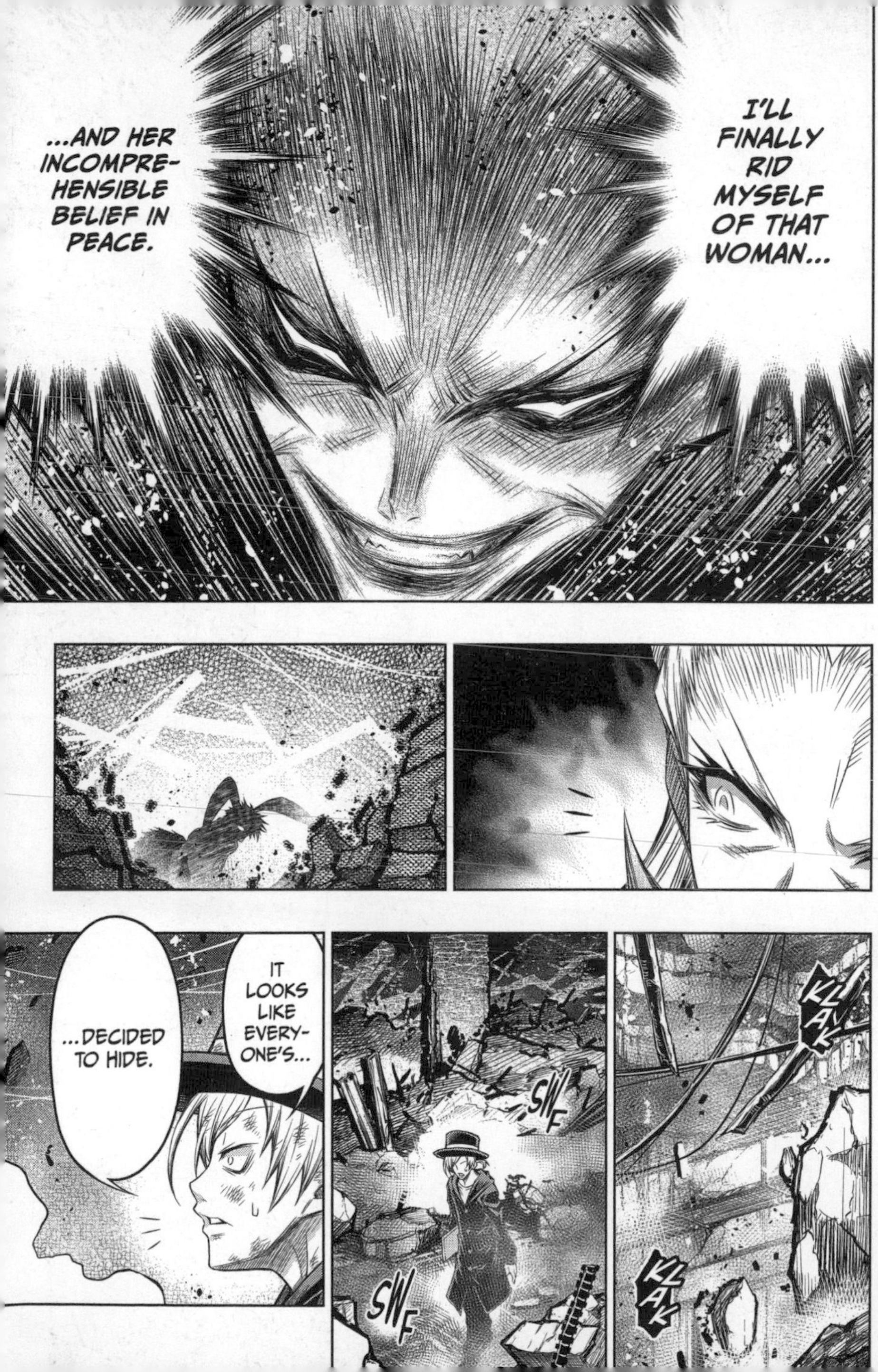
I'LL FINALLY RID MYSELF OF THAT WOMAN...
...AND HER INCOMPRE-HENSIBLE BELIEF IN PEACE.
KLAK
KLAK
SWF
SWF
IT LOOKS LIKE EVERY-ONE'S...
...DECIDED TO HIDE.

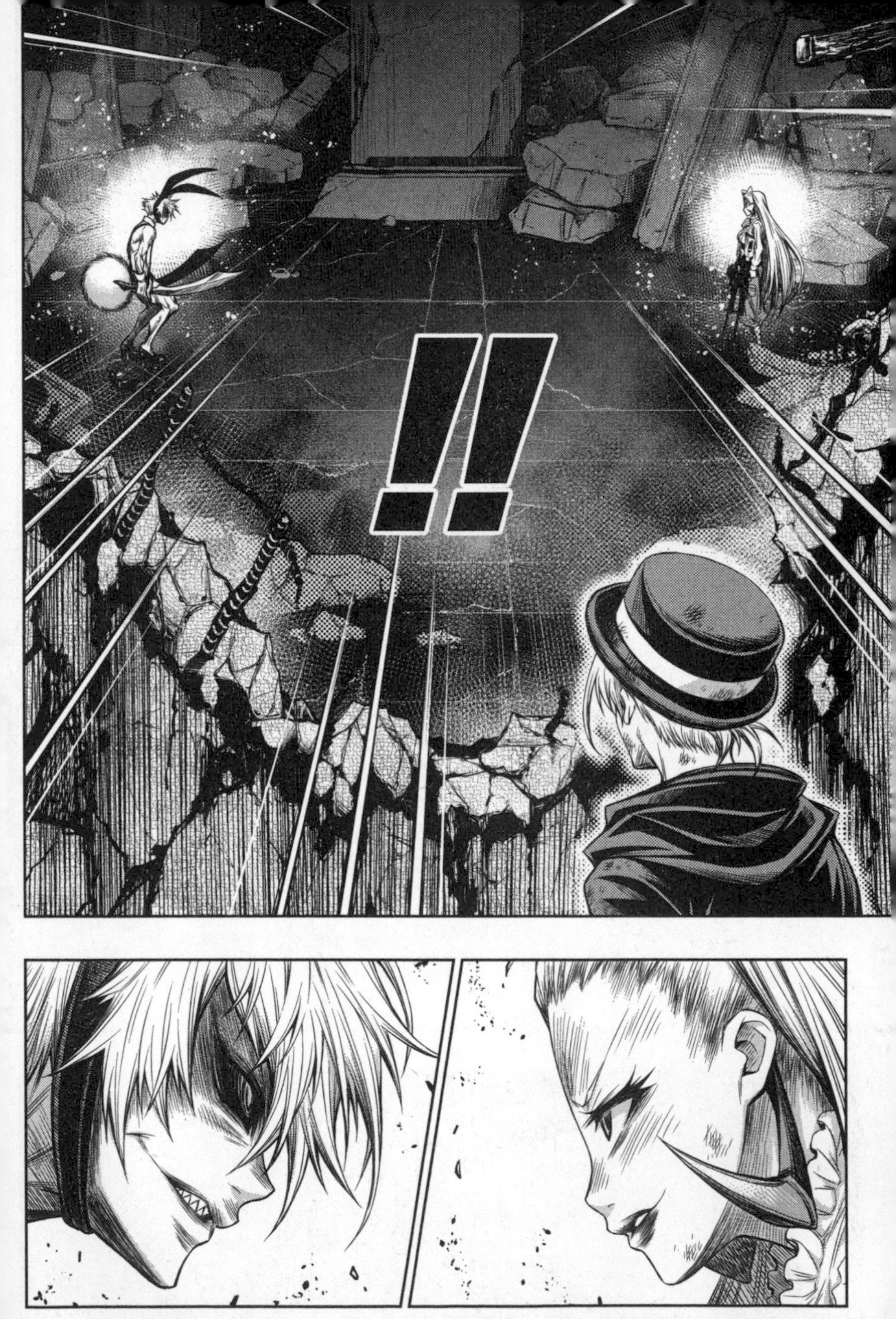
!!

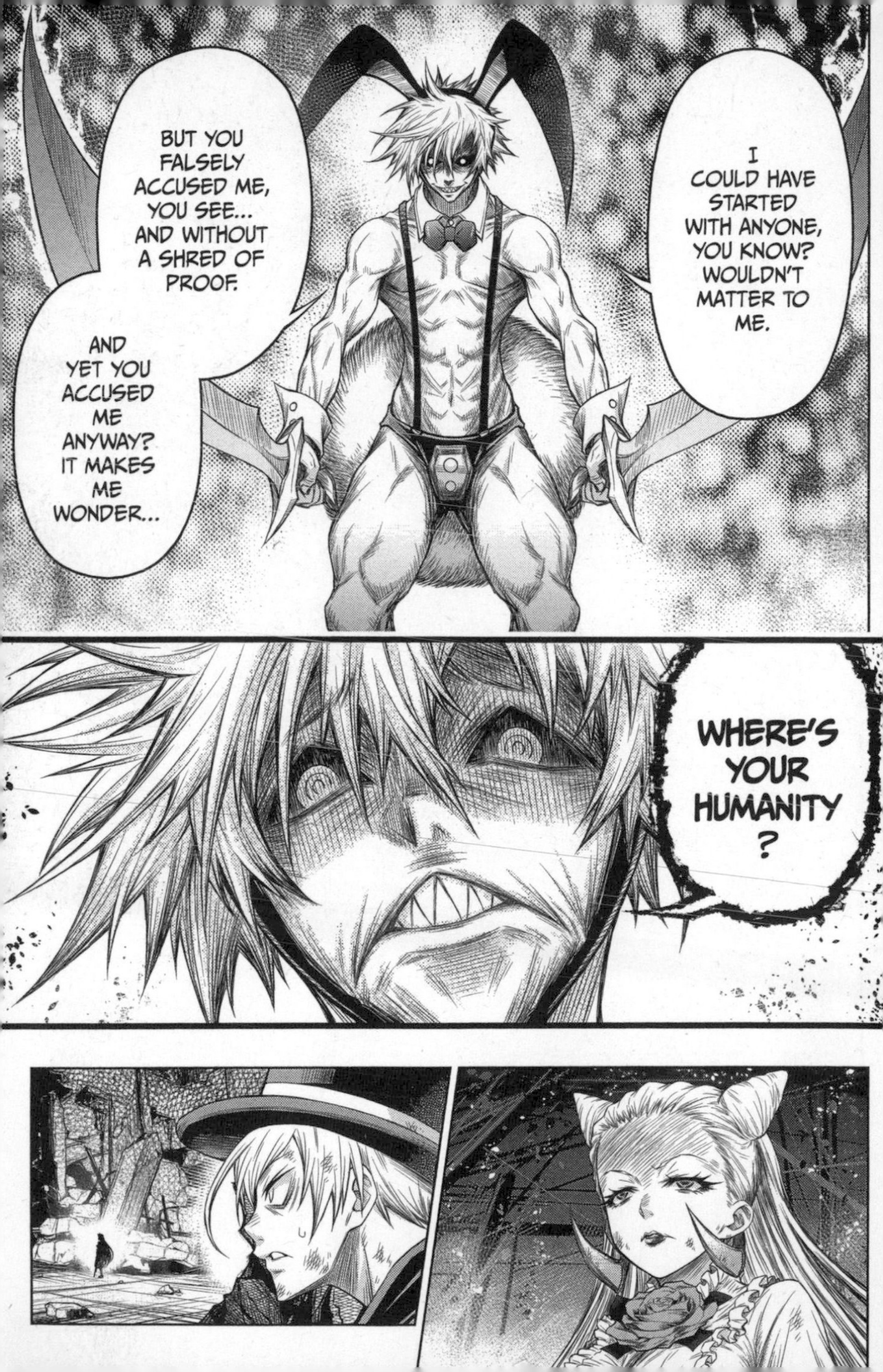
I COULD HAVE STARTED WITH ANYONE, YOU KNOW? WOULDN'T MATTER TO ME.
BUT YOU FALSELY ACCUSED ME, YOU SEE... AND WITHOUT A SHRED OF PROOF.
AND YET YOU ACCUSED ME ANYWAY? IT MAKES ME WONDER...
WHERE'S YOUR HUMANITY?

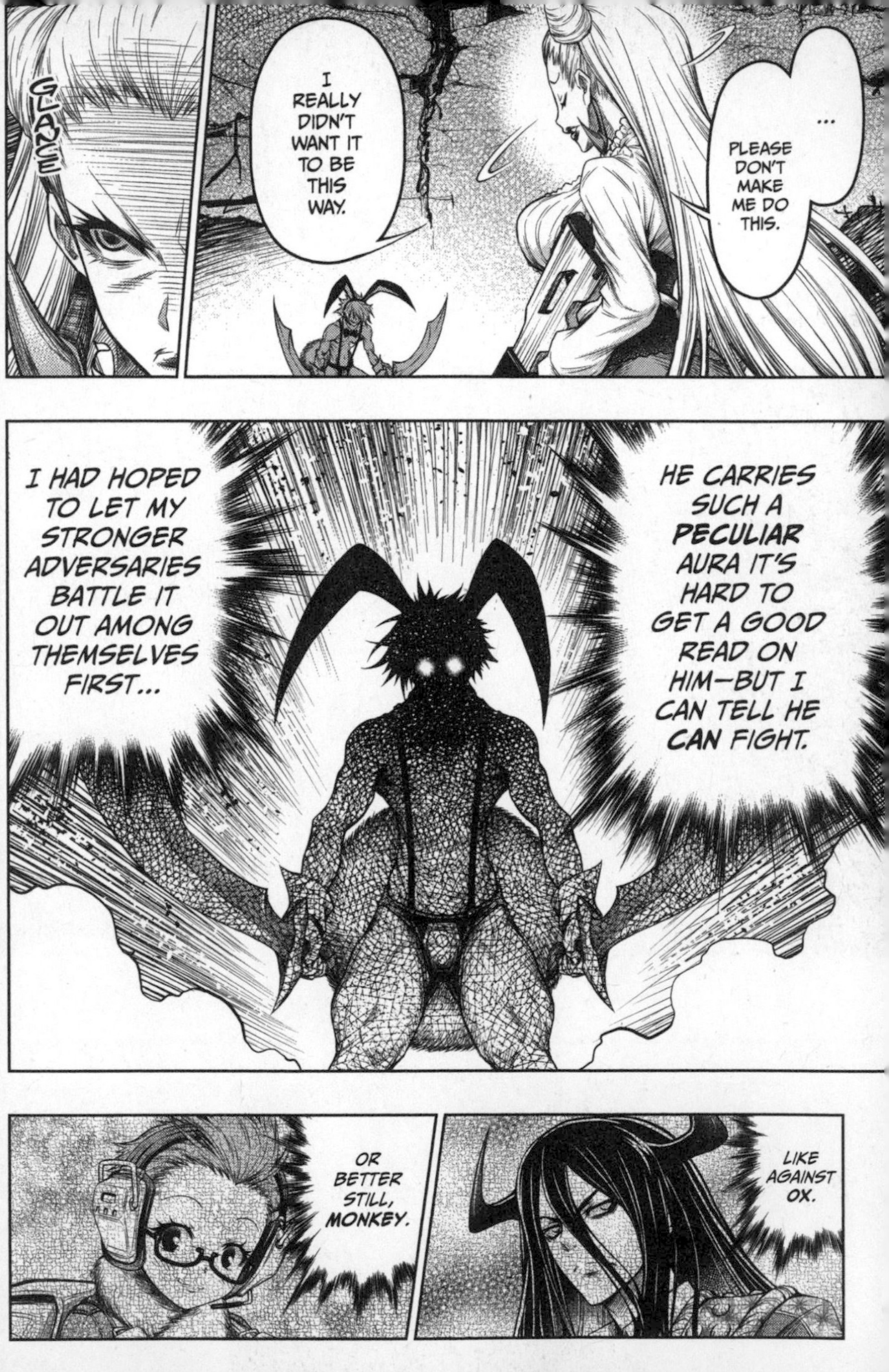
...
PLEASE DON'T MAKE ME DO THIS.
I REALLY DIDN'T WANT IT TO BE THIS WAY.
GLANCE
HE CARRIES SUCH A PECULIAR AURA IT'S HARD TO GET A GOOD READ ON HIM—BUT I CAN TELL HE CAN FIGHT.
I HAD HOPED TO LET MY STRONGER ADVERSARIES BATTLE IT OUT AMONG THEMSELVES FIRST...
LIKE AGAINST OX.
OR BETTER STILL, MONKEY.

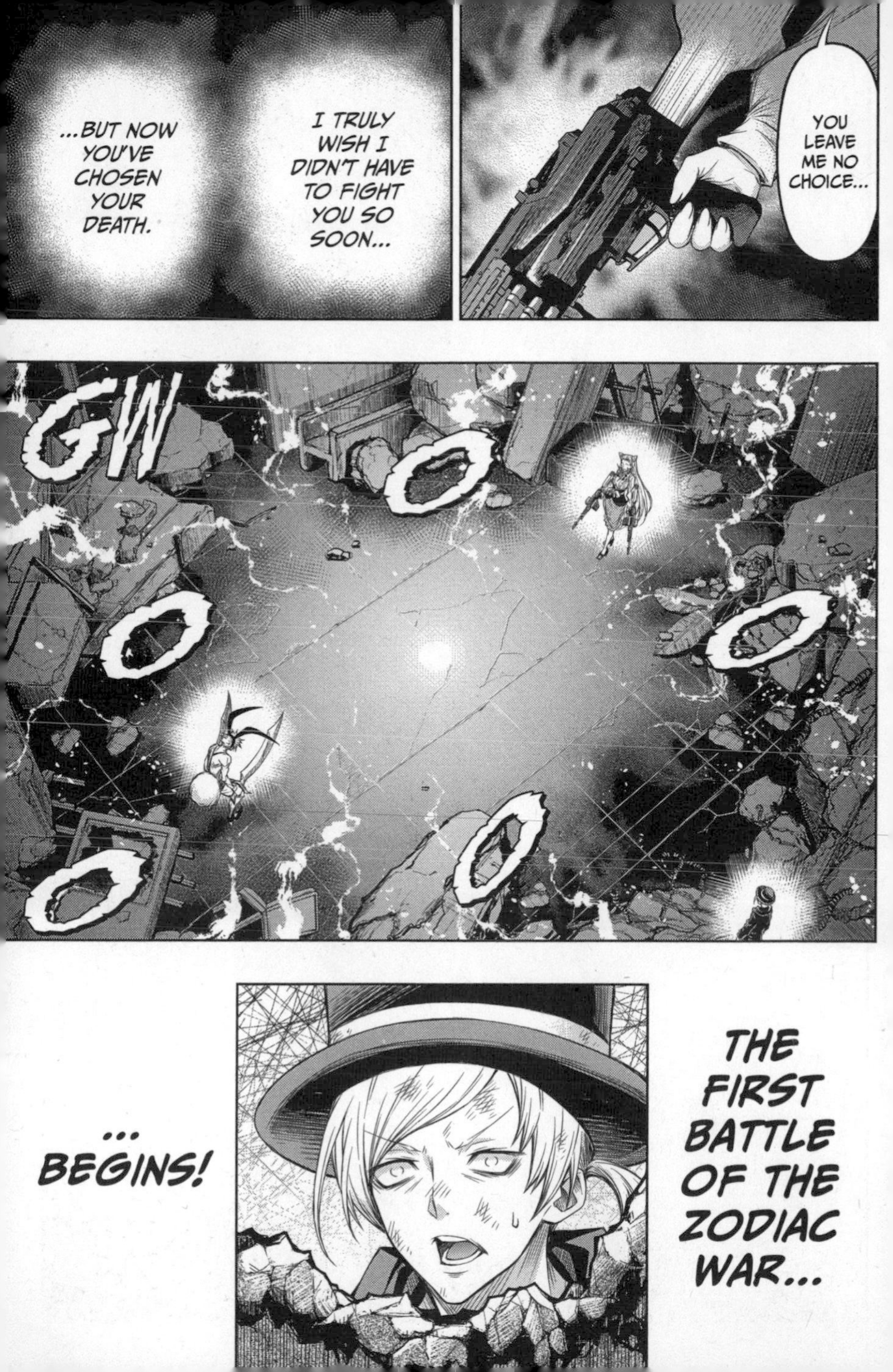
YOU LEAVE ME NO CHOICE...
I TRULY WISH I DIDN'T HAVE TO FIGHT YOU SO SOON...
...BUT NOW YOU'VE CHOSEN YOUR DEATH.
GWOOOOO
THE FIRST BATTLE OF THE ZODIAC WAR...
...BEGINS!

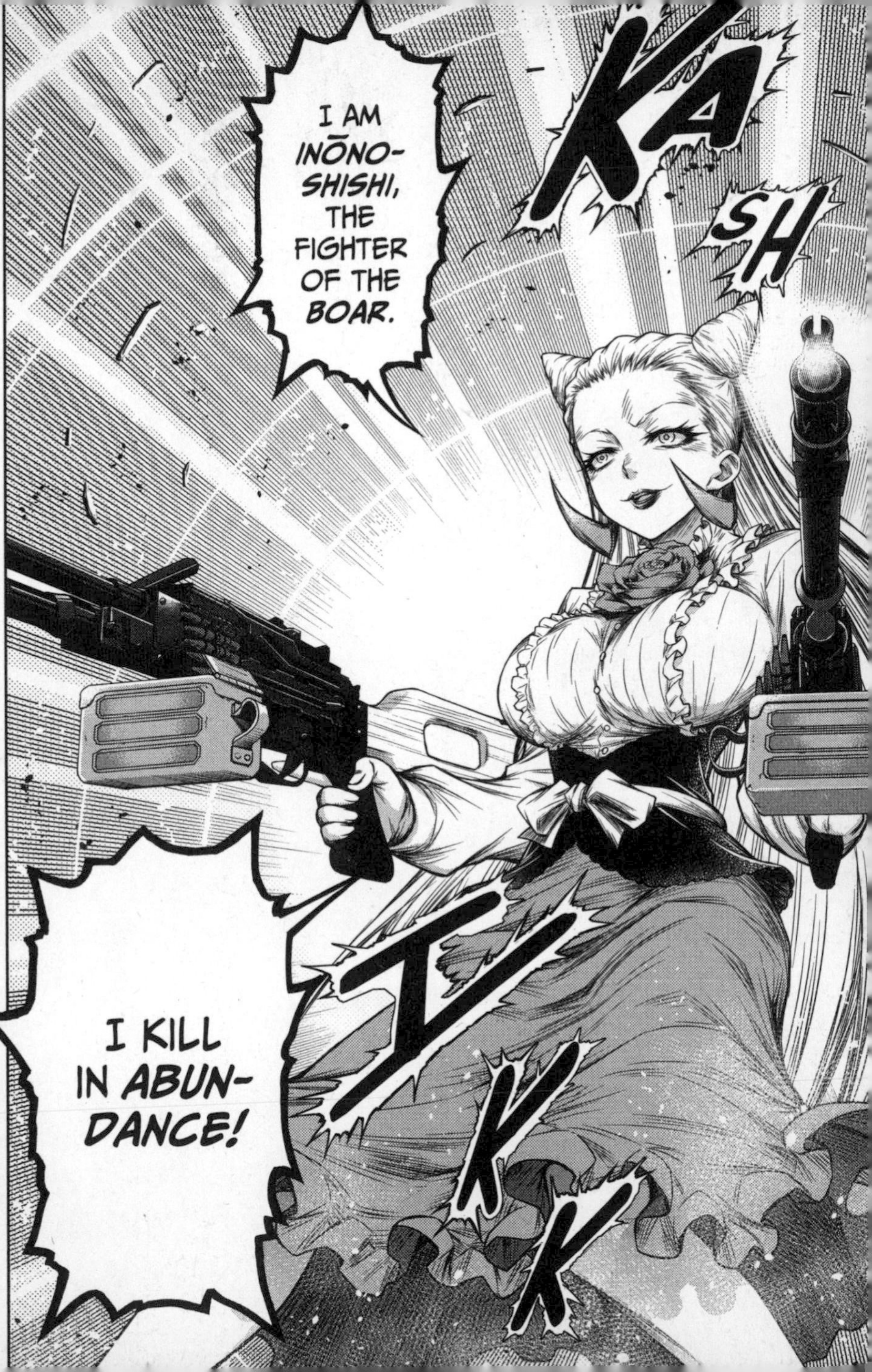
KA
SH
I AM INŌNO-SHISHI, THE FIGHTER OF THE BOAR.
I KILL IN ABUN-DANCE!
I
K
K

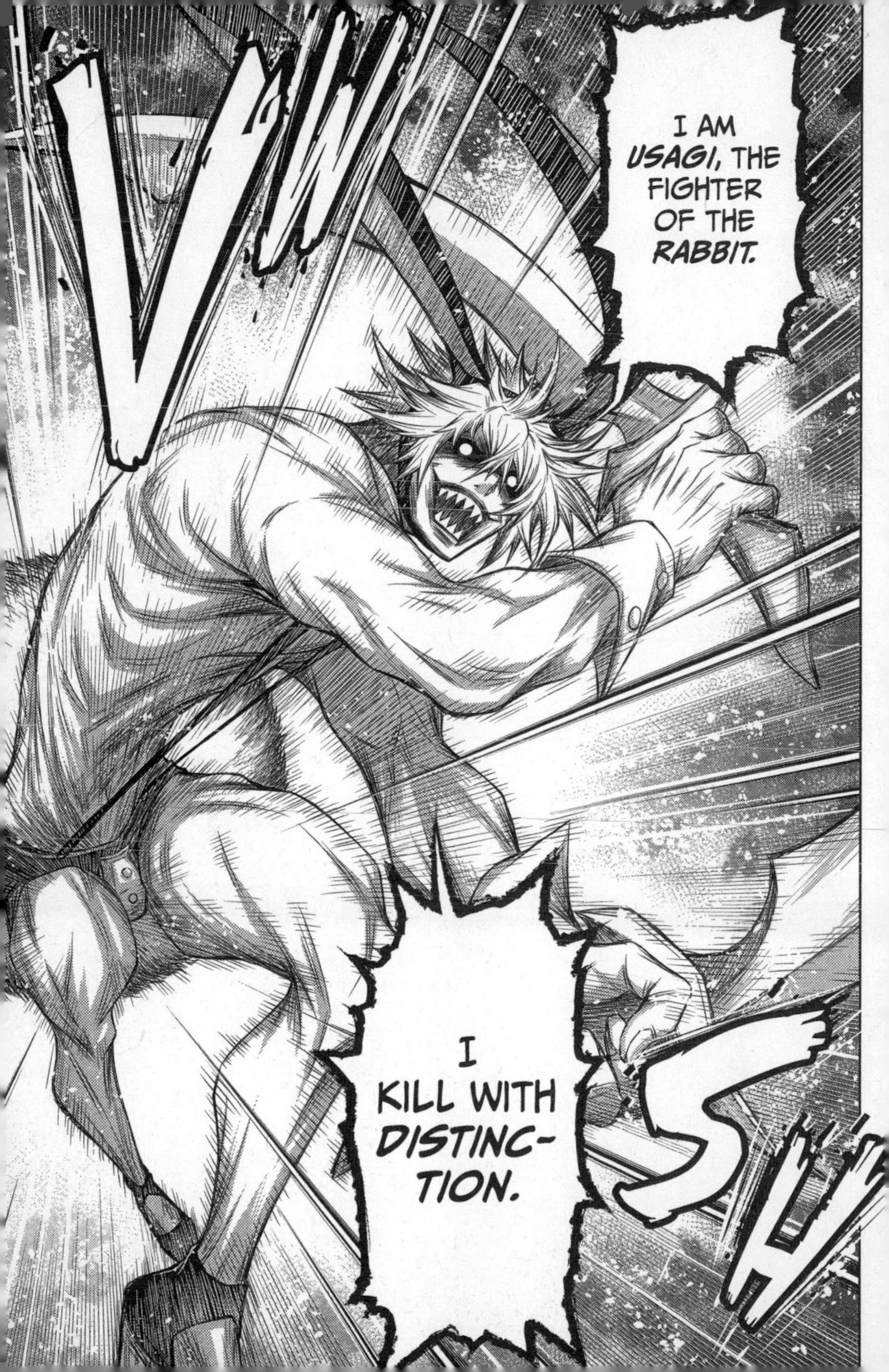

VM
I AM USAGI, THE FIGHTER OF THE RABBIT.
I KILL WITH DISTINCTION.
SH

Luxury was to be made,
not asked for—
such was her philosophy.
This was the time to rise to action—
to graceful action.

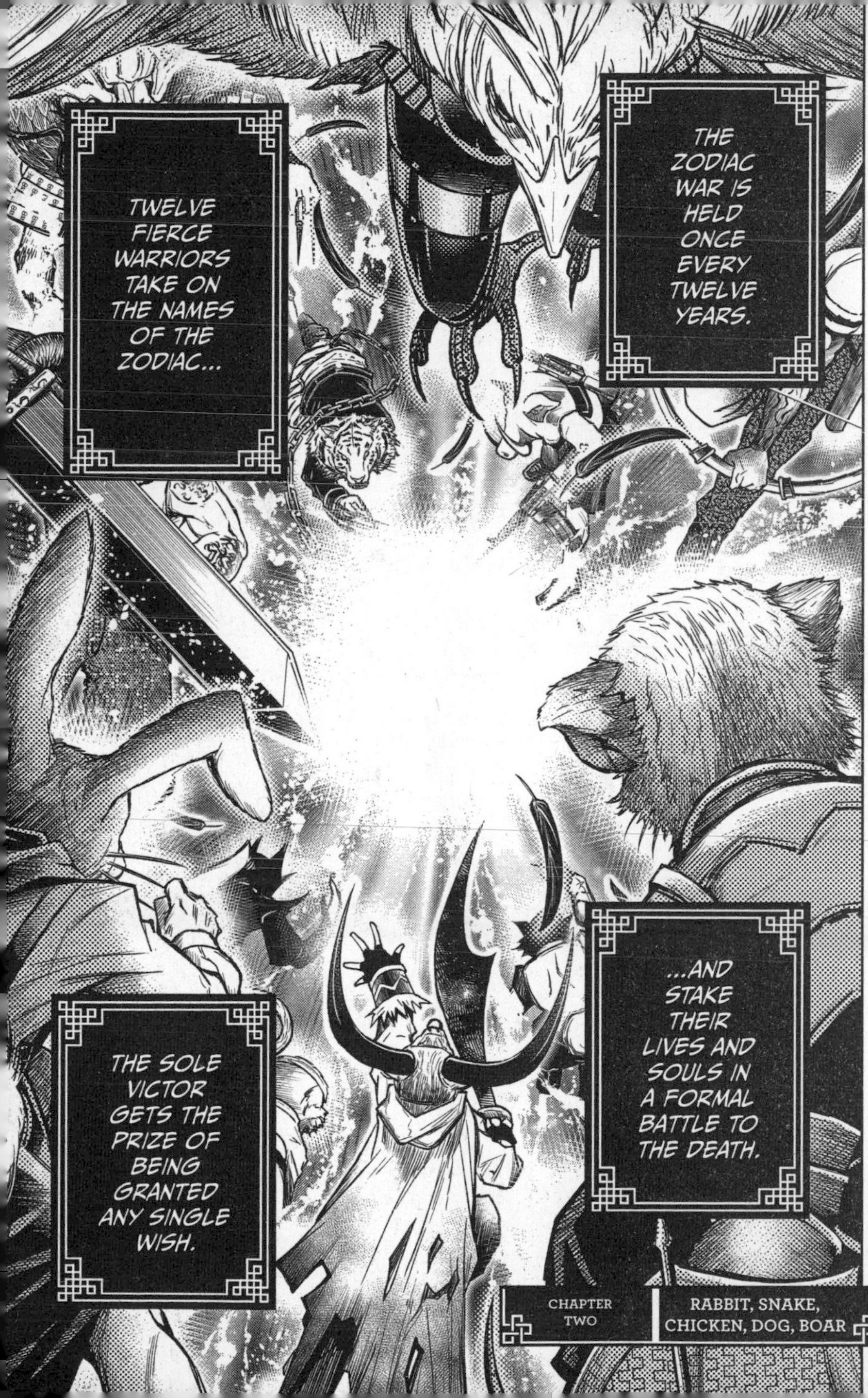
THE ZODIAC WAR IS HELD ONCE EVERY TWELVE YEARS.
TWELVE FIERCE WARRIORS TAKE ON THE NAMES OF THE ZODIAC...
...AND STAKE THEIR LIVES AND SOULS IN A FORMAL BATTLE TO THE DEATH.
THE SOLE VICTOR GETS THE PRIZE OF BEING GRANTED ANY SINGLE WISH.
CHAPTER TWO
RABBIT, SNAKE, CHICKEN, DOG, BOAR

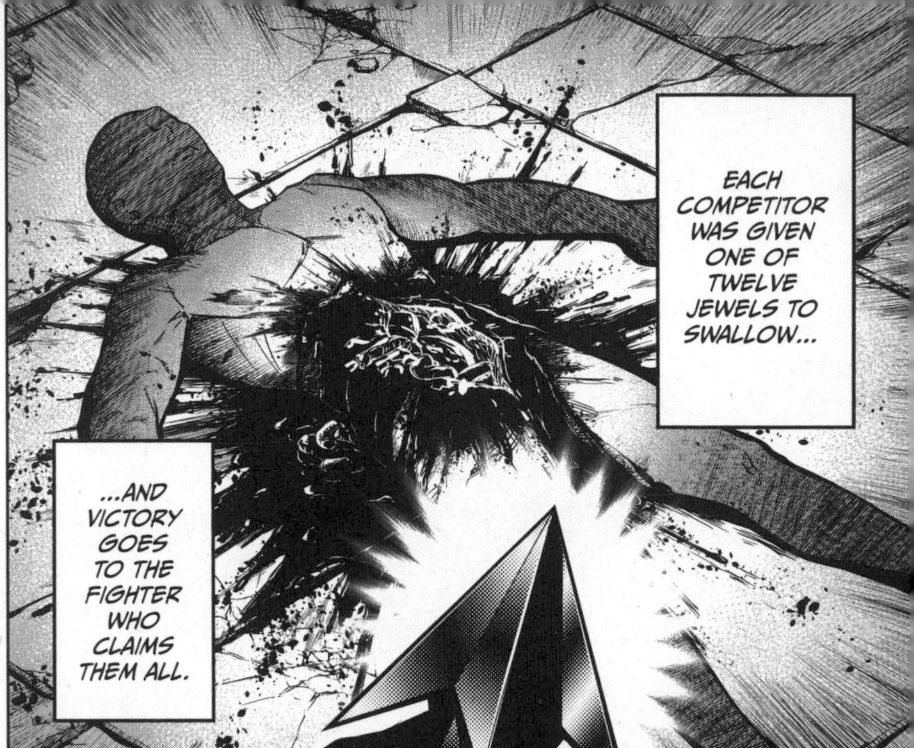
EACH COMPETITOR WAS GIVEN ONE OF TWELVE JEWELS TO SWALLOW...
...AND VICTORY GOES TO THE FIGHTER WHO CLAIMS THEM ALL.

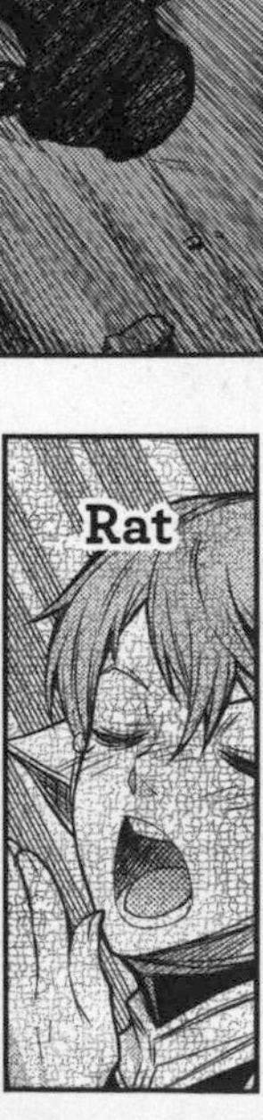
Rat

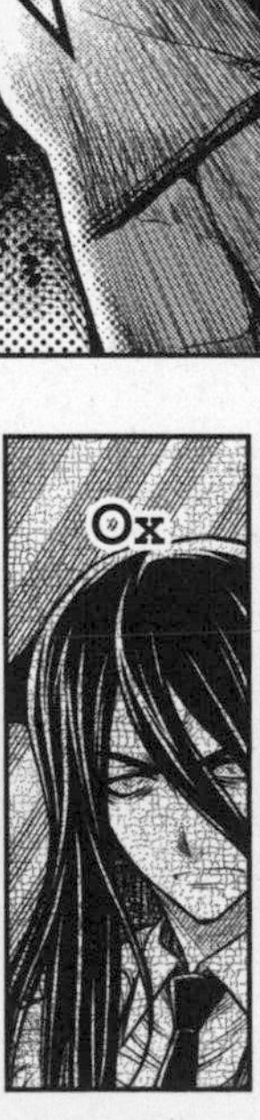
Ox

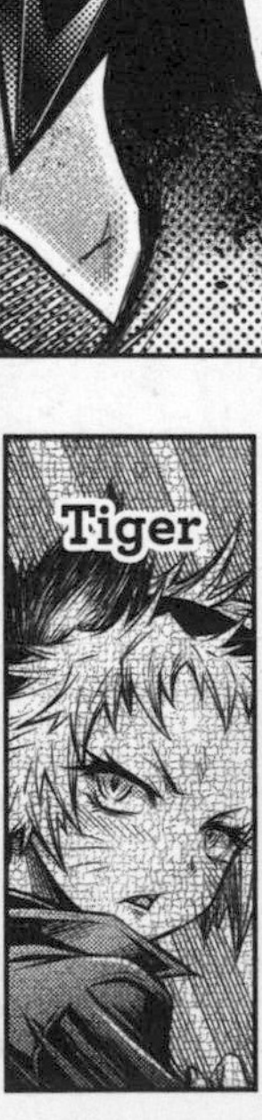
Tiger

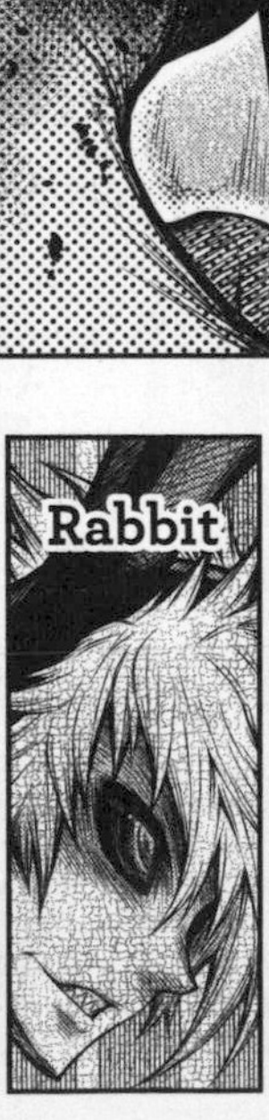
Rabbit

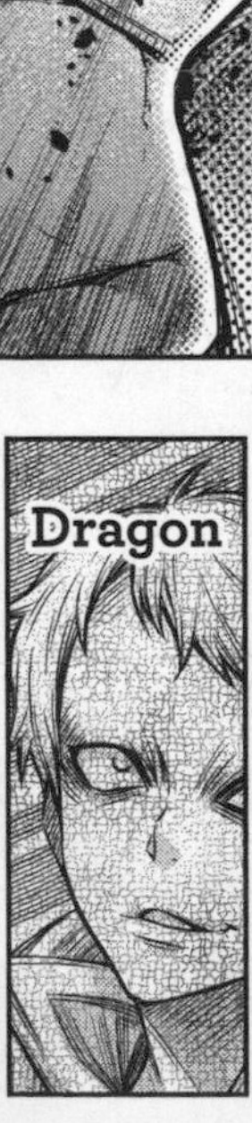
Dragon

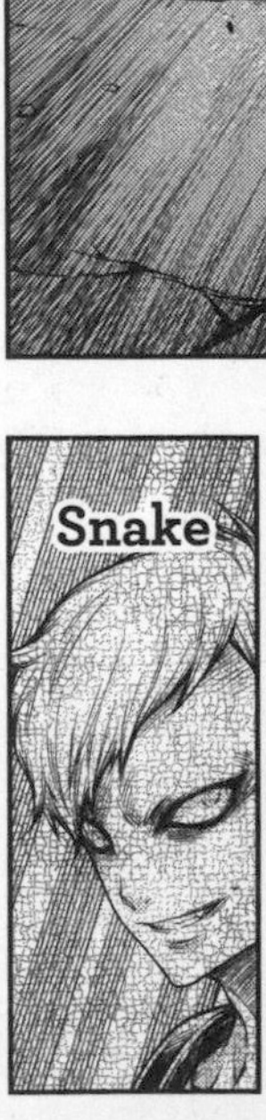
Snake

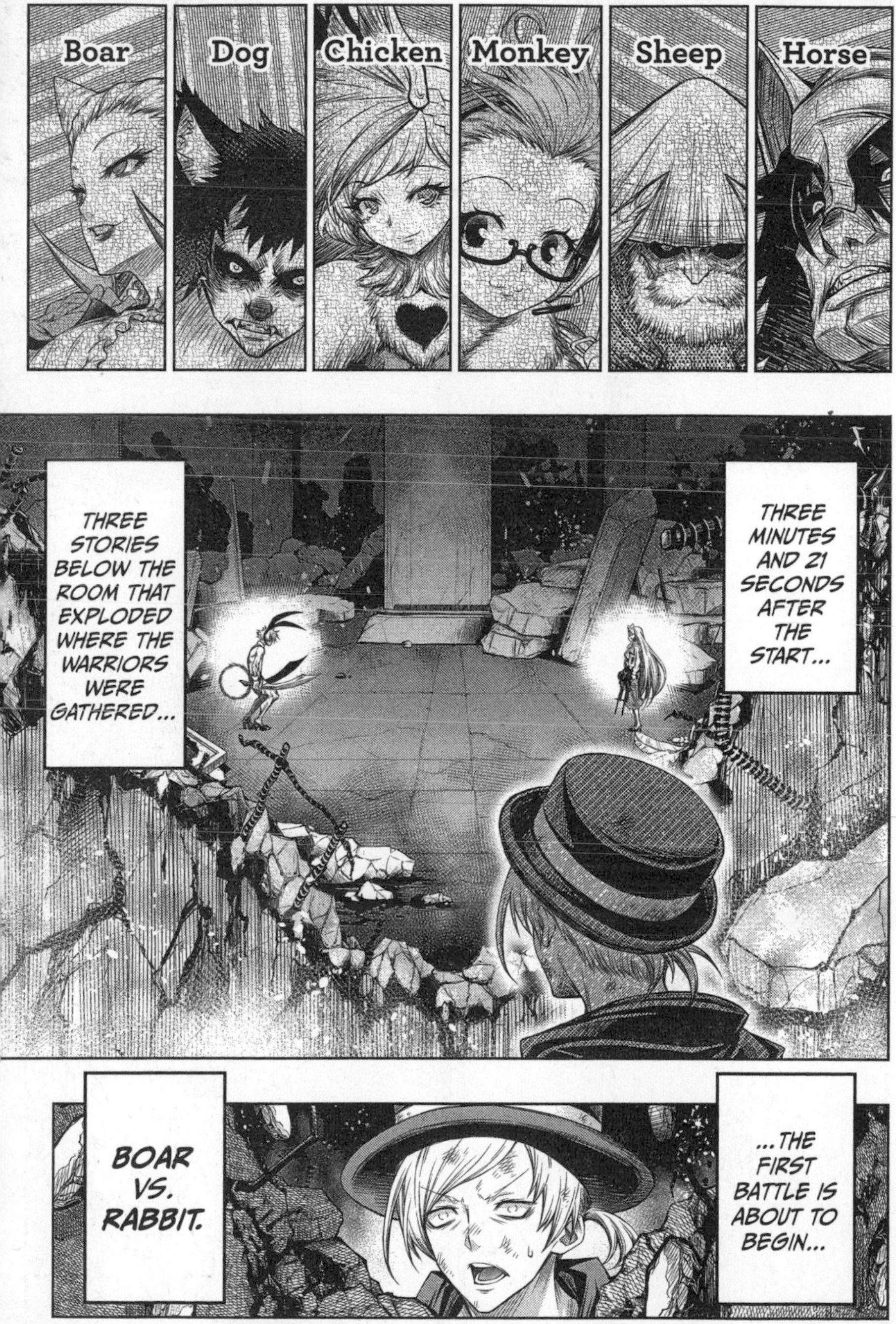
Horse
Sheep
Monkey
Chicken
Dog
Boar
THREE MINUTES AND 21 SECONDS AFTER THE START...
THREE STORIES BELOW THE ROOM THAT EXPLODED WHERE THE WARRIORS WERE GATHERED...
...THE FIRST BATTLE IS ABOUT TO BEGIN...
BOAR VS. RABBIT.

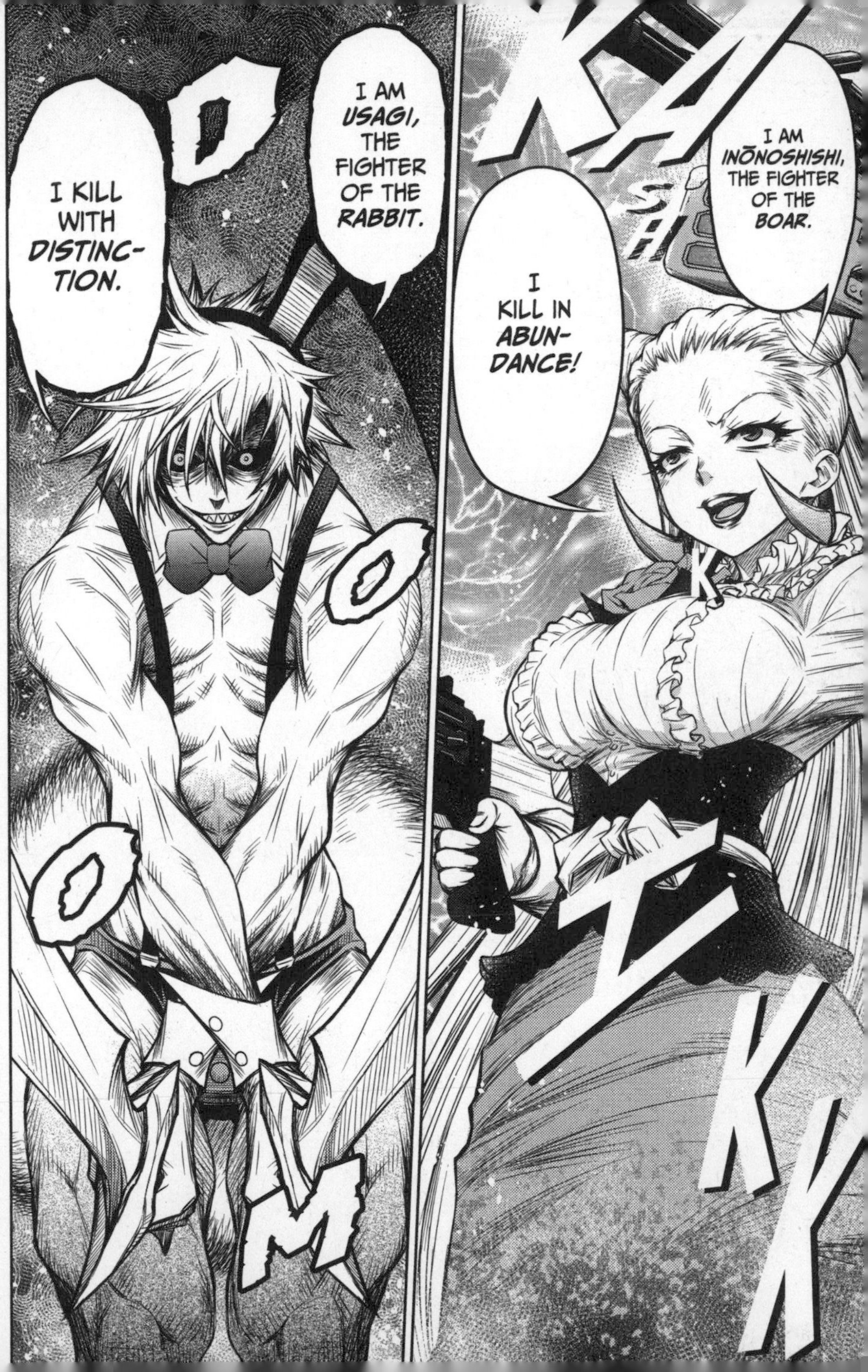
I AM INŌNOSHISHI, THE FIGHTER OF THE BOAR.
KASHI!!
I KILL IN ABUNDANCE!
ZKKK
I AM USAGI, THE FIGHTER OF THE RABBIT.
I KILL WITH DISTINCTION.
DOOM

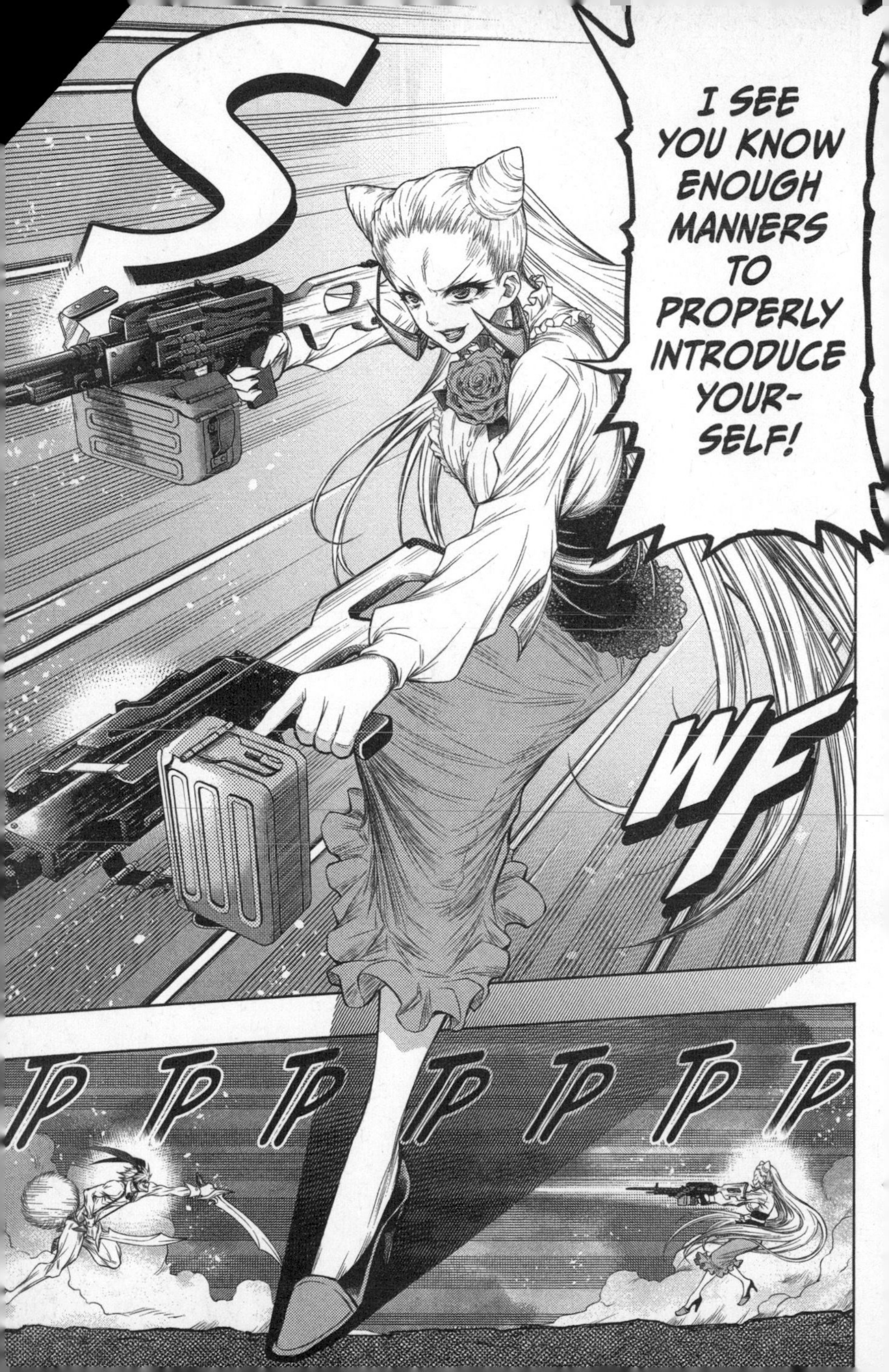
I SEE YOU KNOW ENOUGH MANNERS TO PROPERLY INTRODUCE YOUR-SELF!
S
WF
TP TP TP TP TP TP TP

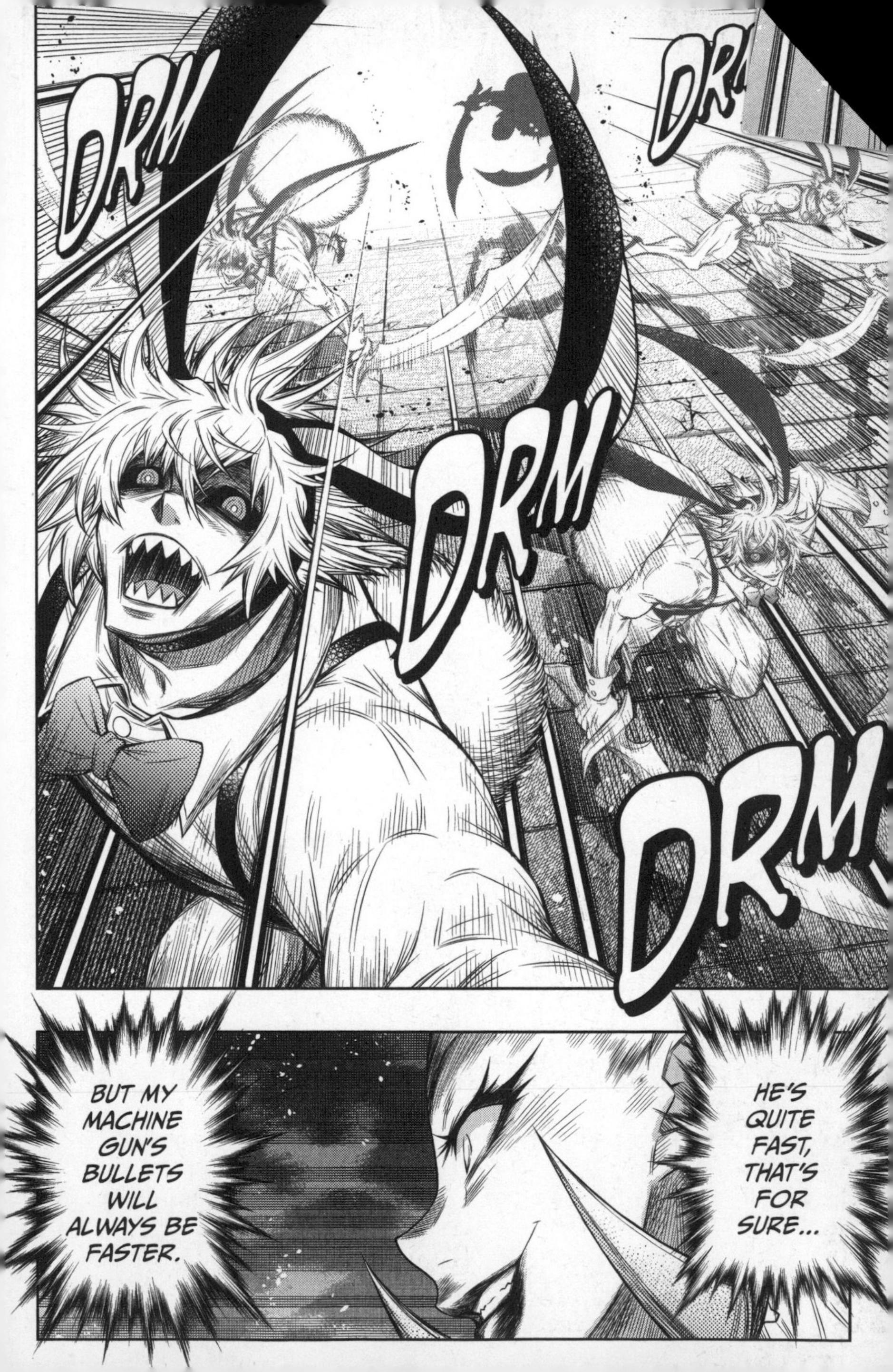
DRM
DRM
DRM
DRM
HE'S QUITE FAST, THAT'S FOR SURE...
BUT MY MACHINE GUN'S BULLETS WILL ALWAYS BE FASTER.

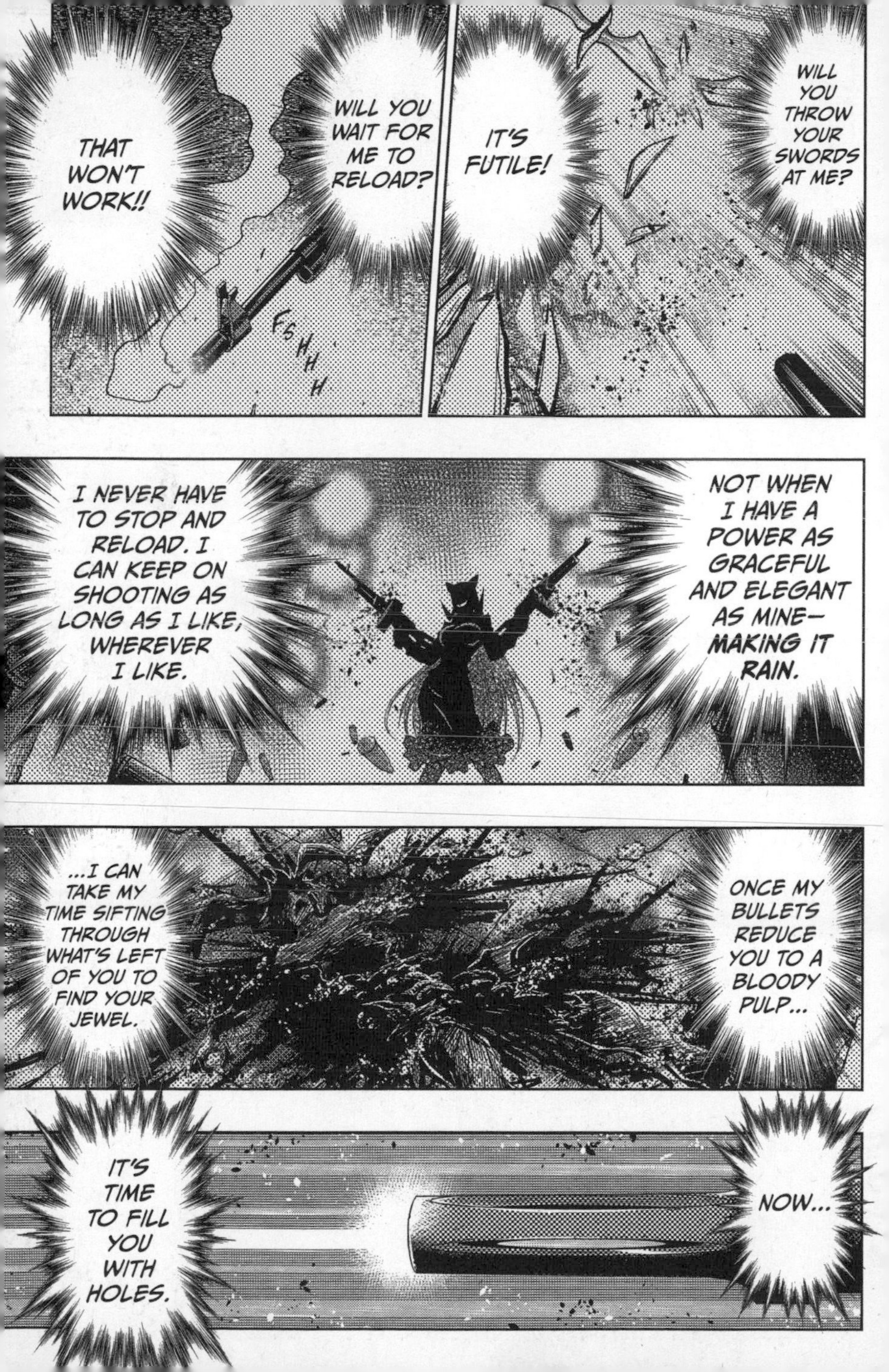
WILL YOU THROW YOUR SWORDS AT ME?
IT'S FUTILE!
WILL YOU WAIT FOR ME TO RELOAD?
THAT WON'T WORK!!
FSHHH
NOT WHEN I HAVE A POWER AS GRACEFUL AND ELEGANT AS MINE— MAKING IT RAIN.
I NEVER HAVE TO STOP AND RELOAD. I CAN KEEP ON SHOOTING AS LONG AS I LIKE, WHEREVER I LIKE.
ONCE MY BULLETS REDUCE YOU TO A BLOODY PULP...
...I CAN TAKE MY TIME SIFTING THROUGH WHAT'S LEFT OF YOU TO FIND YOUR JEWEL.
NOW...
IT'S TIME TO FILL YOU WITH HOLES.

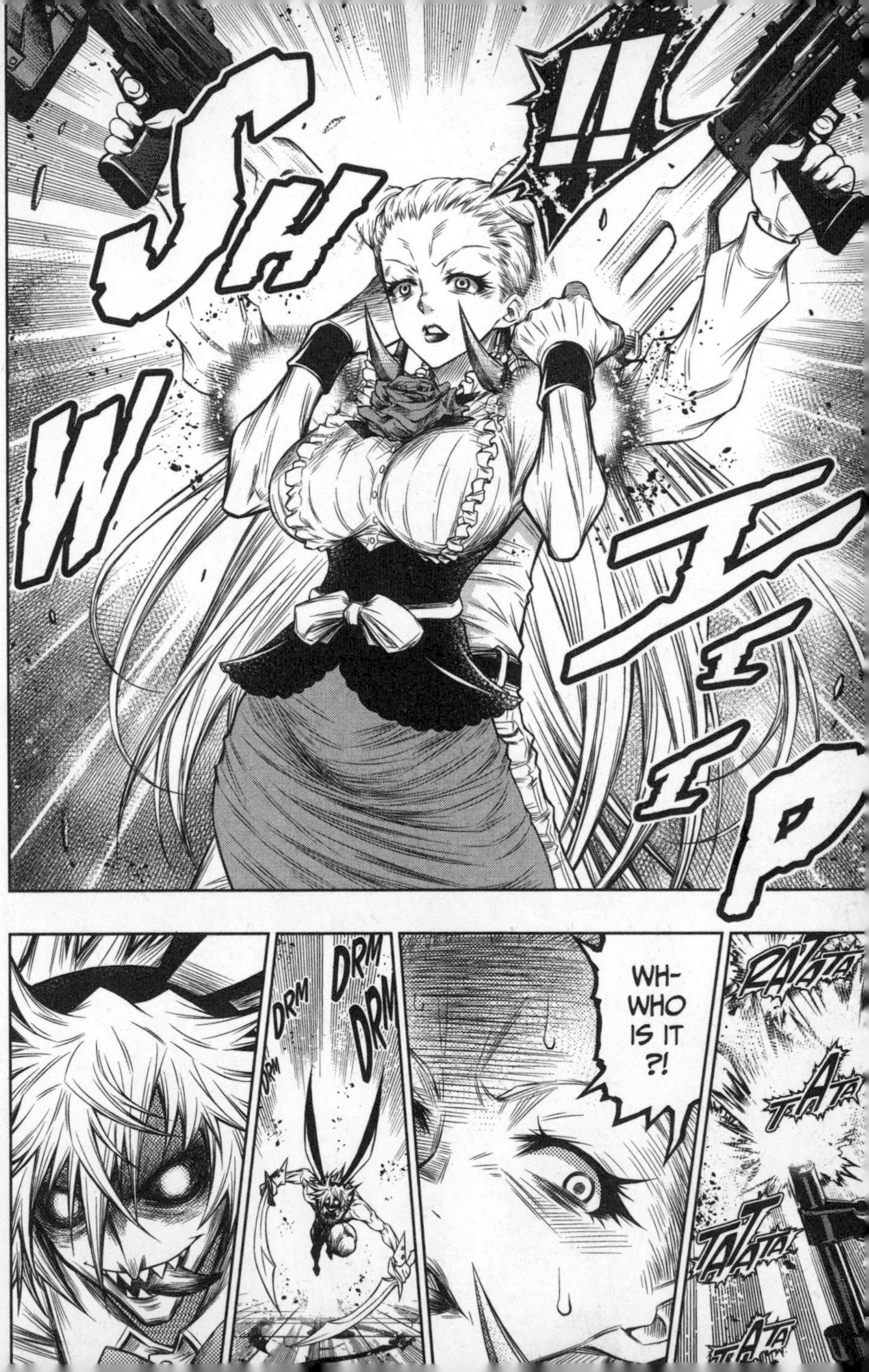
SHWIIIP
!!
RATATA
TATATA
TATATATA
WH- WHO IS IT ?!
DRM DRM
DRM DRM

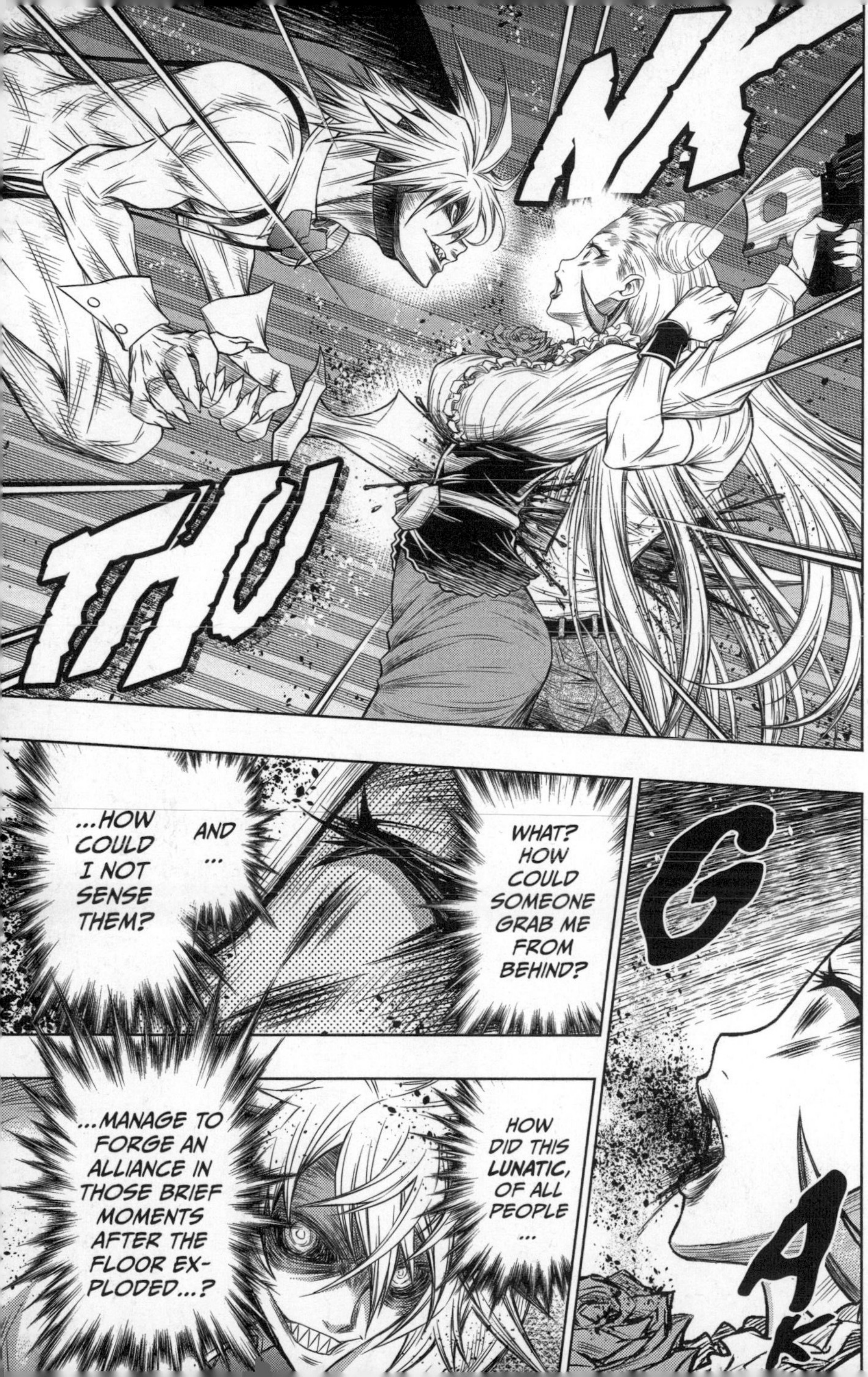
THU
NK
G
A
K
WHAT? HOW COULD SOMEONE GRAB ME FROM BEHIND?
AND ...
...HOW COULD I NOT SENSE THEM?
HOW DID THIS LUNATIC, OF ALL PEOPLE ...
...MANAGE TO FORGE AN ALLIANCE IN THOSE BRIEF MOMENTS AFTER THE FLOOR EX-PLODED...?

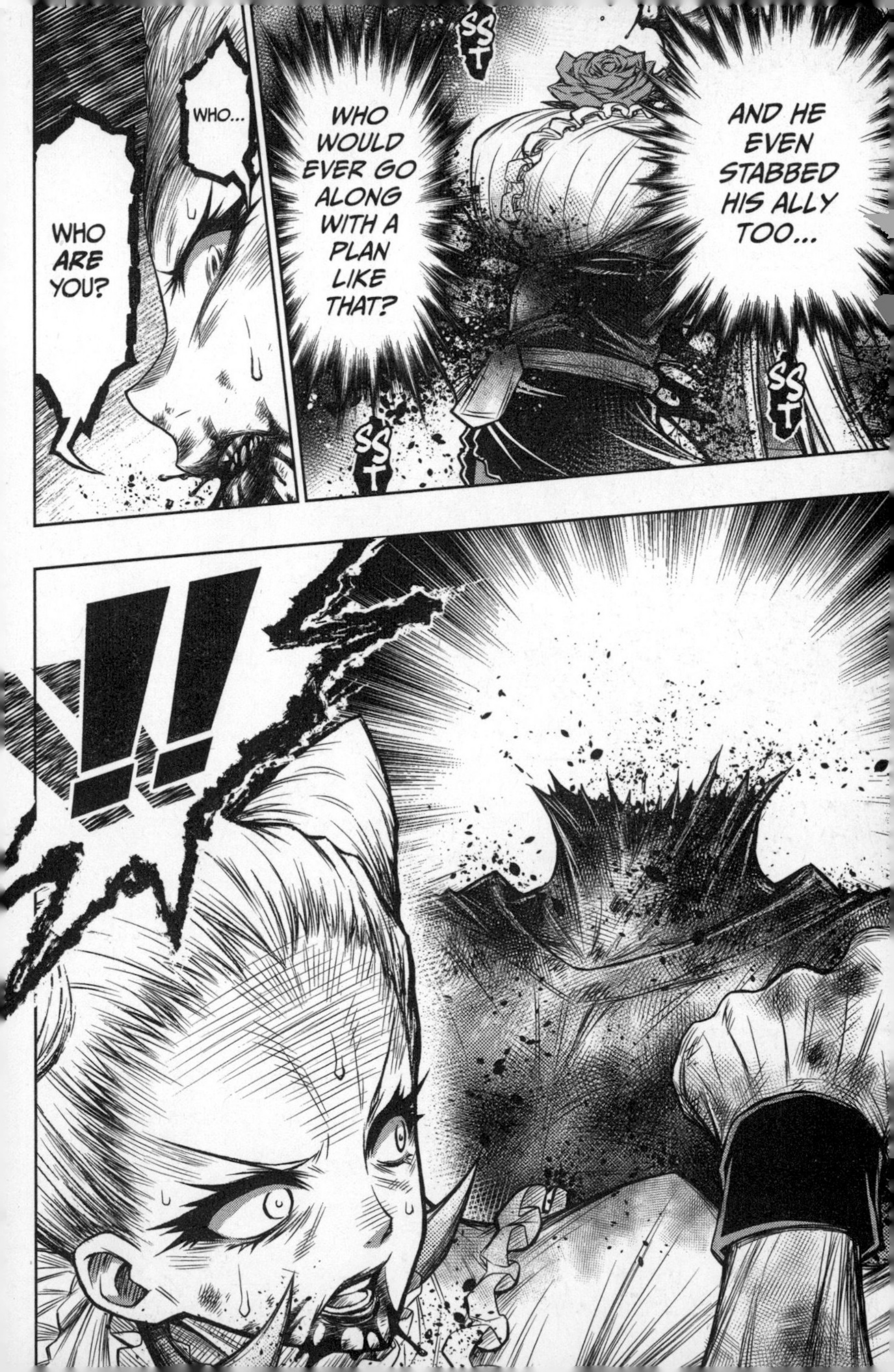
AND HE EVEN STABBED HIS ALLY TOO...
SST
SST
WHO WOULD EVER GO ALONG WITH A PLAN LIKE THAT?
SST
WHO...
WHO ARE YOU?
!!

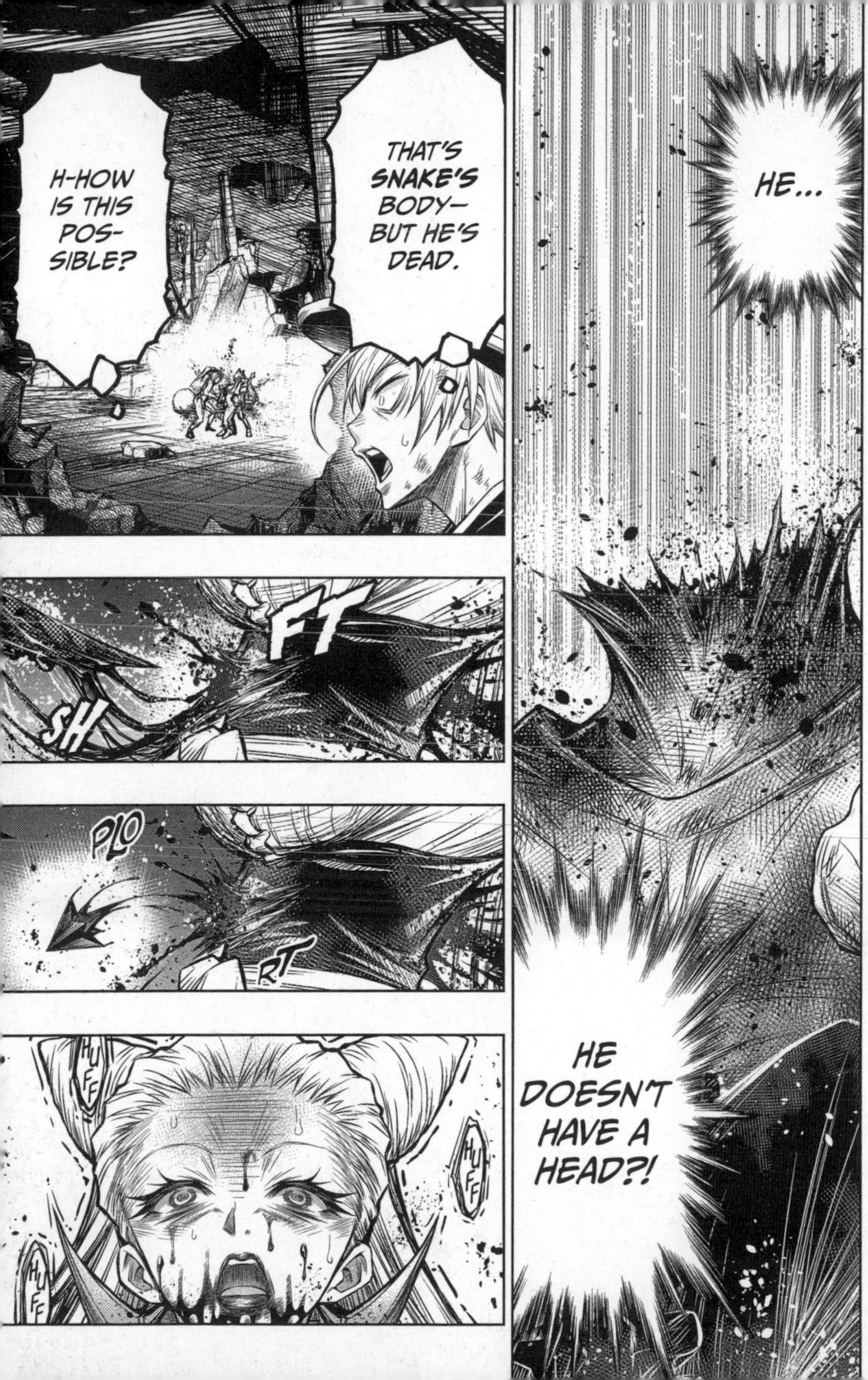
HE...
HE DOESN'T HAVE A HEAD?!
THAT'S SNAKE'S BODY—BUT HE'S DEAD.
H-HOW IS THIS POSSIBLE?
FT
SH
PLO
RT
HUFF
HUFF
HUFF

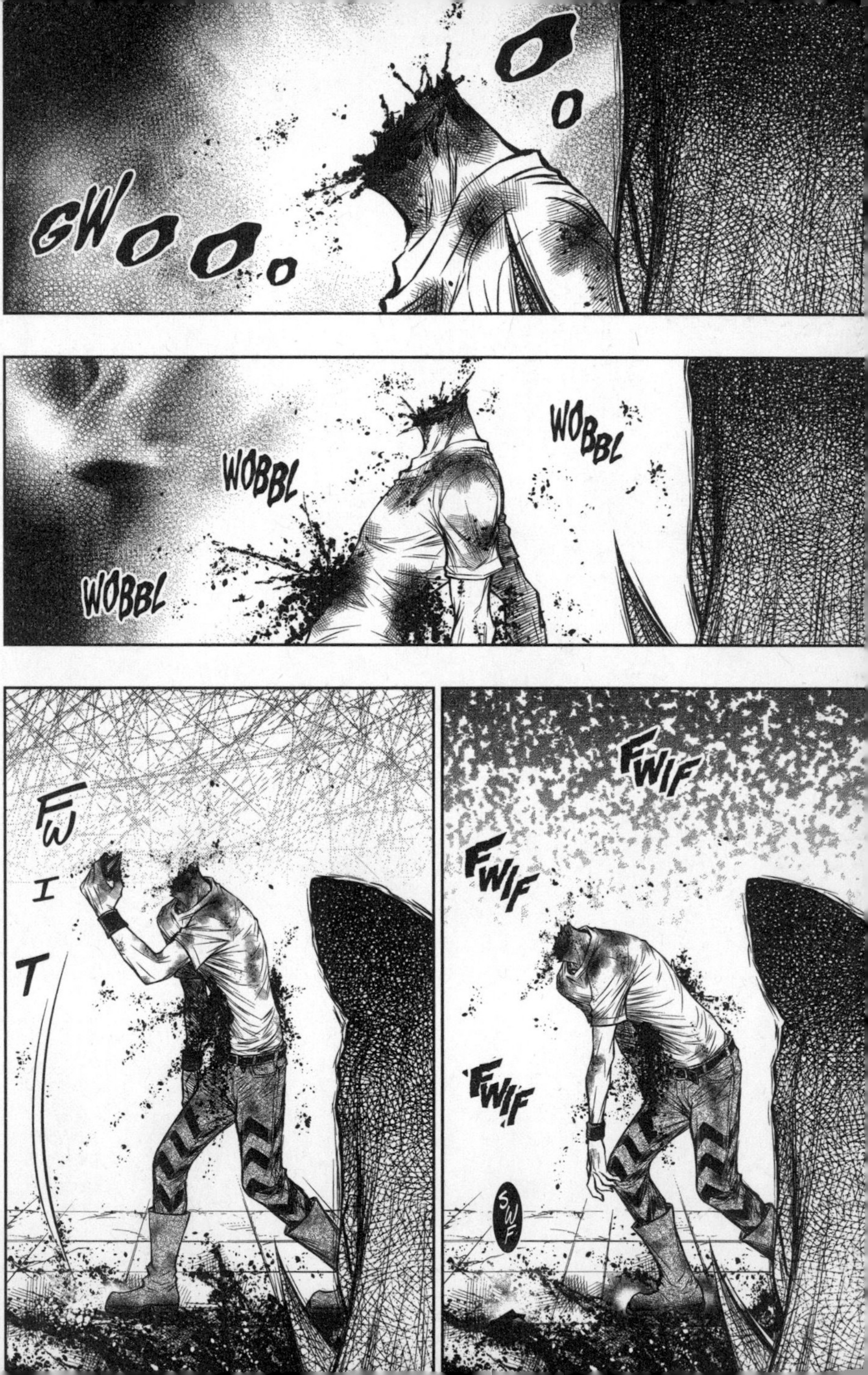
Oo
GWOOOo
WOBBL
WOBBL
WOBBL
FWIF
FWIF
FWIF
SWF
FWIT

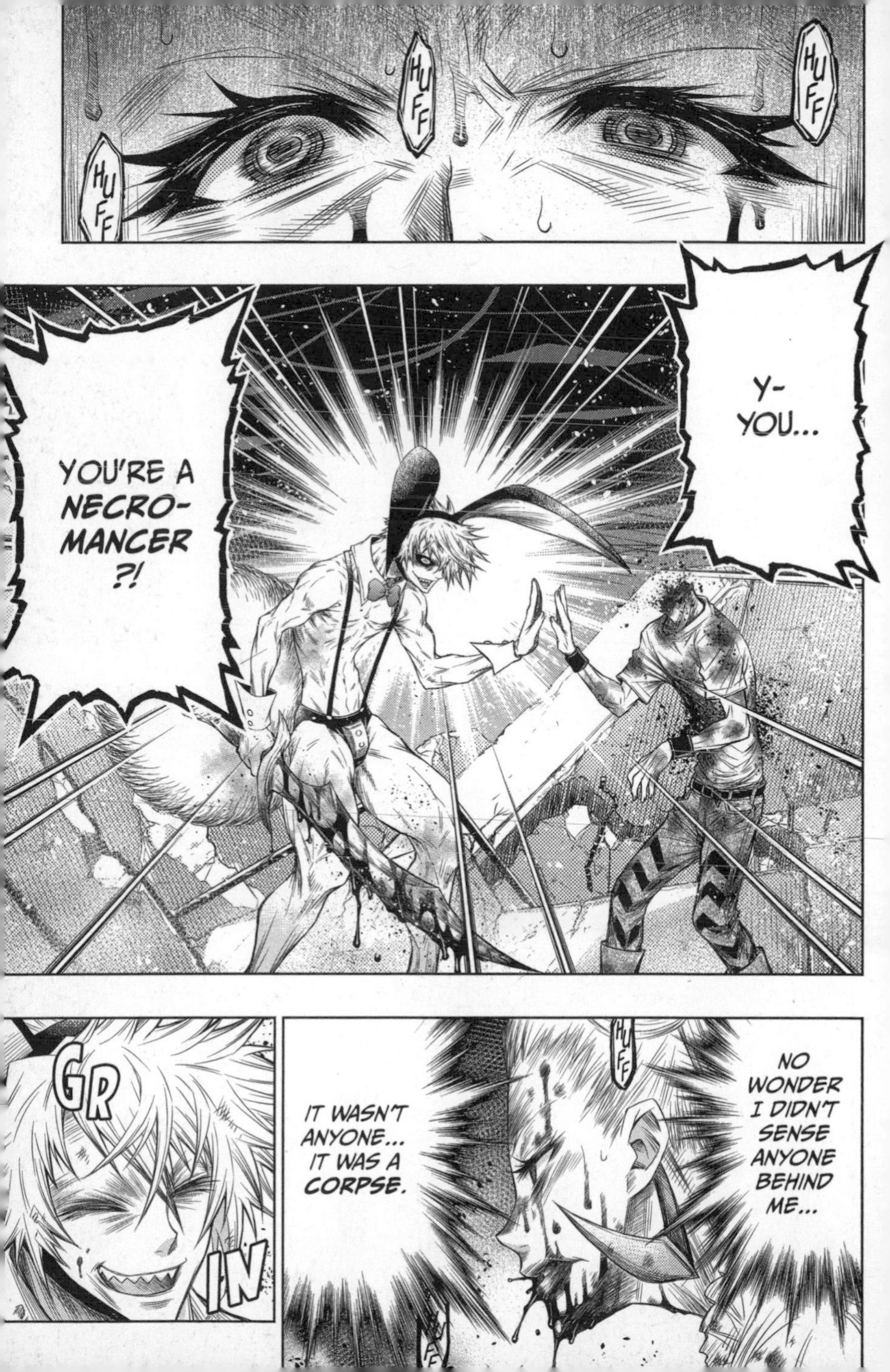
HUFF
HUFF
HUFF
Y- YOU...
YOU'RE A NECROMANCER?!
HUFF
NO WONDER I DIDN'T SENSE ANYONE BEHIND ME...
IT WASN'T ANYONE... IT WAS A CORPSE.
GRIN

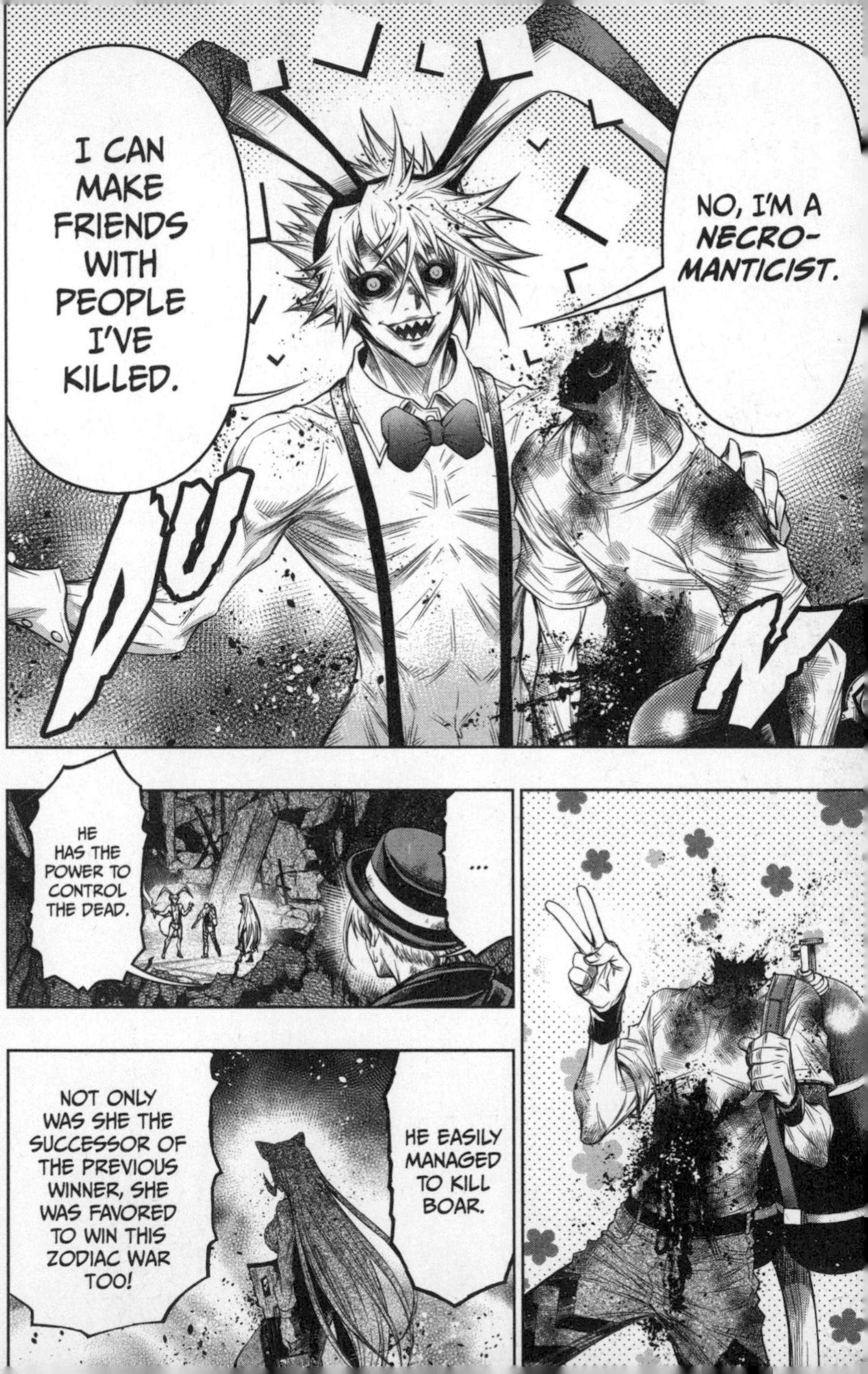
NO, I'M A NECRO-MANTICIST.
I CAN MAKE FRIENDS WITH PEOPLE I'VE KILLED.
DUN
...
HE HAS THE POWER TO CONTROL THE DEAD.
HE EASILY MANAGED TO KILL BOAR.
NOT ONLY WAS SHE THE SUCCESSOR OF THE PREVIOUS WINNER, SHE WAS FAVORED TO WIN THIS ZODIAC WAR TOO!

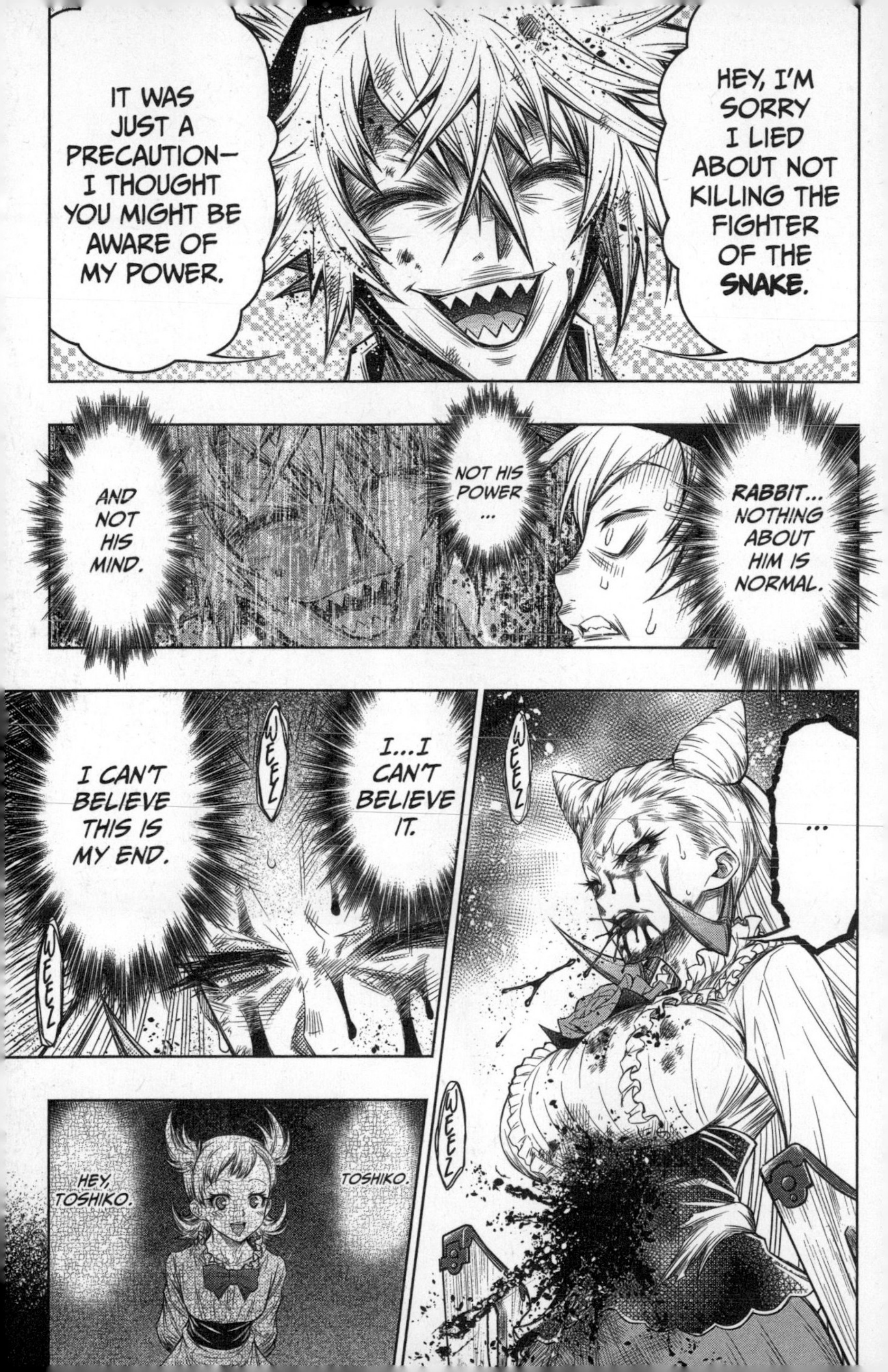
HEY, I'M SORRY I LIED ABOUT NOT KILLING THE FIGHTER OF THE SNAKE.
IT WAS JUST A PRECAUTION— I THOUGHT YOU MIGHT BE AWARE OF MY POWER.
RABBIT... NOTHING ABOUT HIM IS NORMAL.
NOT HIS POWER ...
AND NOT HIS MIND.
WEEZ
...
WEEZ
I...I CAN'T BELIEVE IT.
WEEZ
I CAN'T BELIEVE THIS IS MY END.
WEEZ
TOSHIKO.
HEY, TOSHIKO.

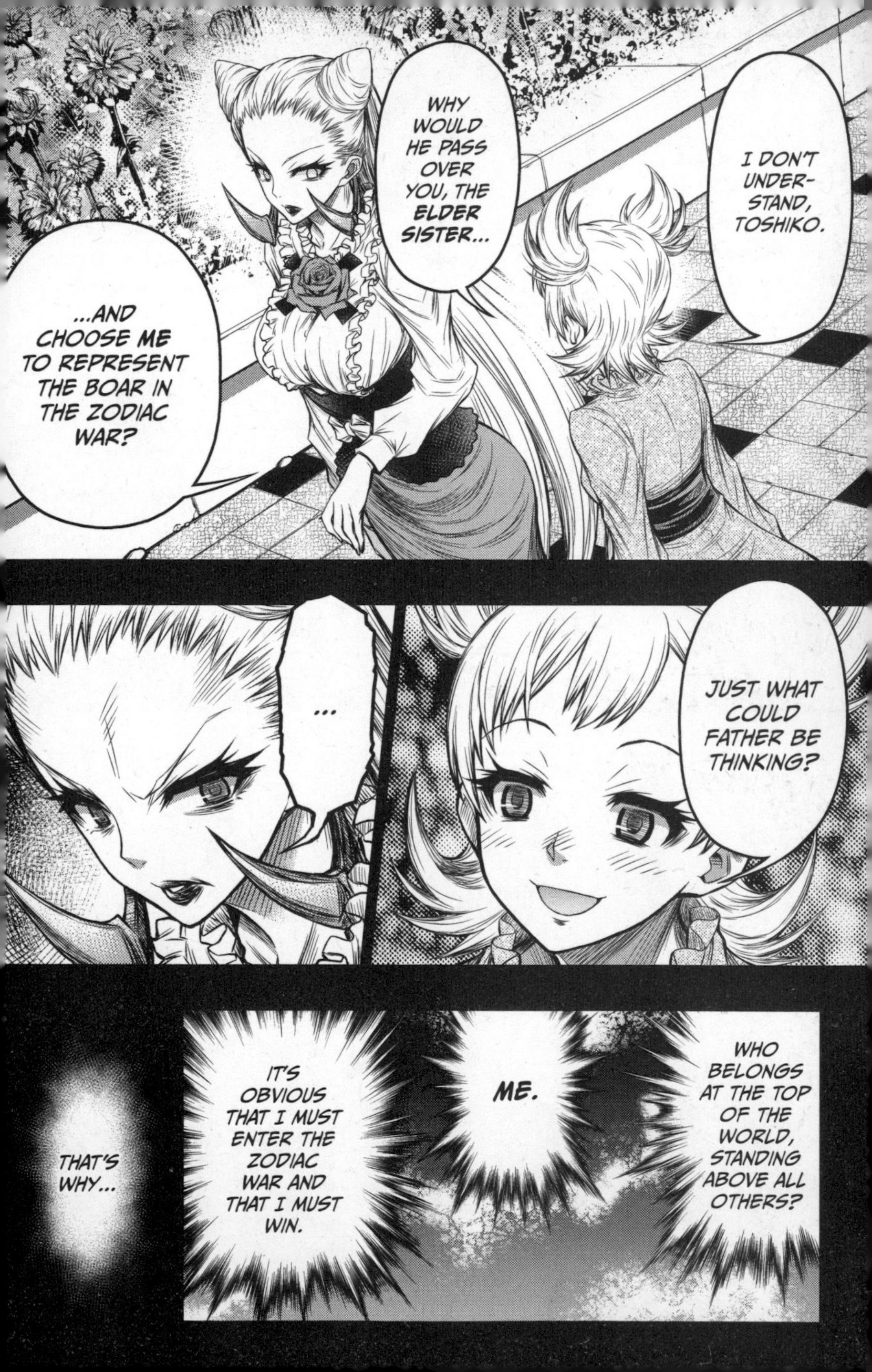
I DON'T UNDER-STAND, TOSHIKO.
WHY WOULD HE PASS OVER YOU, THE ELDER SISTER...
...AND CHOOSE ME TO REPRESENT THE BOAR IN THE ZODIAC WAR?
JUST WHAT COULD FATHER BE THINKING?
...
WHO BELONGS AT THE TOP OF THE WORLD, STANDING ABOVE ALL OTHERS?
ME.
IT'S OBVIOUS THAT I MUST ENTER THE ZODIAC WAR AND THAT I MUST WIN.
THAT'S WHY...

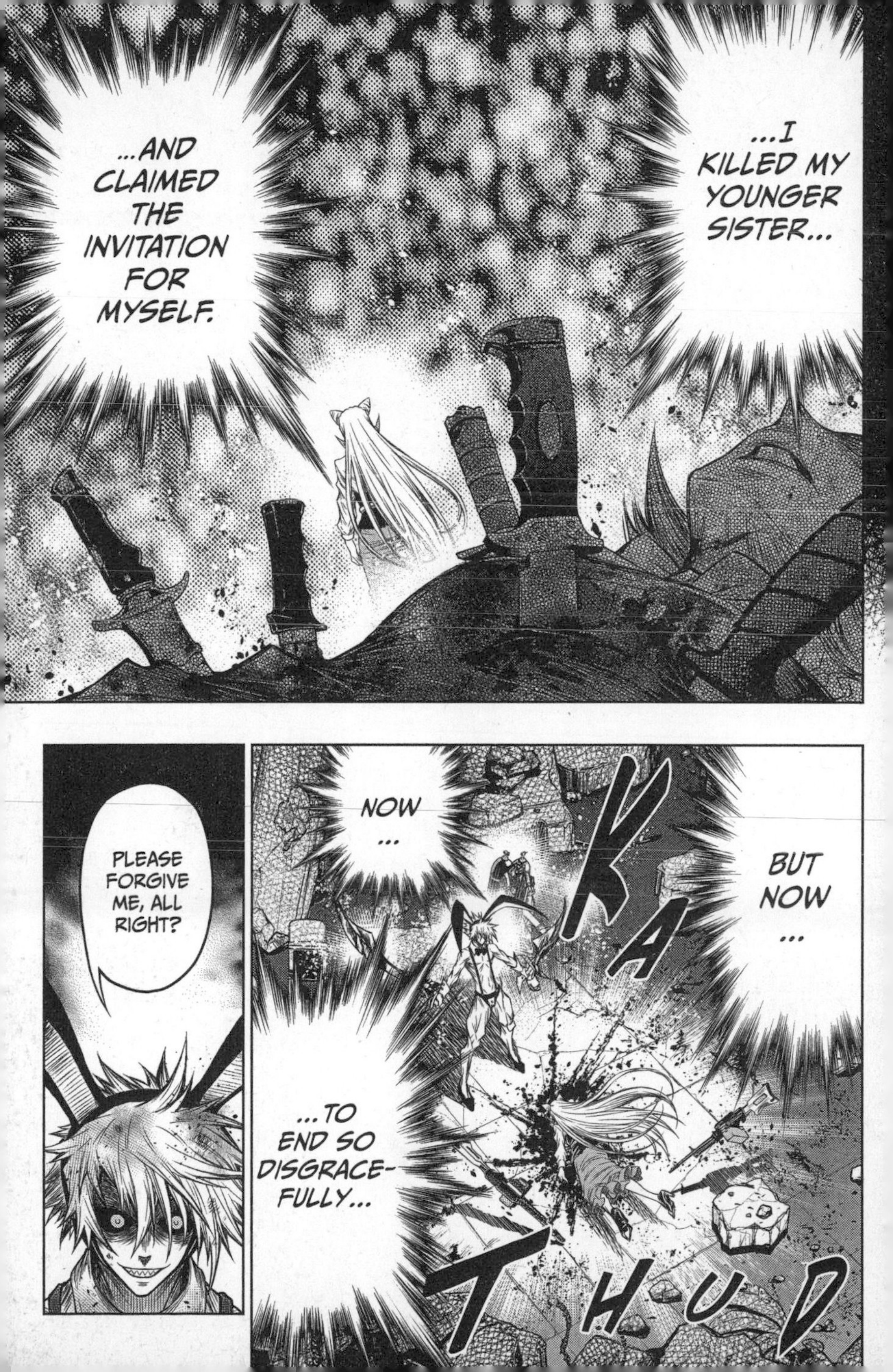
...I KILLED MY YOUNGER SISTER...
...AND CLAIMED THE INVITATION FOR MYSELF.
NOW ...
BUT NOW ...
...TO END SO DISGRACE-FULLY...
KA
THUD
PLEASE FORGIVE ME, ALL RIGHT?

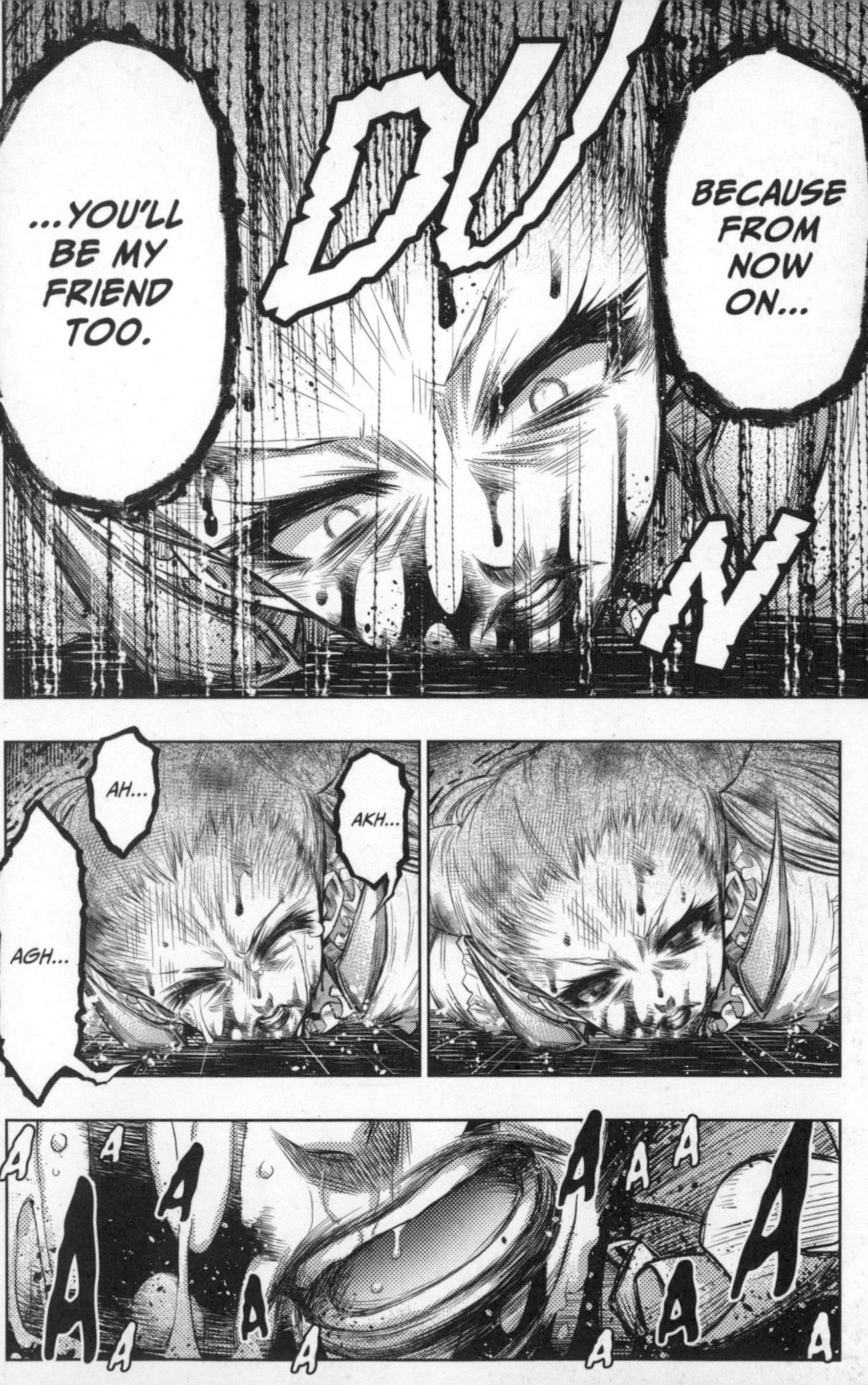
BECAUSE FROM NOW ON...
...YOU'LL BE MY FRIEND TOO.
DON
AKH...
AH...
AGH...
AAAAAAAAAAAAAAAAAAAAAAA

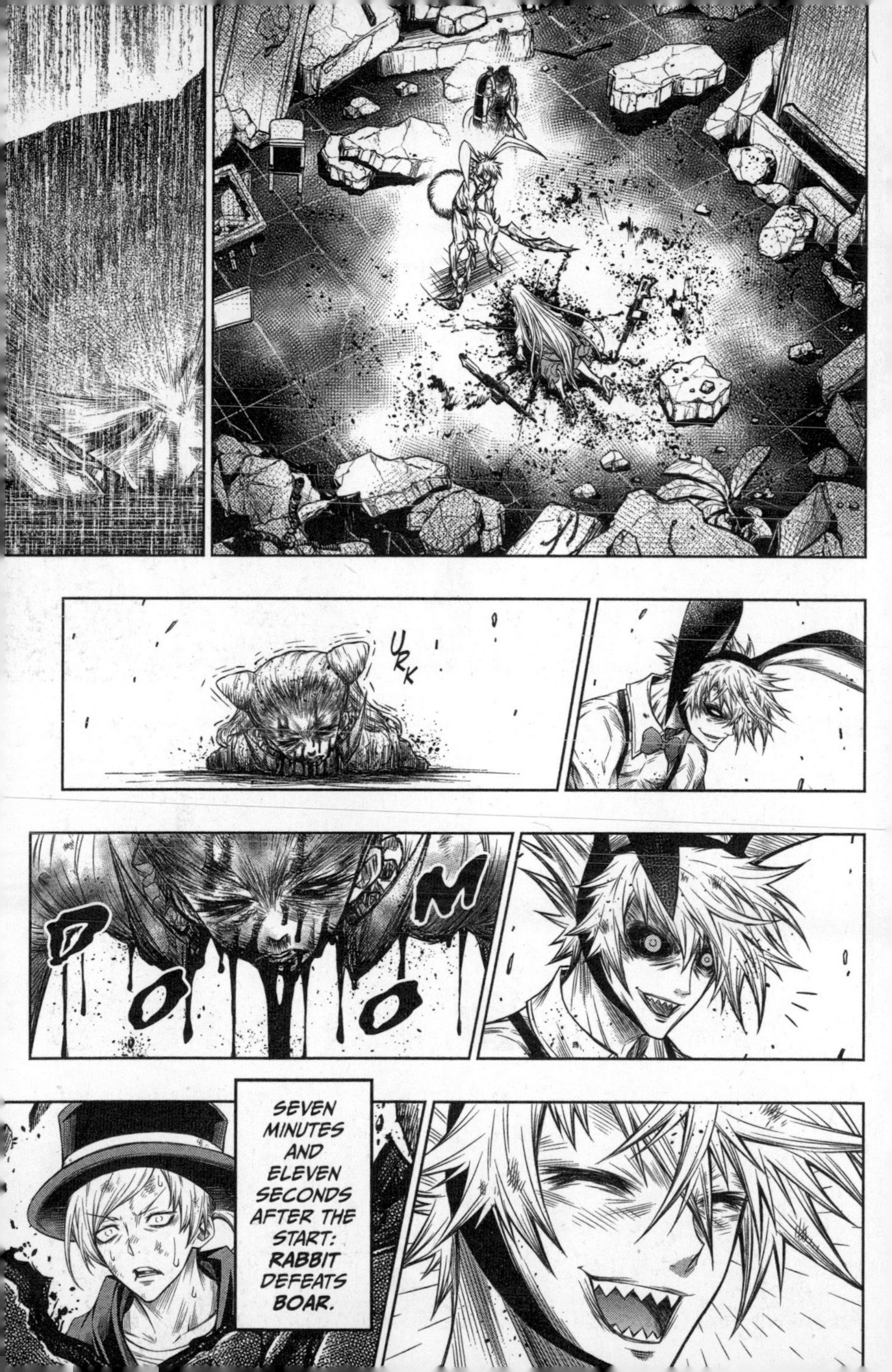
URK
DOOM
SEVEN MINUTES AND ELEVEN SECONDS AFTER THE START: RABBIT DEFEATS BOAR.

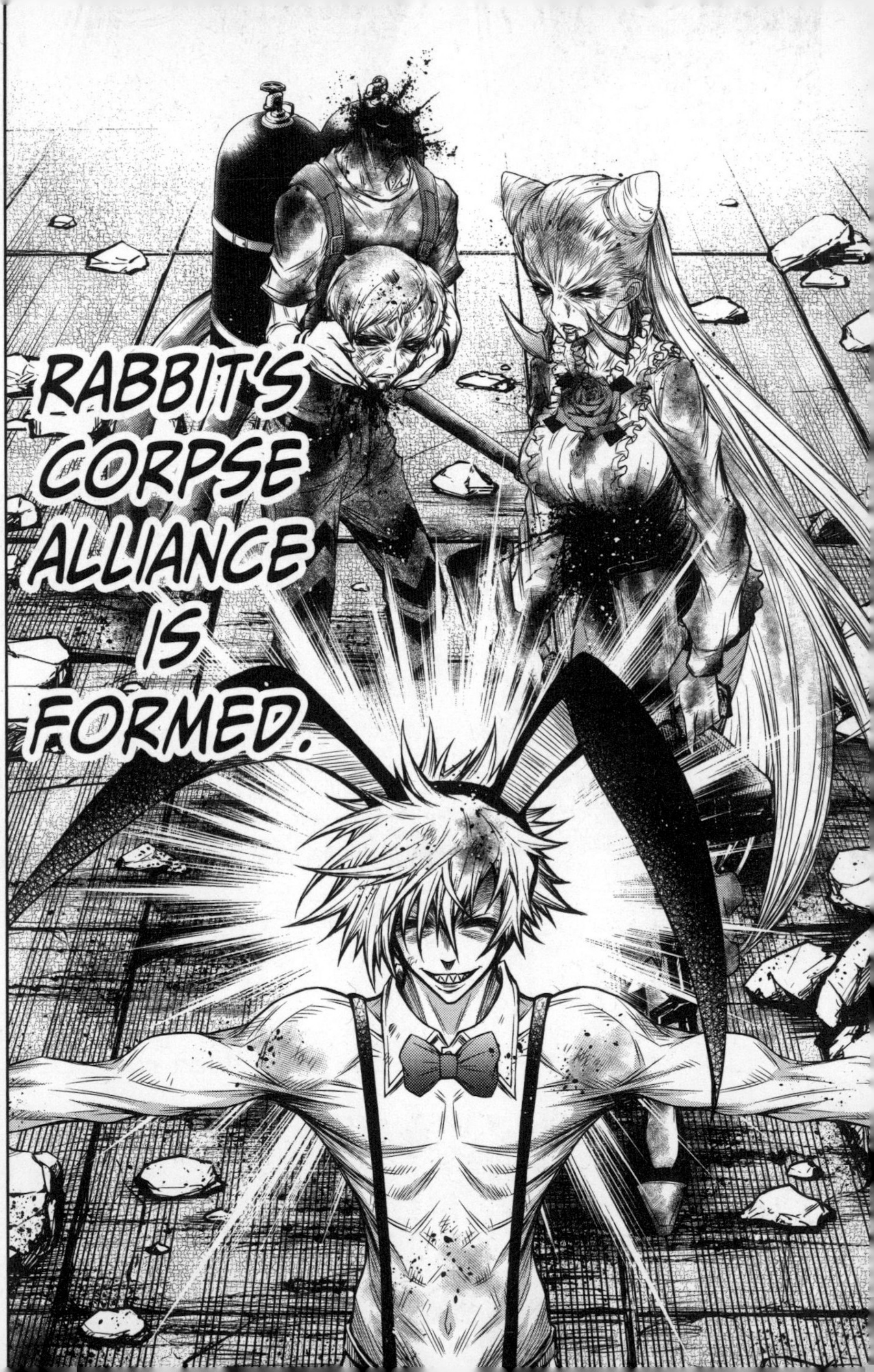
RABBIT'S CORPSE ALLIANCE IS FORMED.

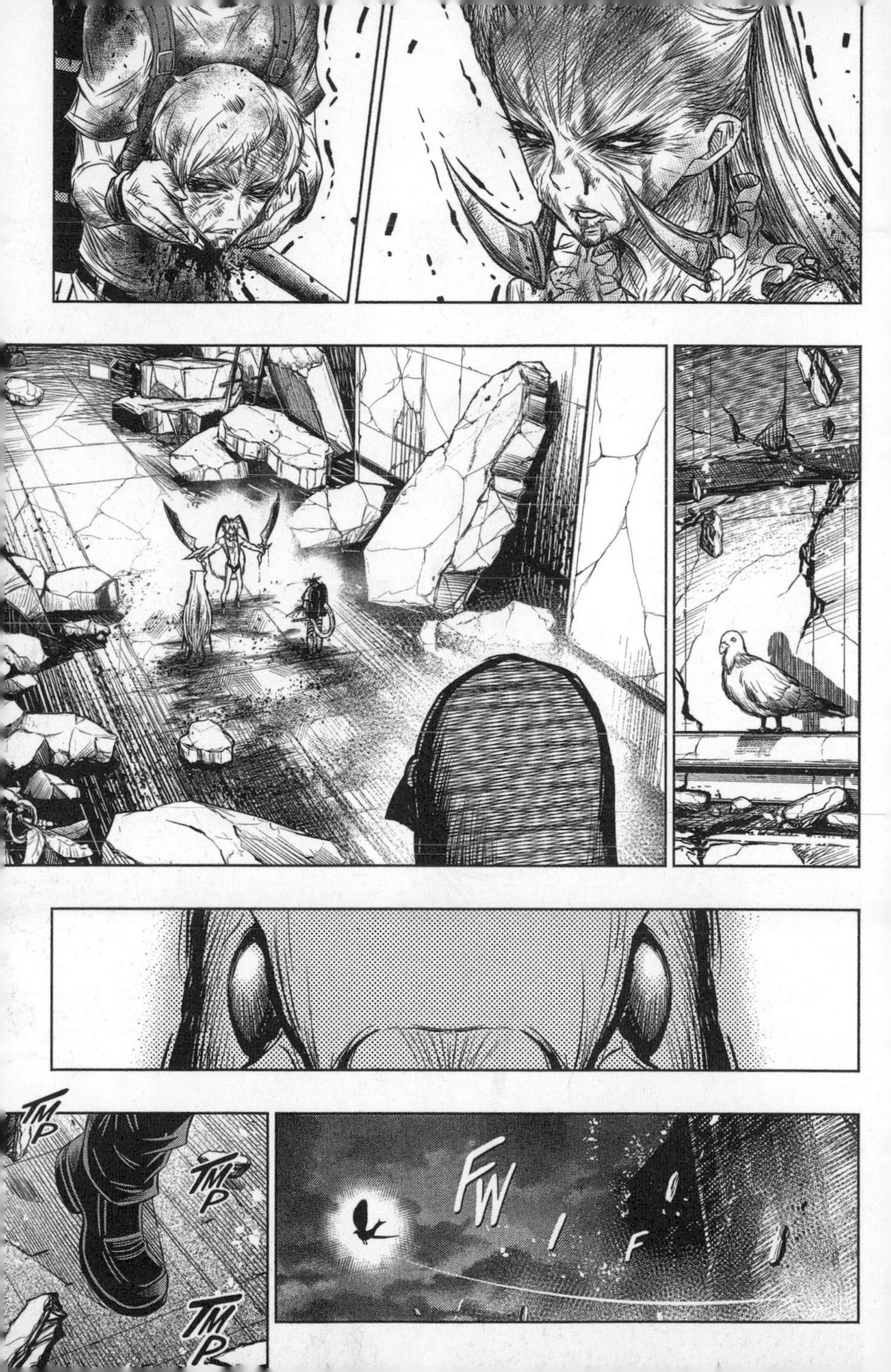
FWIFF
TMP
TMP
TMP

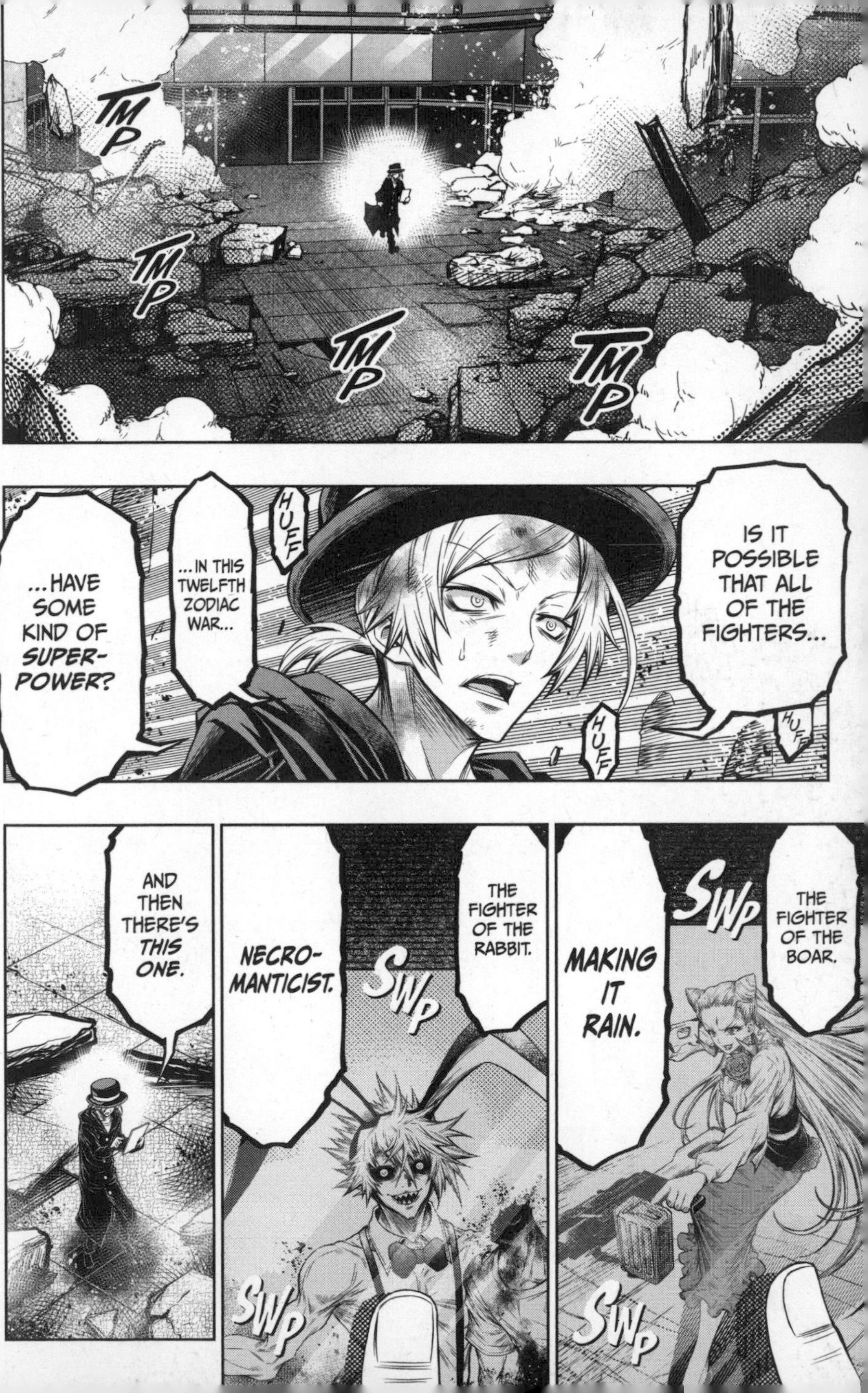
TMP
TMP
TMP
TMP
IS IT POSSIBLE THAT ALL OF THE FIGHTERS...
HUFF
HUFF
...IN THIS TWELFTH ZODIAC WAR...
HUFF
...HAVE SOME KIND OF SUPER-POWER?
SWP
THE FIGHTER OF THE BOAR.
MAKING IT RAIN.
SWP
THE FIGHTER OF THE RABBIT.
SWP
NECRO-MANTICIST.
SWP
AND THEN THERE'S THIS ONE.

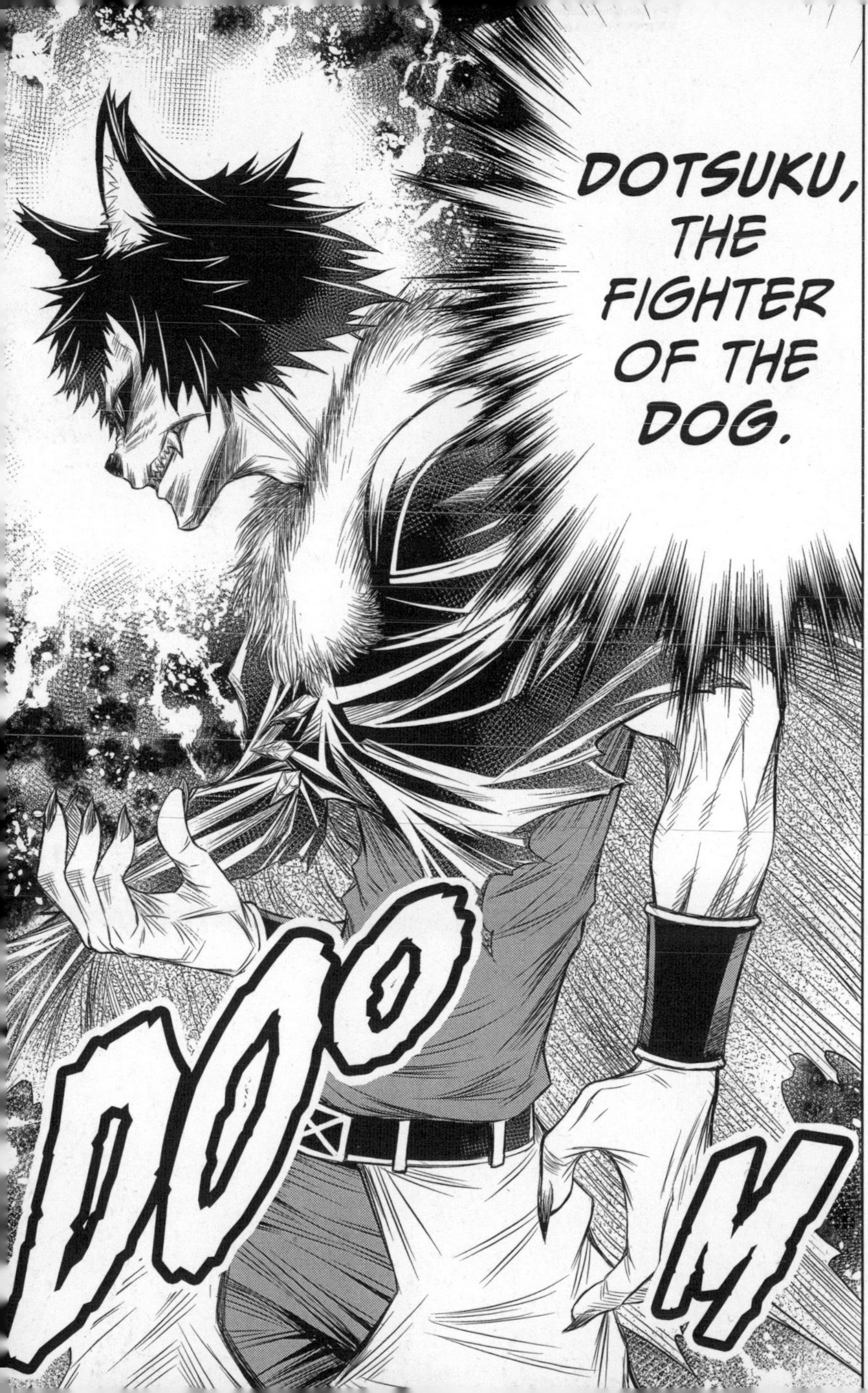
DOTSUKU, THE FIGHTER OF THE DOG.
DOOM

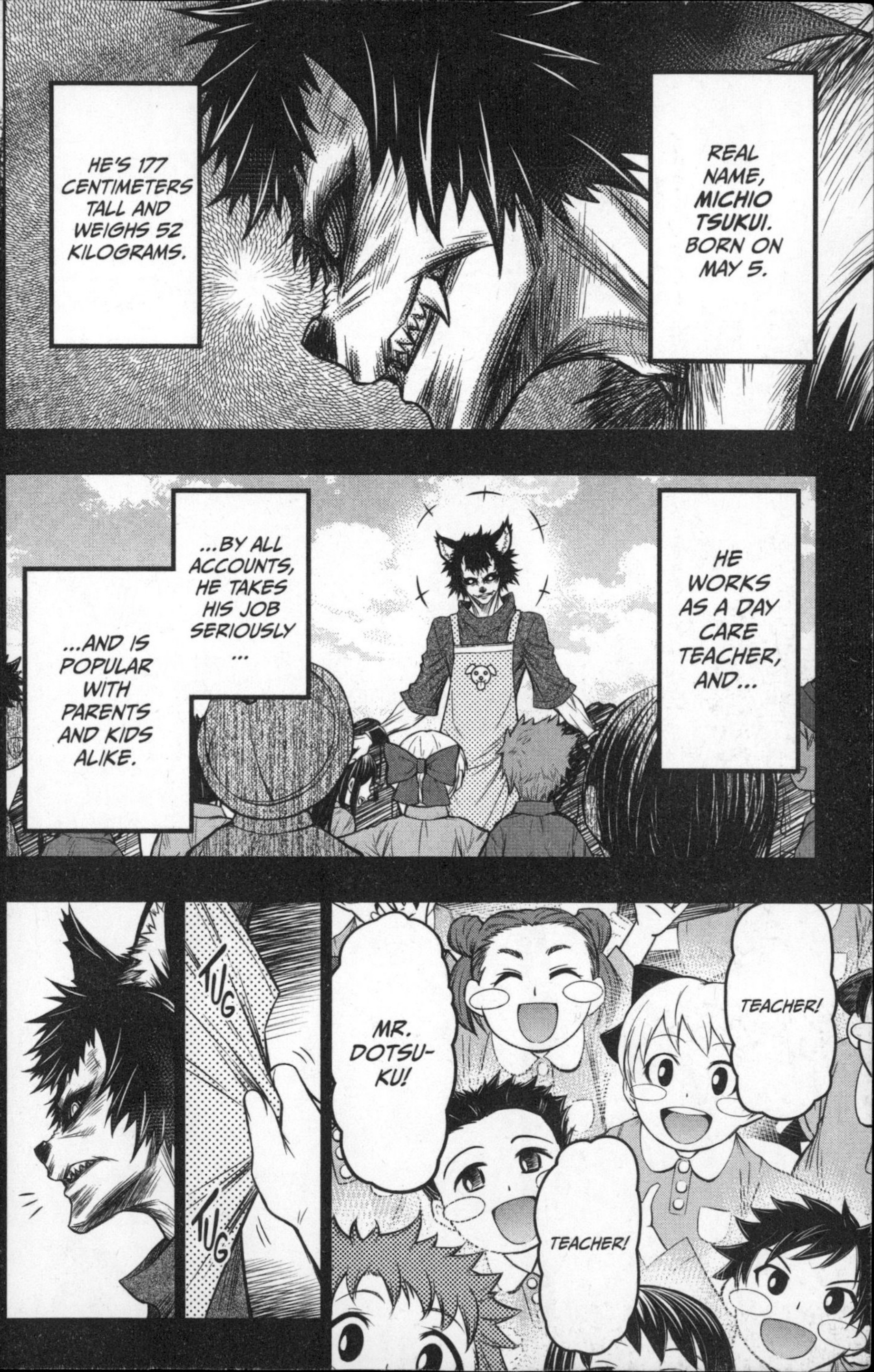
REAL NAME, MICHIO TSUKUI. BORN ON MAY 5.
HE'S 177 CENTIMETERS TALL AND WEIGHS 52 KILOGRAMS.
HE WORKS AS A DAY CARE TEACHER, AND...
...BY ALL ACCOUNTS, HE TAKES HIS JOB SERIOUSLY...
...AND IS POPULAR WITH PARENTS AND KIDS ALIKE.
TEACHER!
MR. DOTSU-KU!
TEACHER!
TUG
TUG

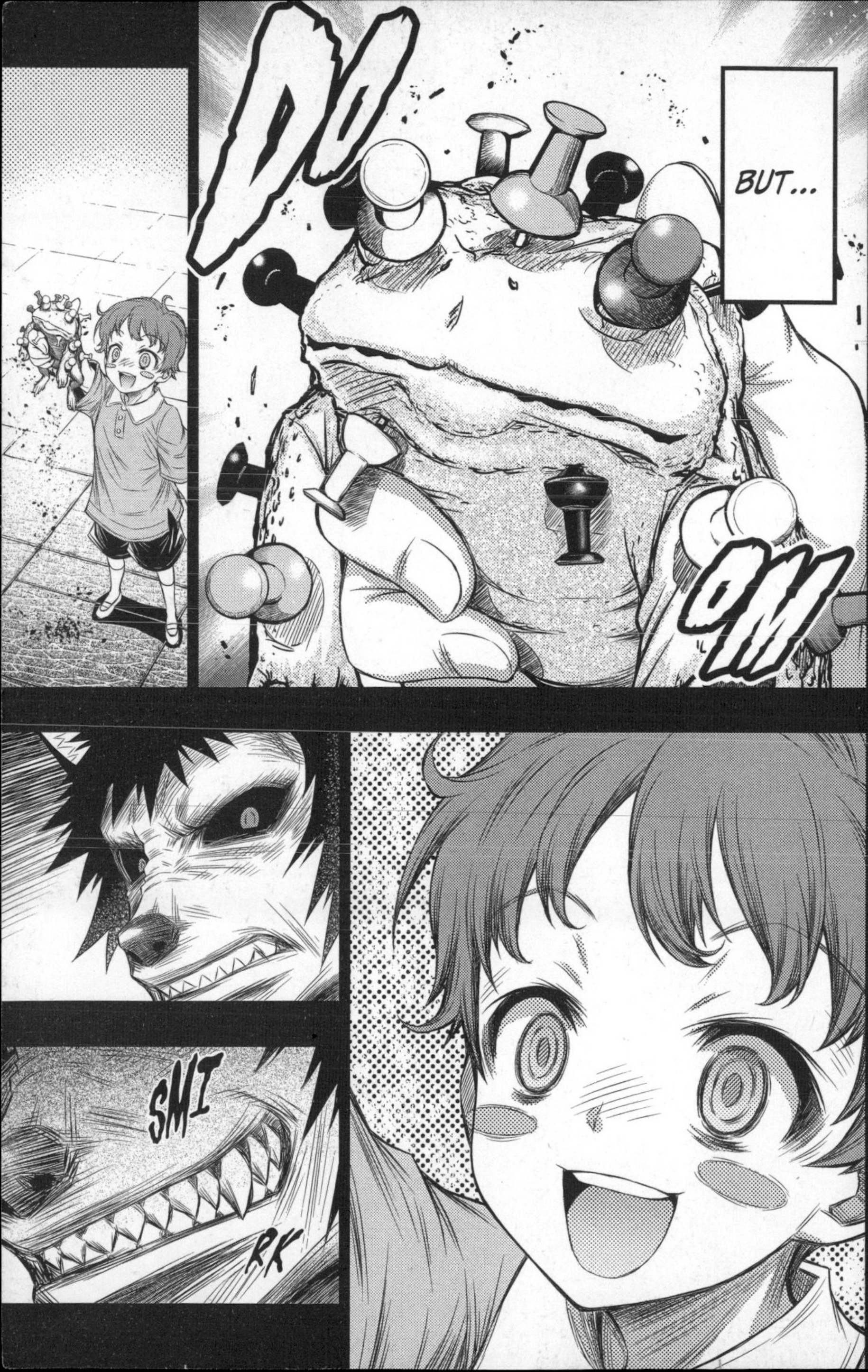
BUT...
DO
OM
SMI
RK

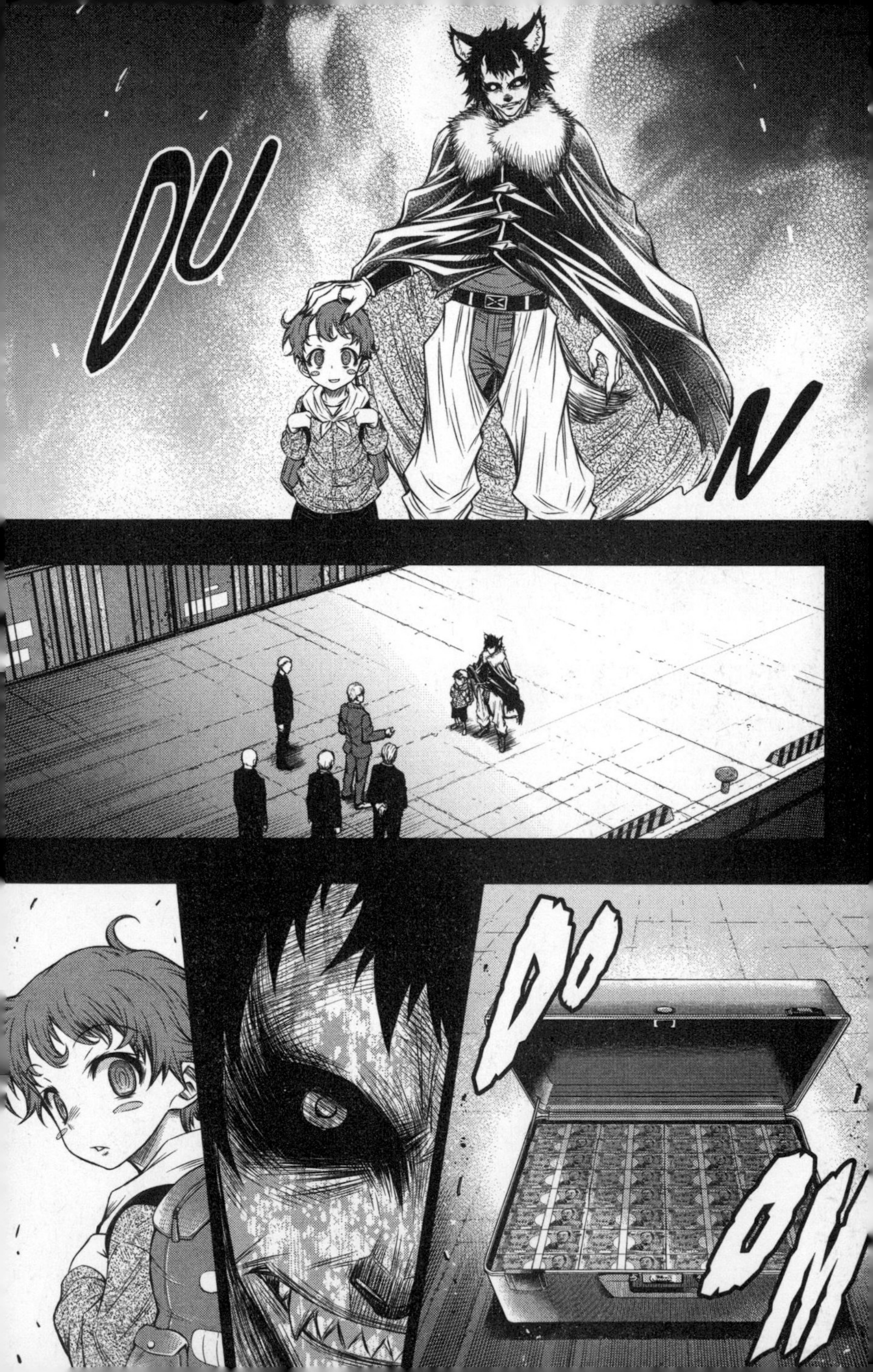
DU
N
DO
OM

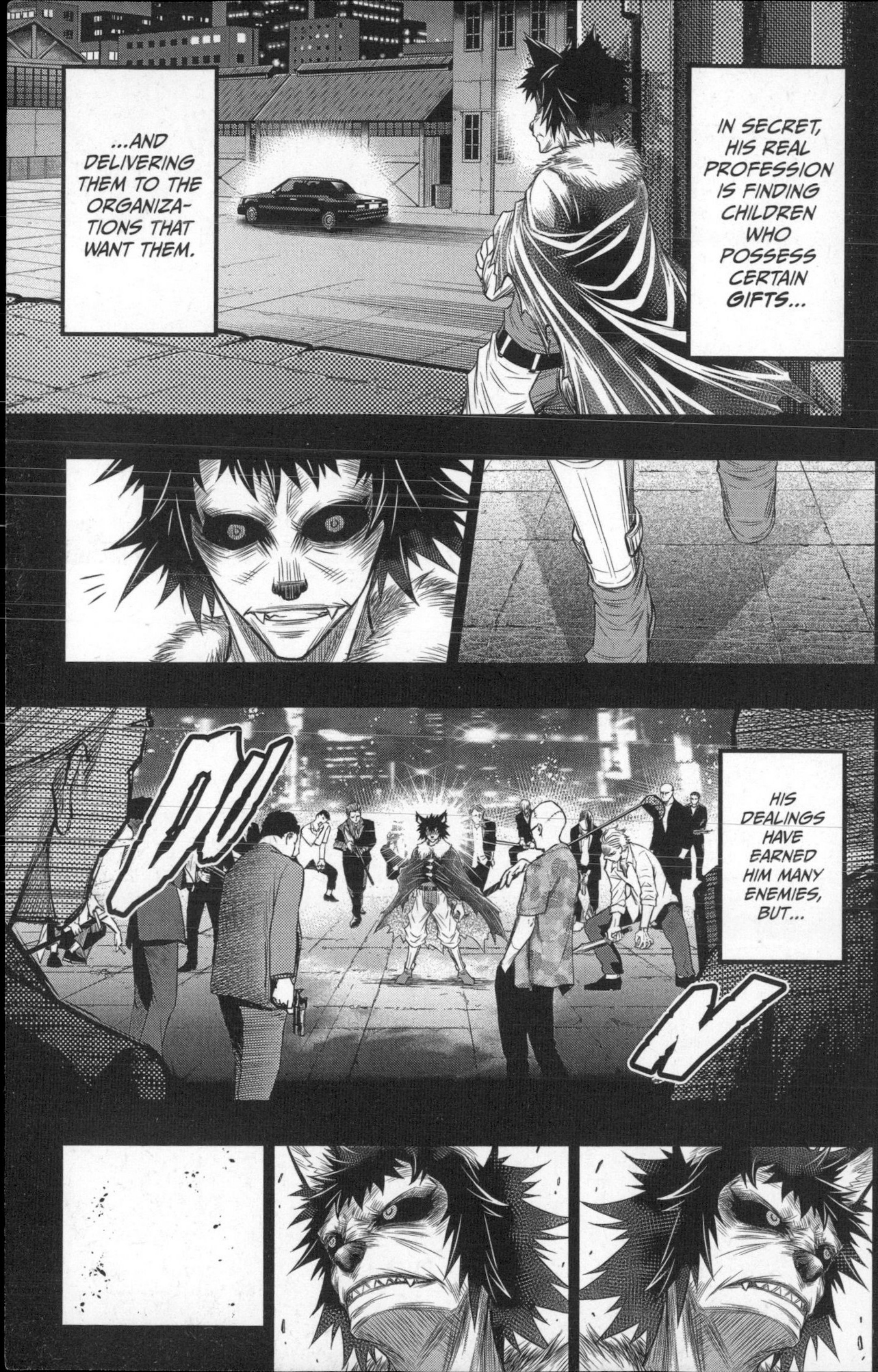
IN SECRET, HIS REAL PROFESSION IS FINDING CHILDREN WHO POSSESS CERTAIN GIFTS...
...AND DELIVERING THEM TO THE ORGANIZATIONS THAT WANT THEM.
HIS DEALINGS HAVE EARNED HIM MANY ENEMIES, BUT...

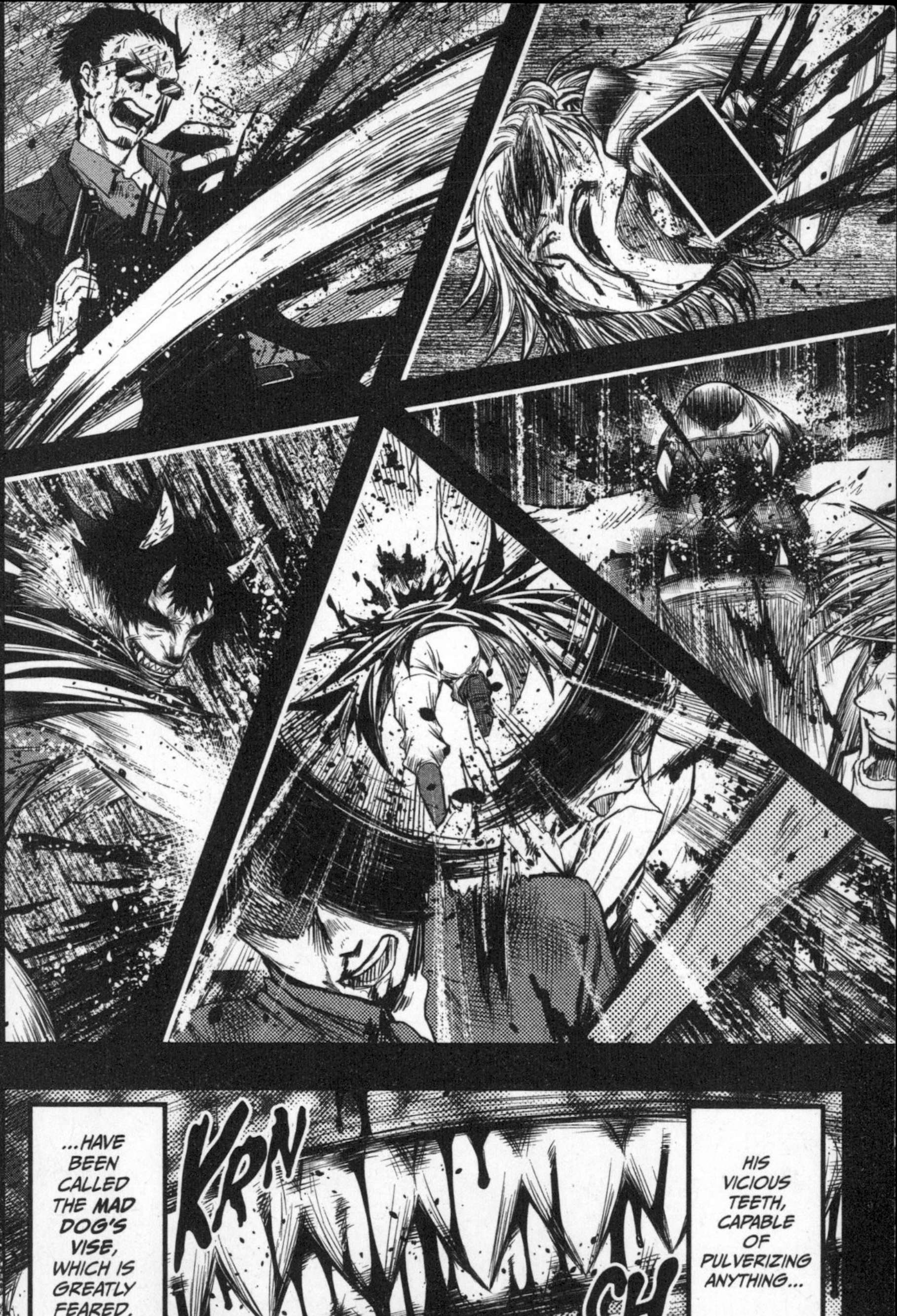
HIS VICIOUS TEETH, CAPABLE OF PULVERIZING ANYTHING...
KRNNNNCH
...HAVE BEEN CALLED THE MAD DOG'S VISE, WHICH IS GREATLY FEARED.

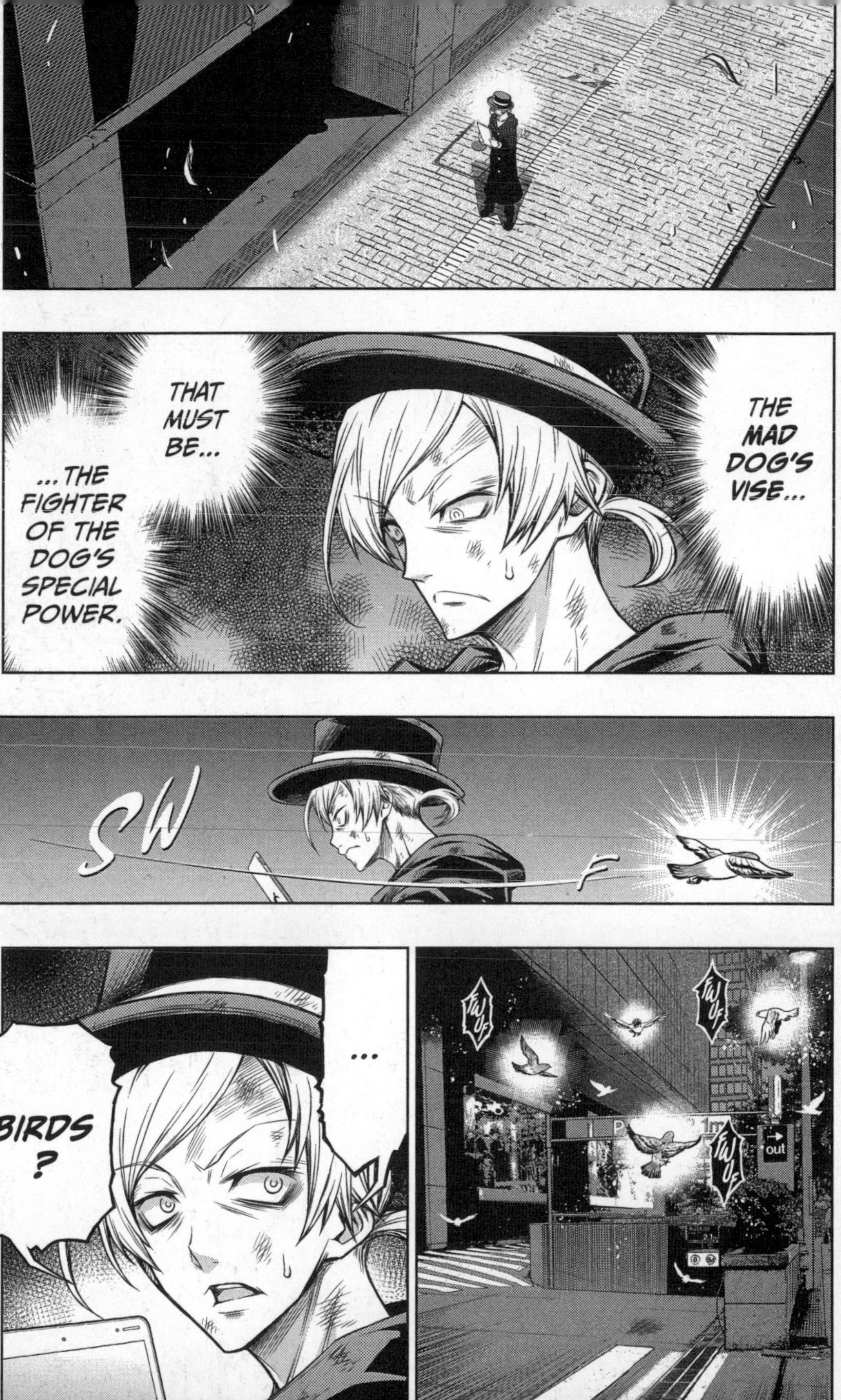
THE MAD DOG'S VISE...
THAT MUST BE...
...THE FIGHTER OF THE DOG'S SPECIAL POWER.
SW
F
FWUF
FWUF
FWUF
out
...
BIRDS?

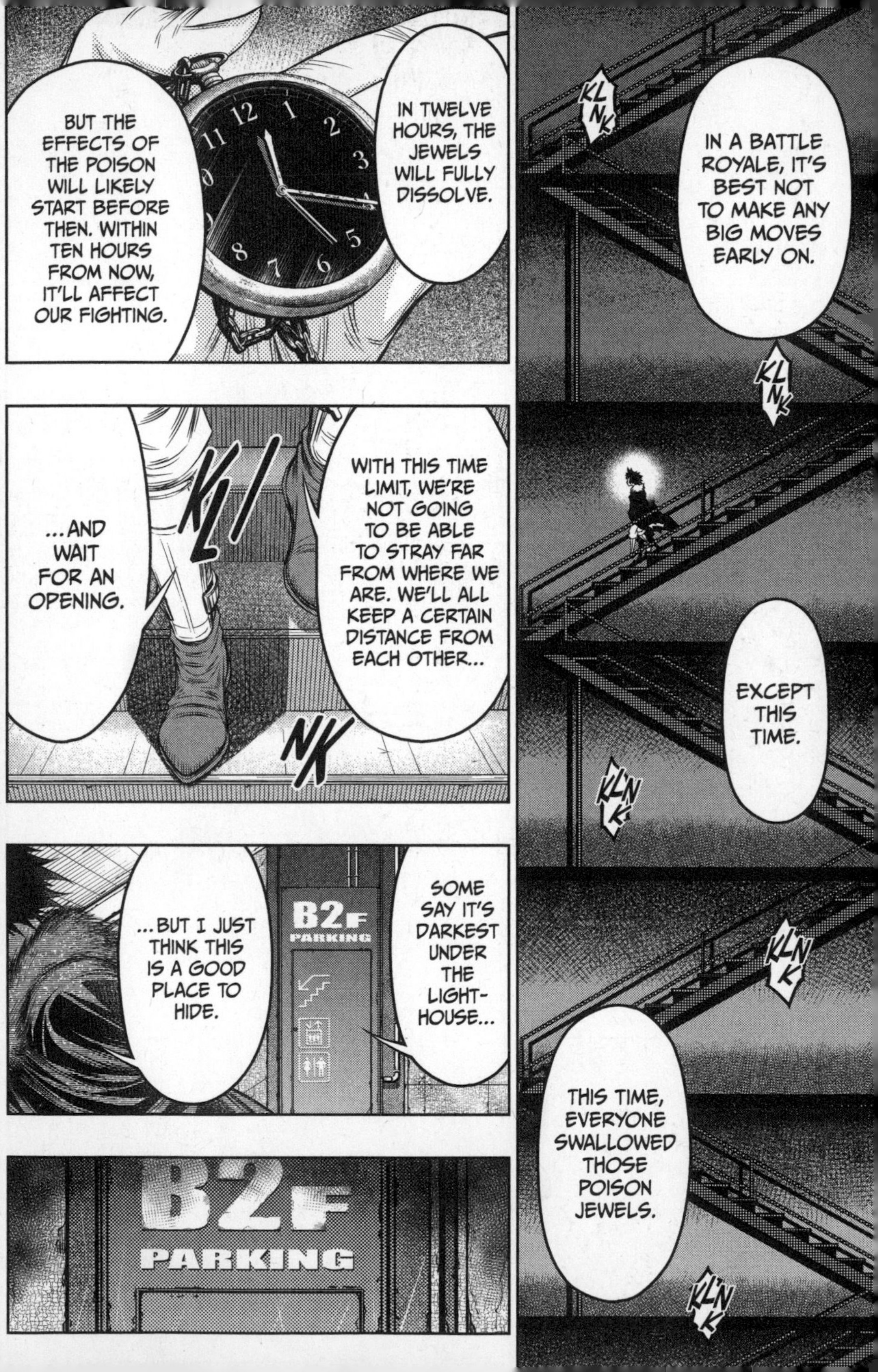
KLNK
IN A BATTLE ROYALE, IT'S BEST NOT TO MAKE ANY BIG MOVES EARLY ON.
KLNK
EXCEPT THIS TIME.
KL'NK
KLNK
THIS TIME, EVERYONE SWALLOWED THOSE POISON JEWELS.
KL'NK
IN TWELVE HOURS, THE JEWELS WILL FULLY DISSOLVE.
BUT THE EFFECTS OF THE POISON WILL LIKELY START BEFORE THEN. WITHIN TEN HOURS FROM NOW, IT'LL AFFECT OUR FIGHTING.
WITH THIS TIME LIMIT, WE'RE NOT GOING TO BE ABLE TO STRAY FAR FROM WHERE WE ARE. WE'LL ALL KEEP A CERTAIN DISTANCE FROM EACH OTHER...
KLINK
...AND WAIT FOR AN OPENING.
B2F PARKING
SOME SAY IT'S DARKEST UNDER THE LIGHTHOUSE...
...BUT I JUST THINK THIS IS A GOOD PLACE TO HIDE.
B2F PARKING

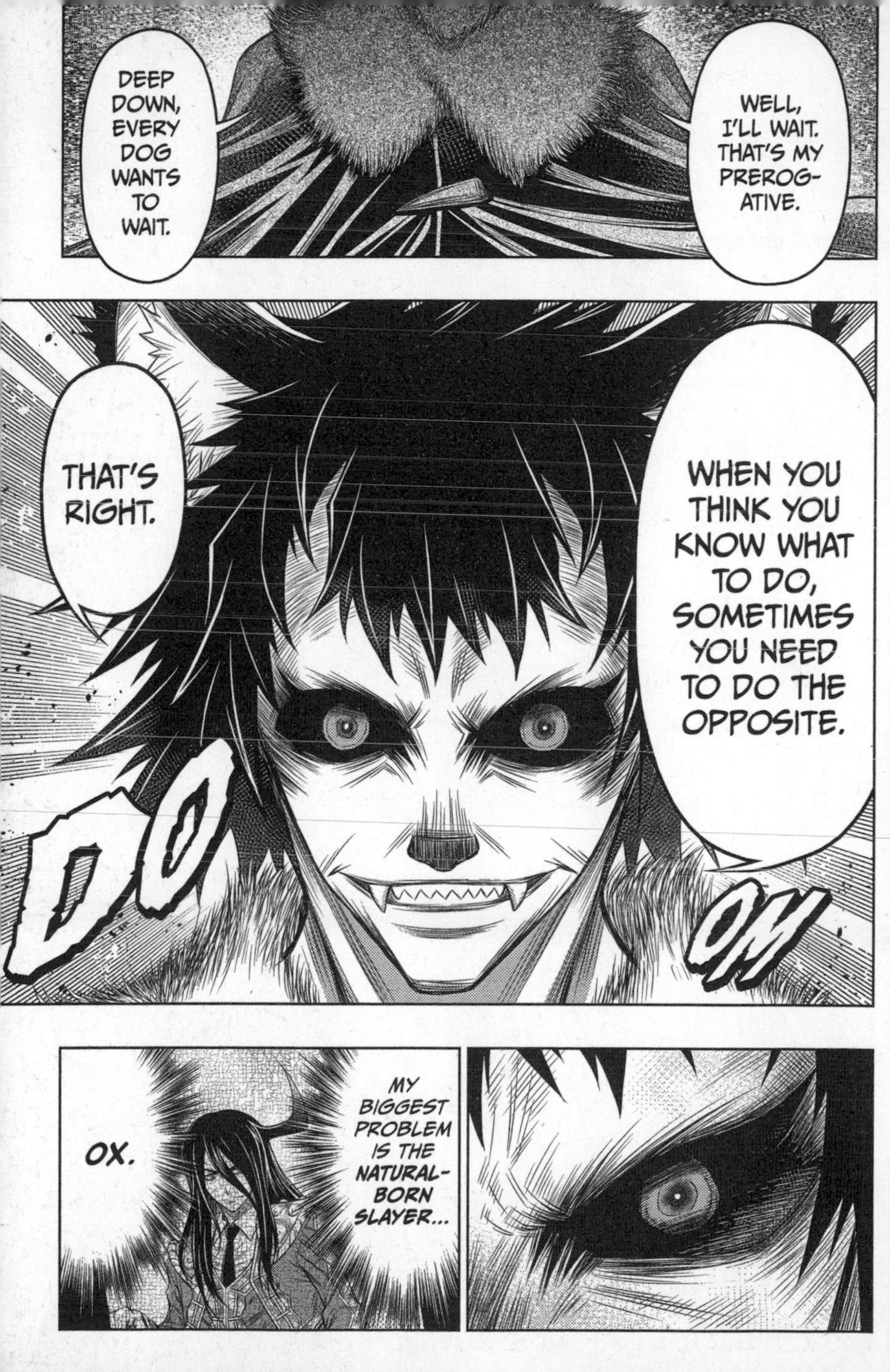
WELL, I'LL WAIT. THAT'S MY PREROG-ATIVE.
DEEP DOWN, EVERY DOG WANTS TO WAIT.
WHEN YOU THINK YOU KNOW WHAT TO DO, SOMETIMES YOU NEED TO DO THE OPPOSITE.
THAT'S RIGHT.
DOOM
MY BIGGEST PROBLEM IS THE NATURAL-BORN SLAYER...
OX.

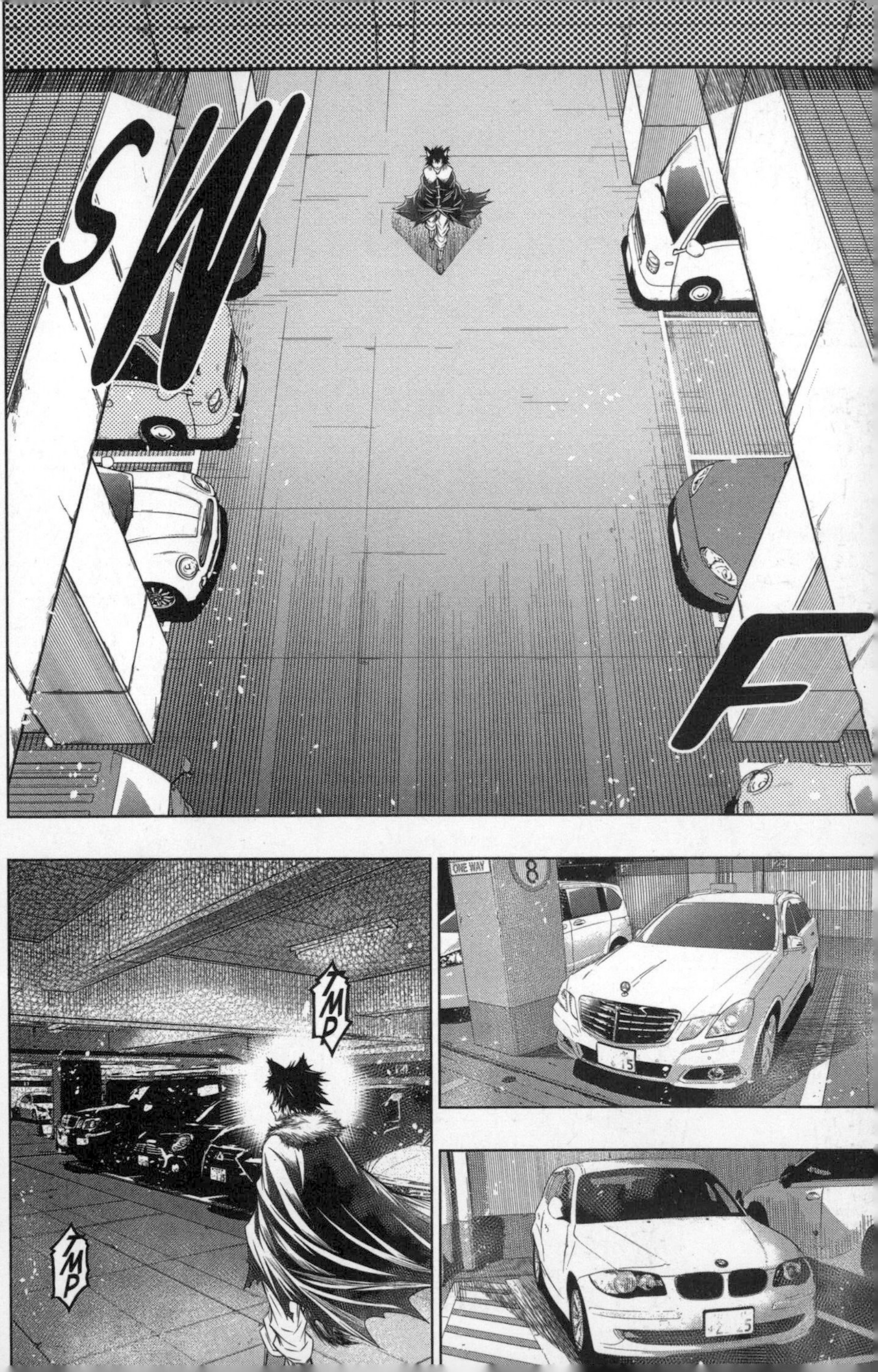
SW
F
ONE WAY
8
TMP
TMP

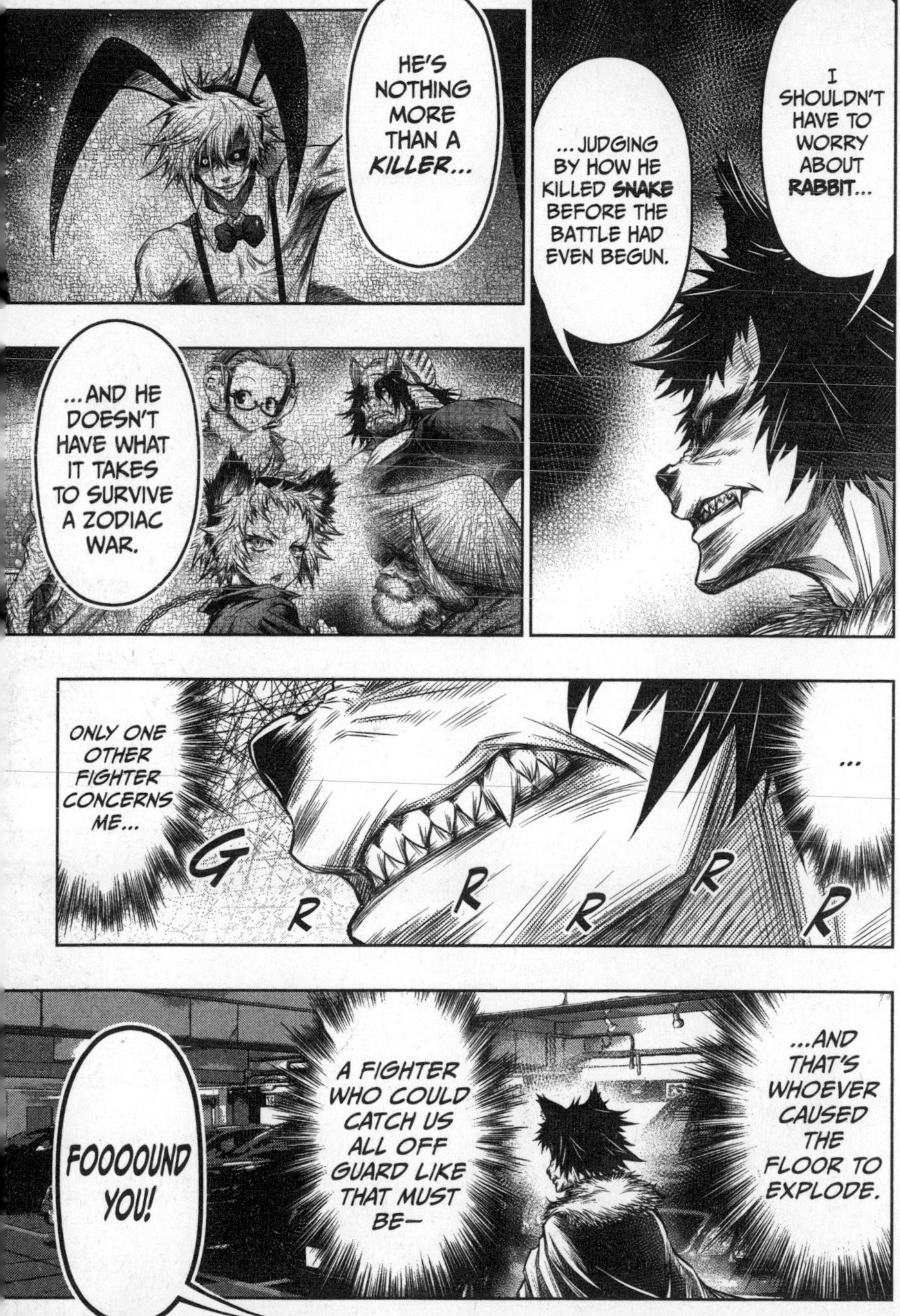
I SHOULDN'T HAVE TO WORRY ABOUT RABBIT...
...JUDGING BY HOW HE KILLED SNAKE BEFORE THE BATTLE HAD EVEN BEGUN.
HE'S NOTHING MORE THAN A KILLER...
...AND HE DOESN'T HAVE WHAT IT TAKES TO SURVIVE A ZODIAC WAR.
...
ONLY ONE OTHER FIGHTER CONCERNS ME...
GRRRRRR
...AND THAT'S WHOEVER CAUSED THE FLOOR TO EXPLODE.
A FIGHTER WHO COULD CATCH US ALL OFF GUARD LIKE THAT MUST BE—
FOOOOUND YOU!

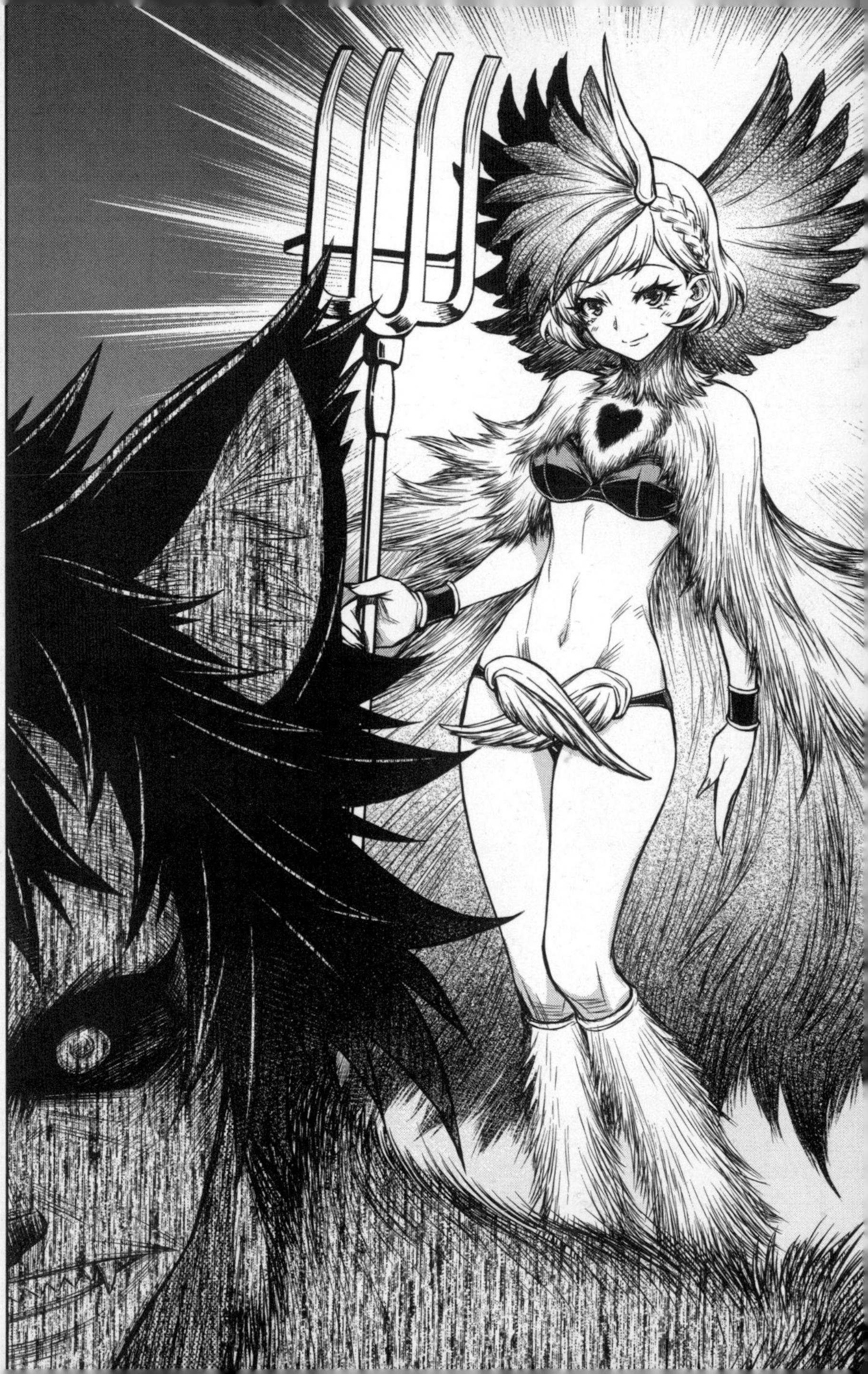

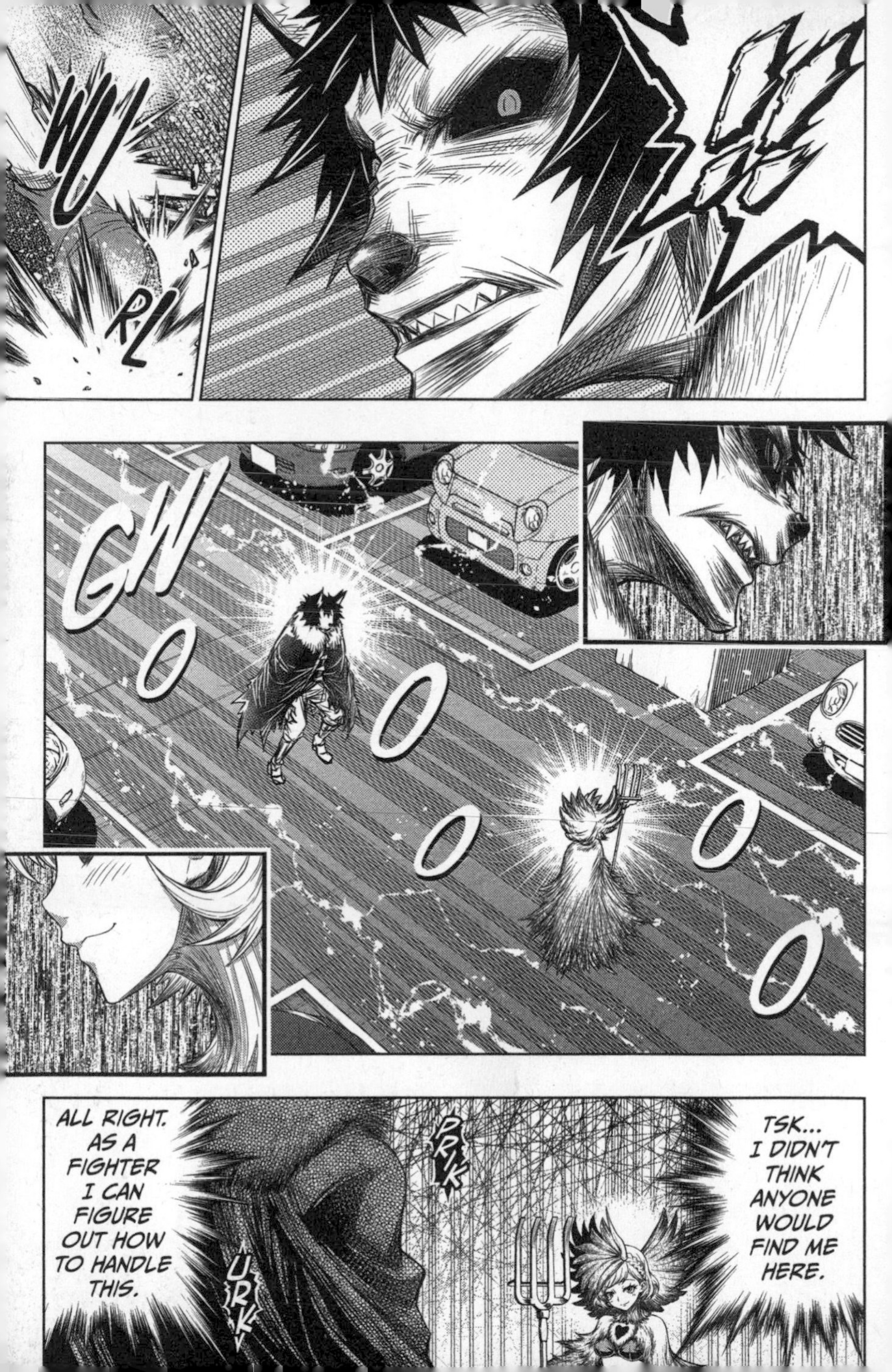
WU
RL
GWOOOOOOO
TSK... I DIDN'T THINK ANYONE WOULD FIND ME HERE.
PRIK
ALL RIGHT. AS A FIGHTER I CAN FIGURE OUT HOW TO HANDLE THIS.
URK

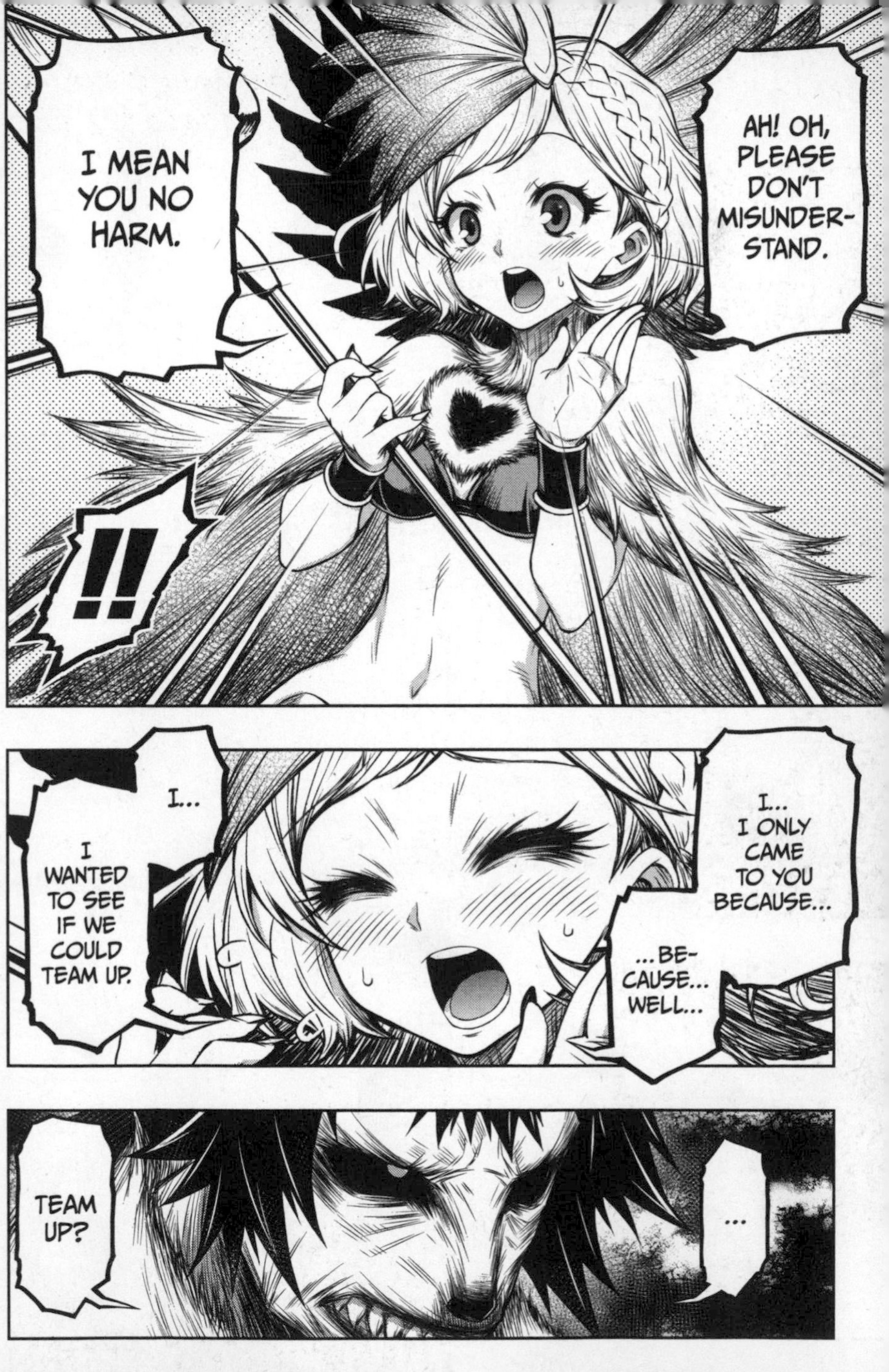
AH! OH, PLEASE DON'T MISUNDERSTAND.
I MEAN YOU NO HARM.
!!
I... I ONLY CAME TO YOU BECAUSE...
...BE-CAUSE... WELL...
I...
I WANTED TO SEE IF WE COULD TEAM UP.
...
TEAM UP?

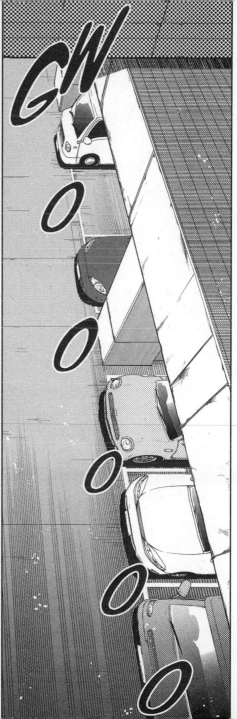

THERE
HE IS.

DOTSUKU,
THE
FIGHTER
OF THE
DOG.

AND
HE'S
NOT
ALONE
...

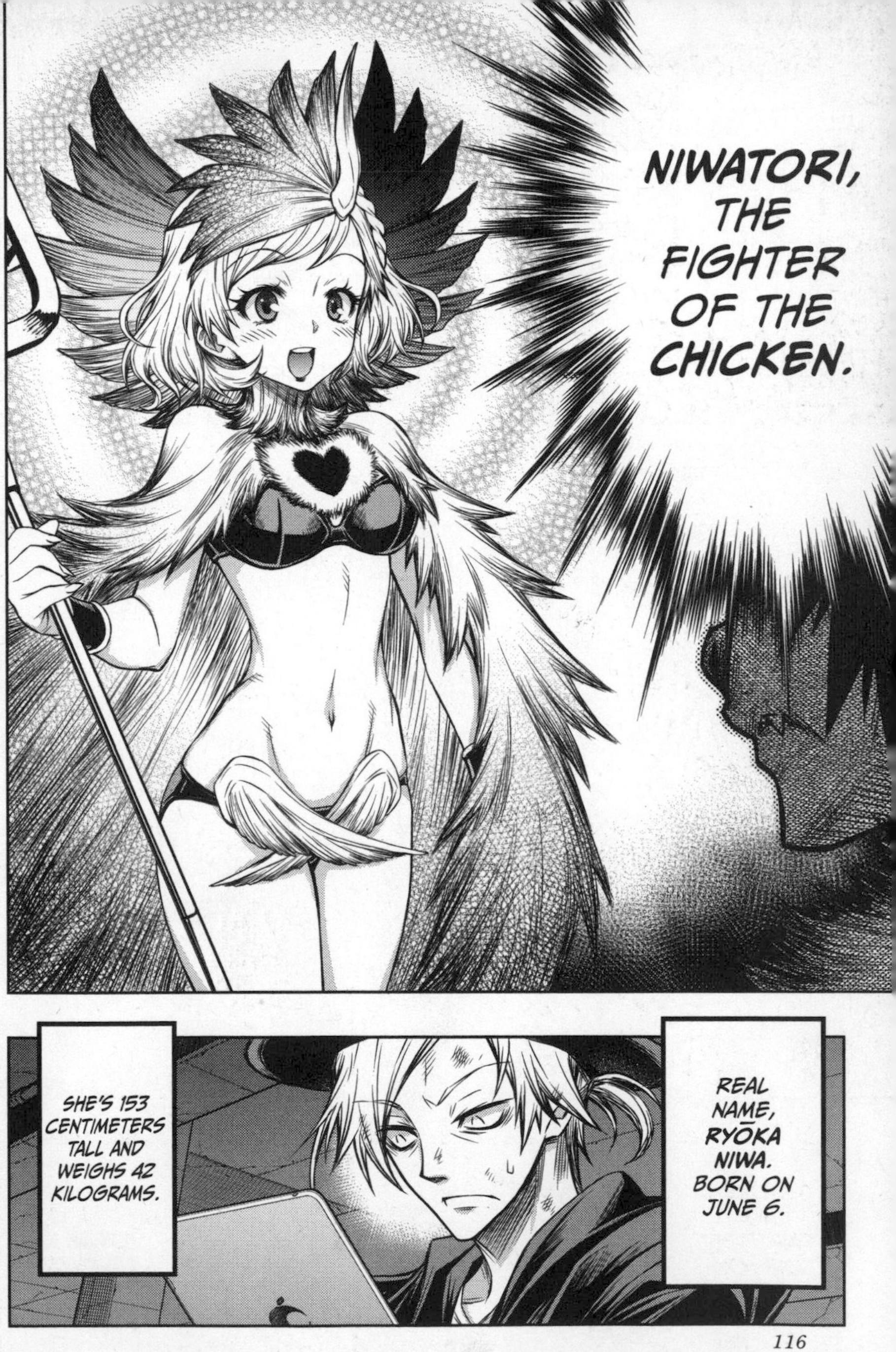
NIWATORI, THE FIGHTER OF THE CHICKEN.
REAL NAME, RYŌKA NIWA. BORN ON JUNE 6.
SHE'S 153 CENTIMETERS TALL AND WEIGHS 42 KILOGRAMS.

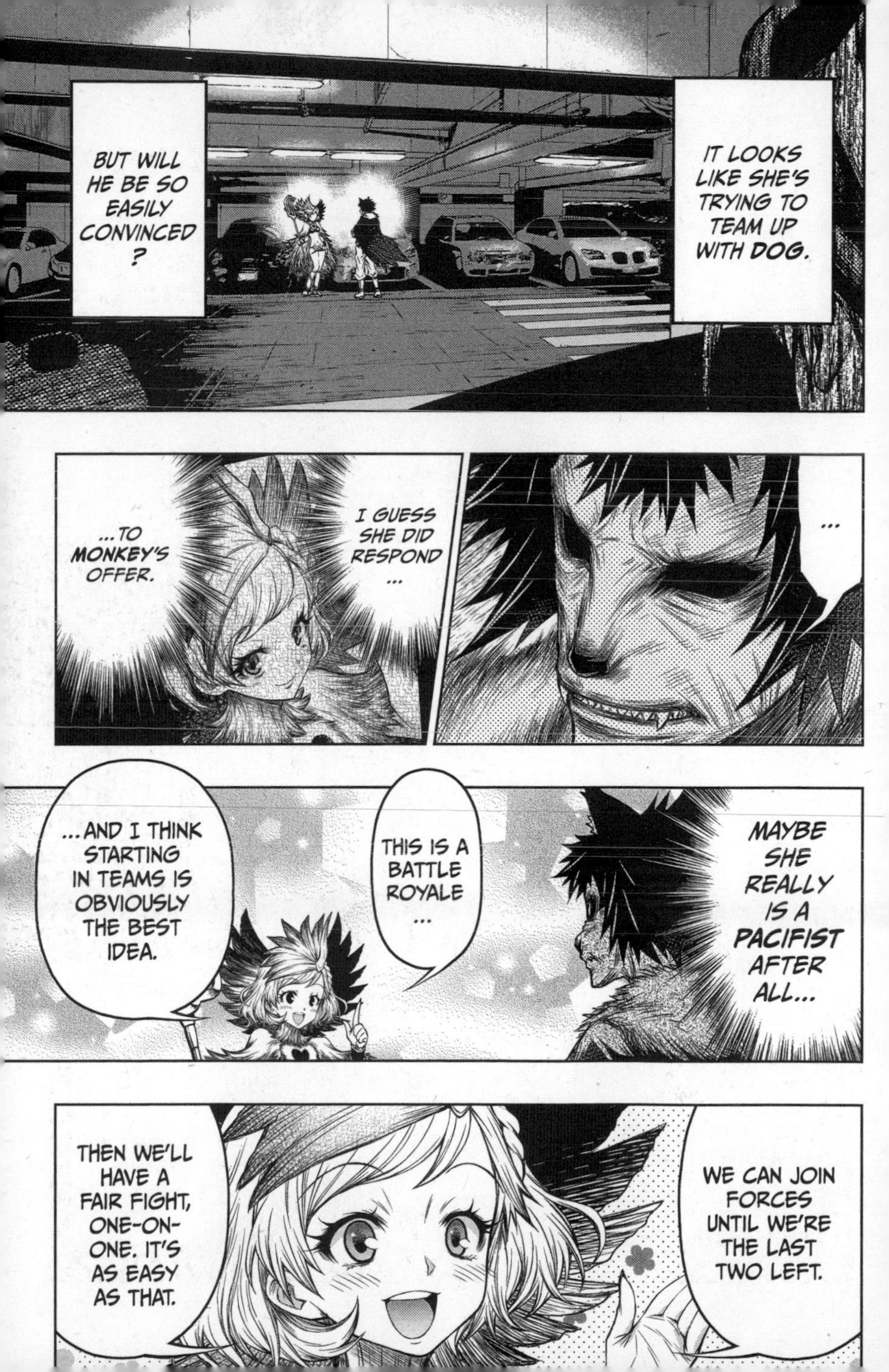
IT LOOKS LIKE SHE'S TRYING TO TEAM UP WITH DOG.
BUT WILL HE BE SO EASILY CONVINCED?
...
I GUESS SHE DID RESPOND...
...TO MONKEY'S OFFER.
MAYBE SHE REALLY IS A PACIFIST AFTER ALL...
THIS IS A BATTLE ROYALE...
...AND I THINK STARTING IN TEAMS IS OBVIOUSLY THE BEST IDEA.
WE CAN JOIN FORCES UNTIL WE'RE THE LAST TWO LEFT.
THEN WE'LL HAVE A FAIR FIGHT, ONE-ON-ONE. IT'S AS EASY AS THAT.

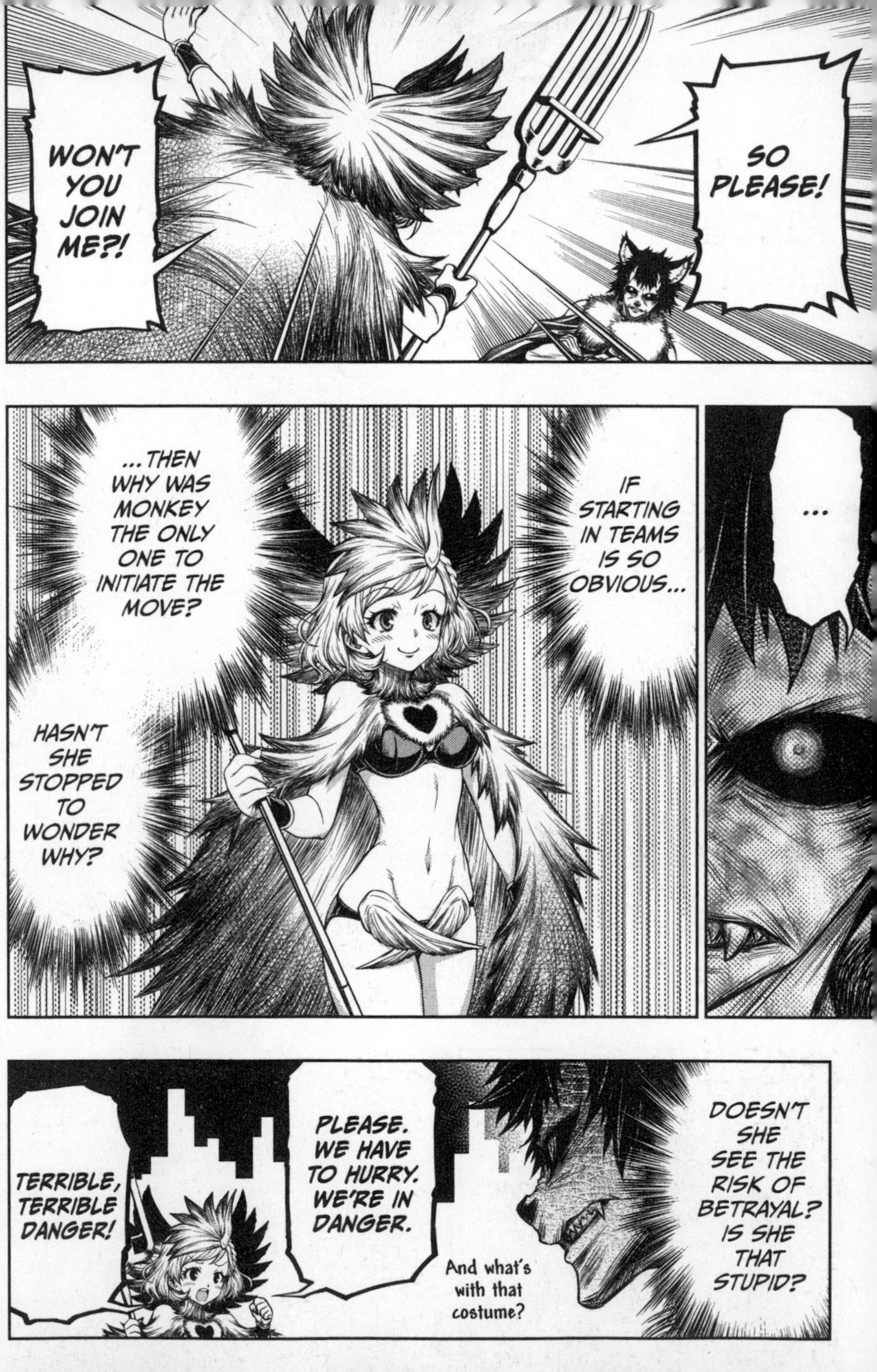
SO PLEASE!
WON'T YOU JOIN ME?!
...
IF STARTING IN TEAMS IS SO OBVIOUS...
...THEN WHY WAS MONKEY THE ONLY ONE TO INITIATE THE MOVE?
HASN'T SHE STOPPED TO WONDER WHY?
DOESN'T SHE SEE THE RISK OF BETRAYAL? IS SHE THAT STUPID?
And what's with that costume?
PLEASE. WE HAVE TO HURRY. WE'RE IN DANGER.
TERRIBLE, TERRIBLE DANGER!

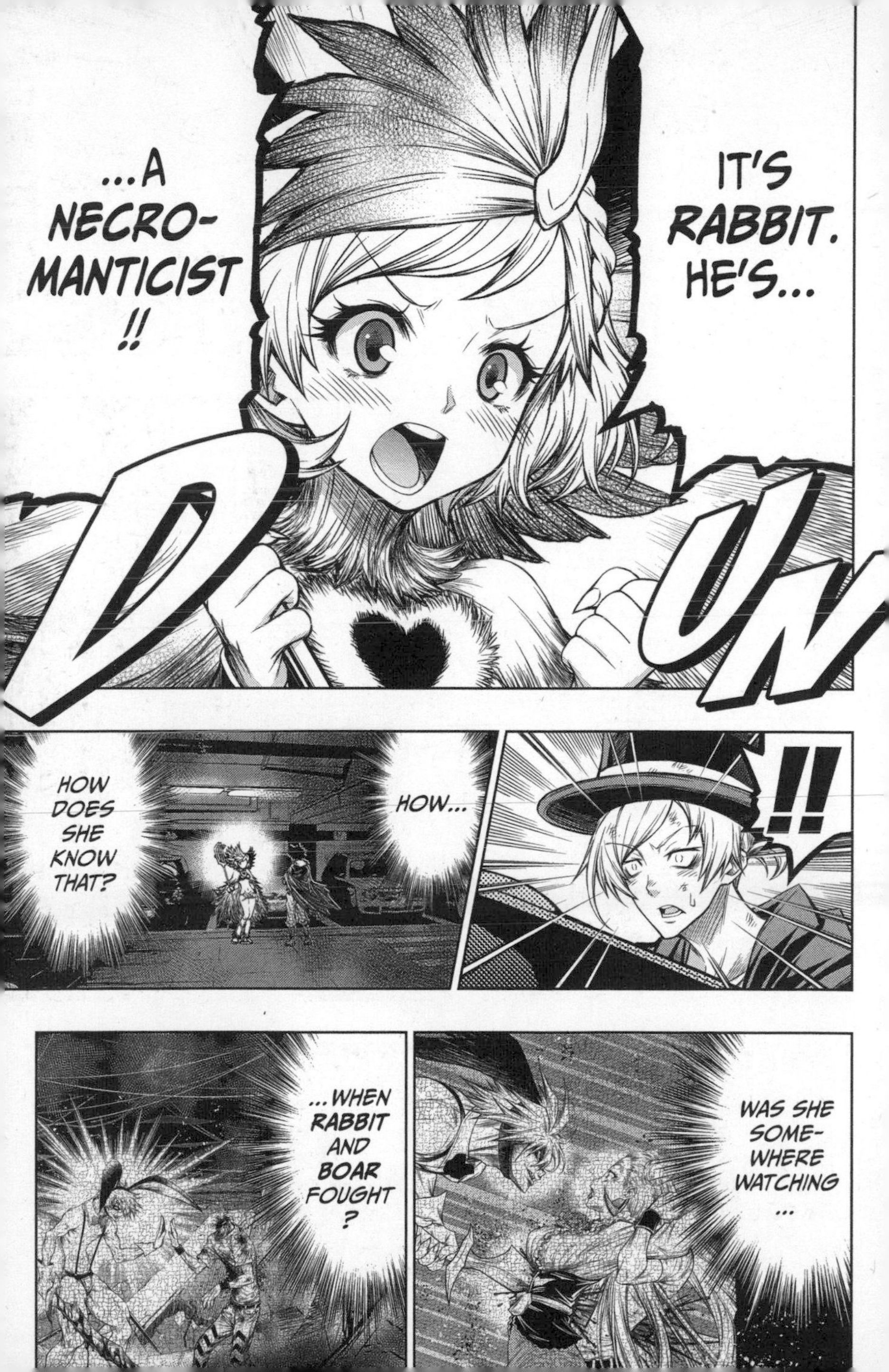
IT'S RABBIT. HE'S...
...A NECRO-MANTICIST !!
DUN
!!
HOW...
HOW DOES SHE KNOW THAT?
WAS SHE SOME-WHERE WATCHING ...
...WHEN RABBIT AND BOAR FOUGHT ?

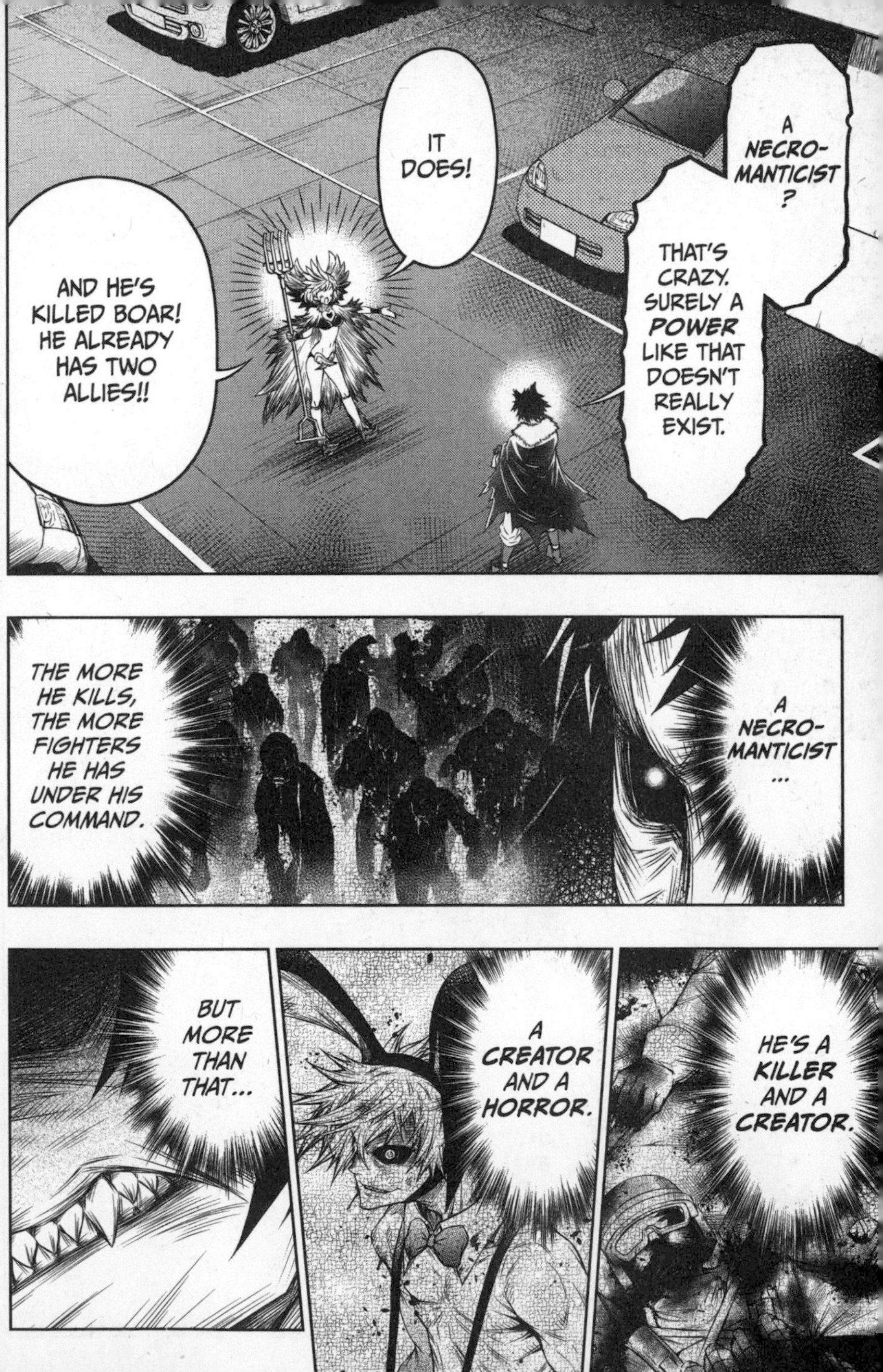
A NECRO-MANTICIST?
THAT'S CRAZY. SURELY A POWER LIKE THAT DOESN'T REALLY EXIST.
IT DOES!
AND HE'S KILLED BOAR! HE ALREADY HAS TWO ALLIES!!
A NECRO-MANTICIST...
THE MORE HE KILLS, THE MORE FIGHTERS HE HAS UNDER HIS COMMAND.
HE'S A KILLER AND A CREATOR.
A CREATOR AND A HORROR.
BUT MORE THAN THAT...

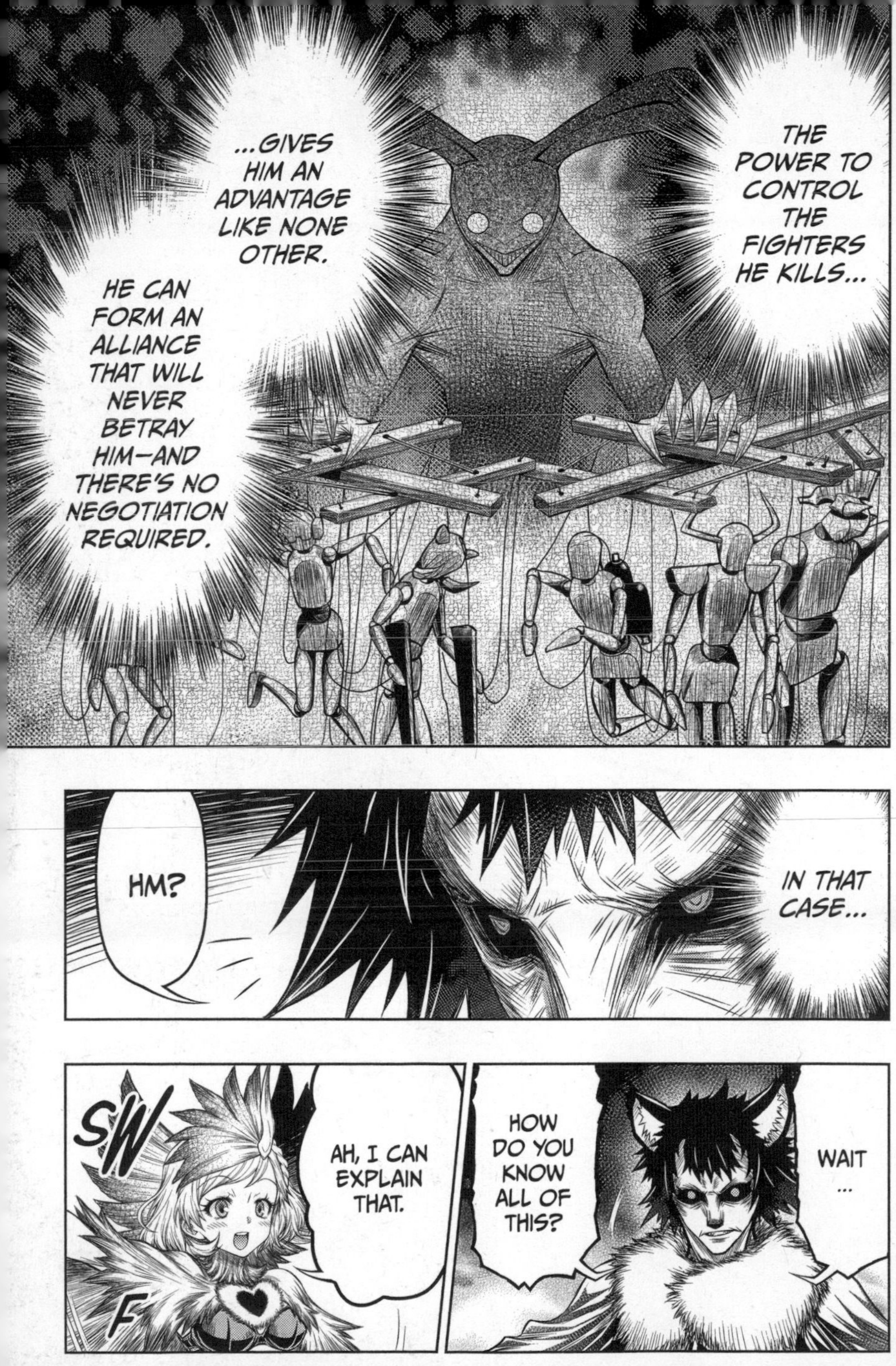
THE POWER TO CONTROL THE FIGHTERS HE KILLS...
...GIVES HIM AN ADVANTAGE LIKE NONE OTHER.
HE CAN FORM AN ALLIANCE THAT WILL NEVER BETRAY HIM—AND THERE'S NO NEGOTIATION REQUIRED.
IN THAT CASE...
HM?
WAIT ...
HOW DO YOU KNOW ALL OF THIS?
AH, I CAN EXPLAIN THAT.
SWF

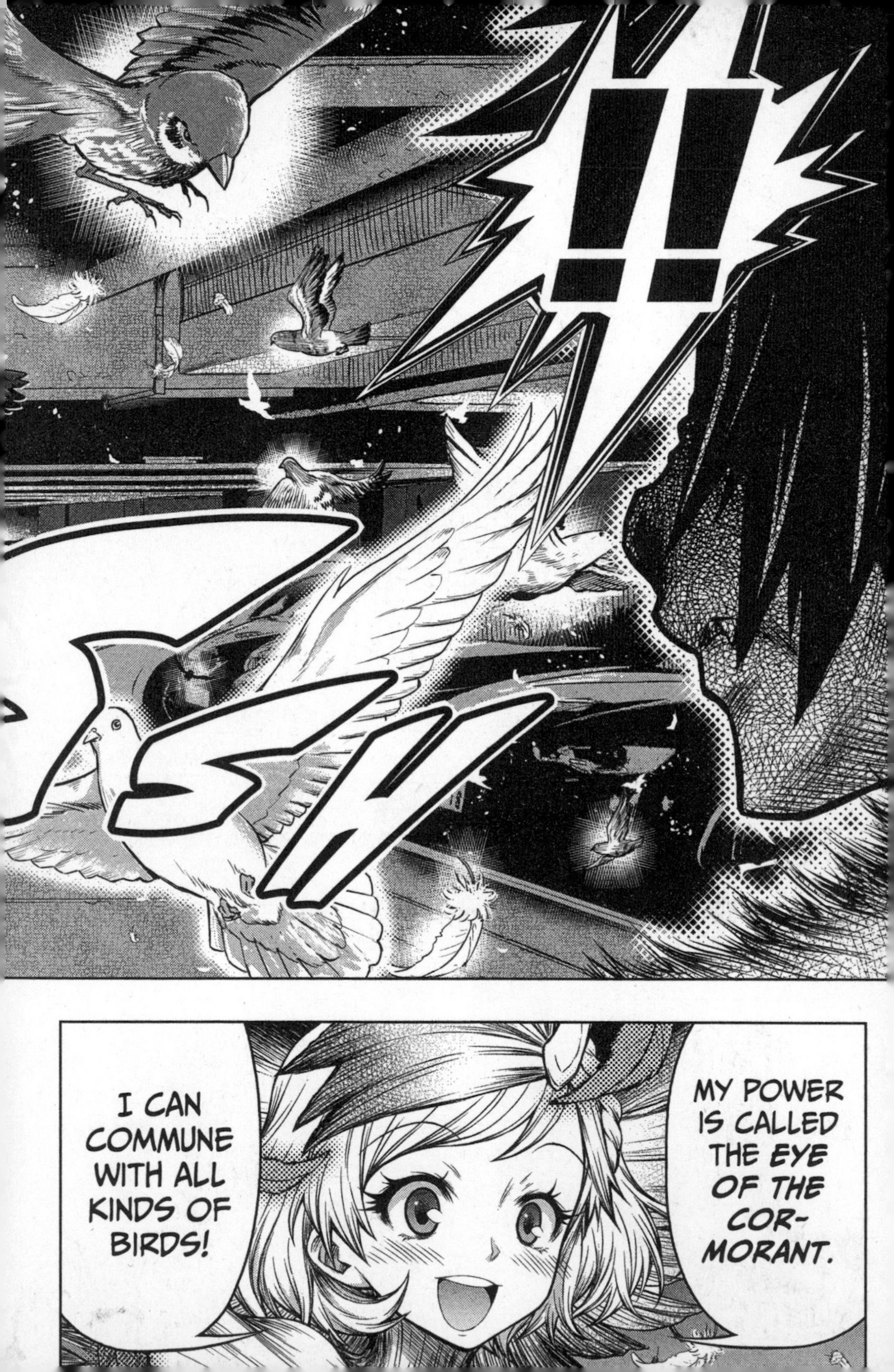
!!
SH
MY POWER IS CALLED THE *EYE OF THE CORMORANT*.
I CAN COMMUNE WITH ALL KINDS OF BIRDS!

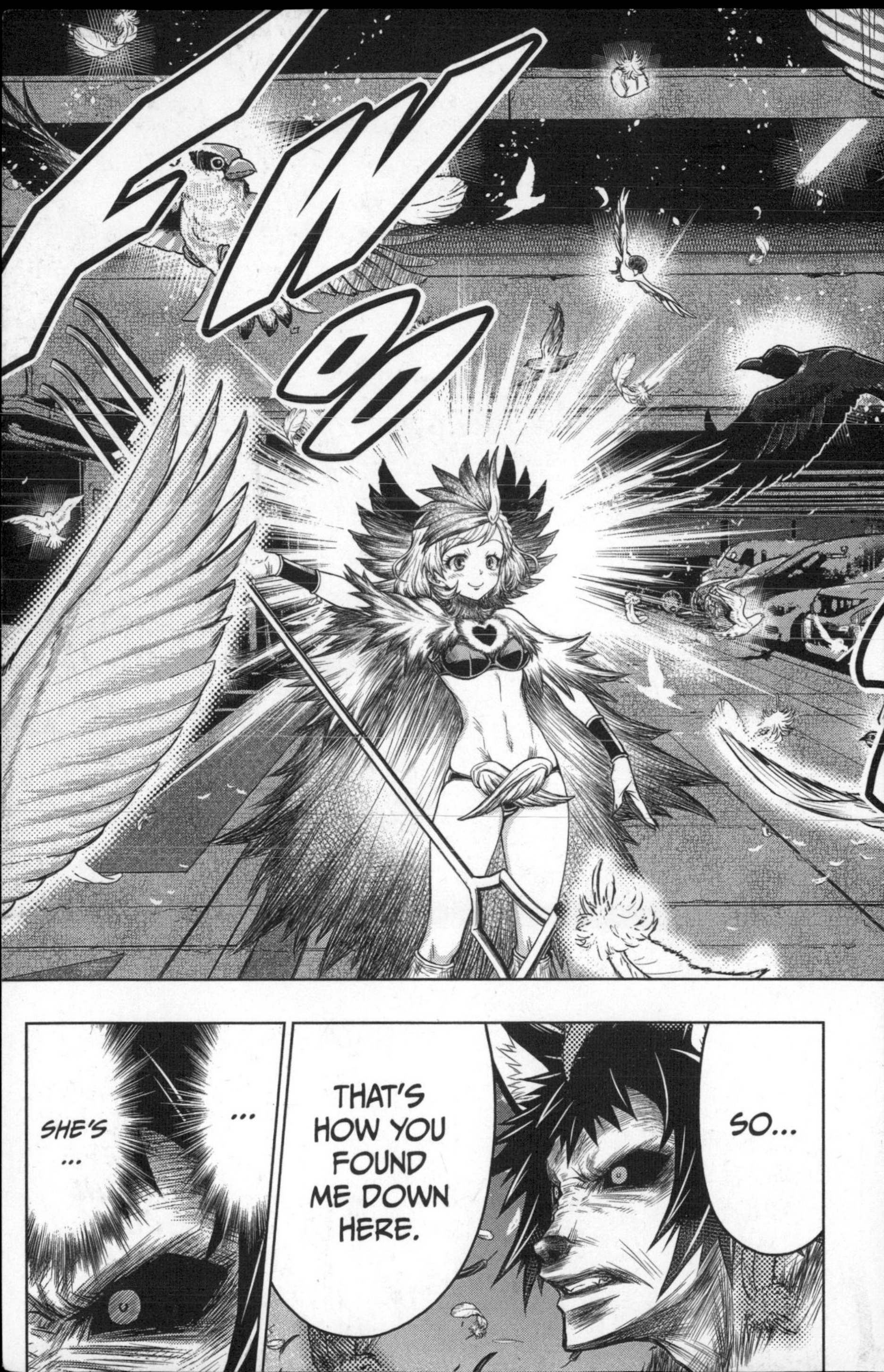
SO...
THAT'S HOW YOU FOUND ME DOWN HERE.
...
SHE'S ...

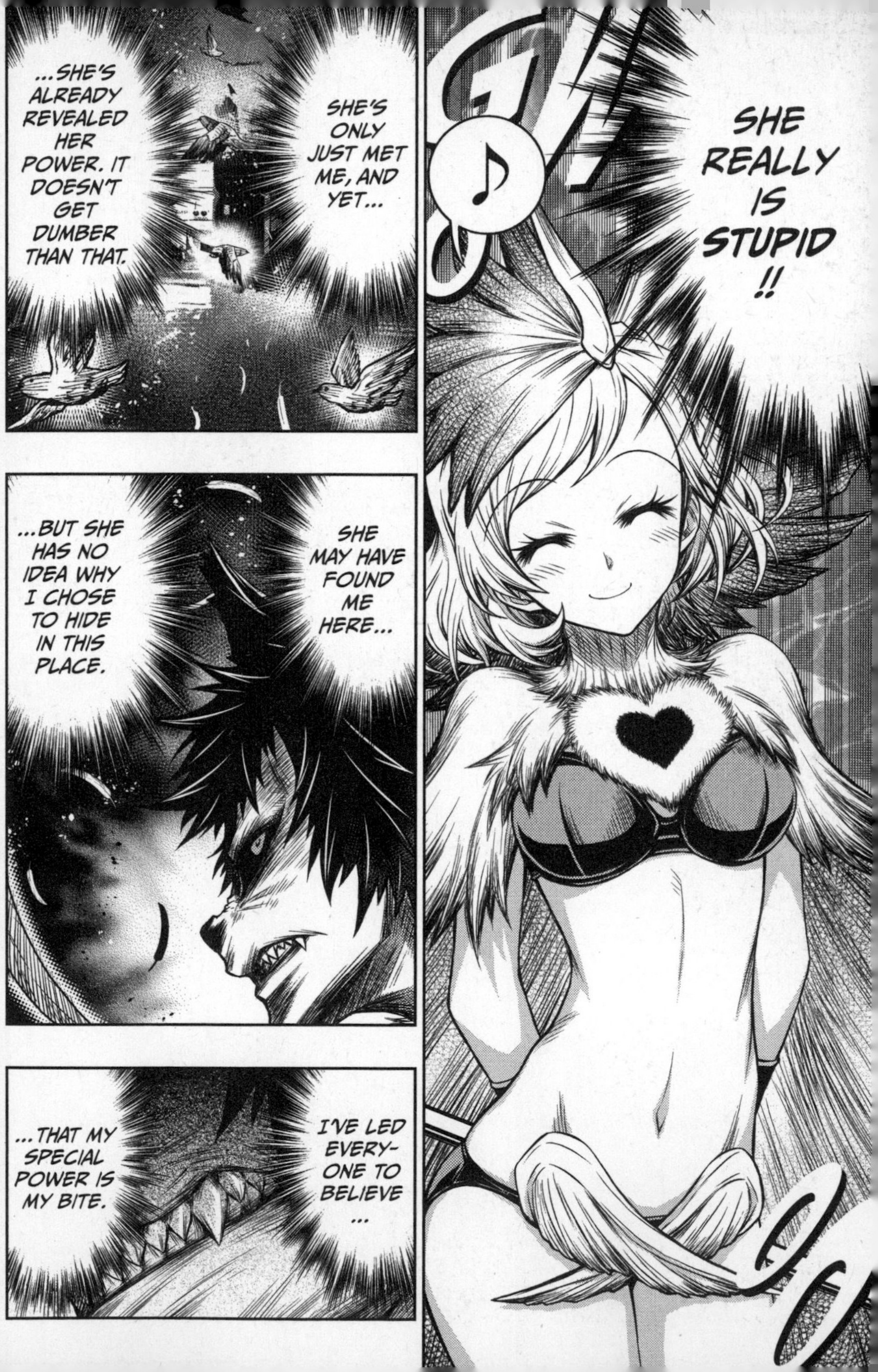
♪
SHE REALLY IS STUPID!!
SHE'S ONLY JUST MET ME, AND YET...
...SHE'S ALREADY REVEALED HER POWER. IT DOESN'T GET DUMBER THAN THAT.
SHE MAY HAVE FOUND ME HERE...
...BUT SHE HAS NO IDEA WHY I CHOSE TO HIDE IN THIS PLACE.
I'VE LED EVERYONE TO BELIEVE...
...THAT MY SPECIAL POWER IS MY BITE.

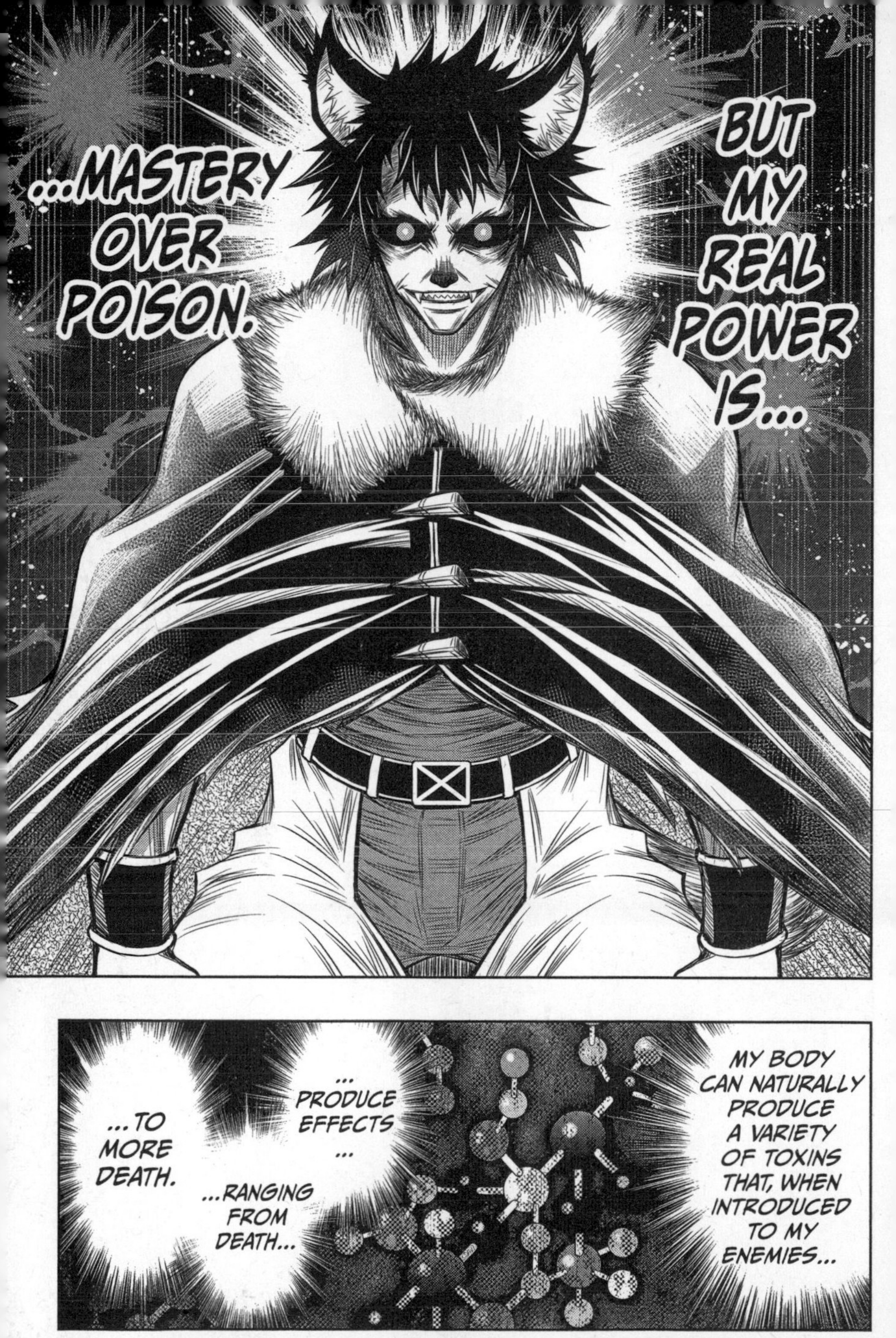
BUT MY REAL POWER IS...
...MASTERY OVER POISON.
MY BODY CAN NATURALLY PRODUCE A VARIETY OF TOXINS THAT, WHEN INTRODUCED TO MY ENEMIES...
...PRODUCE EFFECTS...
...RANGING FROM DEATH...
...TO MORE DEATH.

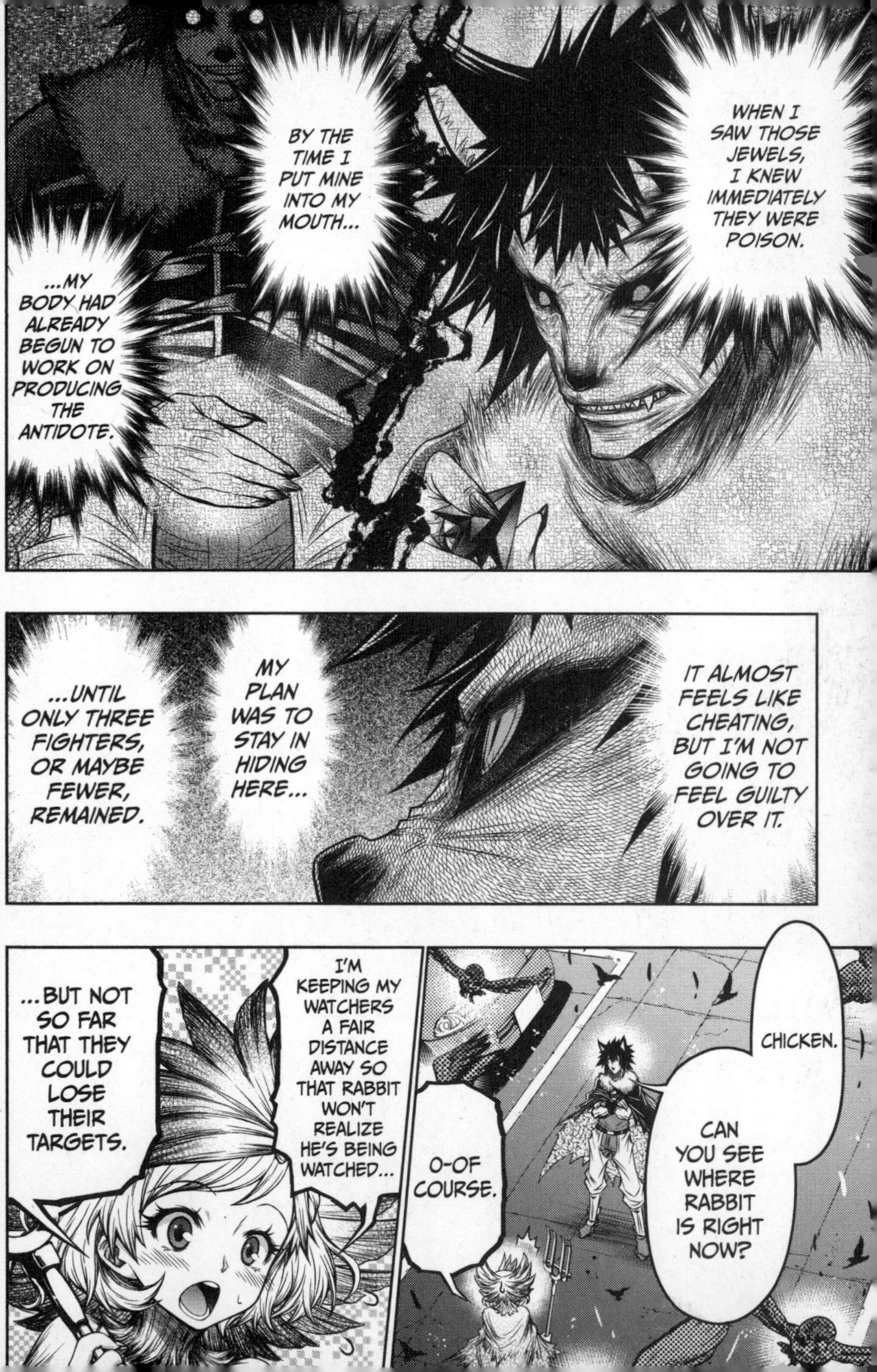
WHEN I SAW THOSE JEWELS, I KNEW IMMEDIATELY THEY WERE POISON.
BY THE TIME I PUT MINE INTO MY MOUTH...
...MY BODY HAD ALREADY BEGUN TO WORK ON PRODUCING THE ANTIDOTE.
IT ALMOST FEELS LIKE CHEATING, BUT I'M NOT GOING TO FEEL GUILTY OVER IT.
MY PLAN WAS TO STAY IN HIDING HERE...
...UNTIL ONLY THREE FIGHTERS, OR MAYBE FEWER, REMAINED.
CHICKEN.
CAN YOU SEE WHERE RABBIT IS RIGHT NOW?
O-OF COURSE.
I'M KEEPING MY WATCHERS A FAIR DISTANCE AWAY SO THAT RABBIT WON'T REALIZE HE'S BEING WATCHED...
...BUT NOT SO FAR THAT THEY COULD LOSE THEIR TARGETS.

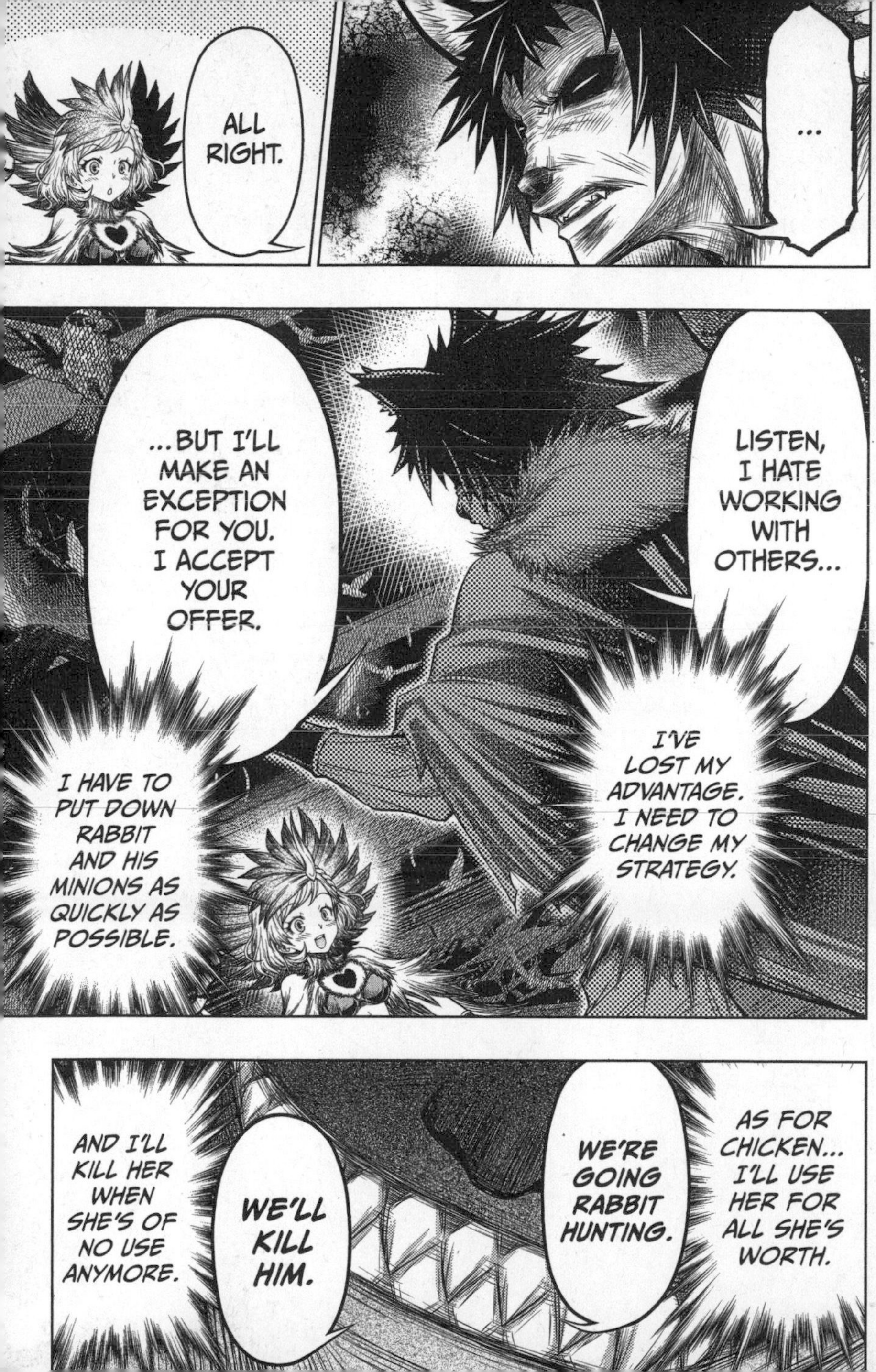
...
ALL RIGHT.
LISTEN, I HATE WORKING WITH OTHERS...
...BUT I'LL MAKE AN EXCEPTION FOR YOU. I ACCEPT YOUR OFFER.
I'VE LOST MY ADVANTAGE. I NEED TO CHANGE MY STRATEGY.
I HAVE TO PUT DOWN RABBIT AND HIS MINIONS AS QUICKLY AS POSSIBLE.
AS FOR CHICKEN... I'LL USE HER FOR ALL SHE'S WORTH.
WE'RE GOING RABBIT HUNTING.
WE'LL KILL HIM.
AND I'LL KILL HER WHEN SHE'S OF NO USE ANYMORE.

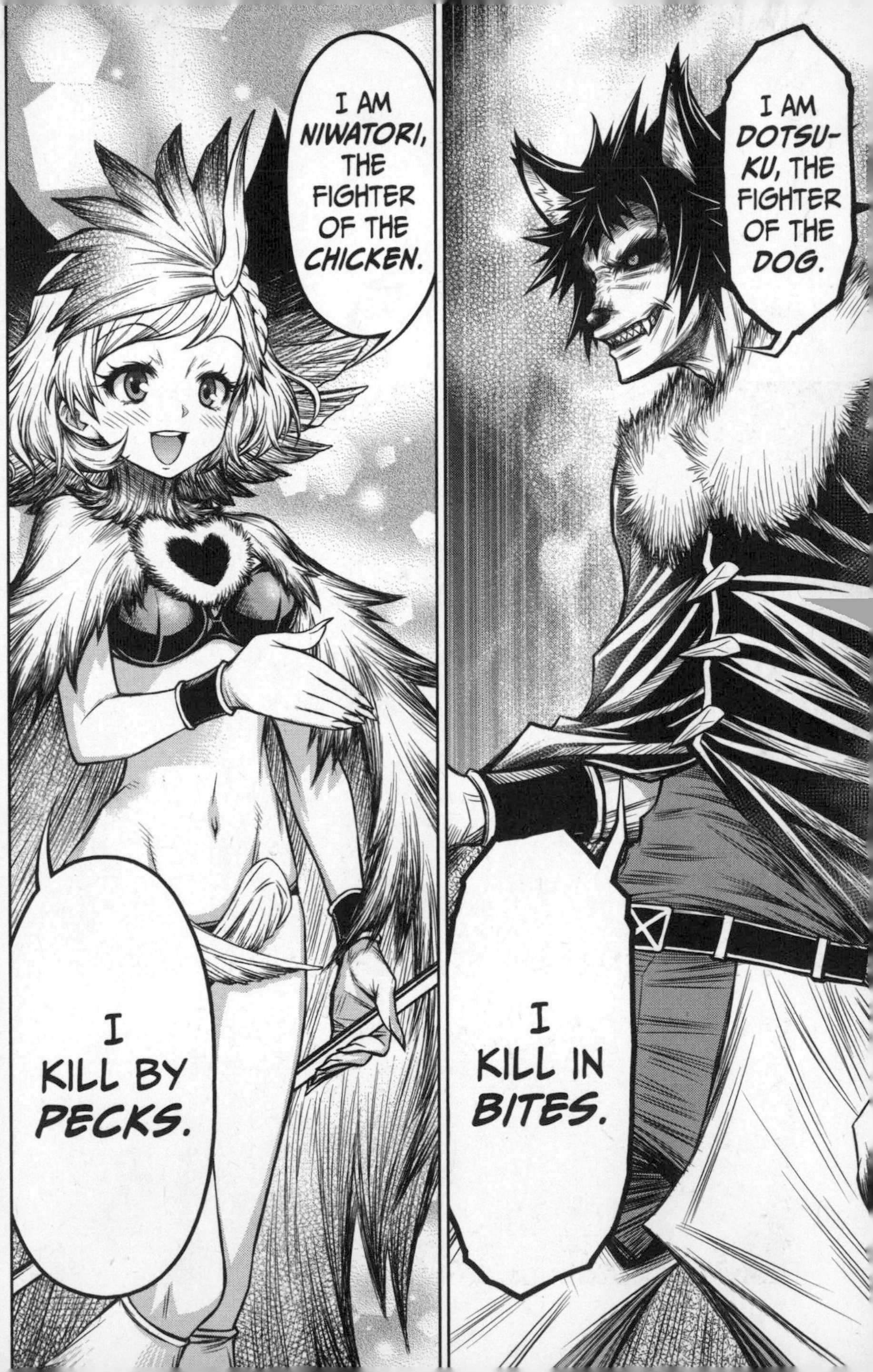
I AM DOTSU-KU, THE FIGHTER OF THE DOG.
I KILL IN BITES.
I AM NIWATORI, THE FIGHTER OF THE CHICKEN.
I KILL BY PECKS.

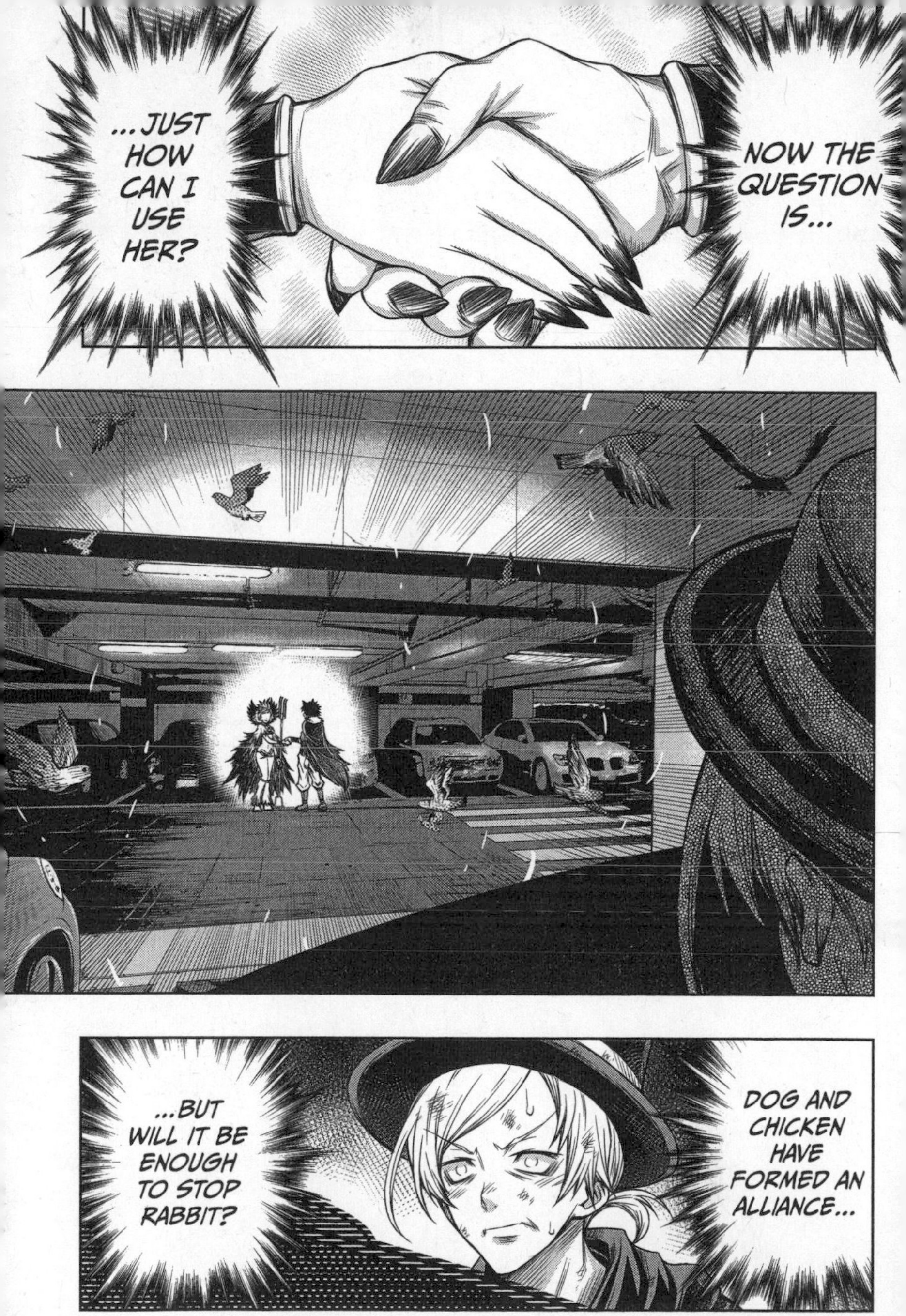
NOW THE QUESTION IS...
...JUST HOW CAN I USE HER?
DOG AND CHICKEN HAVE FORMED AN ALLIANCE...
...BUT WILL IT BE ENOUGH TO STOP RABBIT?

Each fighter held some
advantage over one or another
in the constraints of the battle.
Victory would rely upon how
they used their advantages.

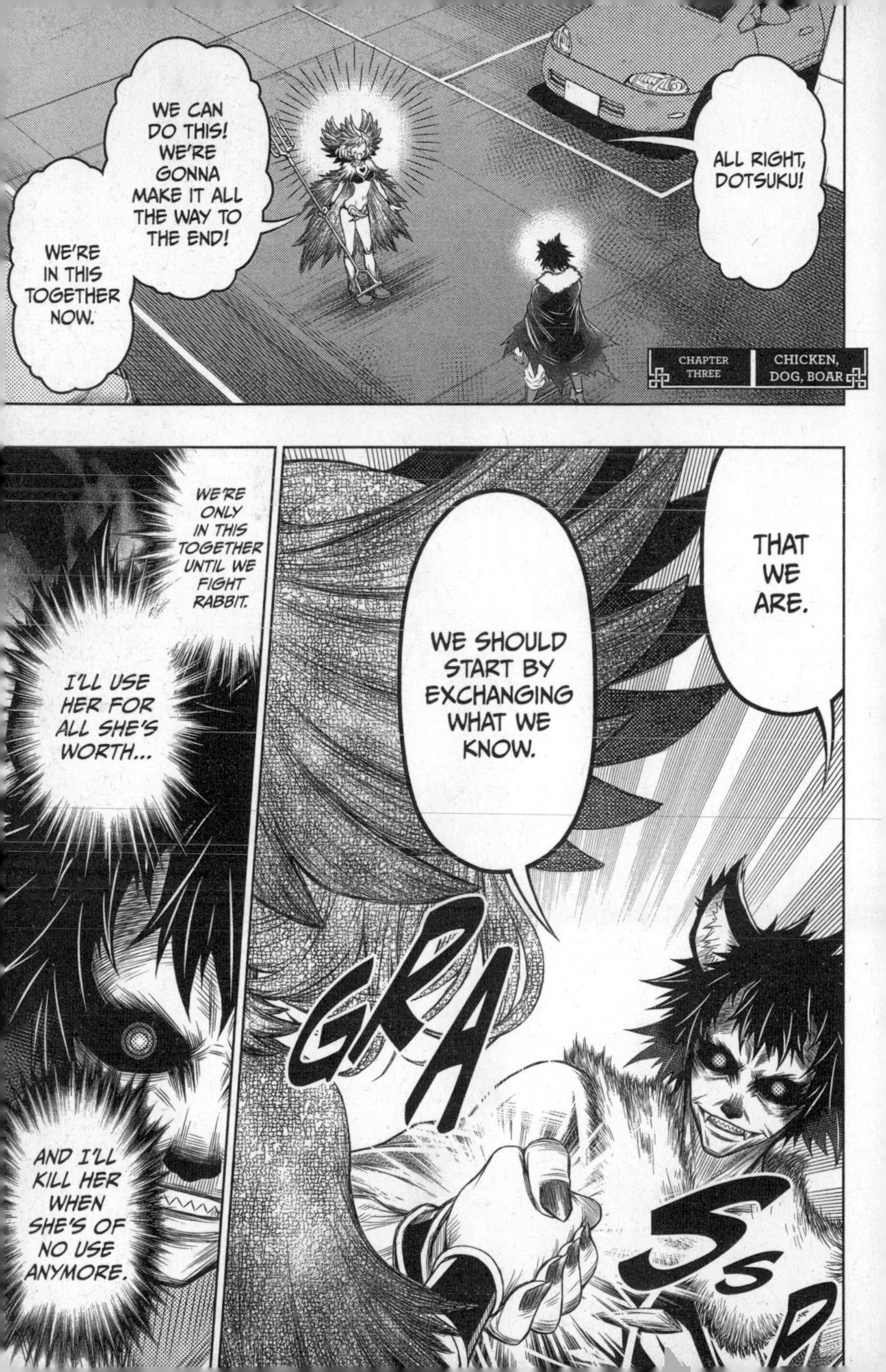
ALL RIGHT, DOTSUKU!
WE CAN DO THIS! WE'RE GONNA MAKE IT ALL THE WAY TO THE END!
WE'RE IN THIS TOGETHER NOW.
CHAPTER THREE
CHICKEN, DOG, BOAR
THAT WE ARE.
WE SHOULD START BY EXCHANGING WHAT WE KNOW.
GRA
SsP
WE'RE ONLY IN THIS TOGETHER UNTIL WE FIGHT RABBIT.
I'LL USE HER FOR ALL SHE'S WORTH...
AND I'LL KILL HER WHEN SHE'S OF NO USE ANYMORE.

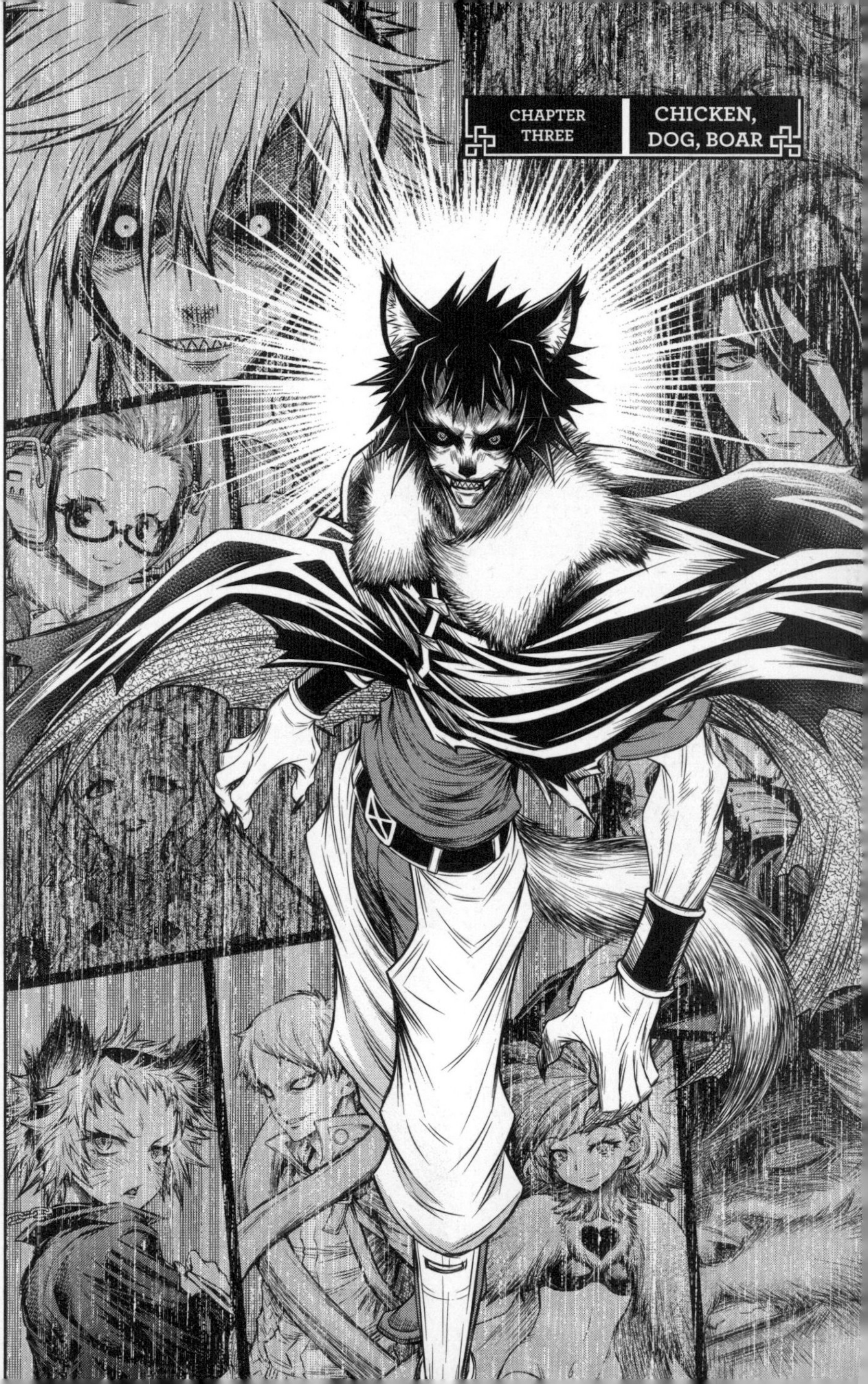
CHAPTER THREE
CHICKEN, DOG, BOAR

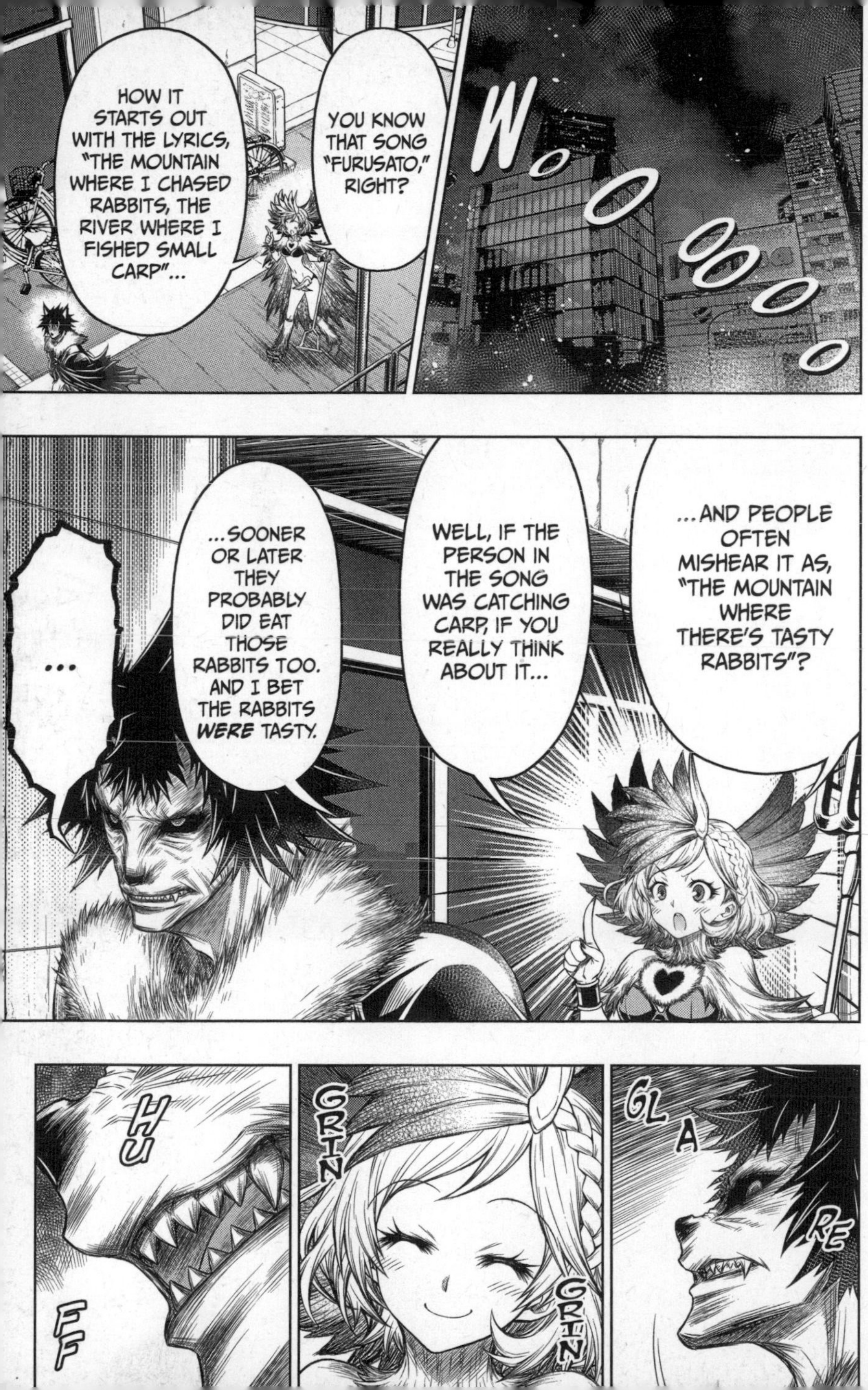
WOOOOOOO
YOU KNOW THAT SONG "FURUSATO," RIGHT?
HOW IT STARTS OUT WITH THE LYRICS, "THE MOUNTAIN WHERE I CHASED RABBITS, THE RIVER WHERE I FISHED SMALL CARP"...
...AND PEOPLE OFTEN MISHEAR IT AS, "THE MOUNTAIN WHERE THERE'S TASTY RABBITS"?
WELL, IF THE PERSON IN THE SONG WAS CATCHING CARP, IF YOU REALLY THINK ABOUT IT...
...SOONER OR LATER THEY PROBABLY DID EAT THOSE RABBITS TOO. AND I BET THE RABBITS *WERE* TASTY.
...
GLARE
GRIN
GRIN
HUFF

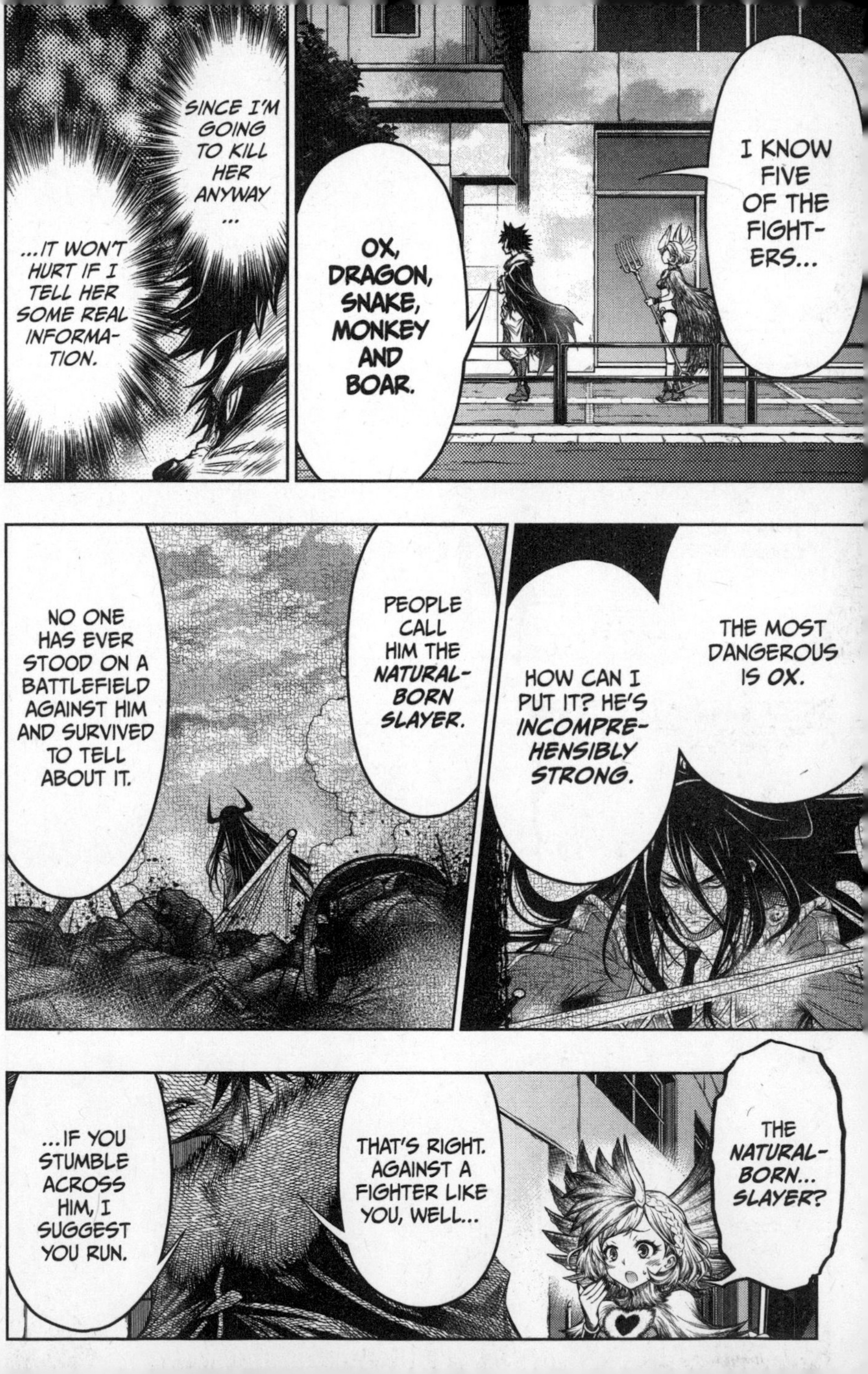
I KNOW FIVE OF THE FIGHTERS...
OX, DRAGON, SNAKE, MONKEY AND BOAR.
SINCE I'M GOING TO KILL HER ANYWAY...
...IT WON'T HURT IF I TELL HER SOME REAL INFORMATION.
THE MOST DANGEROUS IS OX.
HOW CAN I PUT IT? HE'S INCOMPREHENSIBLY STRONG.
PEOPLE CALL HIM THE NATURAL-BORN SLAYER.
NO ONE HAS EVER STOOD ON A BATTLEFIELD AGAINST HIM AND SURVIVED TO TELL ABOUT IT.
THE NATURAL-BORN... SLAYER?
THAT'S RIGHT. AGAINST A FIGHTER LIKE YOU, WELL...
...IF YOU STUMBLE ACROSS HIM, I SUGGEST YOU RUN.

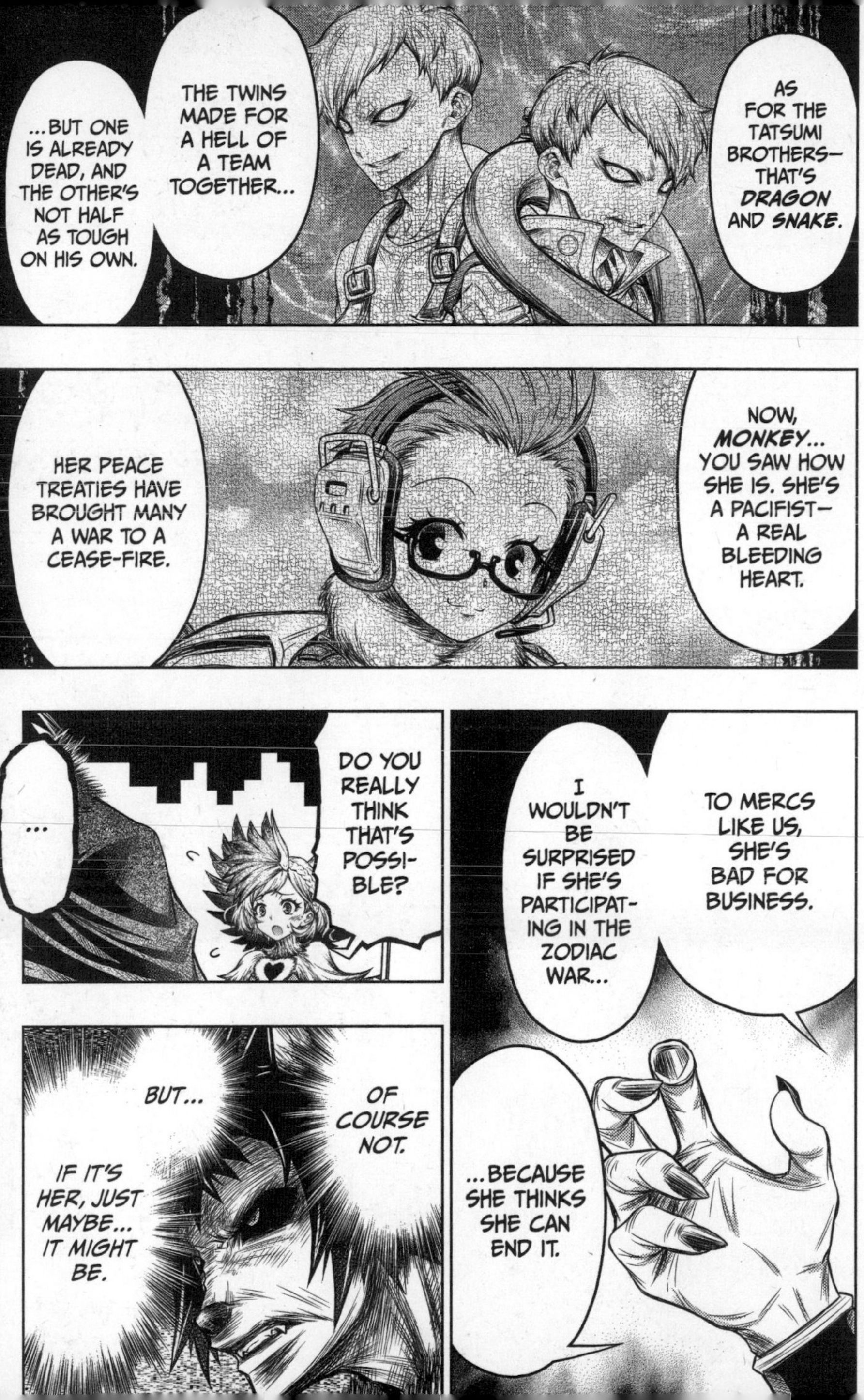
AS FOR THE TATSUMI BROTHERS— THAT'S DRAGON AND SNAKE.
THE TWINS MADE FOR A HELL OF A TEAM TOGETHER...
...BUT ONE IS ALREADY DEAD, AND THE OTHER'S NOT HALF AS TOUGH ON HIS OWN.
NOW, MONKEY... YOU SAW HOW SHE IS. SHE'S A PACIFIST— A REAL BLEEDING HEART.
HER PEACE TREATIES HAVE BROUGHT MANY A WAR TO A CEASE-FIRE.
TO MERCS LIKE US, SHE'S BAD FOR BUSINESS.
I WOULDN'T BE SURPRISED IF SHE'S PARTICIPATING IN THE ZODIAC WAR...
...BECAUSE SHE THINKS SHE CAN END IT.
DO YOU REALLY THINK THAT'S POSSIBLE?
...
OF COURSE NOT.
BUT...
IF IT'S HER, JUST MAYBE... IT MIGHT BE.

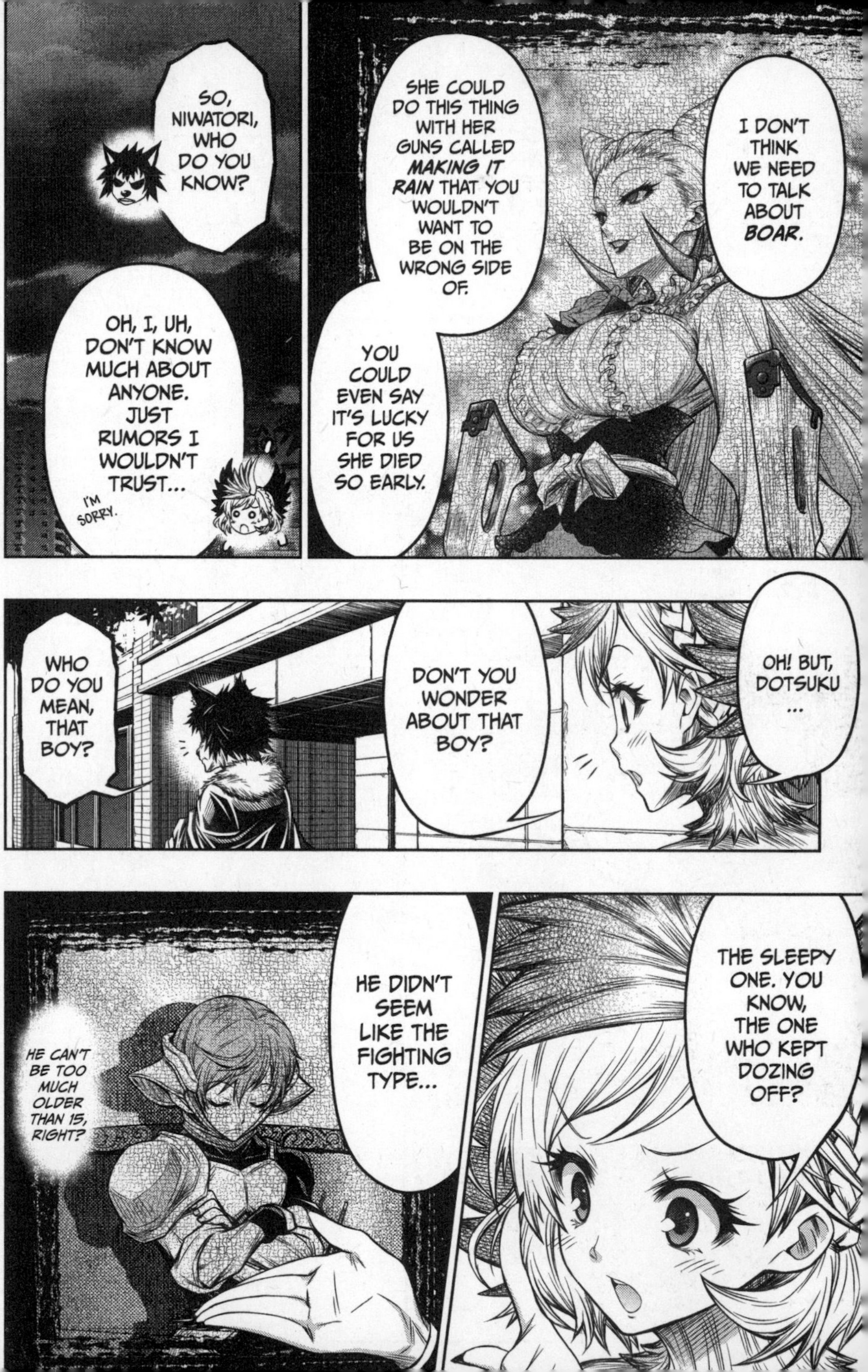
I DON'T THINK WE NEED TO TALK ABOUT BOAR.
SHE COULD DO THIS THING WITH HER GUNS CALLED MAKING IT RAIN THAT YOU WOULDN'T WANT TO BE ON THE WRONG SIDE OF.
YOU COULD EVEN SAY IT'S LUCKY FOR US SHE DIED SO EARLY.
SO, NIWATORI, WHO DO YOU KNOW?
OH, I, UH, DON'T KNOW MUCH ABOUT ANYONE. JUST RUMORS I WOULDN'T TRUST...
I'M SORRY.
OH! BUT, DOTSUKU...
DON'T YOU WONDER ABOUT THAT BOY?
WHO DO YOU MEAN, THAT BOY?
THE SLEEPY ONE. YOU KNOW, THE ONE WHO KEPT DOZING OFF?
HE DIDN'T SEEM LIKE THE FIGHTING TYPE...
HE CAN'T BE TOO MUCH OLDER THAN 15, RIGHT?

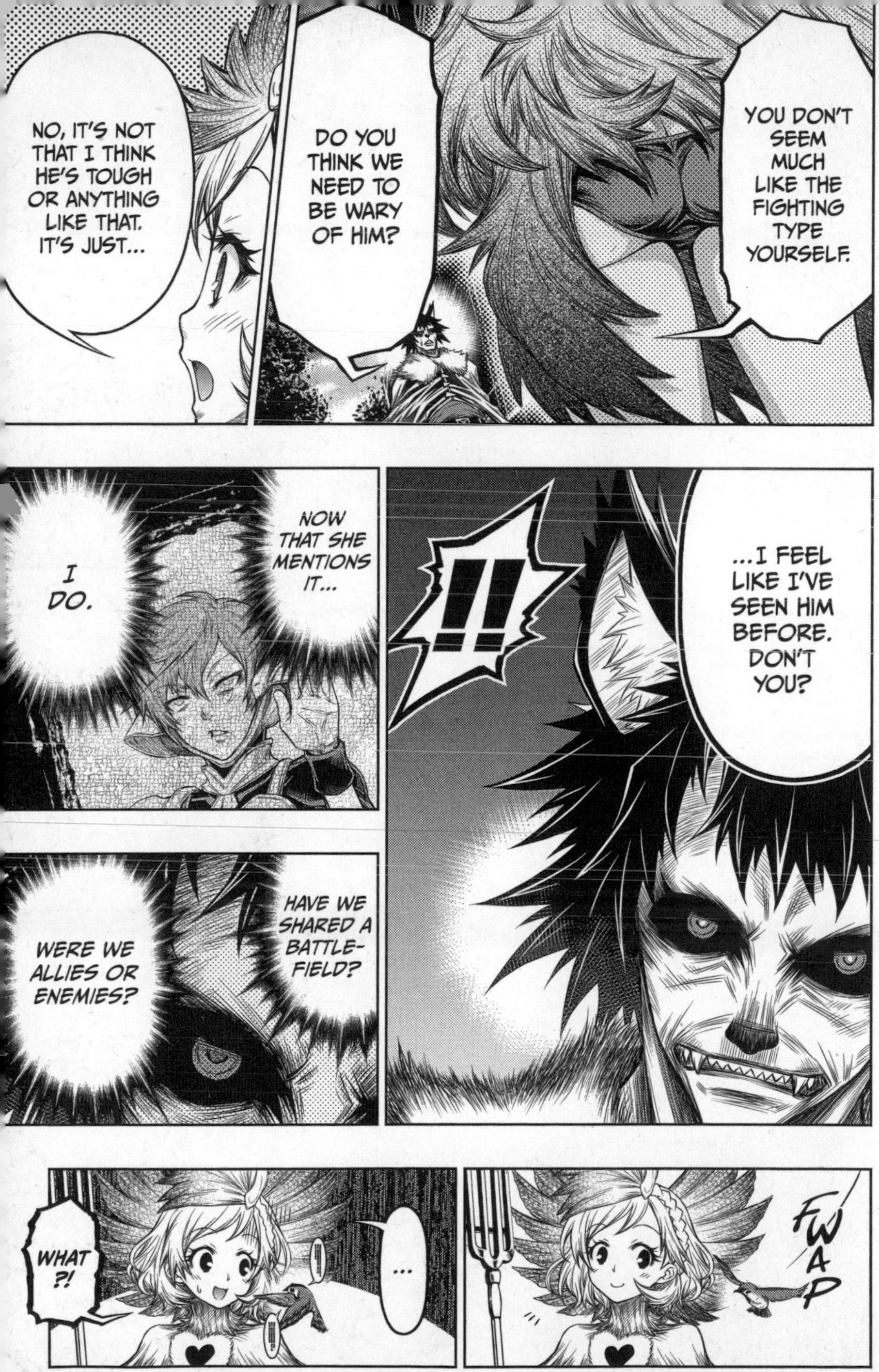
YOU DON'T SEEM MUCH LIKE THE FIGHTING TYPE YOURSELF.
DO YOU THINK WE NEED TO BE WARY OF HIM?
NO, IT'S NOT THAT I THINK HE'S TOUGH OR ANYTHING LIKE THAT. IT'S JUST...
...I FEEL LIKE I'VE SEEN HIM BEFORE. DON'T YOU?
!!
NOW THAT SHE MENTIONS IT...
I DO.
HAVE WE SHARED A BATTLE-FIELD?
WERE WE ALLIES OR ENEMIES?
FWAP
...
WHAT?!

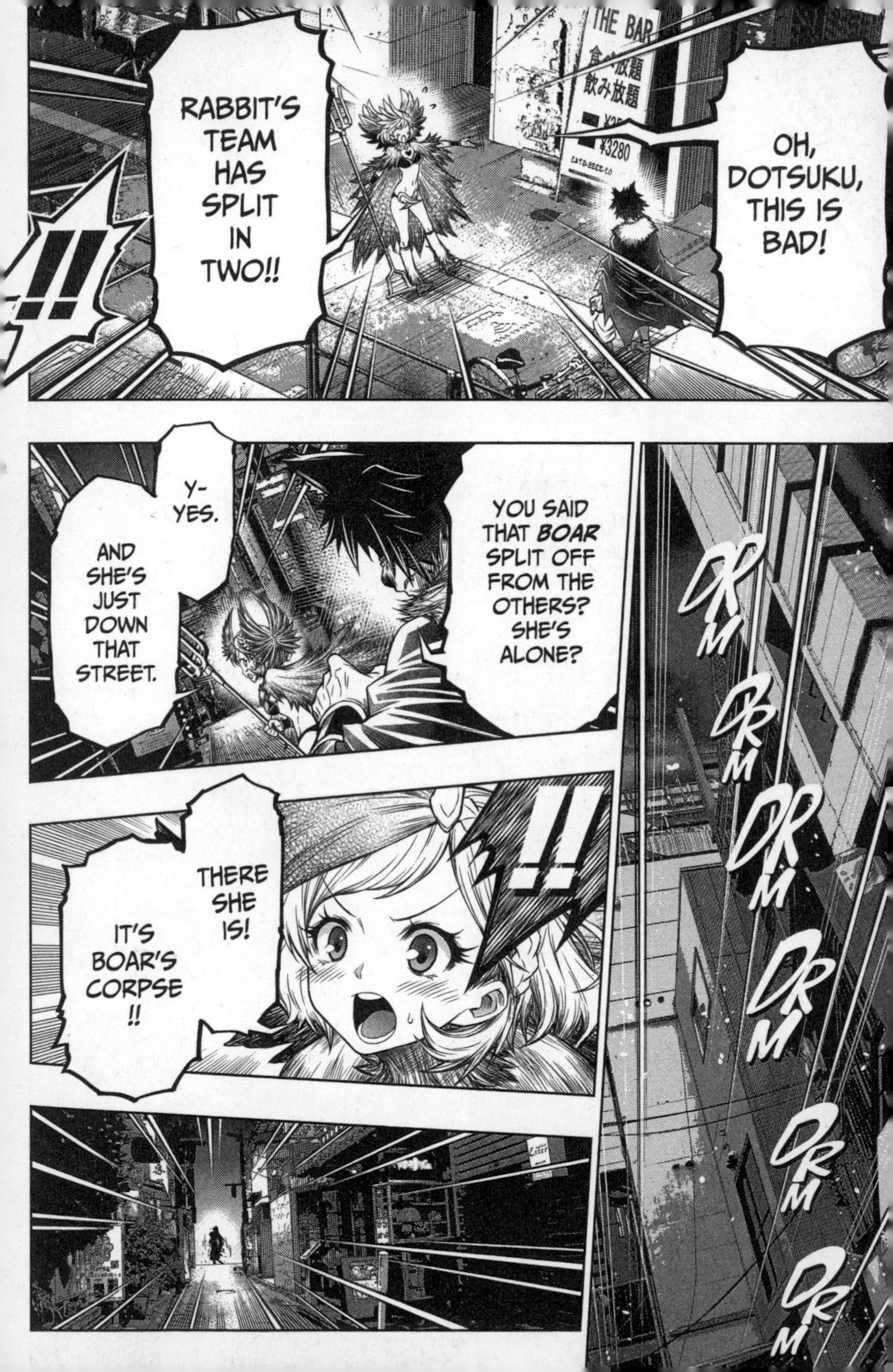
THE BAR
飲み放題
¥3280
OH, DOTSUKU, THIS IS BAD!
RABBIT'S TEAM HAS SPLIT IN TWO!!
!!
DRM DRM DRM DRM DRM DRM DRM
YOU SAID THAT BOAR SPLIT OFF FROM THE OTHERS? SHE'S ALONE?
Y-YES.
AND SHE'S JUST DOWN THAT STREET.
!!
THERE SHE IS!
IT'S BOAR'S CORPSE!!

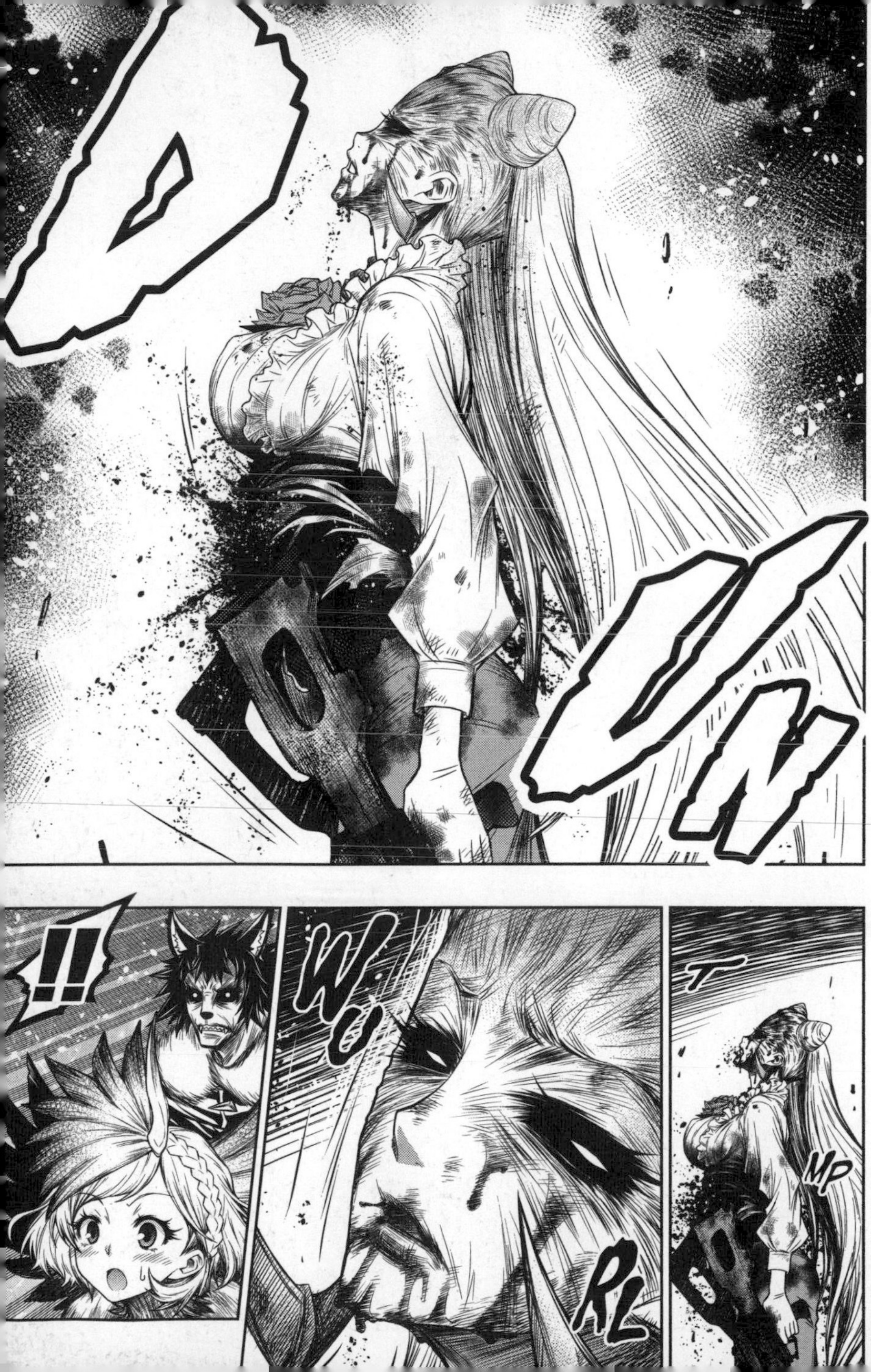
D
UN
T
!
MP
W
RL
!!

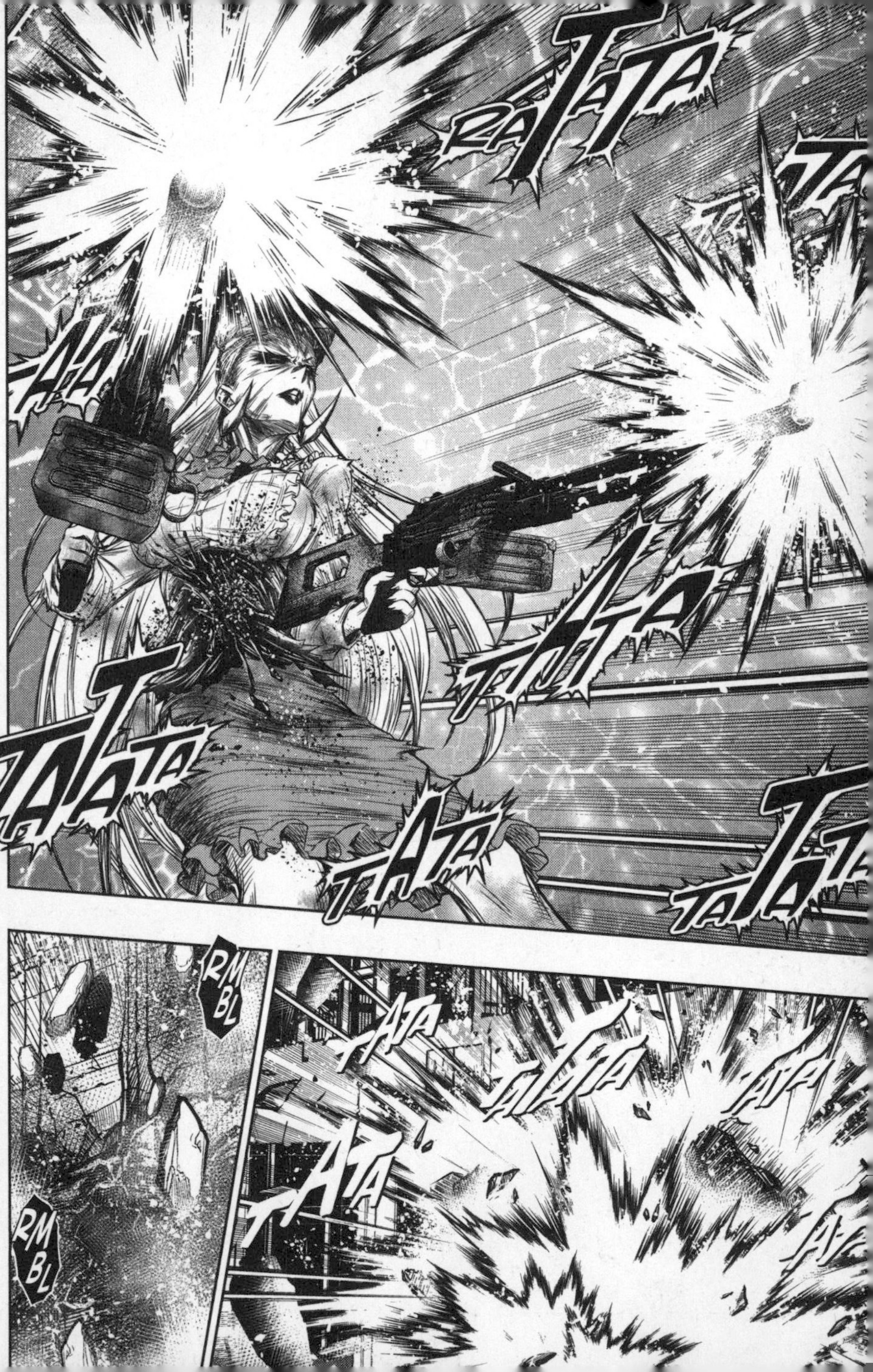
RATATA
TATATA
AAA
TATATA
TATA
TATATA
TATA
TATATA
TATA
RMBL
RMBL

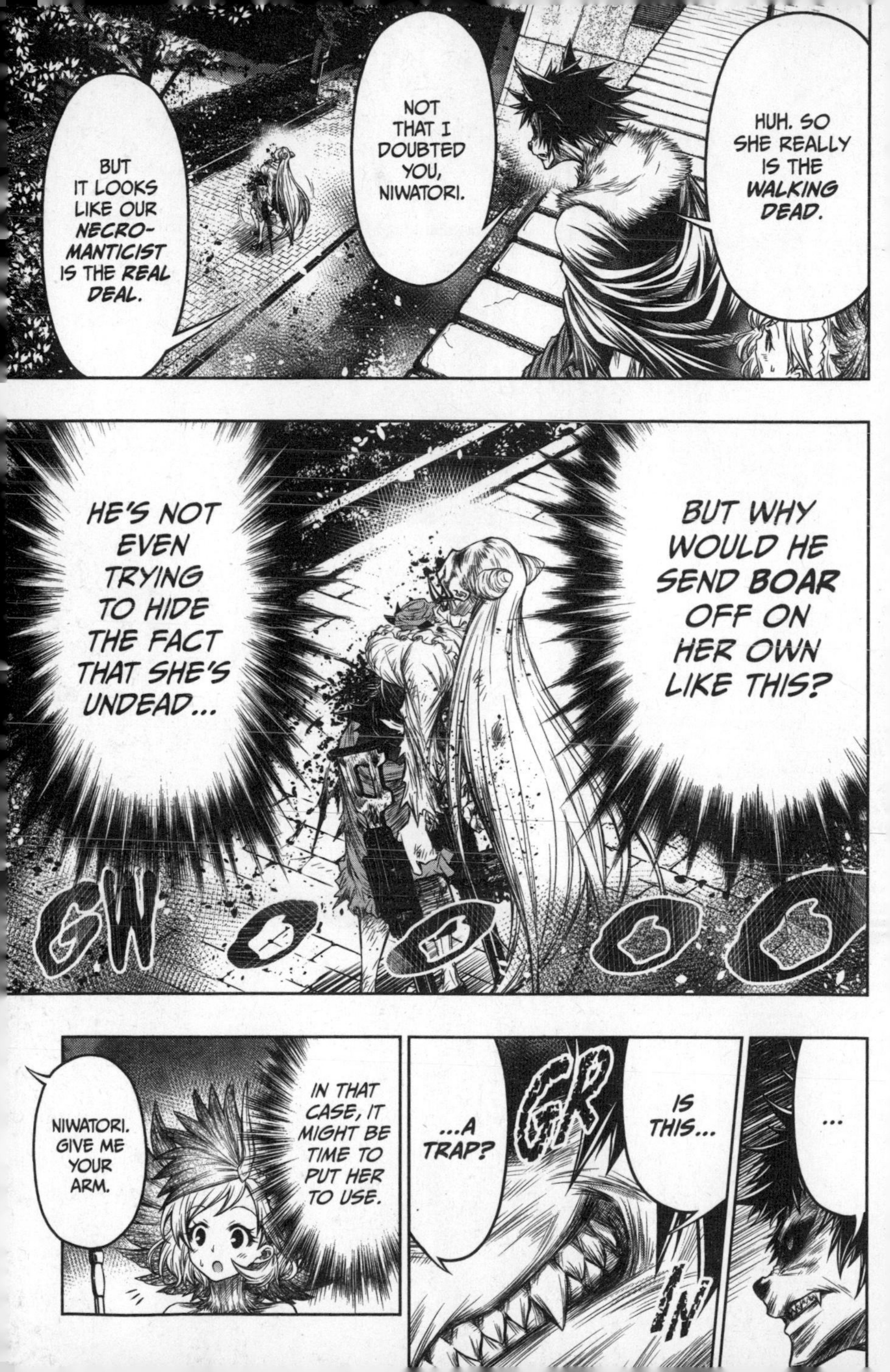
HUH. SO SHE REALLY IS THE WALKING DEAD.
NOT THAT I DOUBTED YOU, NIWATORI.
BUT IT LOOKS LIKE OUR NECRO-MANTICIST IS THE REAL DEAL.
BUT WHY WOULD HE SEND BOAR OFF ON HER OWN LIKE THIS?
HE'S NOT EVEN TRYING TO HIDE THE FACT THAT SHE'S UNDEAD...
GWOOOO
...
IS THIS...
GR
IN
...A TRAP?
IN THAT CASE, IT MIGHT BE TIME TO PUT HER TO USE.
NIWATORI. GIVE ME YOUR ARM.

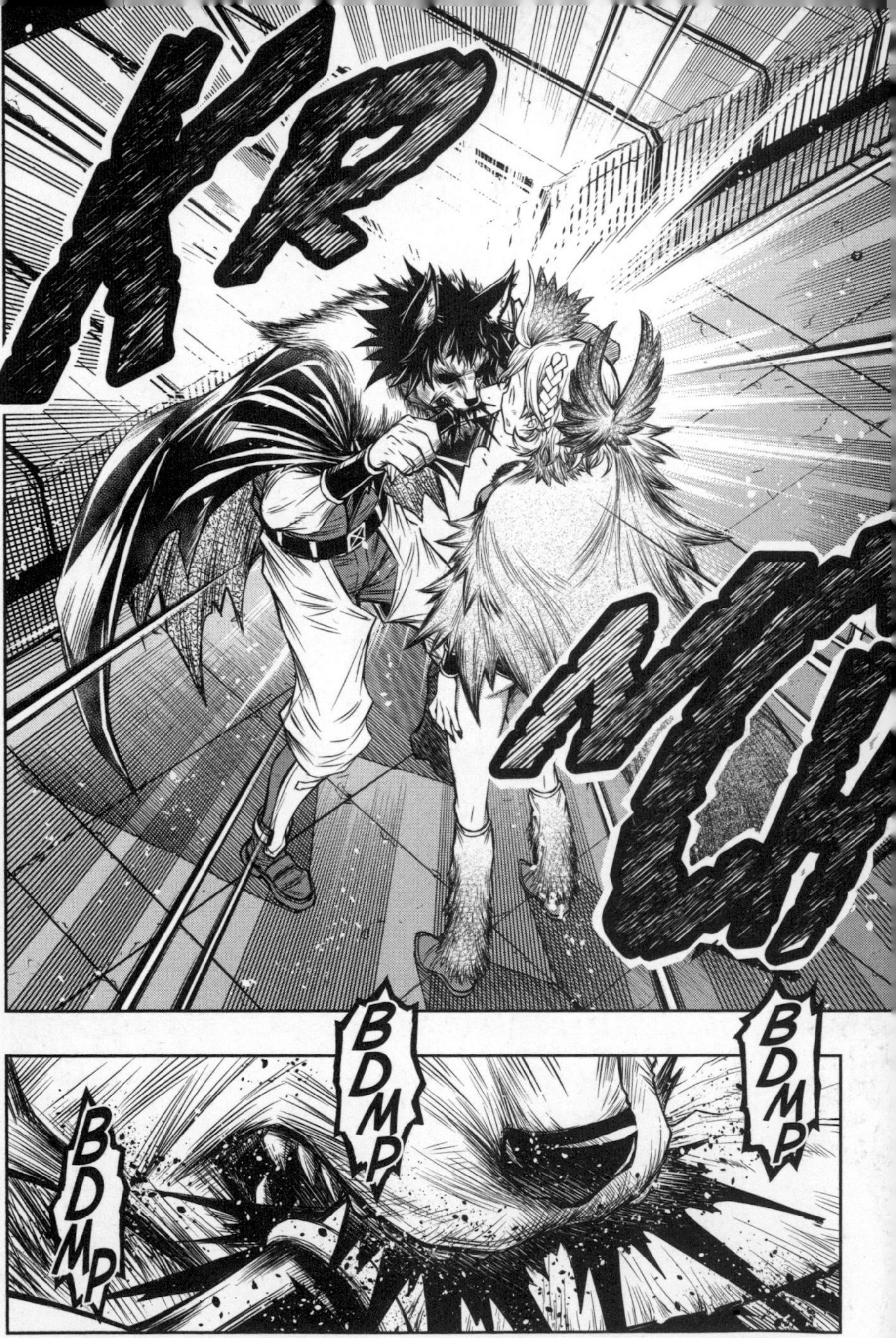
BDMP
BDMP
BDMP

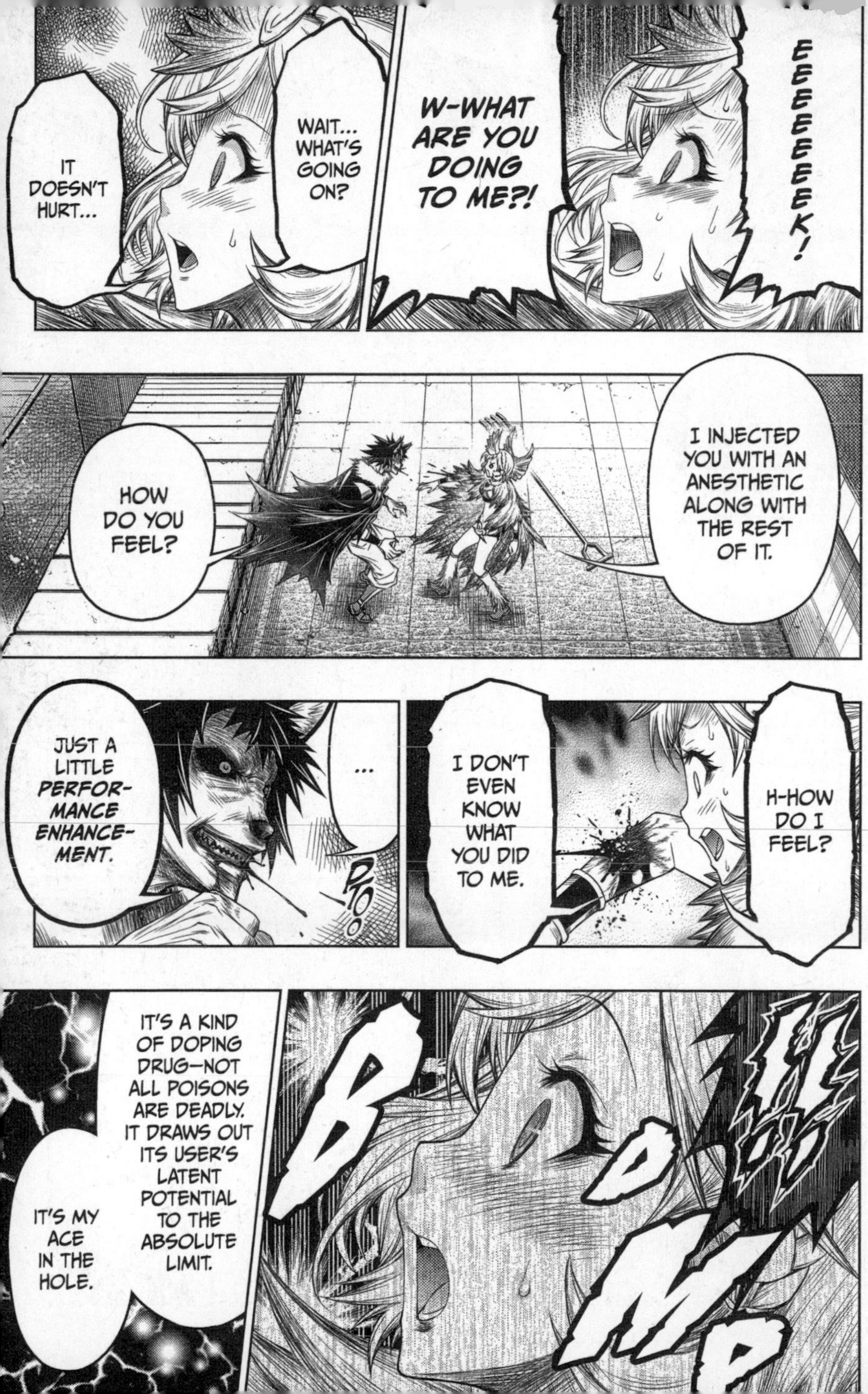
EEEEEEEK!
W-WHAT ARE YOU DOING TO ME?!
WAIT... WHAT'S GOING ON?
IT DOESN'T HURT...
I INJECTED YOU WITH AN ANESTHETIC ALONG WITH THE REST OF IT.
HOW DO YOU FEEL?
H-HOW DO I FEEL?
I DON'T EVEN KNOW WHAT YOU DID TO ME.
...
JUST A LITTLE *PERFORMANCE-ENHANCEMENT*.
IT'S A KIND OF DOPING DRUG—NOT ALL POISONS ARE DEADLY. IT DRAWS OUT ITS USER'S LATENT POTENTIAL TO THE ABSOLUTE LIMIT.
IT'S MY ACE IN THE HOLE.

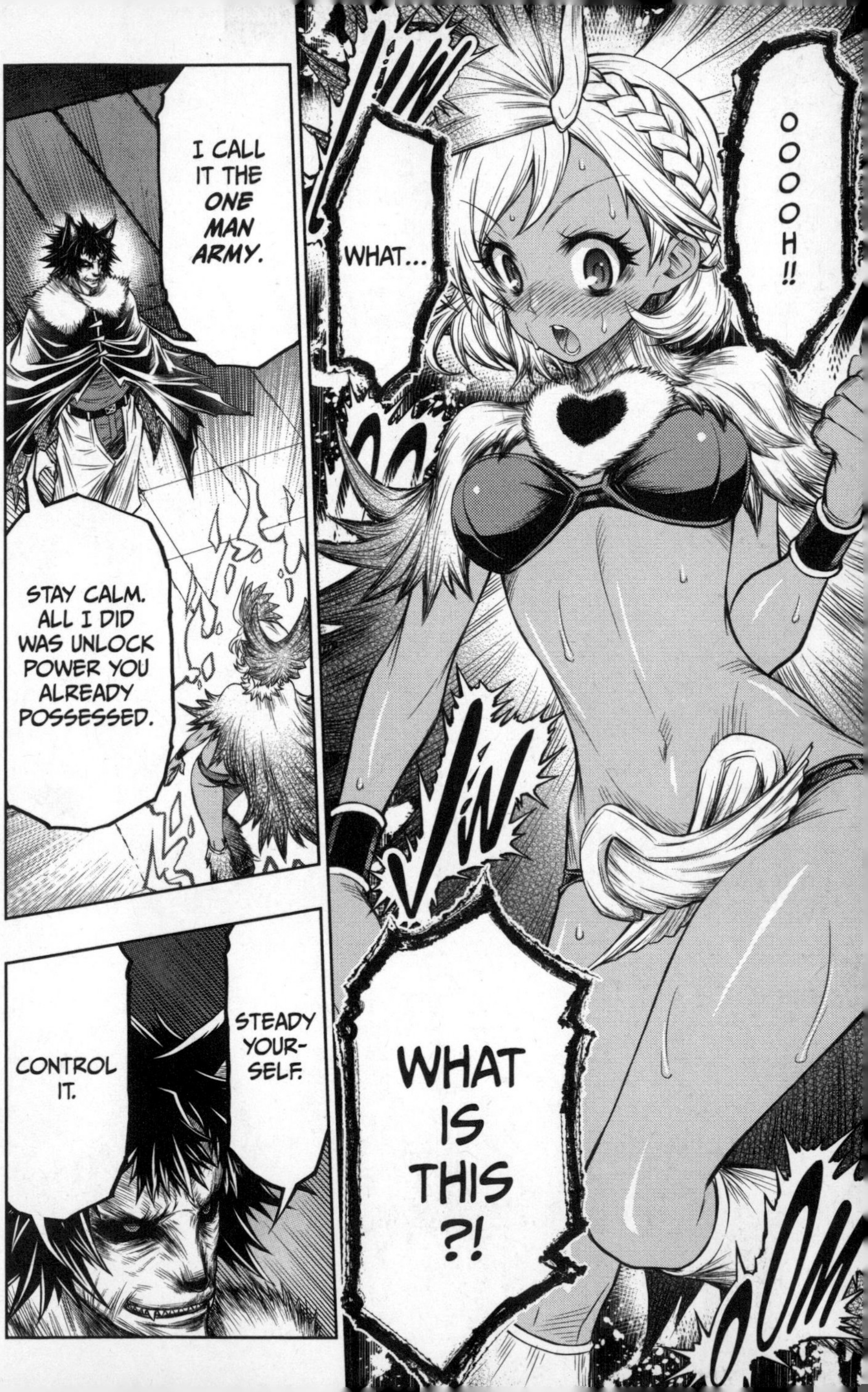
OOOOOH!!
WHAT...
WHAT IS THIS?!
I CALL IT THE ONE MAN ARMY.
STAY CALM. ALL I DID WAS UNLOCK POWER YOU ALREADY POSSESSED.
STEADY YOURSELF.
CONTROL IT.

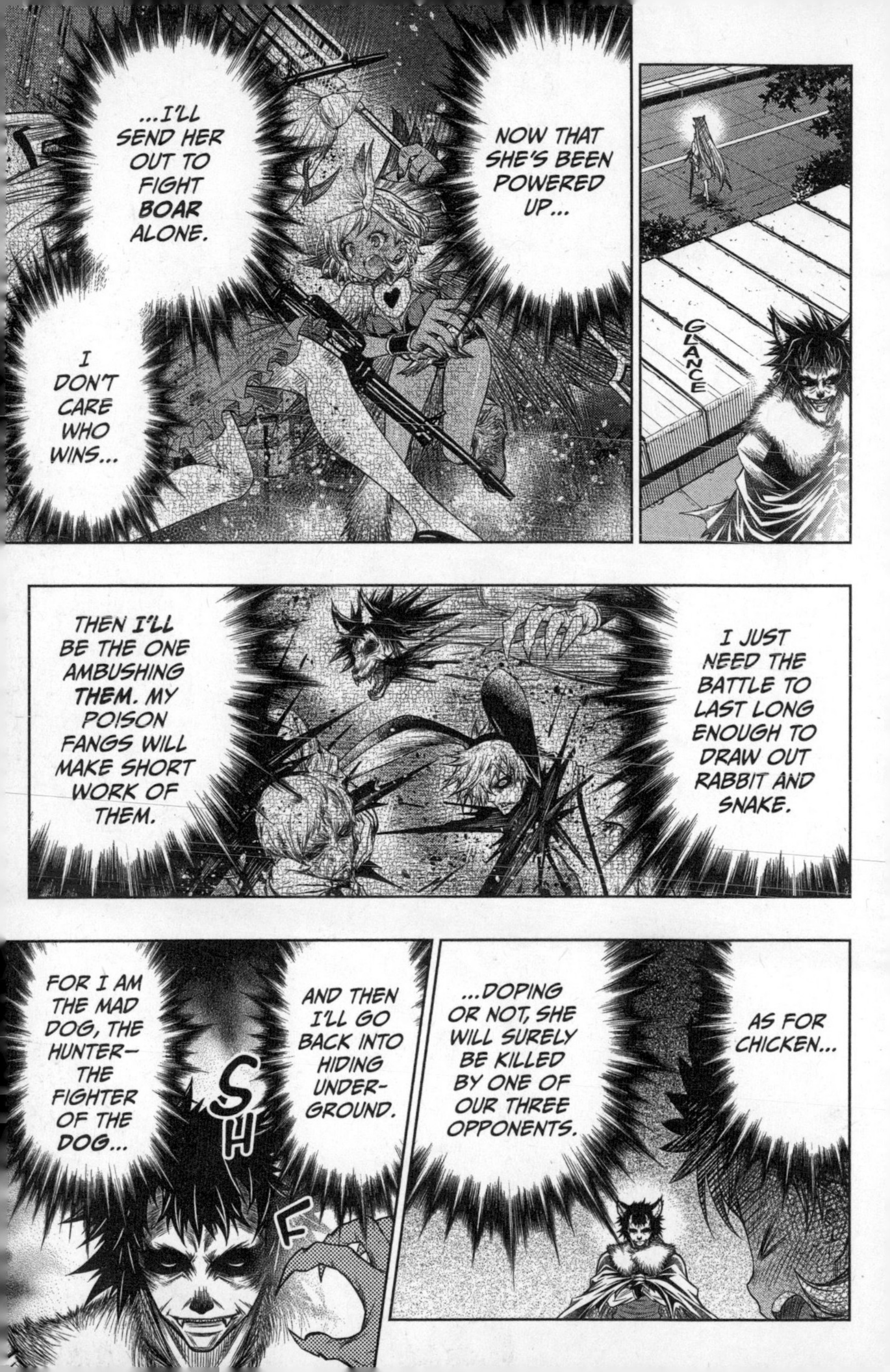
GLANCE
NOW THAT SHE'S BEEN POWERED UP...
...I'LL SEND HER OUT TO FIGHT BOAR ALONE.
I DON'T CARE WHO WINS...
I JUST NEED THE BATTLE TO LAST LONG ENOUGH TO DRAW OUT RABBIT AND SNAKE.
THEN I'LL BE THE ONE AMBUSHING THEM. MY POISON FANGS WILL MAKE SHORT WORK OF THEM.
AS FOR CHICKEN...
...DOPING OR NOT, SHE WILL SURELY BE KILLED BY ONE OF OUR THREE OPPONENTS.
AND THEN I'LL GO BACK INTO HIDING UNDER-GROUND.
FOR I AM THE MAD DOG, THE HUNTER— THE FIGHTER OF THE DOG...
SHF

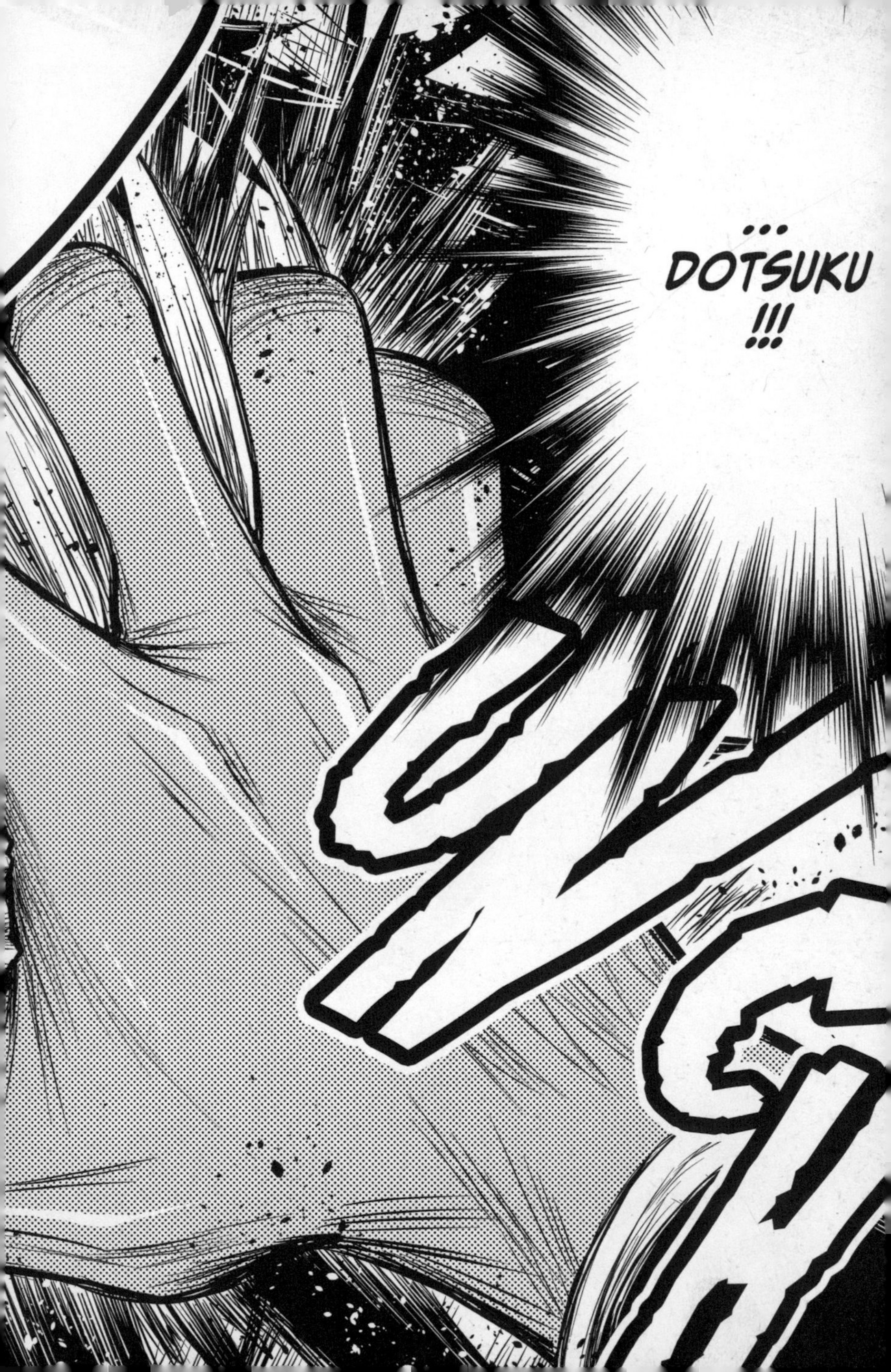
... DOTSUKU !!!

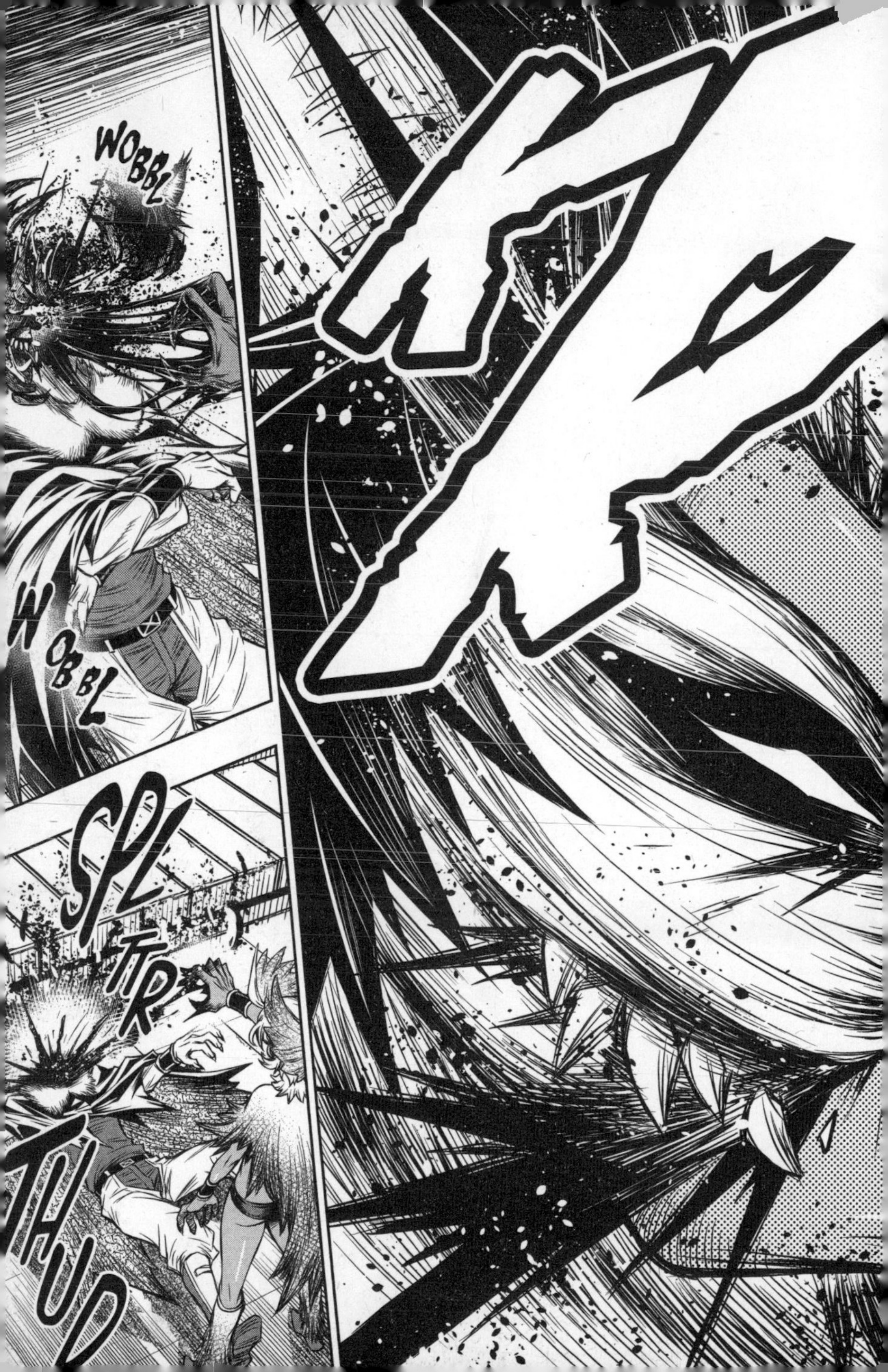
WOBBL
WOBBL
SPLTTR
THUD

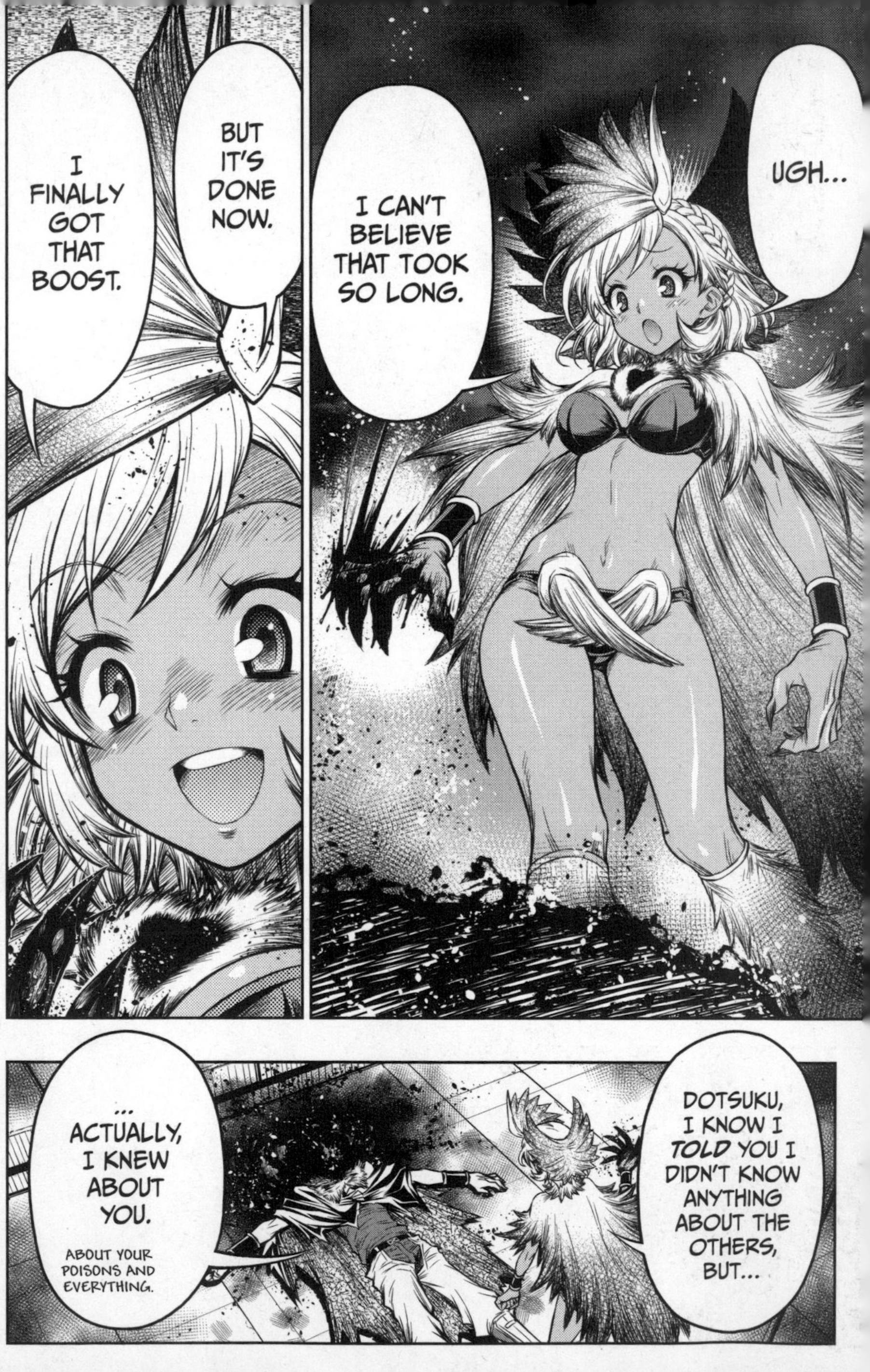
UGH...
I CAN'T BELIEVE THAT TOOK SO LONG.
BUT IT'S DONE NOW.
I FINALLY GOT THAT BOOST.
DOTSUKU, I KNOW I *TOLD* YOU I DIDN'T KNOW ANYTHING ABOUT THE OTHERS, BUT...
...ACTUALLY, I KNEW ABOUT YOU.
ABOUT YOUR POISONS AND EVERYTHING.

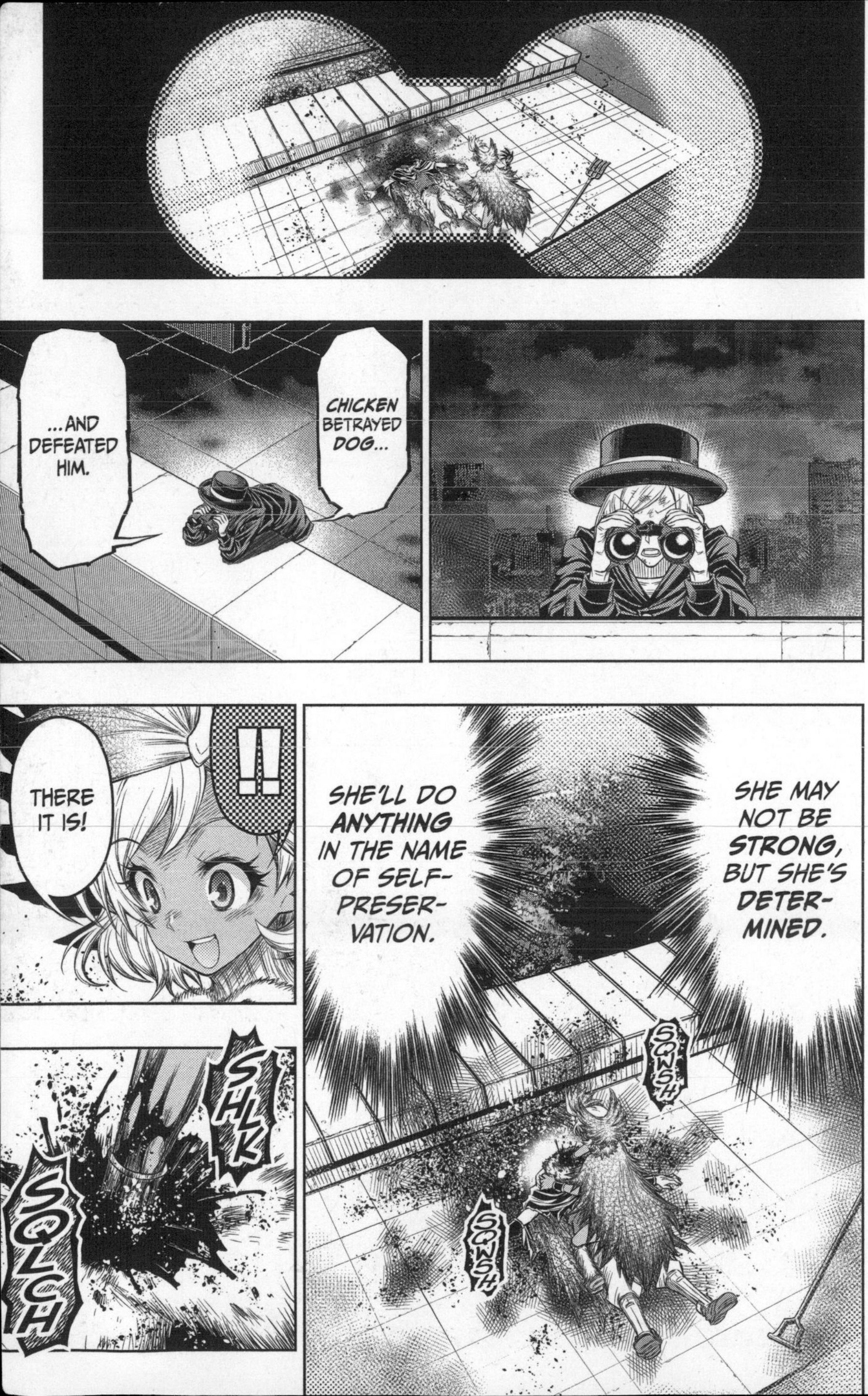
CHICKEN BETRAYED DOG...
...AND DEFEATED HIM.
SHE MAY NOT BE STRONG, BUT SHE'S DETER-MINED.
SHE'LL DO ANYTHING IN THE NAME OF SELF-PRESER-VATION.
SQWSH
SQWSH
!!
THERE IT IS!
SHLK
SQLCH

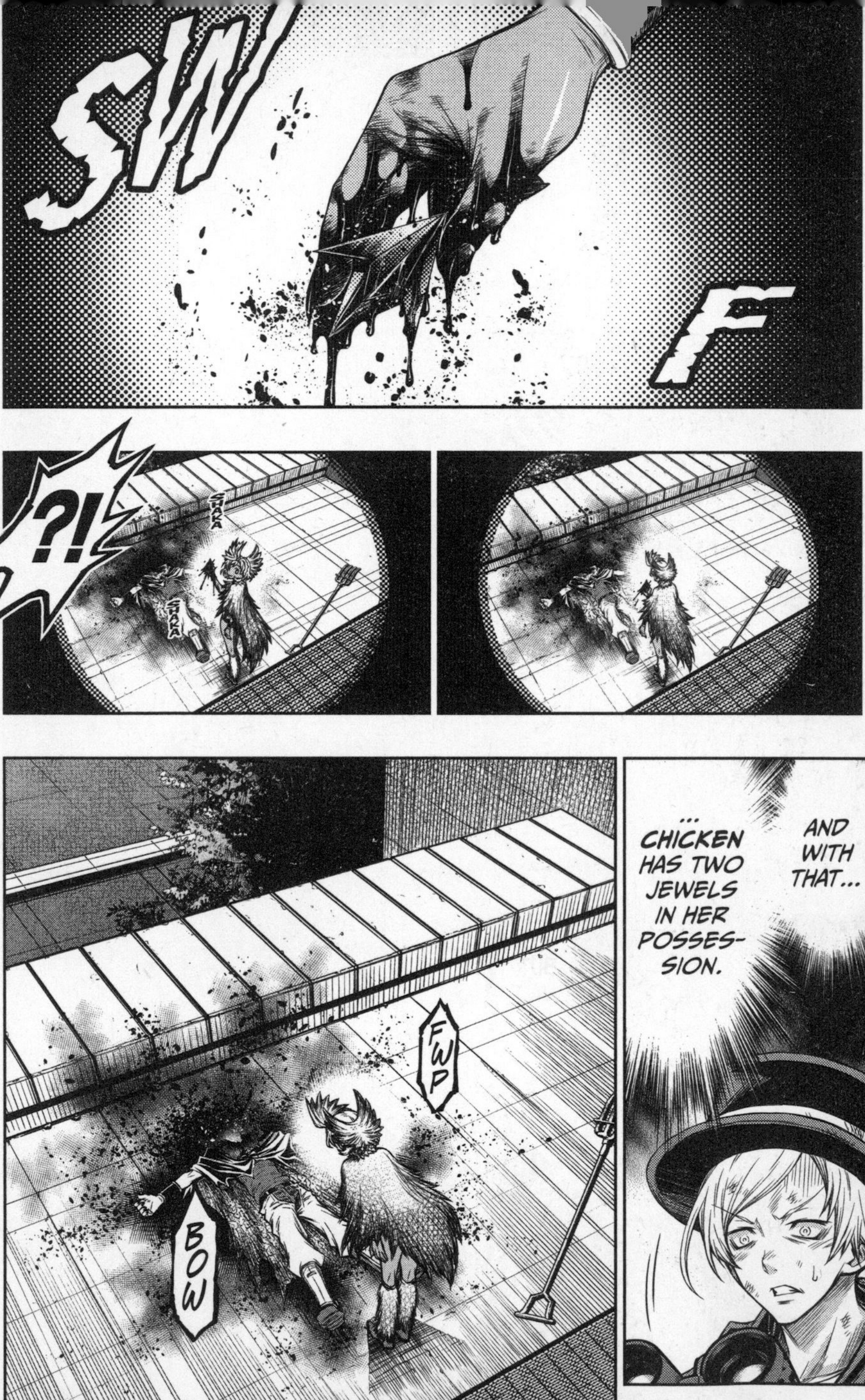
SW
F
?!
SHAKA
SHAKA
AND WITH THAT...
...CHICKEN HAS TWO JEWELS IN HER POSSES-SION.
FWP
BOW

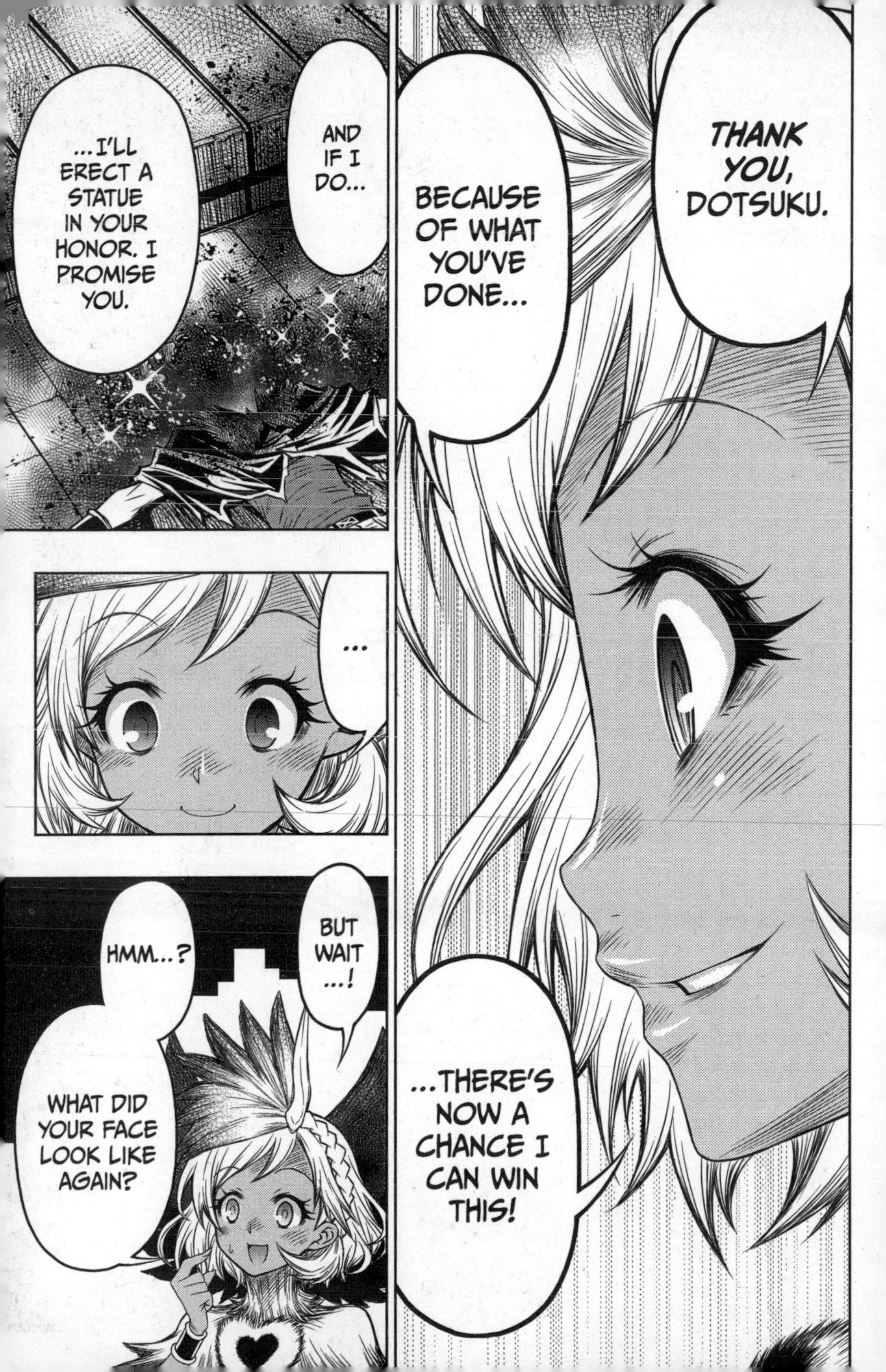
THANK YOU, DOTSUKU.
BECAUSE OF WHAT YOU'VE DONE...
...THERE'S NOW A CHANCE I CAN WIN THIS!
AND IF I DO...
...I'LL ERECT A STATUE IN YOUR HONOR. I PROMISE YOU.
...
BUT WAIT ...!
HMM...?
WHAT DID YOUR FACE LOOK LIKE AGAIN?

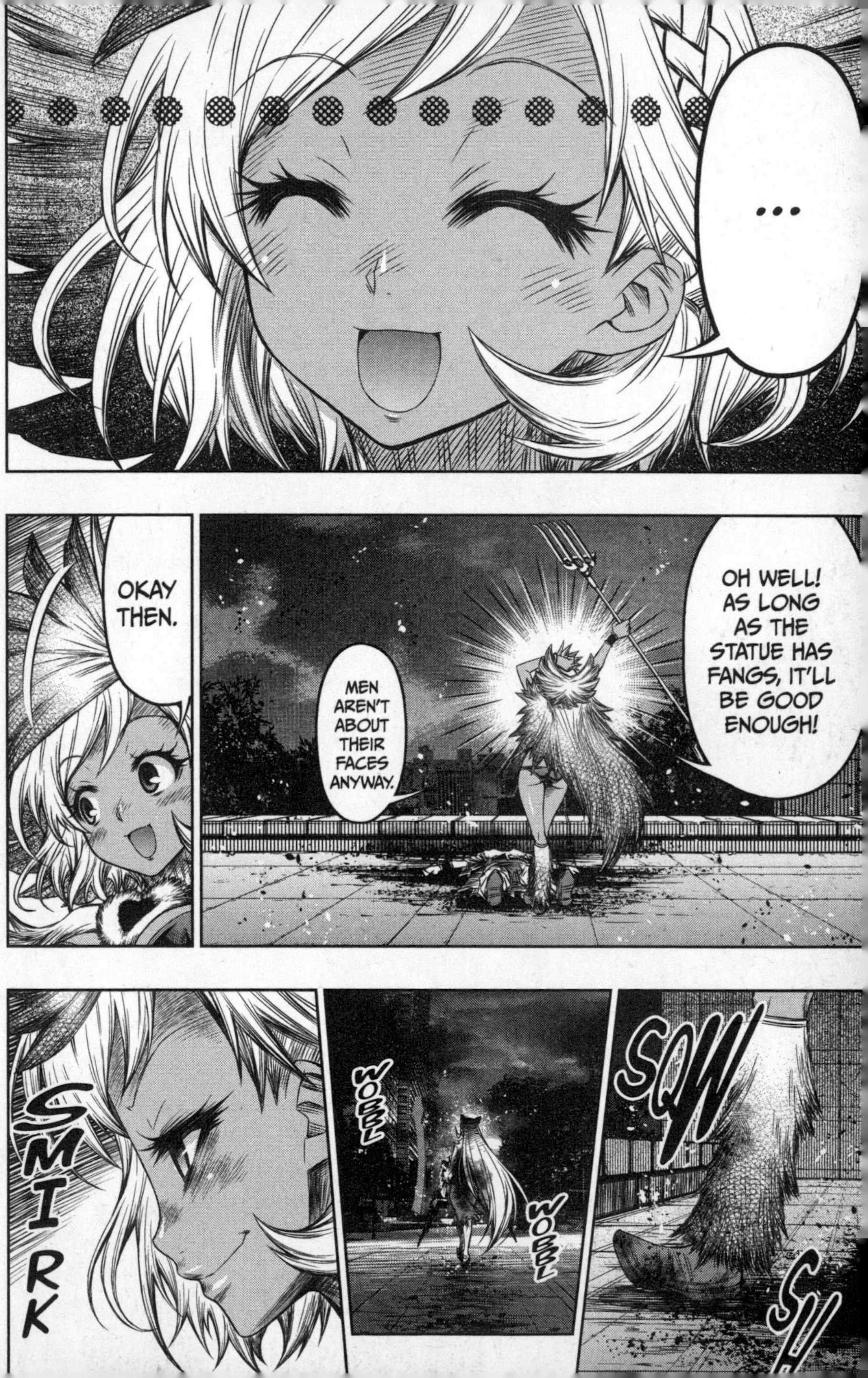
...
OH WELL! AS LONG AS THE STATUE HAS FANGS, IT'LL BE GOOD ENOUGH!
MEN AREN'T ABOUT THEIR FACES ANYWAY.
OKAY THEN.
SQW
SH
WOBBL
WOBBL
SMIRK

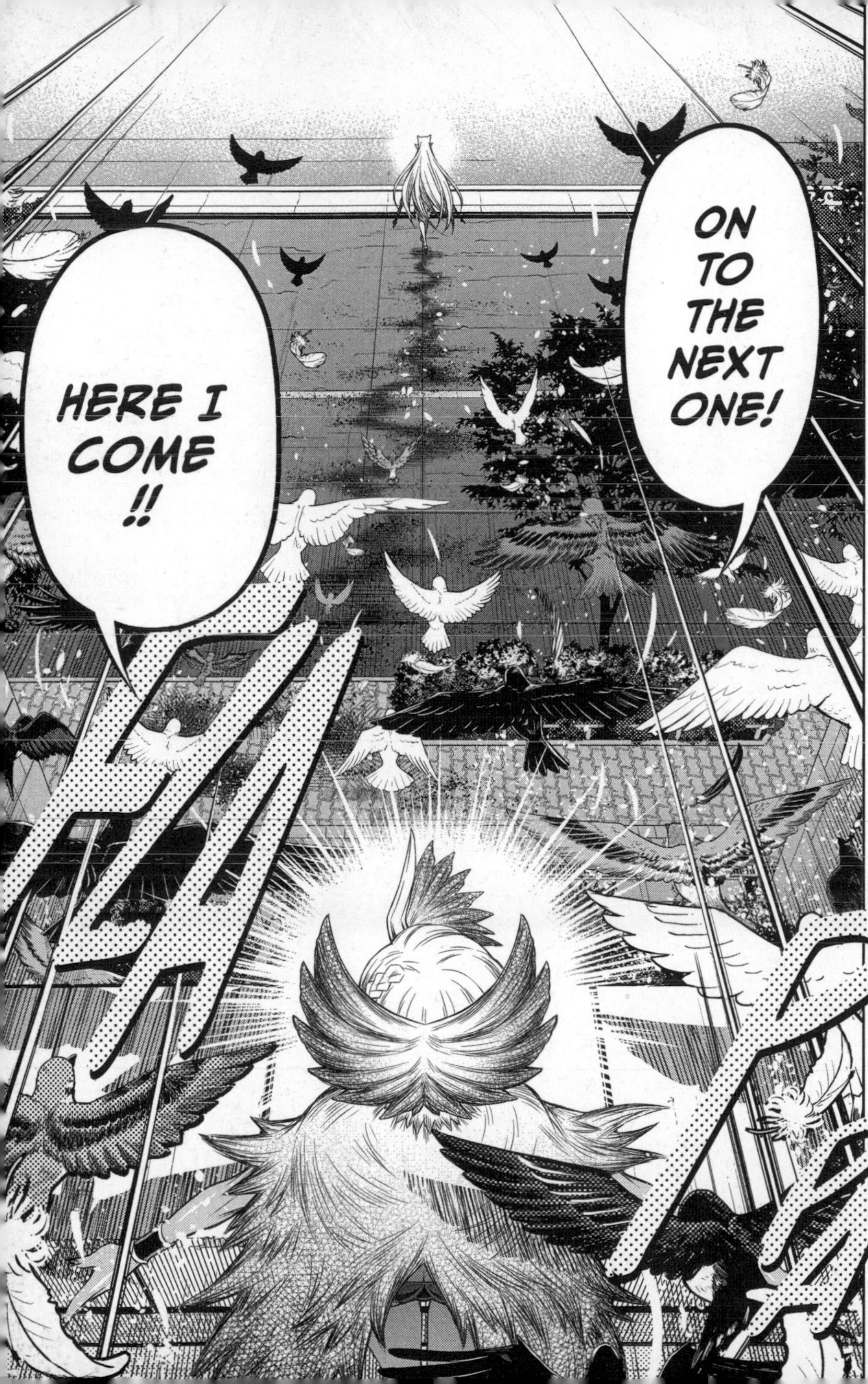
ON TO THE NEXT ONE!
HERE I COME!!

Dog was wrong
to think he could
hide anything from her
Eye of the Cormorant.

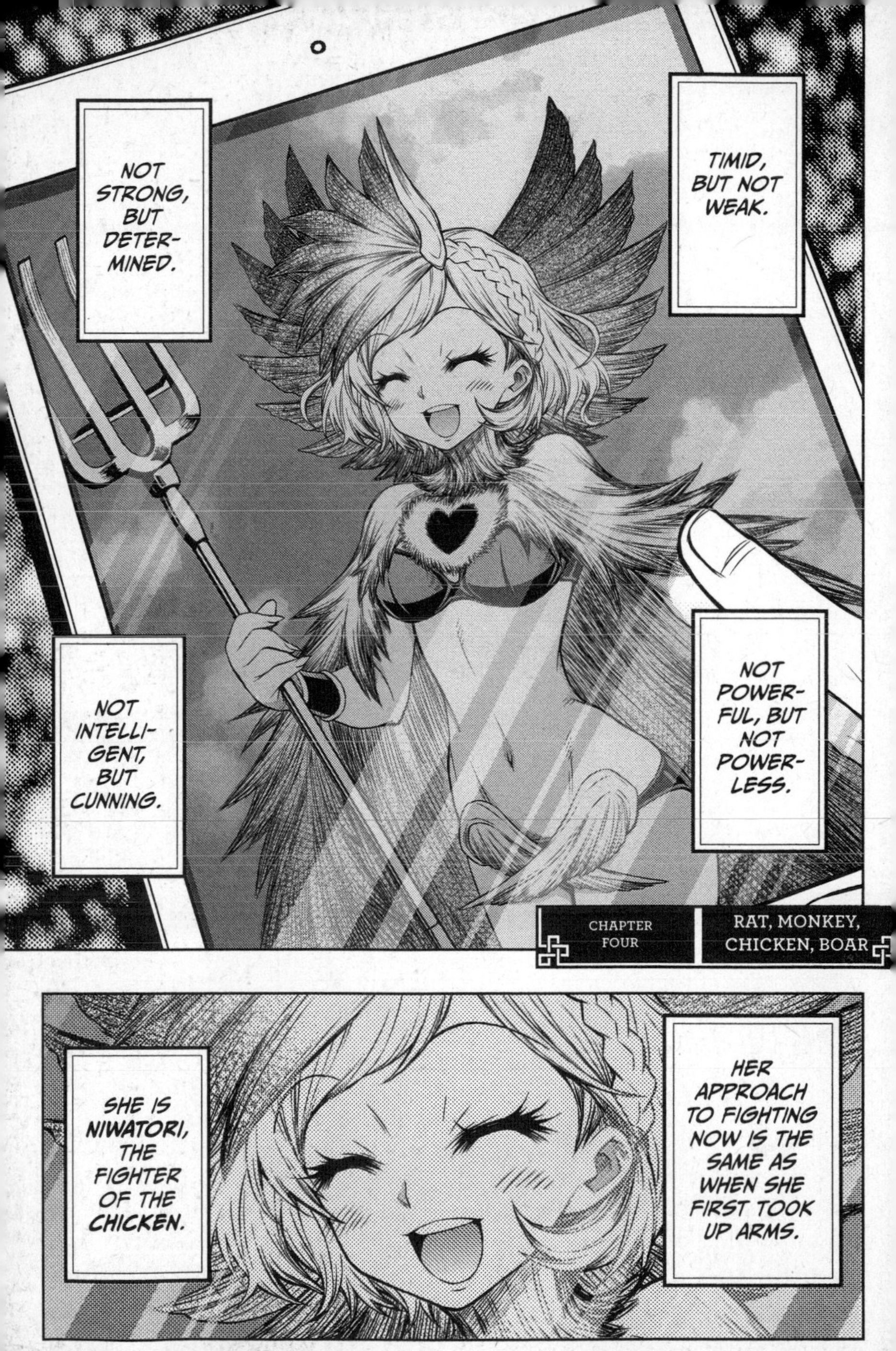
TIMID, BUT NOT WEAK.
NOT STRONG, BUT DETERMINED.
NOT POWERFUL, BUT NOT POWERLESS.
NOT INTELLIGENT, BUT CUNNING.
CHAPTER FOUR
RAT, MONKEY, CHICKEN, BOAR
HER APPROACH TO FIGHTING NOW IS THE SAME AS WHEN SHE FIRST TOOK UP ARMS.
SHE IS NIWATORI, THE FIGHTER OF THE CHICKEN.

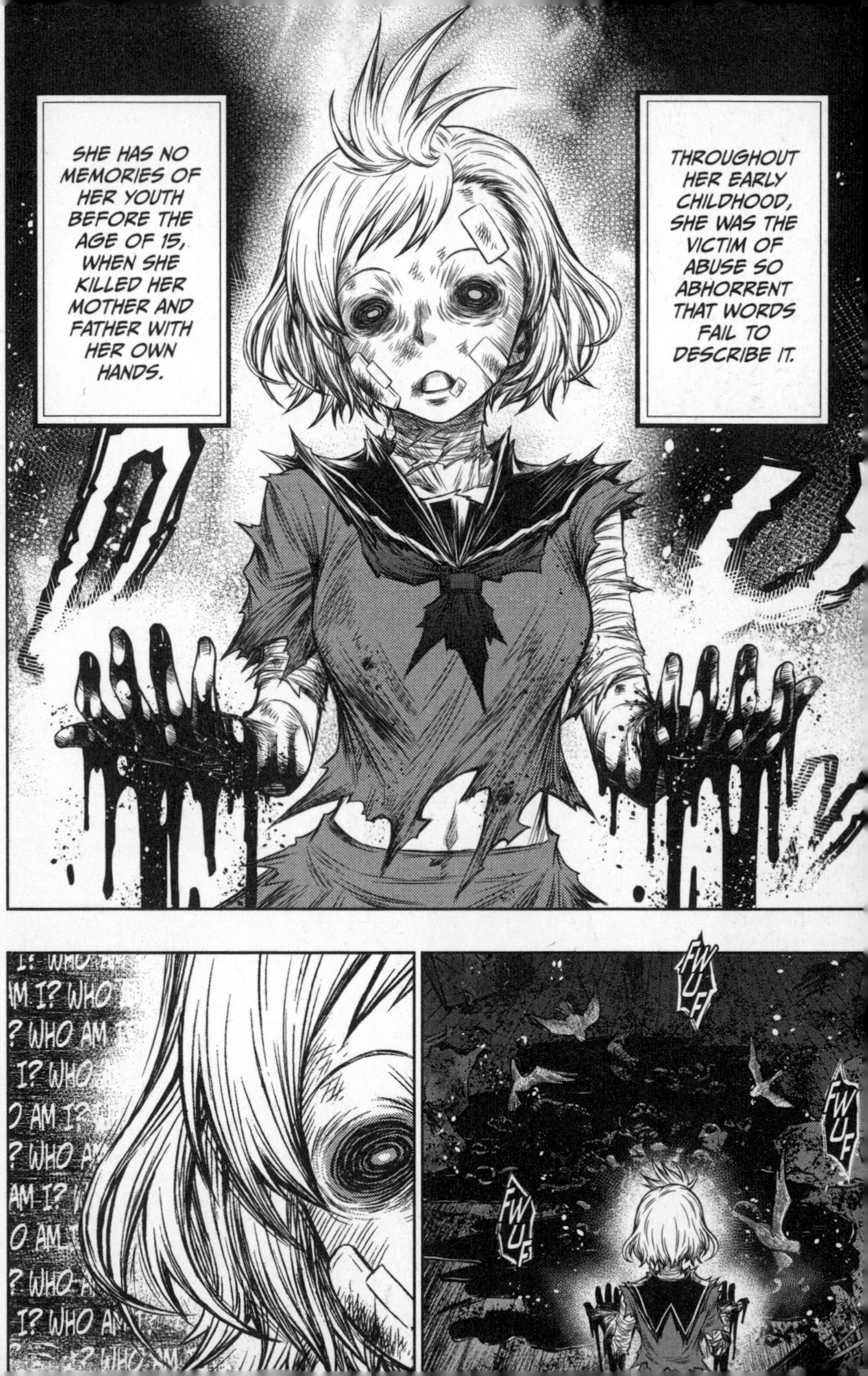
THROUGHOUT HER EARLY CHILDHOOD, SHE WAS THE VICTIM OF ABUSE SO ABHORRENT THAT WORDS FAIL TO DESCRIBE IT.
SHE HAS NO MEMORIES OF HER YOUTH BEFORE THE AGE OF 15, WHEN SHE KILLED HER MOTHER AND FATHER WITH HER OWN HANDS.
FWUF
FWUF
FWUF
AM I? WHO
? WHO AM
I? WHO
O AM I?
? WHO AM
AM I?
? WHO
I? WHO AM
? WHO AM

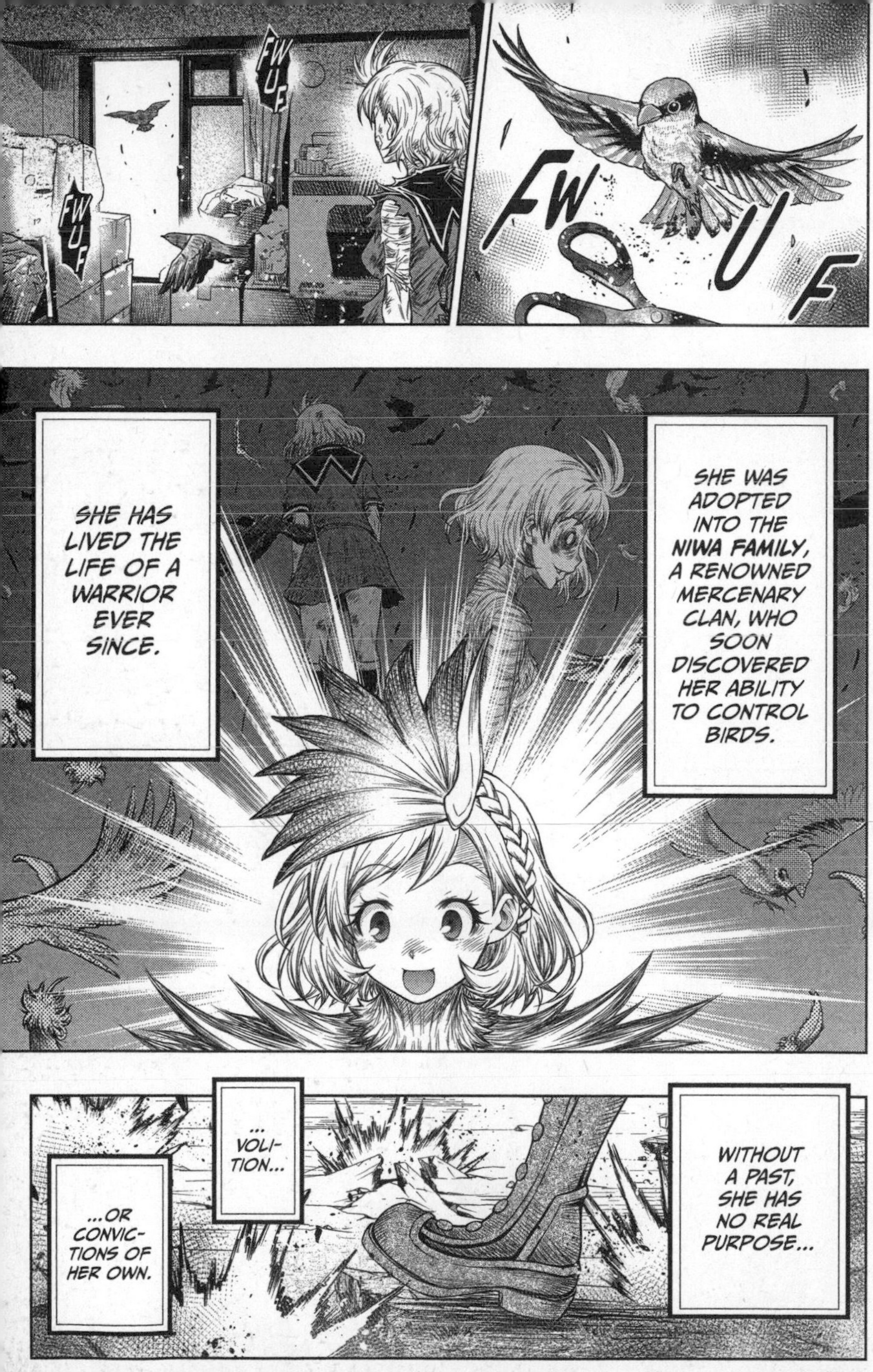
FWUF
FWUF
FWUF
SHE WAS ADOPTED INTO THE NIWA FAMILY, A RENOWNED MERCENARY CLAN, WHO SOON DISCOVERED HER ABILITY TO CONTROL BIRDS.
SHE HAS LIVED THE LIFE OF A WARRIOR EVER SINCE.
WITHOUT A PAST, SHE HAS NO REAL PURPOSE...
...VOLITION...
...OR CONVICTIONS OF HER OWN.

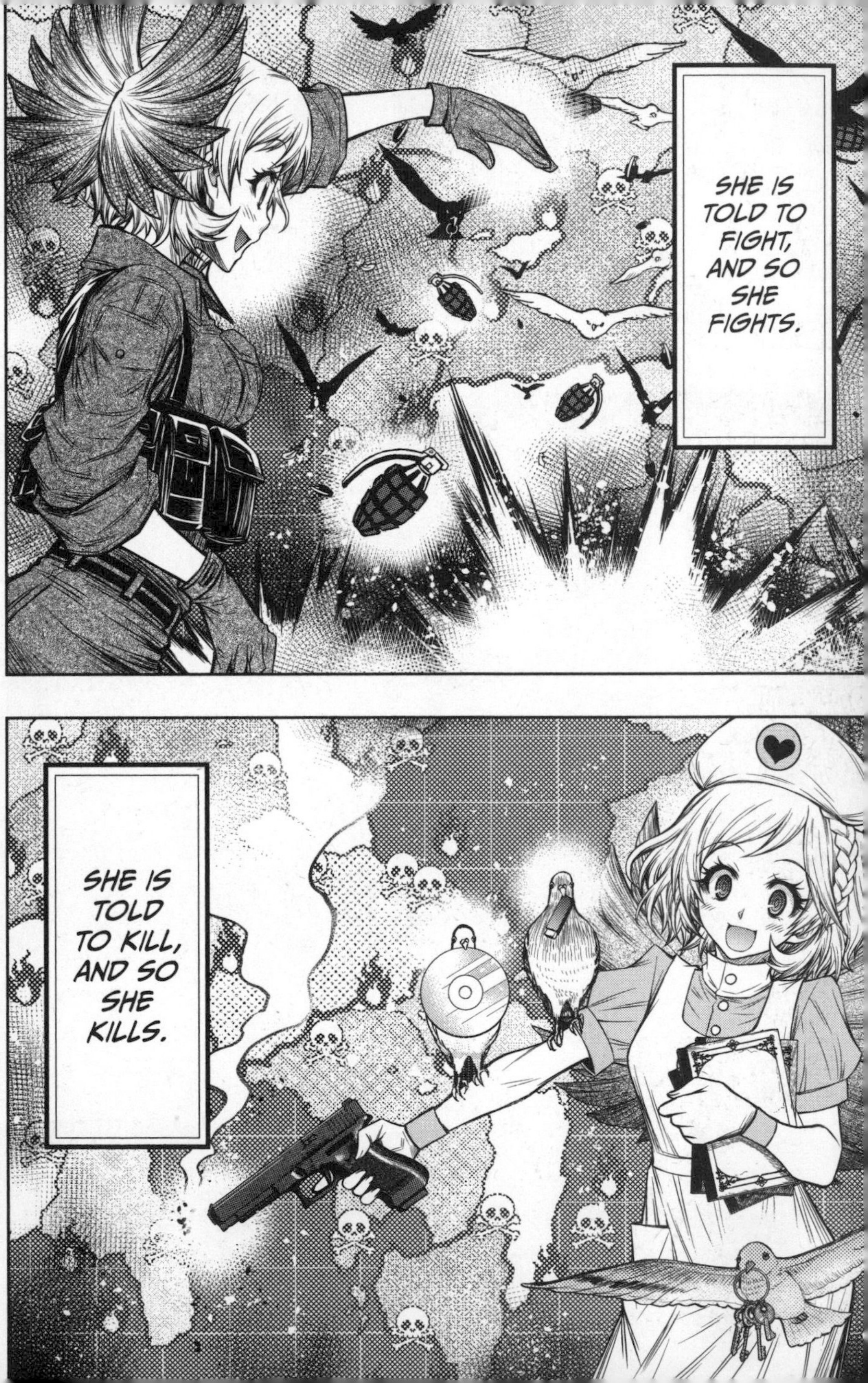
SHE IS TOLD TO FIGHT, AND SO SHE FIGHTS.
SHE IS TOLD TO KILL, AND SO SHE KILLS.

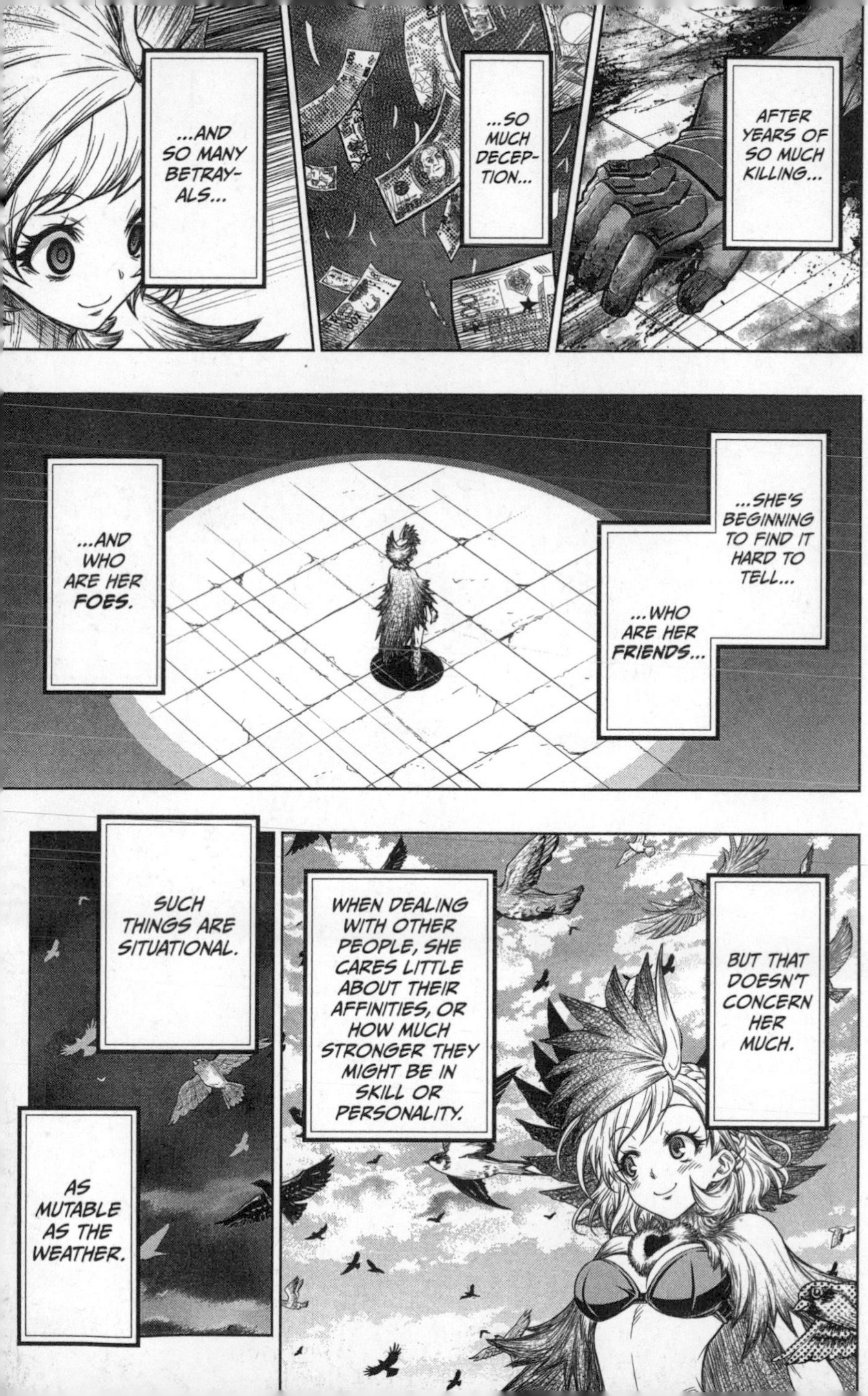
AFTER YEARS OF SO MUCH KILLING...
...SO MUCH DECEPTION...
...AND SO MANY BETRAYALS...
...SHE'S BEGINNING TO FIND IT HARD TO TELL...
...WHO ARE HER FRIENDS...
...AND WHO ARE HER FOES.
BUT THAT DOESN'T CONCERN HER MUCH.
WHEN DEALING WITH OTHER PEOPLE, SHE CARES LITTLE ABOUT THEIR AFFINITIES, OR HOW MUCH STRONGER THEY MIGHT BE IN SKILL OR PERSONALITY.
SUCH THINGS ARE SITUATIONAL.
AS MUTABLE AS THE WEATHER.

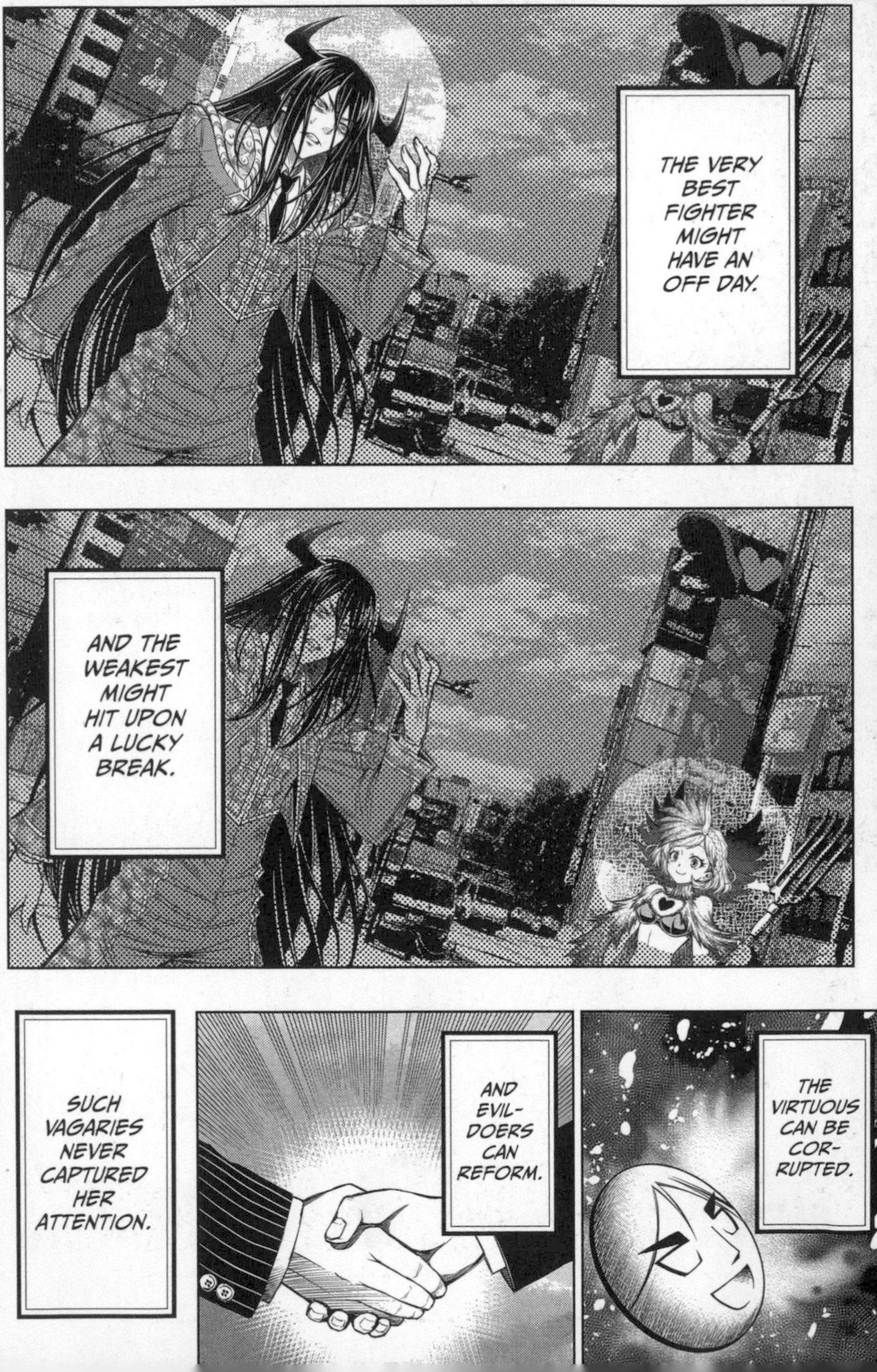
THE VERY BEST FIGHTER MIGHT HAVE AN OFF DAY.
AND THE WEAKEST MIGHT HIT UPON A LUCKY BREAK.
THE VIRTUOUS CAN BE COR-RUPTED.
AND EVIL-DOERS CAN REFORM.
SUCH VAGARIES NEVER CAPTURED HER ATTENTION.

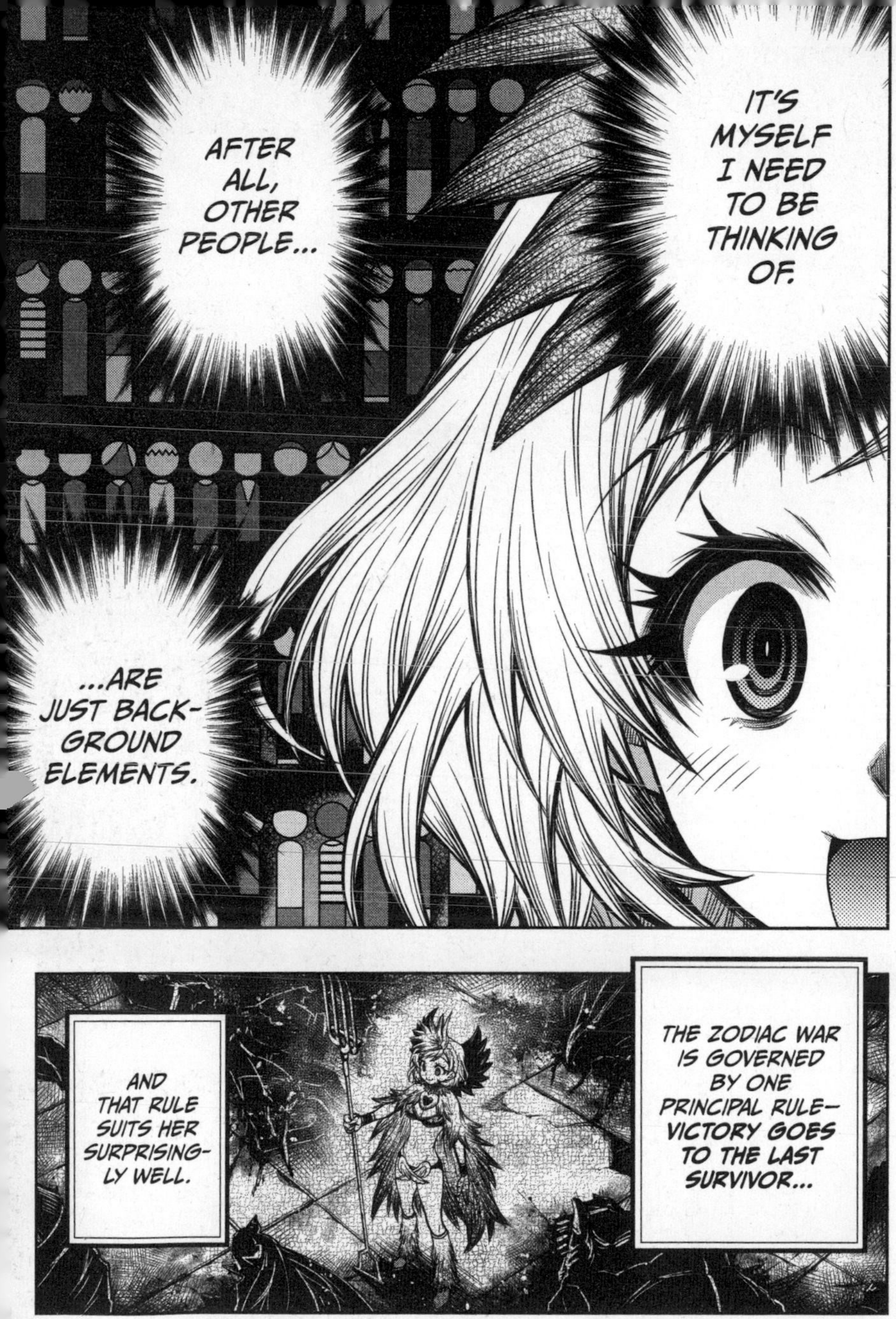
IT'S MYSELF I NEED TO BE THINKING OF.
AFTER ALL, OTHER PEOPLE...
...ARE JUST BACK-GROUND ELEMENTS.
THE ZODIAC WAR IS GOVERNED BY ONE PRINCIPAL RULE— VICTORY GOES TO THE LAST SURVIVOR...
AND THAT RULE SUITS HER SURPRISING-LY WELL.

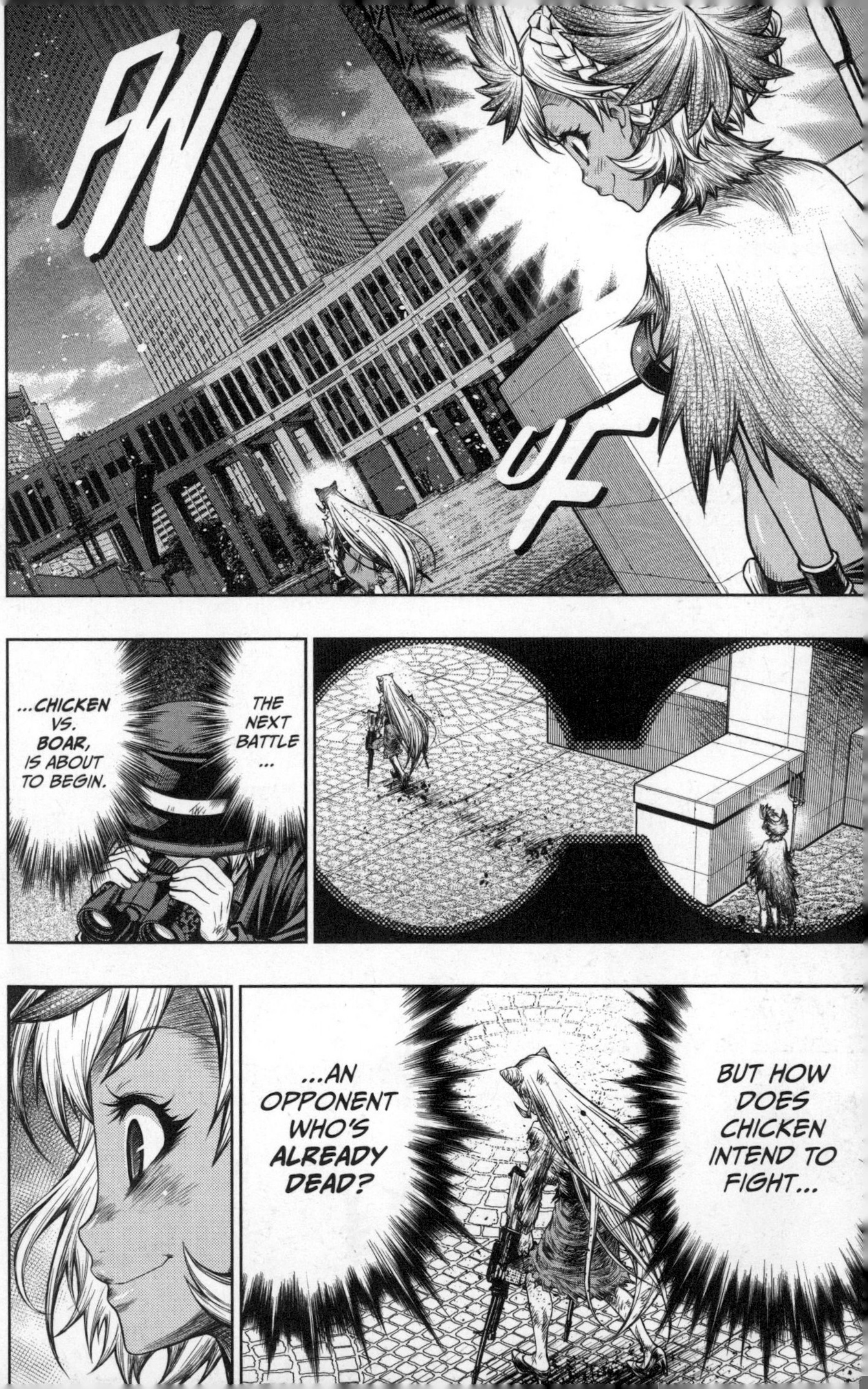
FW
UF
THE NEXT BATTLE ...
...CHICKEN VS. BOAR, IS ABOUT TO BEGIN.
BUT HOW DOES CHICKEN INTEND TO FIGHT...
...AN OPPONENT WHO'S ALREADY DEAD?

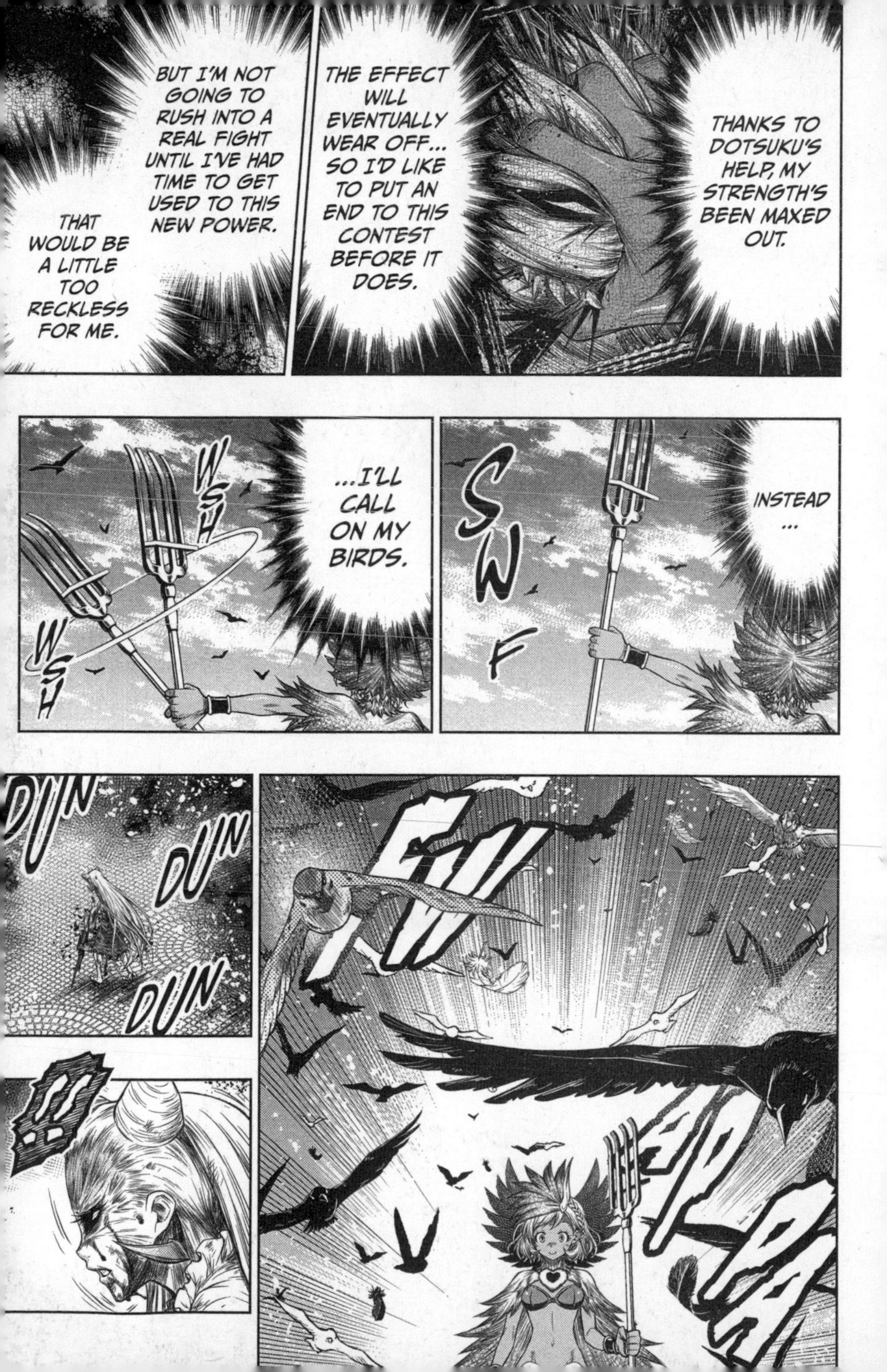
THANKS TO DOTSUKU'S HELP, MY STRENGTH'S BEEN MAXED OUT.
THE EFFECT WILL EVENTUALLY WEAR OFF... SO I'D LIKE TO PUT AN END TO THIS CONTEST BEFORE IT DOES.
BUT I'M NOT GOING TO RUSH INTO A REAL FIGHT UNTIL I'VE HAD TIME TO GET USED TO THIS NEW POWER.
THAT WOULD BE A LITTLE TOO RECKLESS FOR ME.
INSTEAD ...
SWF
...I'LL CALL ON MY BIRDS.
WSH
WSH
FW
AA
DUN
DUN
DUN
!?

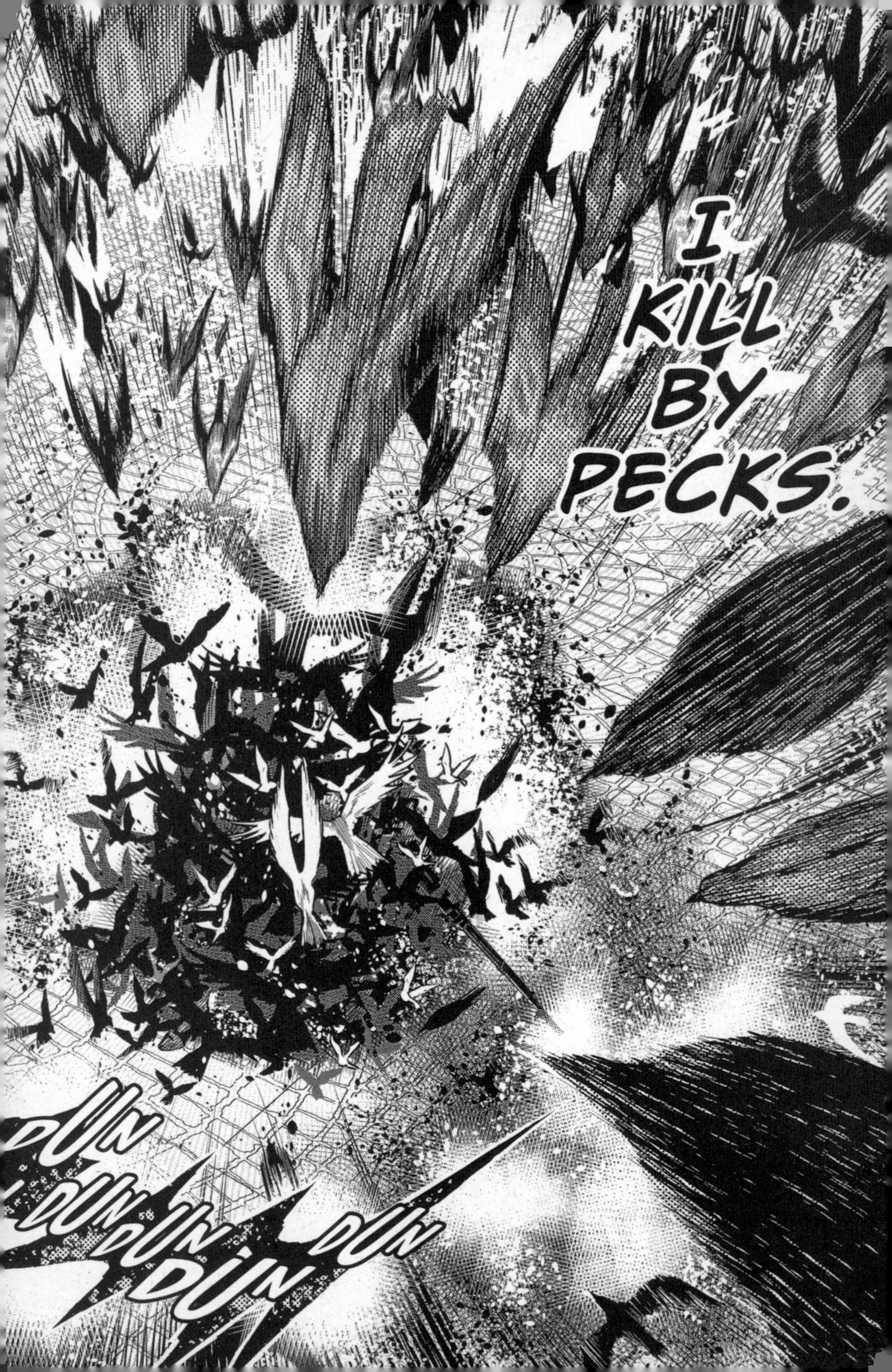
I KILL BY PECKS.

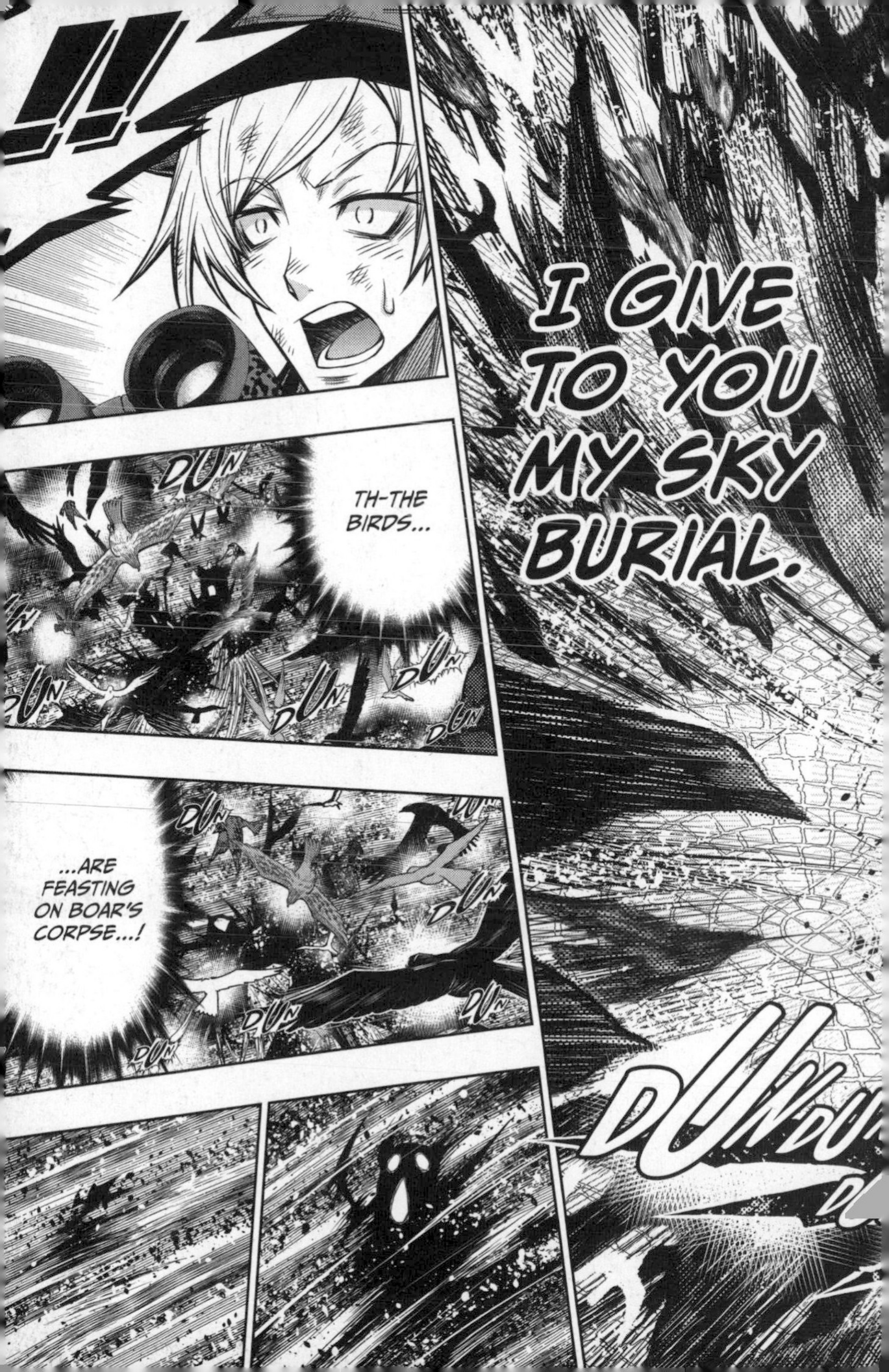
I GIVE TO YOU MY SKY BURIAL.
DUN DUN
!!
TH-THE BIRDS...
DUN DUN DUN DUN DUN DUN DUN
...ARE FEASTING ON BOAR'S CORPSE...!
DUN DUN DUN DUN DUN DUN DUN

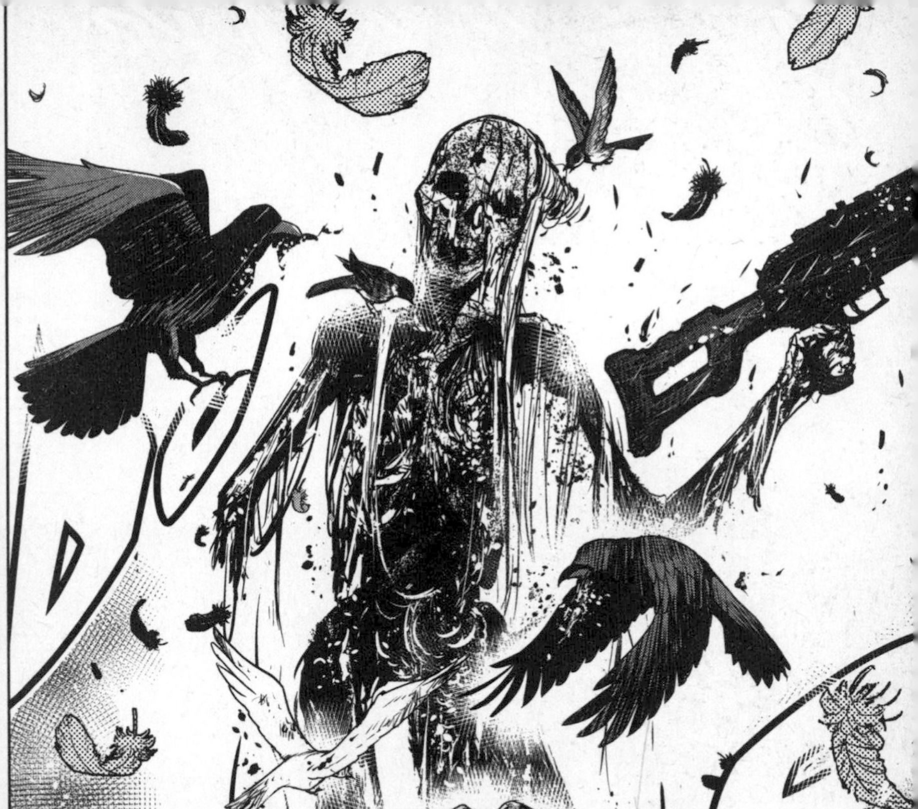

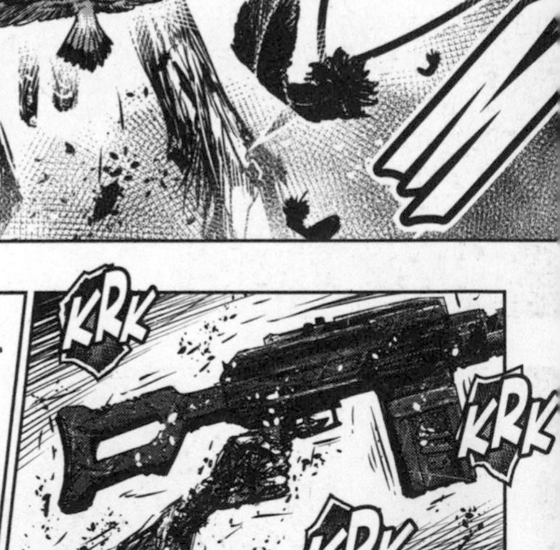
KRK
KRK
KRK

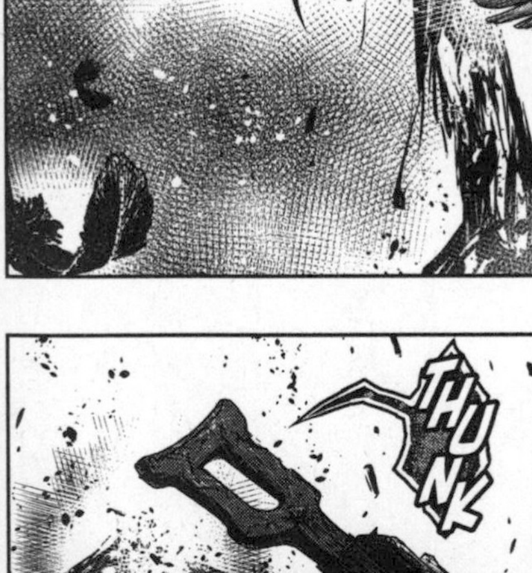
THUNK

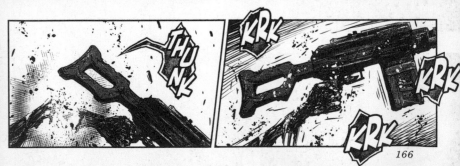

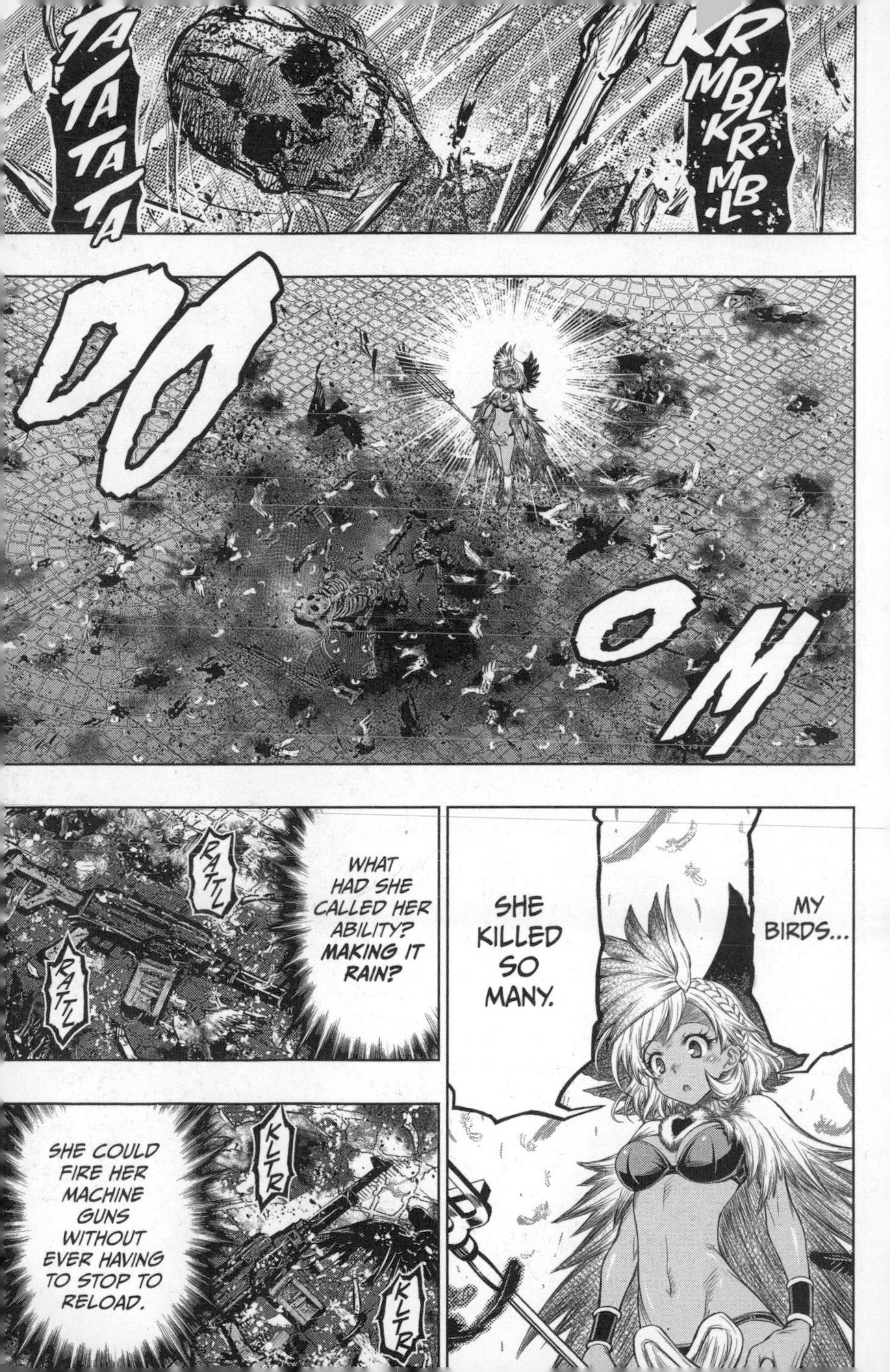
KRMBL KRMBL
TATATATATA
DOOM
MY BIRDS...
SHE KILLED SO MANY.
WHAT HAD SHE CALLED HER ABILITY? MAKING IT RAIN?
RATTL
RATTL
SHE COULD FIRE HER MACHINE GUNS WITHOUT EVER HAVING TO STOP TO RELOAD.
KLTR
KLTR

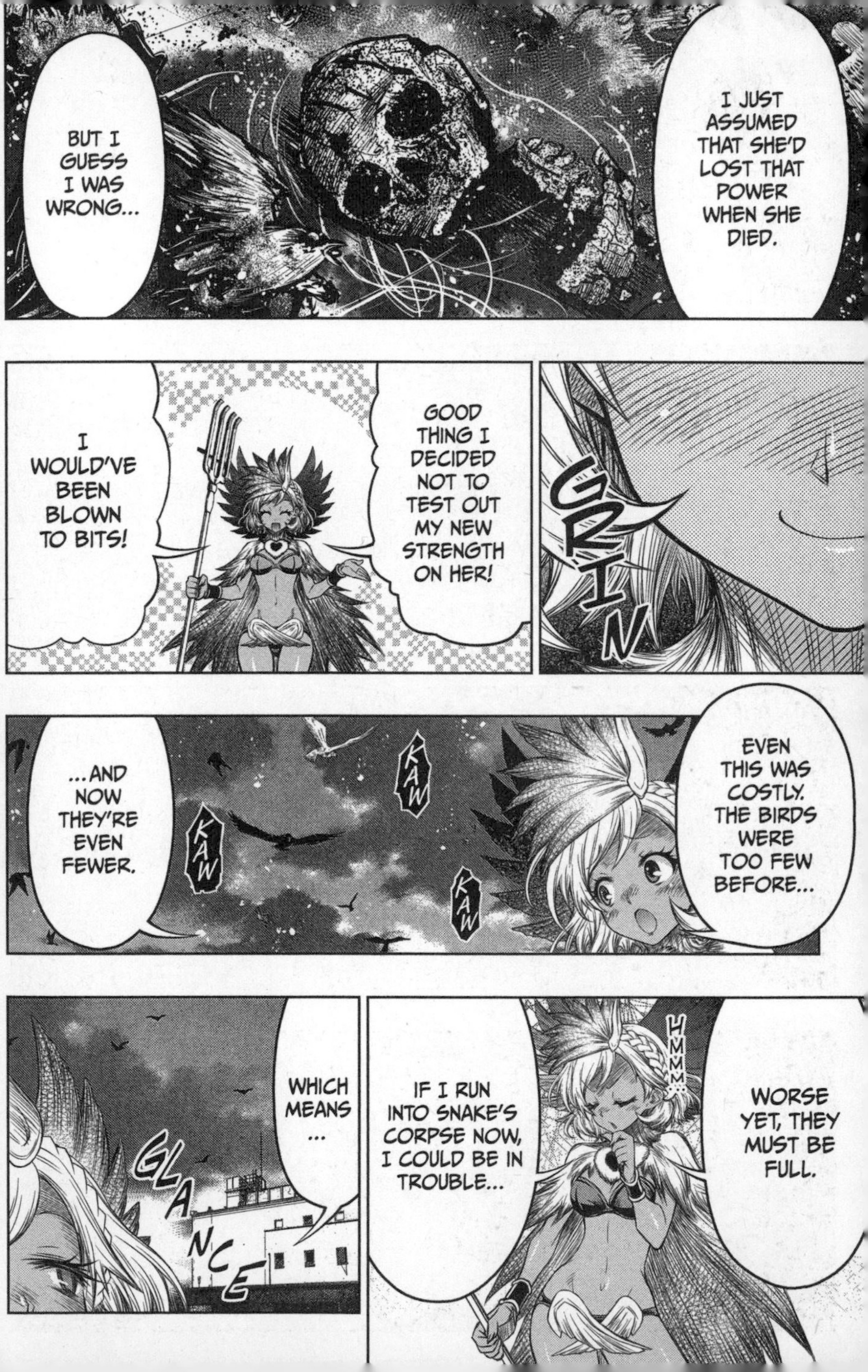
I JUST ASSUMED THAT SHE'D LOST THAT POWER WHEN SHE DIED.
BUT I GUESS I WAS WRONG...
GRIN
GOOD THING I DECIDED NOT TO TEST OUT MY NEW STRENGTH ON HER!
I WOULD'VE BEEN BLOWN TO BITS!
EVEN THIS WAS COSTLY. THE BIRDS WERE TOO FEW BEFORE...
KAW
KAW
KAW
...AND NOW THEY'RE EVEN FEWER.
WORSE YET, THEY MUST BE FULL.
HMMM...
IF I RUN INTO SNAKE'S CORPSE NOW, I COULD BE IN TROUBLE...
WHICH MEANS ...
GLANCE

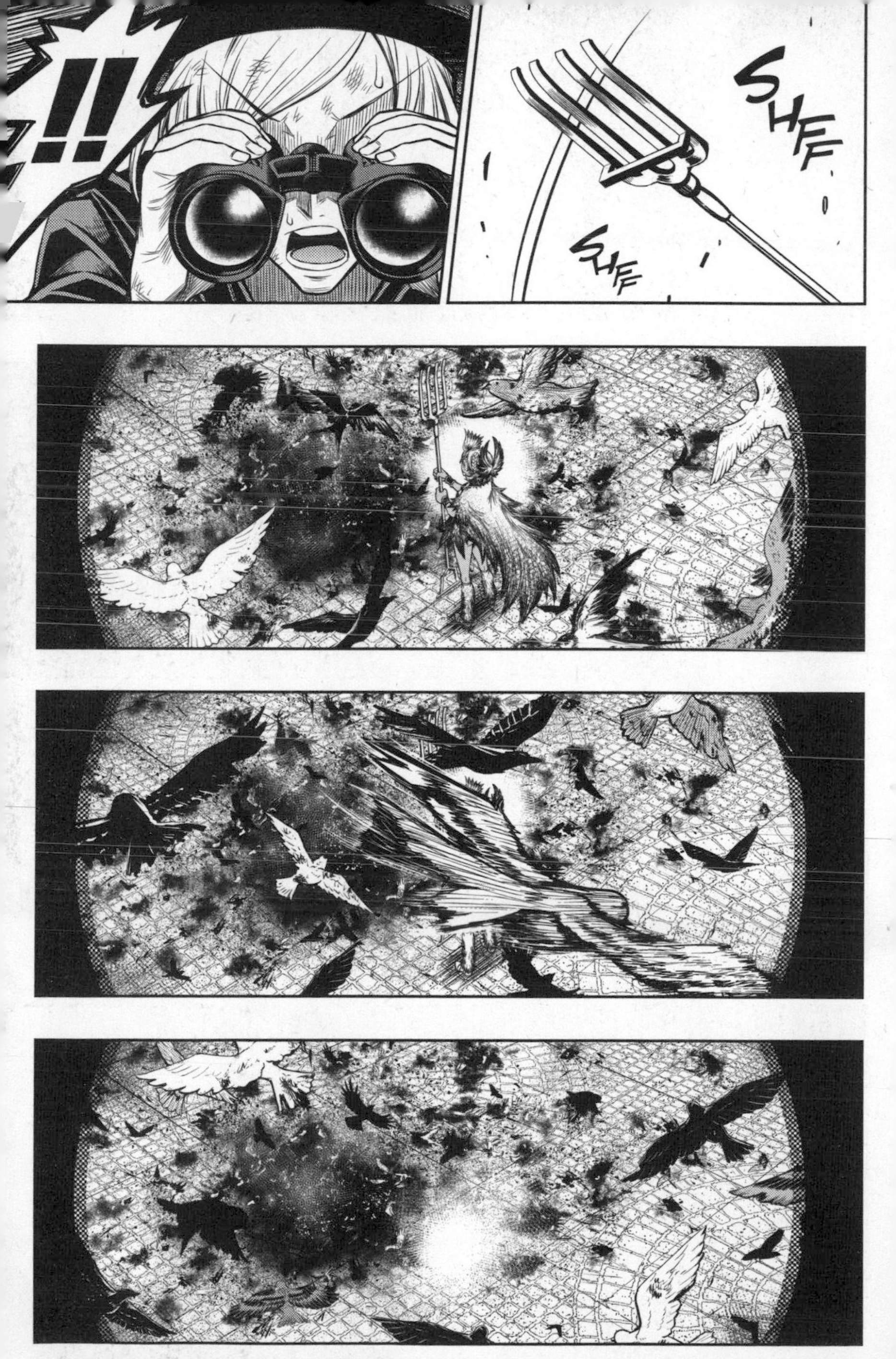
SHFF
SHFF
!!

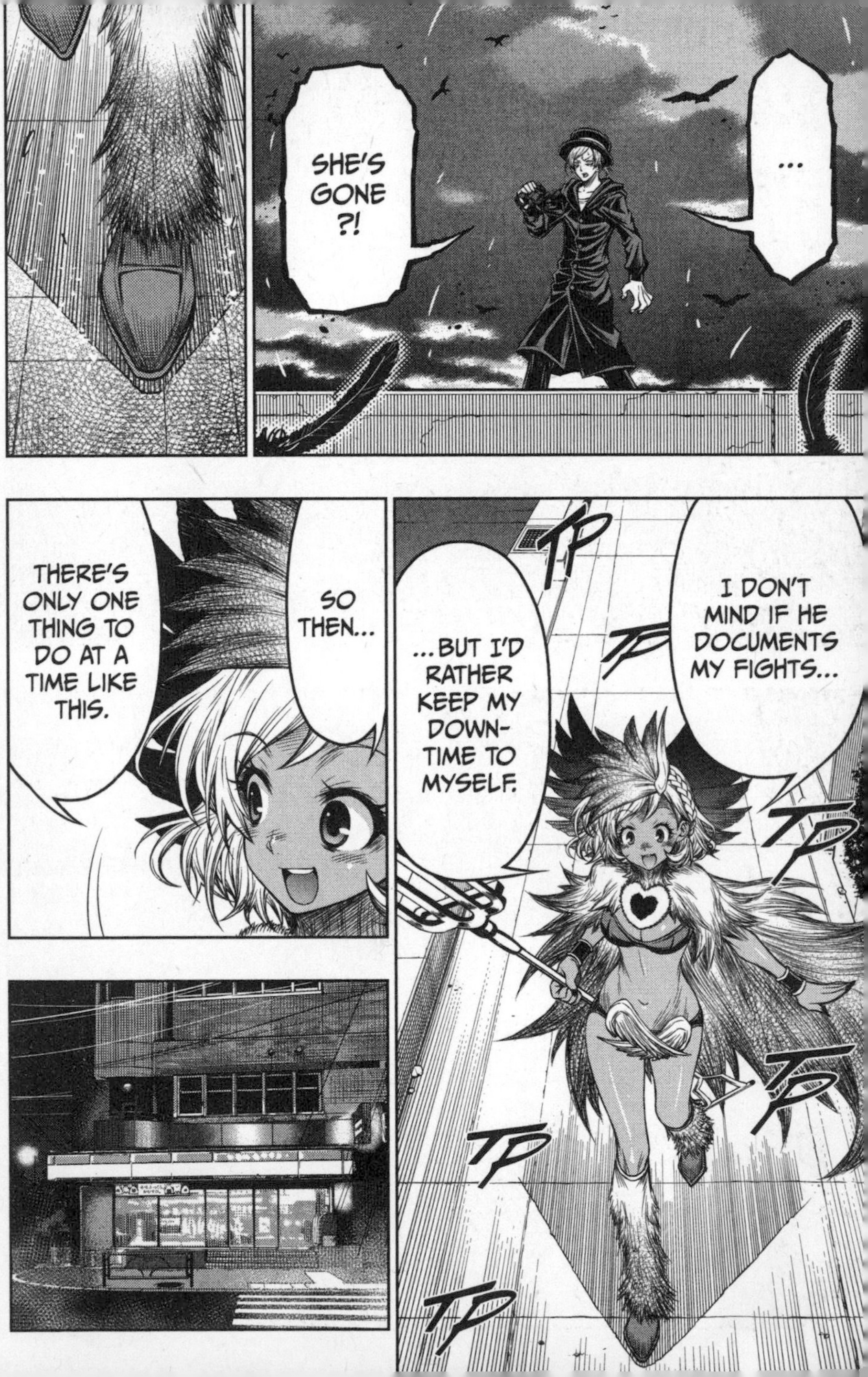
...
SHE'S GONE ?!
TP
TP
I DON'T MIND IF HE DOCUMENTS MY FIGHTS...
...BUT I'D RATHER KEEP MY DOWN-TIME TO MYSELF.
TP
TP
TP
TP
SO THEN...
THERE'S ONLY ONE THING TO DO AT A TIME LIKE THIS.

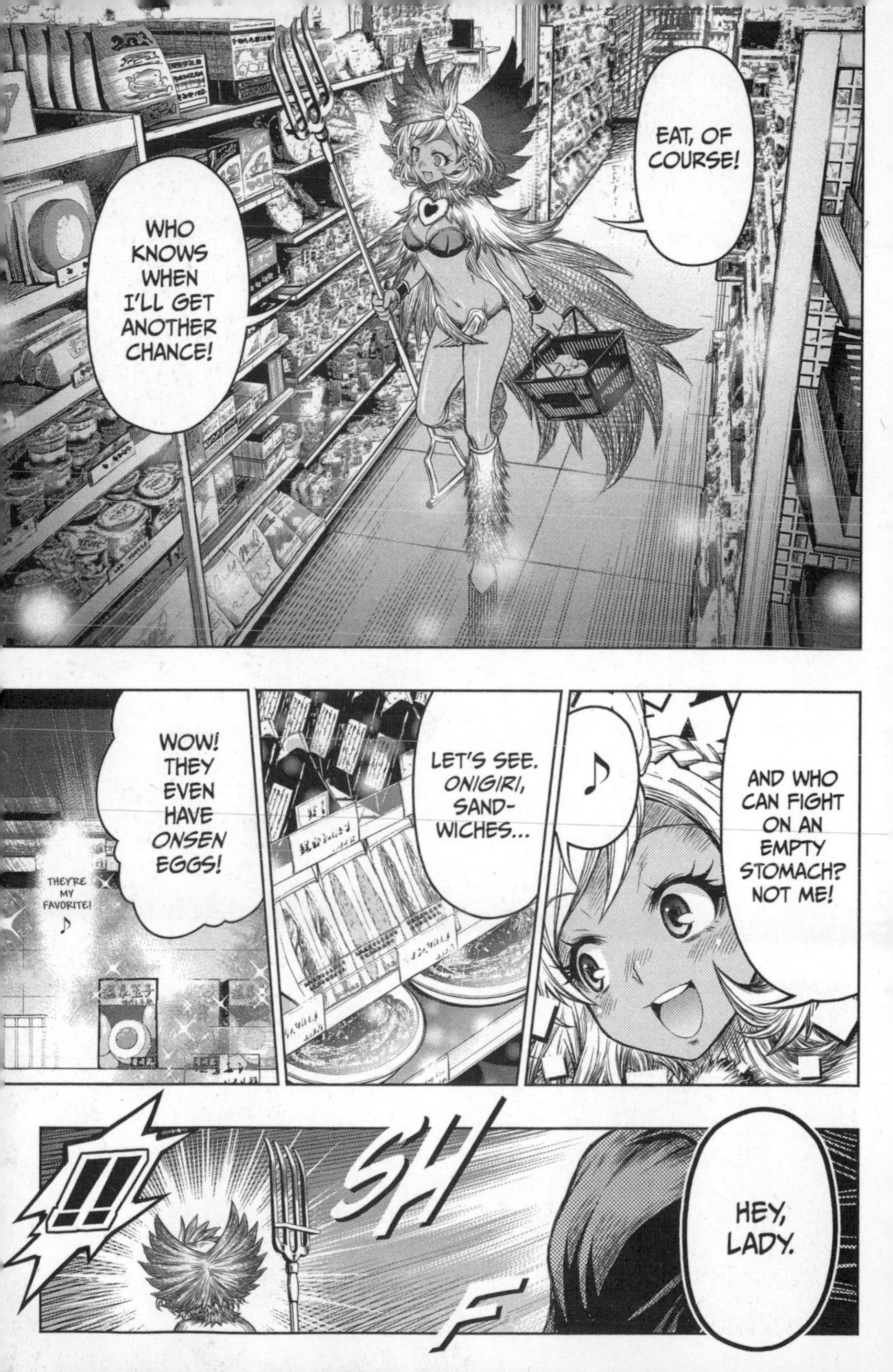
EAT, OF COURSE!
WHO KNOWS WHEN I'LL GET ANOTHER CHANCE!
AND WHO CAN FIGHT ON AN EMPTY STOMACH? NOT ME!
♪
LET'S SEE. ONIGIRI, SANDWICHES...
WOW! THEY EVEN HAVE ONSEN EGGS!
THEY'RE MY FAVORITE! ♪
HEY, LADY.
SH
F
!!

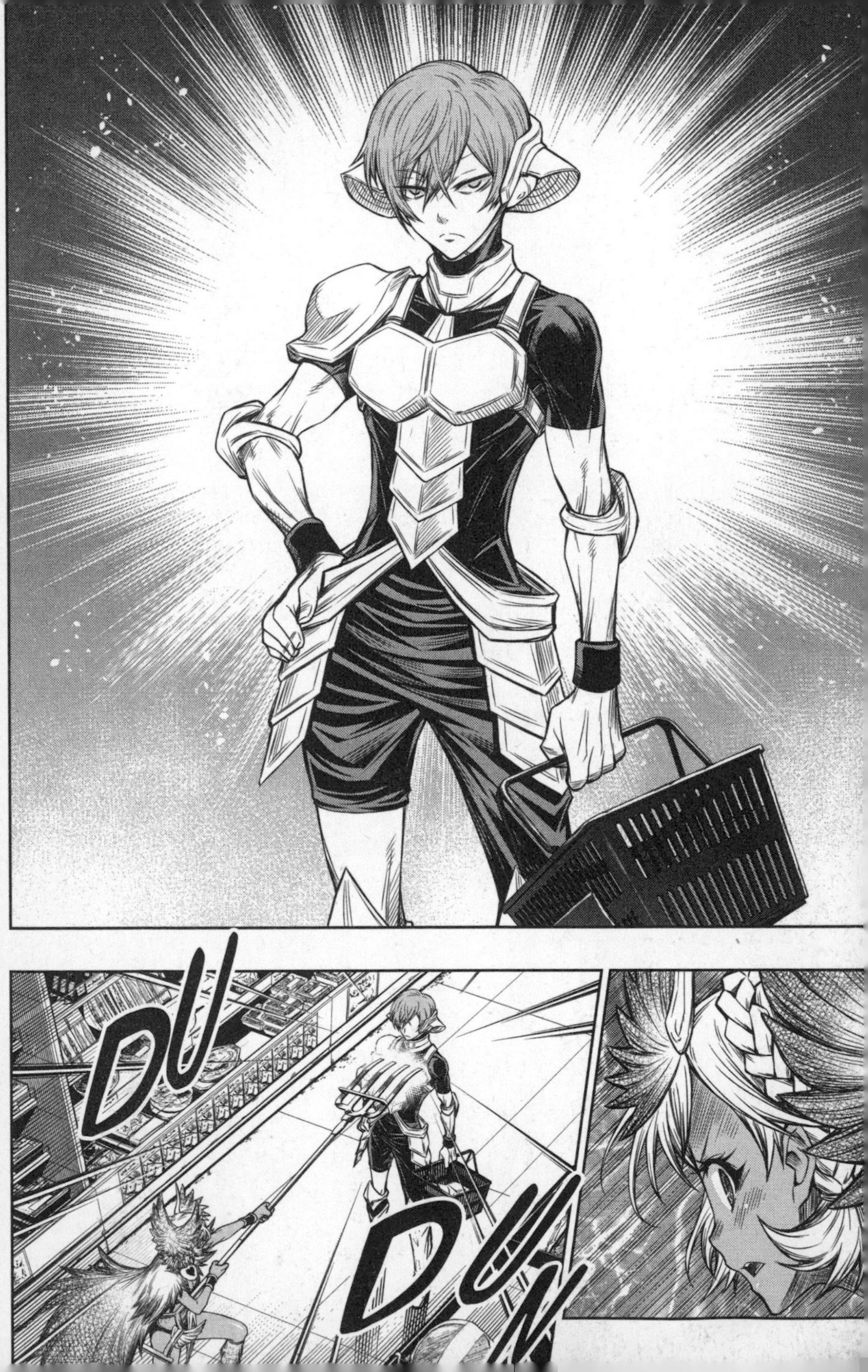
DU
DUN

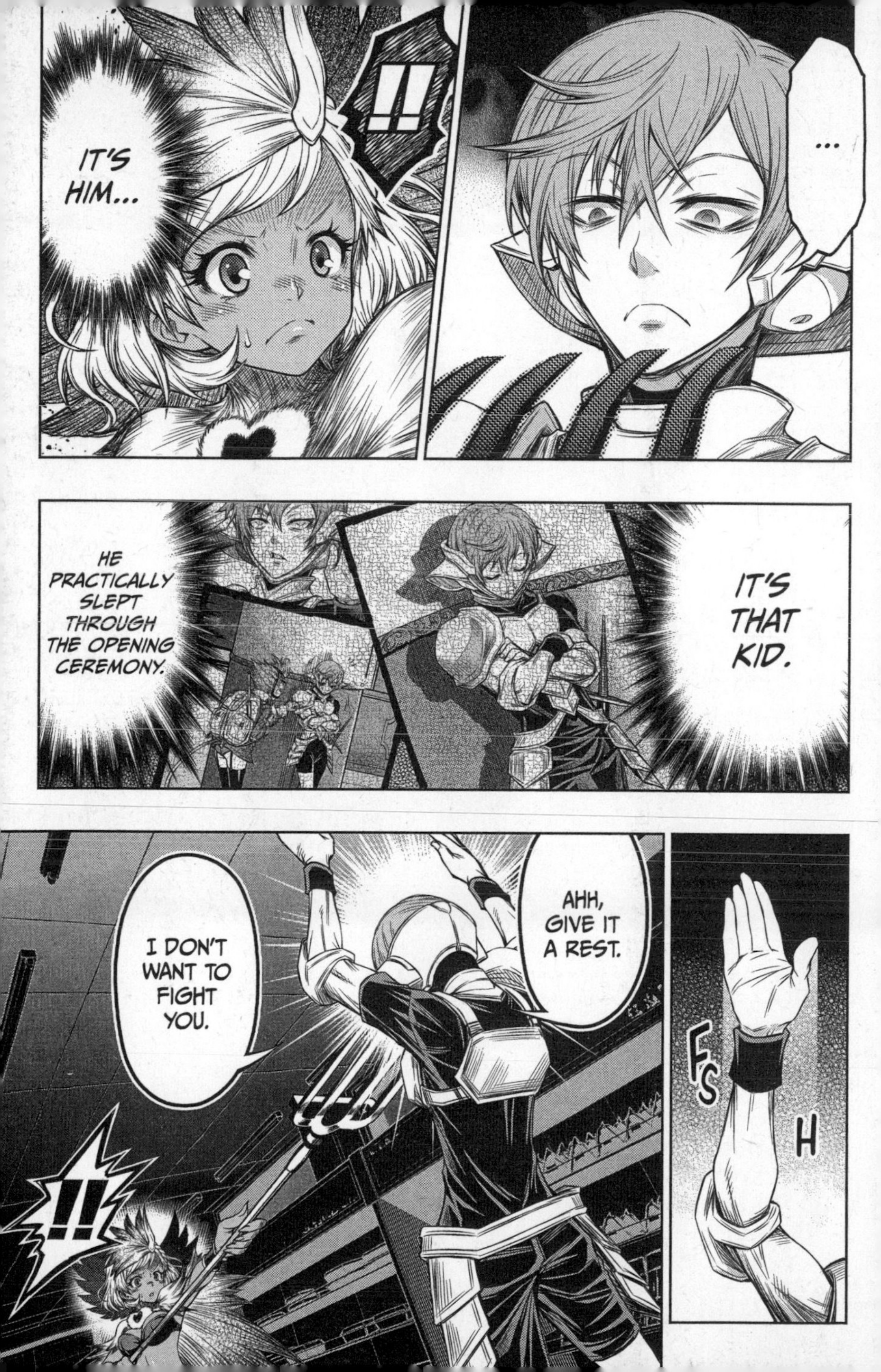
...
!!
IT'S HIM...
IT'S THAT KID.
HE PRACTICALLY SLEPT THROUGH THE OPENING CEREMONY.
FSH
AHH, GIVE IT A REST.
I DON'T WANT TO FIGHT YOU.
!!

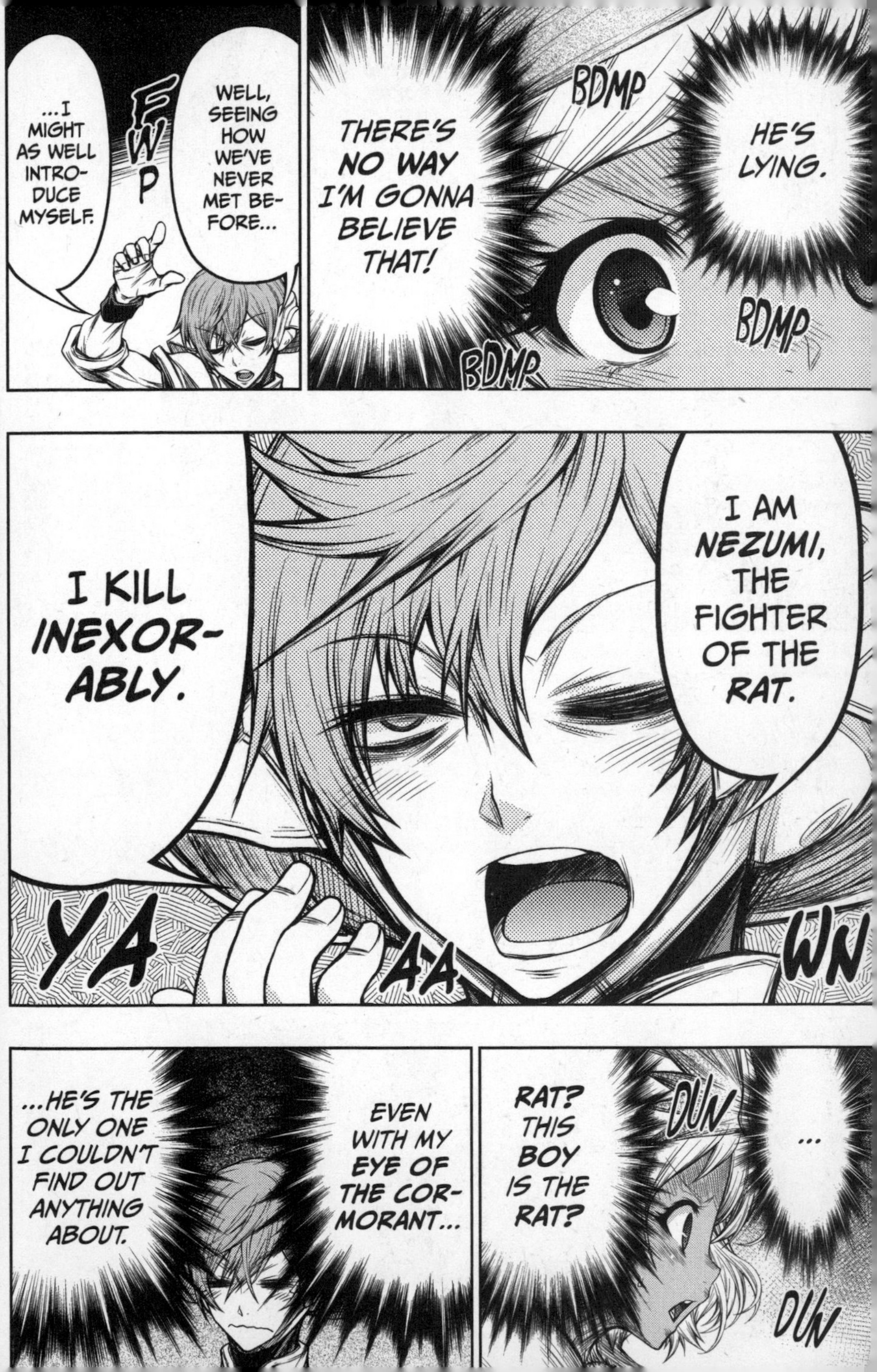
BDMP
HE'S LYING.
THERE'S NO WAY I'M GONNA BELIEVE THAT!
BDMP
BDMP
WELL, SEEING HOW WE'VE NEVER MET BEFORE...
FWP
...I MIGHT AS WELL INTRODUCE MYSELF.
I AM NEZUMI, THE FIGHTER OF THE RAT.
I KILL INEXORABLY.
YAAAWN
...
DUN
RAT? THIS BOY IS THE RAT?
DUN
EVEN WITH MY EYE OF THE CORMORANT...
...HE'S THE ONLY ONE I COULDN'T FIND OUT ANYTHING ABOUT.

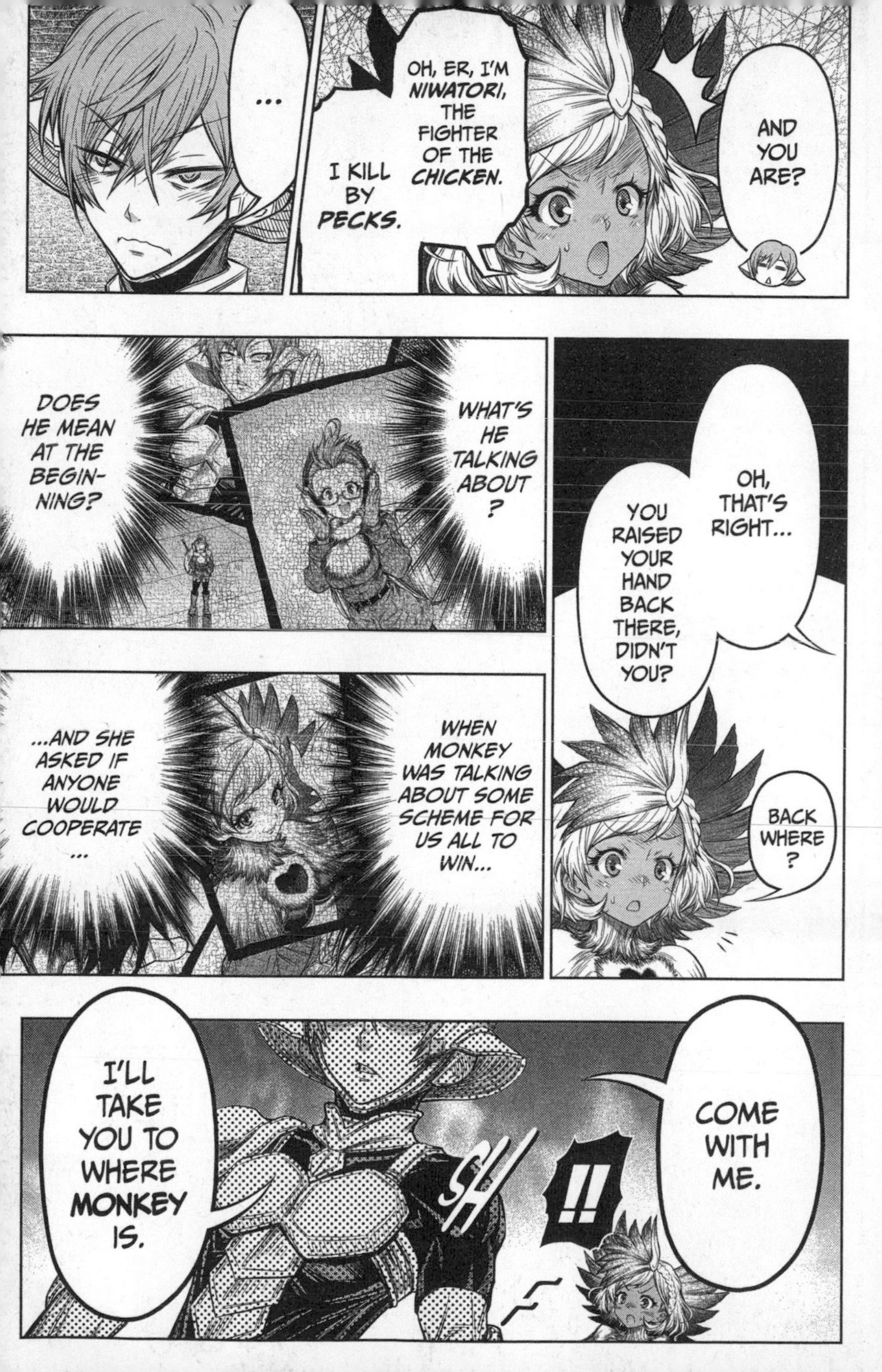
AND YOU ARE?
OH, ER, I'M NIWATORI, THE FIGHTER OF THE CHICKEN.
I KILL BY PECKS.
...
OH, THAT'S RIGHT...
YOU RAISED YOUR HAND BACK THERE, DIDN'T YOU?
BACK WHERE?
WHAT'S HE TALKING ABOUT?
DOES HE MEAN AT THE BEGIN-NING?
WHEN MONKEY WAS TALKING ABOUT SOME SCHEME FOR US ALL TO WIN...
...AND SHE ASKED IF ANYONE WOULD COOPERATE...
COME WITH ME.
SH
!!
I'LL TAKE YOU TO WHERE MONKEY IS.

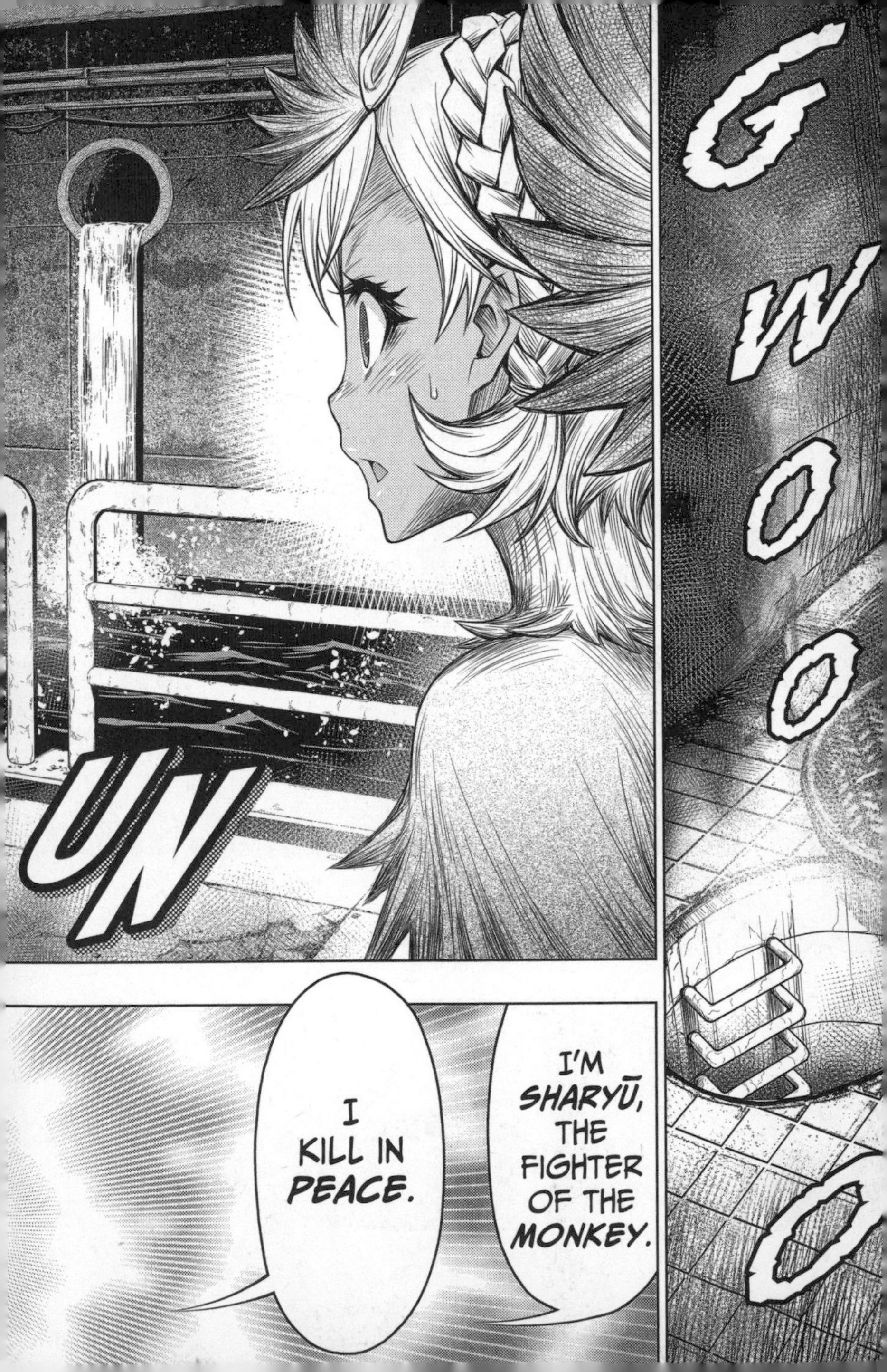
GWOOO
UN
I'M SHARYŪ, THE FIGHTER OF THE MONKEY.
I KILL IN PEACE.

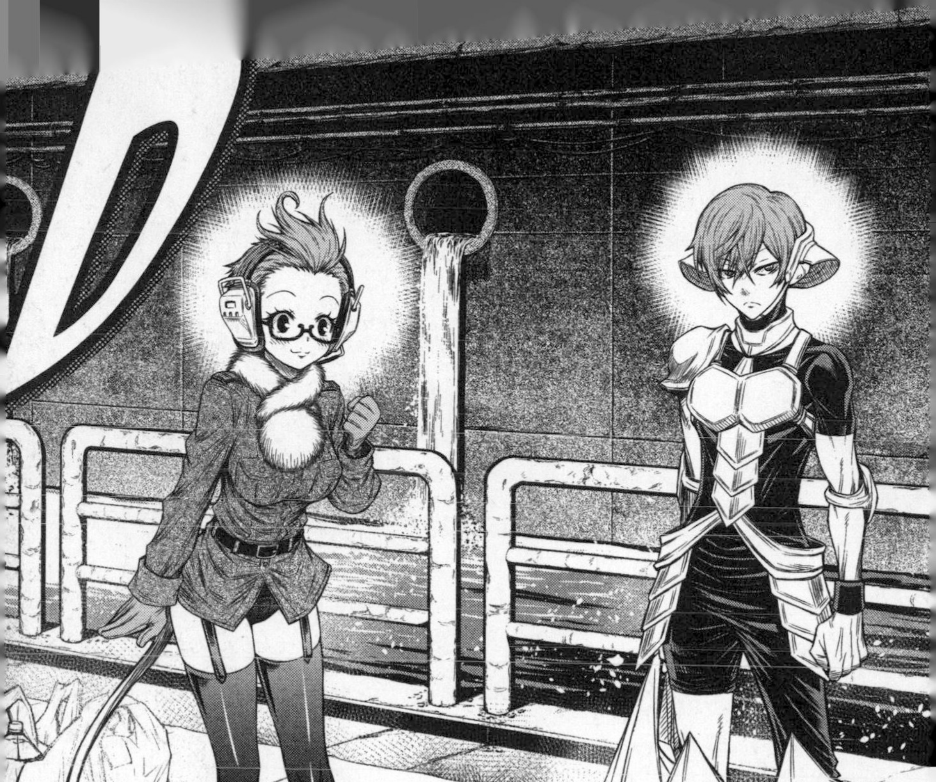

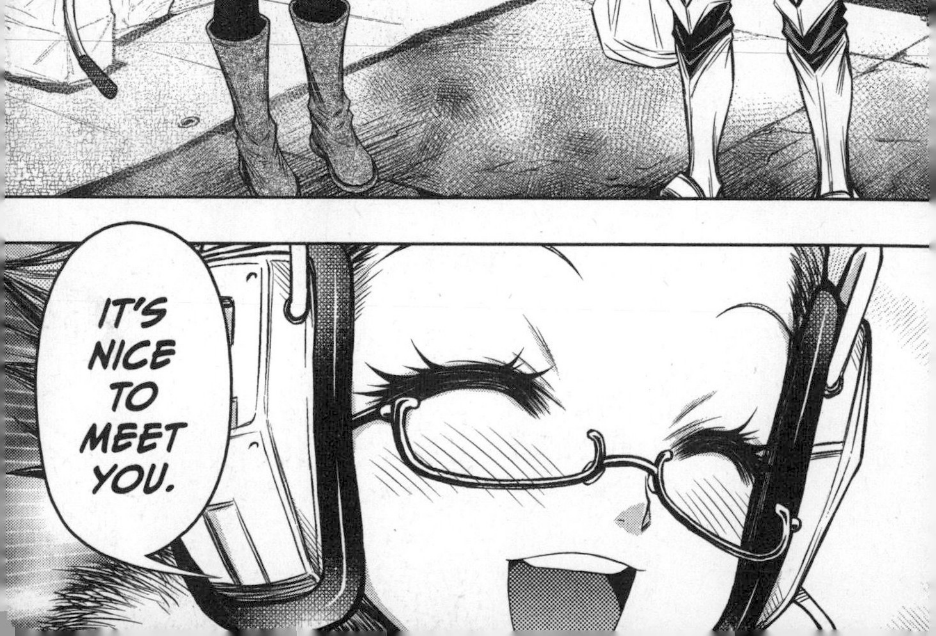
IT'S NICE TO MEET YOU.

INŌNOSHISHI,
THE FIGHTER
OF THE BOAR

REAL NAME:
TOSHIKO INŌ

HEIGHT:
176 CM
WEIGHT:
60 KG

"I wish for love."

"I wish to win."

DOTSUKU,
THE FIGHTER
OF THE DOG

REAL NAME:
MICHIO
TSUKUI

HEIGHT:
177 CM
WEIGHT:
52 KG

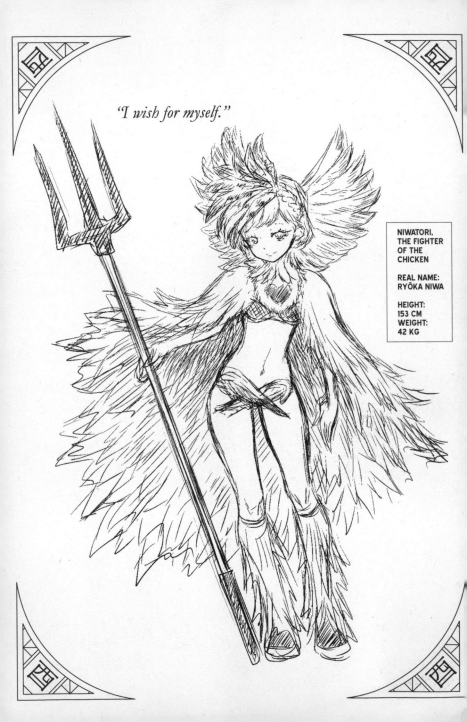

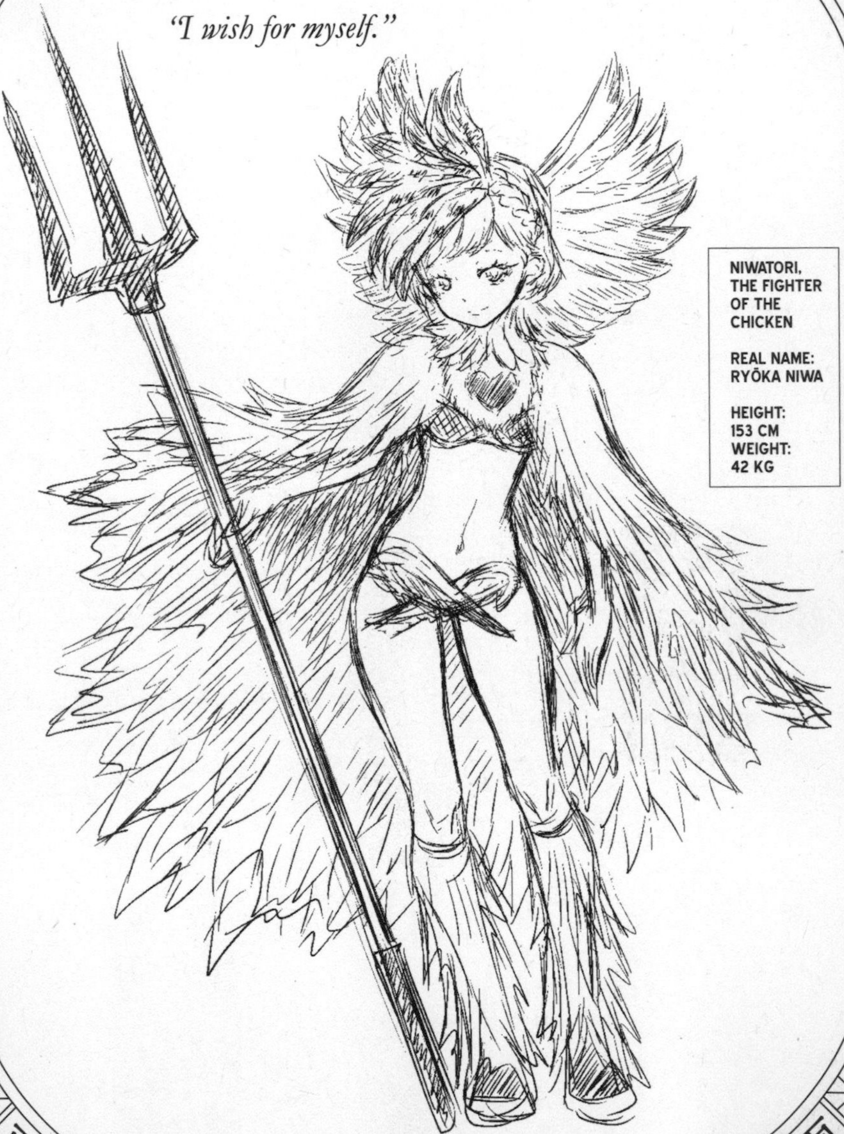
"I wish for myself."
NIWATORI, THE FIGHTER OF THE CHICKEN
REAL NAME: RYŌKA NIWA
HEIGHT: 153 CM
WEIGHT: 42 KG

"I wish for peace."

SHARYŪ,
THE FIGHTER
OF THE
MONKEY

REAL NAME:
MISAKI YŪKI

HEIGHT:
150 CM
WEIGHT:
40 KG

Although this is my third manga collaboration with NISIOISIN (*Medaka Box* and *Shōnen Shōjo* were the other two), it's also my first manga based on an existing novel, and through this work I'm once again experiencing a beginner's nervousness.

At the same time, I'm tremendously enjoying my return to drawing battle scenes, even if I sometimes get carried away and cause more destruction to the city than needed. (*lol*)

Whether you are a fan of the original novel, or if you were brought in through the anime, or if this manga is your introduction to the Zodiac War, I hope you'll go on this journey with me until the very end. I'll be doing my best!

—Akira Akatsuki

AKIRA AKATSUKI

Born 1977, Akira Akatsuki made his manga debut in 2003 with *Z-XL Dai* in *Akamaru Jump*. He later published a number of one shots, such as *Angel Agent*, *Contractor M&Y* and *Little Brave Pukateriosu*, in *Jump the Revolution!*, *Weekly Shonen Jump* and *Akamaru Jump*, respectively. His most notable work and first major collaboration with NISIOISIN, *Medaka Box*, premiered in *Weekly Shonen Jump* in 2009 and concluded in 2013. He published two more one shots, *Toshokan Kyuuseishu Kurabu* (*Library Savior Club*) and *Musume Iri-Hako* (*The Girl in the Box*), the latter of which was another collaboration with NISIOISIN, before starting work on *Juni Taisen: Zodiac War* in 2017 on *Jump+*.

NISIOISIN

Born 1981. In 2002, NISIOISIN's novel *The Beheading Cycle* won the 23rd Mephisto Prize and became his debut publication. Among his numerous novels are the *Zaregoto* series, the *Monogatari* series, the *Densetsu* series, and the *Bōkyaku Tantei* series. He also wrote the manga tie-in novel *Death Note: Another Note*. As a manga writer, he has appeared in the *Weekly Shonen Jump* magazine with his series *Medaka Box* and his *Ōgiri* series of one-shot manga stories have seen the pages of *Weekly Shonen Jump*, *Jump SQ*, *Weekly Young Jump* and *Bessatsu Margaret*.

HIKARU NAKAMURA

Born 1984. Illustrator Hikaru Nakamura made her debut in 2001 with her manga *Kairi no Sue* in the *Monthly Gangan Wing* magazine. Her other works include *Arakawa Under the Bridge*, published in *Young Gangan*, and 2009 Tezuka Osamu Cultural Prize winner *Saint Young Men*, published in *Monthly Morning Two*. She previously collaborated with NISIOISIN for his *Ōgiri* series with "The One Wish I Really Want to Come True, and the Ninety-Nine Others I Don't So Much."

JUNI TAISEN

ZODIAC WAR

1

SHONEN JUMP MANGA EDITION

MANGA BY
AKIRA AKATSUKI

BASED ON THE NOVEL BY
NISIOISIN

CHARACTER DESIGNS BY
HIKARU NAKAMURA

TRANSLATION
Nathan A. Collins

LETTERING
Mark McMurray

RETOUCH
James Gaubatz

DESIGN
Alice Lewis

EDITOR
Marlene First

JUUNI TAISEN © 2017 by NISIOISIN, Hikaru Nakamura, Akira Akatsuki
All rights reserved. First published in Japan in 2017 by SHUEISHA Inc., Tokyo.
English translation rights arranged by SHUEISHA Inc.

The stories, characters and incidents mentioned in this publication
are entirely fictional.

Printed in the U.S.A.

Published by VIZ Media, LLC
P.O. Box 77010
San Francisco, CA 94107

10 9 8 7 6 5 4 3 2 1
First Printing, October 2018

viz.com

shonenjump.com

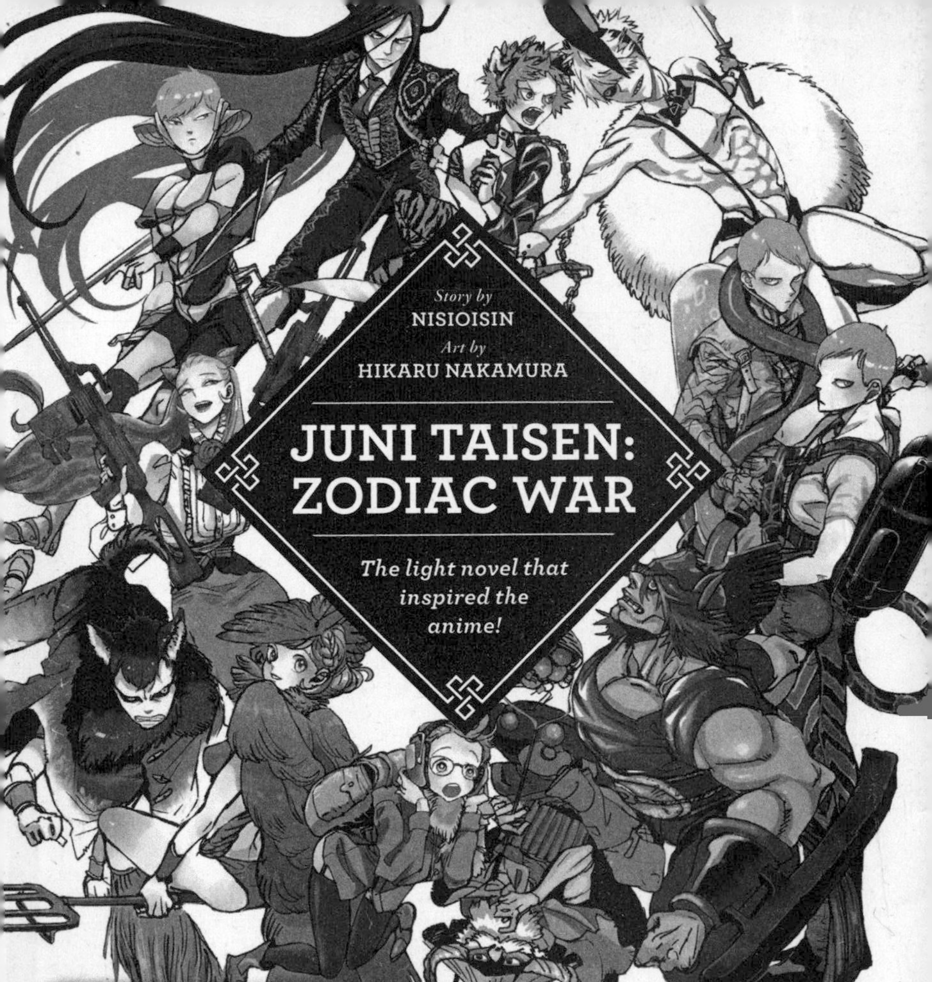
Story by
NISIOISIN
Art by
HIKARU NAKAMURA
JUNI TAISEN:
ZODIAC WAR
The light novel that
inspired the
anime!

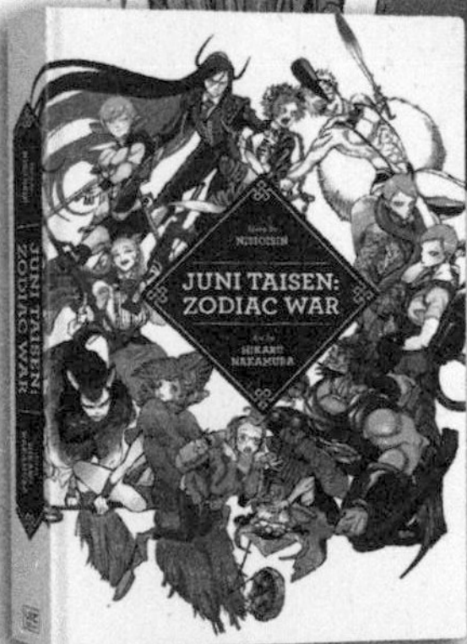
NISIOISIN
JUNI TAISEN:
ZODIAC WAR
HIKARU
NAKAMURA

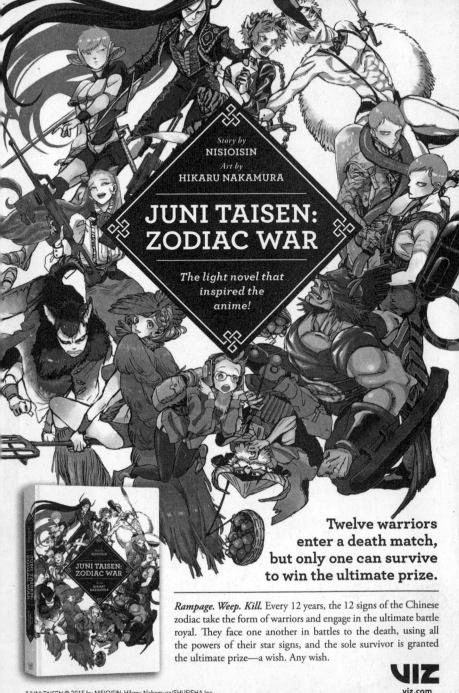

ASTRA
LOST IN SPACE

CAN EIGHT TEENAGERS FIND THEIR WAY HOME FROM 5,000 LIGHT-YEARS AWAY?

It's the year 2063, and interstellar space travel has become the norm. Eight students from Caird High School and one child set out on a routine planet camp excursion. While there, the students are mysteriously transported 5,000 light-years away to the middle of nowhere! Will they ever make it back home?!

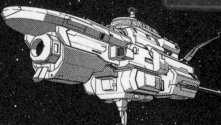

DEATH NOTE
ALL-IN-ONE EDITION

Story by **Tsugumi Ohba** | Art by **Takeshi Obata**

Light Yagami is an ace student with great prospects—and he's bored out of his mind. But all that changes when he finds the Death Note, a notebook dropped by a rogue Shinigami death god. Any human whose name is written in the notebook dies, and now Light has vowed to use the power of the Death Note to rid the world of evil. But when criminals begin dropping dead, the authorities send the legendary detective L to track down the killer. With L hot on his heels, will Light lose sight of his noble goal...or his life?

Includes a NEW epilogue chapter!

All 12 volumes in ONE monstrously large edition!

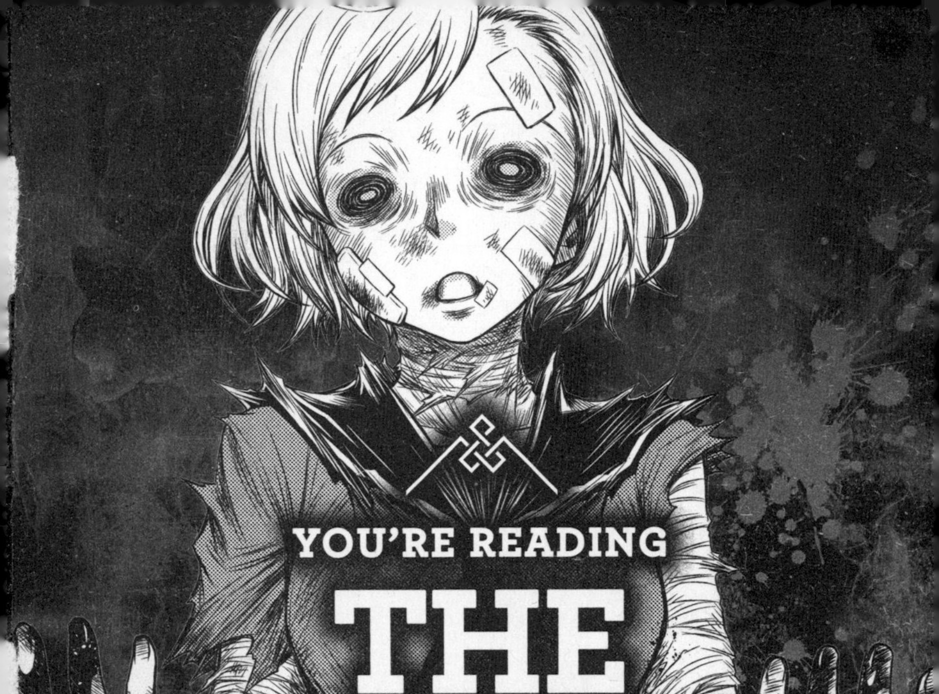

YOU'RE READING THE WRONG WAY!

Juni Taisen: Zodiac War reads from right to left, starting in the upper-right corner.

Japanese is read from right to left, meaning that action, sound effects, and word-balloon order are completely reversed from English order.

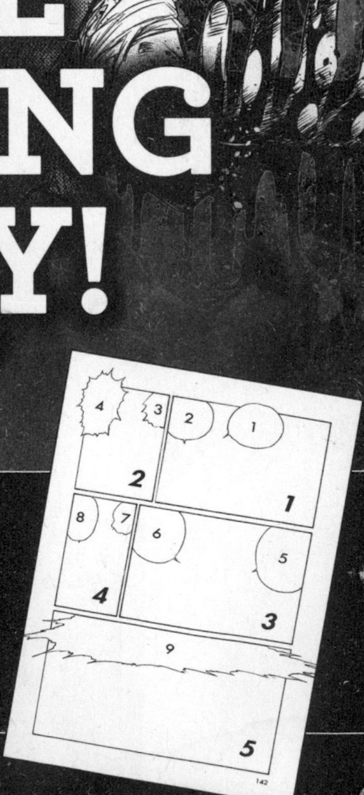
1
2
3
4
5
1
2
3
4
5
6
7
8
9